LIBRARY OF HEBREW BIBLE/ OLD TESTAMENT STUDIES

574

Formerly Journal for the Study of the Old Testament Supplement Series

READING JOB INTERTEXTUALLY

edited by

Katharine Dell

and

Will Kynes

B L O O M S B U R Y

NEW YORK · LONDON · NEW DELHI · SYDNEY

Bloomsbury T&T Clark

An imprint of Bloomsbury Publishing Plc

175 Fifth Avenue	50 Bedford Square
New York	London
NY 10010	WC1B 3DP
USA	UK

www.bloomsbury.com

First published 2013

© Katharine Dell, Will Kynes and contributors, 2013

"Be-hippatah shaʾarê mawet" ("When the Gates of Death Open"), by Aaron Zeitlin, reproduced in translation with permission from the Bialik Institute.

Library of Congress Cataloging-in-Publication Data
A catalog record for this book is available from the Library of Congress.

ISBN: HB: 978-0-567-48552-6

Typeset by Forthcoming Publications Ltd (www.forthpub.com)
Printed and bound in the United States of America

CONTENTS

Part II
JOB IN DIALOGUE WITH THE PROPHETS

Part III
JOB IN DIALOGUE WITH THE WRITINGS

Part IV
JOB'S DIALOGUE BEYOND THE HEBREW BIBLE

PREFACE

The idea for this book was conceived after much discussion of inter-textuality in the book of Job by the editors and out of the realization that the piecemeal forays into intertextuality in Job deserved a more comprehensive treatment, and that only the gathered expertise of a broad group of scholars could do the vast subject justice. It is hoped that this volume will be of interest and of use to scholars and students of Job alike. The editors would like to thank warmly all those who have contributed to this book, especially for being prepared to write at relatively short notice within busy schedules. They also thank a few who dropped by the wayside for their initial willingness and continued support for the project. Finally they would like to thank the co-editors of the LHBOTS series, Andrew Mein and Claudia Camp, for taking this project on board and bringing it to fruition. Job is a book that continues to tantalize and tease the more we study it, and it is hoped that this volume adds some illumination to this continuing enigma without which world literature would be much the poorer.

Katharine Dell
Will Kynes

ABBREVIATIONS

AB	Anchor Bible
ABD	*Anchor Bible Dictionary*. Edited by D. N. Freedman. 6 vols. New York, 1992
AugStud	*Augustinian Studies*
BDB	Brown, F., S. R. Driver, and C. A. Briggs. *A Hebrew and English Lexicon of the Old Testament*. Oxford, 1907
BEATAJ	Beiträge zur Erforschung des Alten Testaments und des antiken Judentums
BETL	Bibliotheca ephemeridum theologicarum lovaniensium
Bib	*Biblica*
BibInt	*Biblical Interpretation*
BJRL	*Bulletin of the John Rylands University Library of Manchester*
BJS	Brown Judaic Studies
BKAT	Biblischer Kommentar, Altes Testament. Edited by M. Noth and H. W. Wolff
BZ	*Biblische Zeitschrift*
BZAW	Beihefte zur Zeitschrift für die alttestamentliche Wissenschaft
CBQMS	Catholic Biblical Quarterly Monograph Series
COS	*The Context of Scripture*. Edited by W. W. Hallo. 3 vols. Leiden, 1997–2002
CSEL	Corpus scriptorum ecclesiasticorum latinorum
ET	English translation
ExAud	*Ex Auditu*
ExpTim	*Expository Times*
FAT	Forschungen zum Alten Testament
FRLANT	Forschungen zur Religion und Literatur des Alten und Neuen Testaments
HAT	Handbuch zum Alten Testament
HBS	Herders biblische Studien
HUCA	*Hebrew Union College Annual*
ICC	International Critical Commentary
JBL	*Journal of Biblical Literature*
JSOT	*Journal for the Study of the Old Testament*
JSOTSup	Journal for the Study of the Old Testament Supplement Series
JSS	*Journal of Semitic Studies*
KAI	*Kanaanäische und aramäische Inschriften*. H. Donner and W. Röllig. 2d ed. Wiesbaden, 1966–69

LHBOTS	Library of Hebrew Bible Old Testament Studies
LXX	Septuagint
MT	Masoretic text
NETS	New English Translations of the Septuagint
NICOT	New International Commentary on the Old Testament
OTL	Old Testament Library
OtSt	Oudtestamentische Studiën
RevExp	*Review and Expositor*
RSV	Revised Standard Version
SBLSP	*Society of Biblical Literature Seminar Papers*
SBS	Stuttgarter Bibelstudien
SemeiaSt	Semeia Studies
StJ	Studies in Judaism
VT	*Vetus Testamentum*
VTSup	Vetus Testamentum Supplement Series
WBC	Word Biblical Commentary
ZAW	*Zeitschrift für die alttestamentliche Wissenschaft*

CONTRIBUTORS

Dr James K. Aitken, Lecturer in Hebrew, Old Testament and Second Temple Studies, University of Cambridge

Professor Samuel Balentine, Professor of Old Testament, Union Presbyterian Seminary

Professor John Barton, Oriel and Laing Professor of the Interpretation of the Holy Scripture, Oriel College, University of Oxford

Dr John Burnight, Assistant Professor, Philosophy & World Religions, University of Northern Iowa

Professor James L. Crenshaw, Robert L. Flowers Emeritus Professor of Old Testament, Duke University

Dr Katharine Dell, Senior Lecturer in Old Testament Studies, University of Cambridge and Fellow of St Catharine's College, Cambridge

Professor Christian Frevel, Chair of Old Testament Studies, Ruhr-University Bochum

Professor Edward L. Greenstein, Professor of Biblical Studies and Head of the Institute for Jewish Biblical Interpretation, Bar-Ilan University

Dr Christopher B. Hays, D. Wilson Moore Associate Professor of Ancient Near Eastern Studies, Fuller Theological Seminary

Dr Raik Heckl, Associate Professor of Old Testament, University of Leipzig

Professor J. Gerald Janzen, MacAllister-Petticrew Professor Emeritus of Old Testament, Christian Theological Seminary

Professor Paul M. Joyce, Samuel Davidson Professor of Old Testament/ Hebrew Bible, King's College London

Dr Will Kynes, Departmental Lecturer in Old Testament Studies, St Peter's College, University of Oxford

Dr Michael Lyons, Associate Professor of Old Testament, Simpson University

Dr Hilary Marlow, Affiliate Lecturer, University of Cambridge and Research Associate, Cambridge Inter-faith Programme

Professor J. Clinton McCann, Evangelical Professor of Biblical Interpretation, Eden Theological Seminary

Professor James D. Nogalski, Professor and Director of Graduate Studies in Religion, Baylor University

Professor Gabrielle Oberhänsli, Chair of Jewish Studies, Albert-Ludwigs-University Freiburg (Germany)

Professor Manfred Oeming, Professor of Old Testament Theology, University of Heidelberg

Dr Anathea Portier-Young, Associate Professor of Old Testament, Duke University

Professor Richard L. Schultz, Blanchard Professor of Old Testament, Wheaton College

Dr Susannah Ticciati, Lecturer in Systematic Theology, King's College London

Professor Markus Witte, Chair of Exegesis and Literary History of the Old Testament, Humboldt University Berlin

INTRODUCTION

Katharine Dell and Will Kynes

Long before Julia Kristeva coined the term "intertextuality" in the late 1960s, biblical commentators recognized that the book of Job was, in some sense, a "mosaic of quotations."[1] After listing fifteen pages of parallels between Job and passages across the canon, Samuel Lee (1837, 86) surmised that "either the language and sentiments of this book must have been accessible to the sacred writers ever since the times of Moses, or else the Book of Job must have been written subsequent to them all, and so have borrowed in all this abundance from them."[2] Lee thought the latter possibility "an opinion which the wildest of theorists would scarcely adopt," instead arguing that the fact that "David, Solomon, the prophets generally, and even Moses himself, have cited, or alluded to, this book" proves "it was in existence, and recognised as of canonical authority, prior to the times of them all…that it was looked upon as a sort of treasury of divinity, and worthy of all acceptation at all times, ever since its first publication" (67).[3] However, he expressed a wish that "some good Hebrew scholar, who has leisure and judgment sufficient for the task, would thoroughly investigate this question" (86 n. 1).

The present volume is a collective attempt to fulfill Lee's wish. In the essays that follow the intertextual links between Job and texts from across the Hebrew Bible, from the Law, Prophets, and Writings, are "thoroughly investigated." However, unlike Lee, and instead following

---

1. Kristeva 1980b, 66.
2. Edward Kissane (1939, xlix) similarly observes a century later that the "enormous number of parallels to passages in other books of the Old Testament" suggest "either the writer of Job showed an intimate knowledge of the rest of Hebrew literature, or that he exerted a deep influence on subsequent writers."
3. John Mason Good (1812, xlvii) likewise claimed that Job "is occasionally quoted or copied by almost every Hebrew writer who had an opportunity of referring to it, from the age of Moses to that of Malachi; especially by the Psalmist, Isaiah, Jeremiah, and Ezekiel."

Bateson Wright (1883, 11), the contributors to this volume think it "improbable" that "Job should be the vast storehouse of Hebrew expression on philosophical and theological problems, to which all Hebrew poets and philosophers are indebted." Because Job is now widely considered the product of the postexilic period, holding this view no longer makes them the "the wildest of theorists."

A revised understanding of the date of Job is not the only difference between the approach to Job's intertextual connections practiced in the essays to follow and that of Lee and his nineteenth-century colleagues.[4] First, as Lee's comments demonstrate, this discussion of parallels between Job and other biblical texts was primarily concerned with determining the date of Job. Lists of parallels like the one he provided, though rarely as extensive, were standard fare in the introductions of Job commentaries into the early twentieth century, but, after contributing to an argument for the book's date, those parallels rarely reappeared in the exegetical comments which followed. Possible quotations and allusions were considered primarily of historical interest. Firmly under the aegis of "influence," these scholars rarely investigated the hermeneutical value of the inner-biblical connections criss-crossing the book of Job. In the essays to follow, the historical value of these connections is not ignored (the date of Job relative to some texts in the Hebrew Bible is after all still debated), but, thanks to the influence of the development of intertextuality, the emphasis has shifted from history to hermeneutics.

Second, whereas nineteenth-century interpreters focused their efforts on identifying parallels between Job and other texts in the Hebrew Bible, as well as ancient Near Eastern "Wisdom" texts after their discovery around the turn of the twentieth century, in the service of this historical quest, the investigation of the intertextual significance of Job need not be restricted to canonical, or even ancient Near Eastern, boundaries.[5] Job, like all texts, is part of an infinite intertextual web. Although, to make this study manageable, we have restricted it to later texts that are linked explicitly with Job, even these subsequent texts can offer readers new insight into the meaning of the book.

This points to a third difference between this volume and "intertextual" studies over a century ago. In the intervening years, the reader has emerged as a recognized participant in interpretation, and intertextuality

---

4.   For a fuller discussion of the history of intertextual interpretation of Job, with a focus on connections between Job and the Psalms, see Kynes 2012, Chapter 1.

5.   This is one reason we prefer "intertextuality" over "inner-biblical exegesis" or "inner-biblical allusion" to describe the approaches taken in this volume.

has contributed to this development. The degree to which the reader, as opposed to the author, is the focus in an intertextual study has become a distinguishing feature between what are commonly characterized as the two major approaches to intertextual method: the "diachronic" and the "synchronic" (see G. D. Miller 2011, 286). The essays in this volume take different approaches to this question, but all, to some degree, incorporate aspects of both, demonstrating that the diametric opposition between them is a false dichotomy (see below).

Intertextuality has also contributed to a difference between the approaches taken in this volume and those common in the bulk of the twentieth century. Concurrent with the rise of form criticism in the early twentieth century, those lists of parallels in Job commentaries disappeared.[6] It seems likely the emphasis on generalized formal comparisons between texts was a contributing cause, as the focus in Job scholarship moved to comparing "forms" evident in Job and other texts.[7] But intertextuality returned interest in connections between specific texts. The term was first explicitly applied to Job's connections with earlier texts by Tryggve Mettinger (1993), though Michael Fishbane's *Biblical Interpretation in Ancient Israel* (1985) is often credited with introducing an intertextual approach into the study of the Hebrew Bible (despite the fact that he never mentions the term).[8] Mettinger claims Job "draws on literary material from a very wide range of backgrounds: wisdom, law, cult, psalmody, etc." (75), and a number of studies of intertextual connections between Job and specific texts have followed, demonstrating this to be the case.[9]

These connections with texts across the canon suggest another development of nineteenth- and twentieth-century critical scholarship that may have obscured the type of intertextual insight pursued in this study. It was only in the mid-nineteenth century that Job was placed in the category "Wisdom Literature" (see Bruch 1851; Sheppard 2000, 372). As time has progressed, that categorization has led to the book being isolated in that category, with connections between it and the rest of the canon overlooked. The widespread interaction between Job and texts

---

6. The last are Driver and Gray 1921, lxvii–lxviii; Dhorme 1967 [French 1926], clix–clxviii.

7. E.g. Baumgärtel 1933; Westermann 1981 [German 1956]; Fohrer 1963; Dell 1991.

8. A list of parallels reappears soon after in the Job commentary by Hartley (1988). Already in 1971, Fishbane had provided what is now considered an important "intertextual" study of Job 3 and Gen 1 (Fishbane 1971).

9. E.g. Köhlmoos 1999, 15; Pyeon 2003, 66; Schmid 2007; Heckl 2010b.

across the canon demonstrated in this volume point to the need to reintegrate Job with the rest of the Hebrew Bible.[10]

Thus, in thoroughly investigating the question of intertextuality in Job, this volume unearths both historical *and* hermeneutical insight, addresses texts across the canon *and* beyond, and attends to the roles of both the author *and* the reader as it examines not merely formal similarities but connections between specific texts, demonstrating how Job breaks the bounds of the "Wisdom Literature" category, its meaning shaped by the diverse texts to which it alludes and illuminated by the intertextual dialogue initiated by texts that refer to or resonate with it.

Intertextual Approaches

In the first essay, John Barton provides an incisive overview of the state of intertextual studies in Hebrew Bible scholarship. He describes the widely accepted description of an opposition between "diachronic" and "synchronic" approaches, the former often associated with "author-oriented" and "historical" interpretation and the latter with "reader-oriented" and "literary" reading. He criticizes both the terms and those equivalences, suggesting a distinction instead between relations envisioned in time for the former, and in space for the latter, may be more helpful. We agree with him that "diachronic" and "synchronic" are not ideal terms, but we believe their ubiquity in this discussion makes them unavoidable, and they can still serve as helpful descriptors of different approaches to relations between texts if properly nuanced.

Barton points out, however, that "the absolute polarization of these two approaches is probably exaggerated." The following essays strongly support this observation. Both "diachronic" and "synchronic" concerns contribute to some degree in every essay.[11] For some, this integration of approaches is explicit and central to their approaches. Will Kynes demonstrates how the two approaches can be put into dialogue to push beyond the scholarly impasse on the relative dating of Job and Isa 40–55 and provide new exegetical insight into both texts. Kynes's argument hinges on recognizing the parodic use of Isa 40–55 in Job's speeches, and Edward Greenstein similarly focuses on parody in his discussion of allusions to Deut 32 in Job. Greenstein points out that even parody,

---

10. Dell (2006, 188) makes a similar argument in relation to Proverbs. See her comments in the present volume, as well as those of Witte.

11. Thus, instead of binary opposition it would be better to refer to a spectrum or "a range of intertextualities" (Stead 2009, 18).

which would appear to be undeniably diachronically oriented, depends on "a reader's interpretation of intertextual relations." J. Clinton McCann explicitly demonstrates this interaction of diachronic and synchronic intertextual approaches by reading the intertextual links between Marjorie Kemper's short story "God's Goodness" and Job first from an author-oriented perspective and then reflecting on what that intersection means for him as a reader. Paul Joyce similarly devotes separate sections of his examination of Job and Ezekiel to considering author- and reader-oriented questions. Though he concludes that a direct literary connection between Job and the only other book in the Hebrew Bible to mention the character is unlikely, he argues this does not preclude readers from employing their imaginations to explore the intertextual network opened up by this link.

Other contributors acknowledge the ways both reading strategies implicitly inform their studies. Michael Lyons observes that even in his comprehensive analysis of the author's use of *intra*textual quotation and allusion within Job as part of his "communicational strategy," a "reader-oriented" feature exists "inasmuch as all texts must be construed by readers." In her study of Job and the "confessions" of Jeremiah, Katharine Dell "make[s] no apology for a more diachronic intertextual approach that seeks to explore connections between texts within a viable historical and literary biblical world." However, she claims that even her choice of these two texts, "where some parallels exist though none are strong enough to be obvious on a purely diachronic reading," adds a synchronic element "of lateral comparison that the diachronic approach alone does not have the flexibility to allow." Raik Heckl's essay has a similar lateral element, as he argues that "intended intertextual links" at the beginning of Job to the opening of 1 Samuel serve as "a signal for the reader to read both books as related to each other and to compare the framed book of Job with the books of Samuel and Kings." Christian Frevel "bridges the (false opposition) between the diametrical concepts of 'author-centered' and 'reader-oriented' methodologies" in his essay by acknowledging that "the reading processes of the authors are established or (re-)constructed by (modern) readers again." Through a survey of the "disintegrative textual signals which change the direction of reading for the (model and modern) reader," he investigates the significance of reading Ps 104 as "one of the hypotexts beneath the book of Job."

Even contributions that fall more naturally at opposite ends of the diachronic–synchronic spectrum may incorporate aspects of the opposite approach. John Burnight's approach is mainly diachronic, as he argues that Job's opening speech (chs. 3–4) involves a series of "rhetorical 'reversals'" of traditions of Israel's *Heilsgeschichte*. Although he argues that the Job poet makes use of his audience's familiarity with traditional biblical themes "in the pursuit of his rhetorical ends," he discovers these reversals predominantly through identifying aspects of the Joban text that are "puzzling" to the reader; these are puzzles that a recognition of earlier intertexts helps to solve.

On the reader-oriented end of the spectrum, J. D. Nogalski reads the dialogue between Bildad and Job in Job 8–10 and Joel together to compare how the verb שׁוב functions differently within the texts, and "this synchronic approach puts into relief the theological claims of these three characters." Though his analysis of these specific connections "exhibits no interest in the intentions of the author," his study as a whole does contribute to our understanding of the intended meaning of the texts as it demonstrates "how intricately the characters of the two books are tied to their own competing theologies," in which Job as protest literature "seeks to make traditional theological paradigms problematic" and Joel "instructs its readers in corporate versions of the very traditions against which Job protests." When J. Gerald Janzen analyzes Job, Deutero-Isaiah, and several New Testament texts according to what he calls a "hermeneutics of resonance," engaging in a "thick reading" of the texts that suggests a new understanding of the message of the book of Job, he acknowledges that this "interpretation of texts in synchronic interplay may be attributable to action occurring solely as overtones within the interpreter's own 'cave of resonant signification.'" And yet, his argument does not violate diachronic possibility. It *could* have been what the author of Job intended.

A number of the essays demonstrate how diachronic and synchronic approaches are intertwined while putting an intertextual spin on more traditional approaches to biblical criticism. Two interact in different ways with ancient Near Eastern comparisons. Christopher B. Hays discusses how Job "*adapted* Egyptianizing mythological imagery in various ways" to create a dialogue about death and the afterlife. The goal of his comparative study is not merely to identify the borrowing of Egyptian motifs, but, following Kristeva's "transformational/intertextual method," "to understand a text's cultural context well enough to appreciate how it functioned within that context," which, he claims, "reinforces the sub-field's best tendencies." Manfred Oeming, however, argues that biblical scholars have placed unwarranted emphasis on imaginative connections with ancient Near Eastern mythology in their interpretation of statements about the "Urmensch" in the book of Job. Instead, in his interpretation of אדם in Job, he claims a more compelling source for the author's ideas is Gen 2–3.

James Crenshaw "grafts intertextual concerns with tradition criticism," as in his analysis of Job 5:17–18 he begins with the close parallel in Prov 3:11–12, but expands his search for lexemes related to the tradition of divine discipline both across Proverbs and throughout the canon, so that they "become threads sewing together disparate texts from Job to 2 Samuel to the epistle to the Hebrews." The study of the diachronic development of this tradition over time brings all the related texts to bear synchronically on the reading of the Job passage. Markus Witte combines intertextuality with redaction criticism as he traces "references to Deuteronomy in each literary layer in Job in order to show how Deuteronomy is repeatedly alluded to in the multiple redactional layers of Job as the book developed."

As Samuel Balentine observes, "[i]ntertextual studies do not typically concern themselves with reception history issues," but several essays in this volume demonstrate the interpretive value of doing so. Thus Balentine incorporates the frequent depiction of Job as a priest in art and iconography into his reading of themes from Priestly literature (and perhaps even Priestly texts) in Job. Anathea Portier-Young argues that the author of *Testament of Job*, a close relative of the biblical book, offers a "glossotelic" intertextual reading of Job, as he "transposes, transforms, and transvalues" language (*glossa*) from Old Greek Job with a purpose (*telos*): "to provide its readers a means for their own mystical transformation." Susannah Ticcati explores the "unexpected deeper resonances" between Job and Augustine's anti-Pelagian writings. Though Augustine's use of Joban texts may at first appear to be proof-texting, she identifies "three successive moments of rapprochement between the worlds of Augustine and Job, the final one leading to the opening up of new meaning within Job." In a more expanded examination of the history of interpretation, Gabrielle Oberhänsli traces the reception of Job in talmudic-rabbinic, modern, and post-modern Jewish literature. This places the texts in this tradition not only in dialogue with Job, but also with each other and reveals a diachronic development in the way the biblical story is represented, with hatred drowning out hope.

Many of the essays involve reevaluations of purported intentional allusions between Job and other texts as posited by earlier scholars. In some cases, the evidence is found wanting, but this does not preclude the hermeneutical potential of intertextual comparison. James Aitken, for example, draws on rabbinic interpretation to demonstrate the "inevitability" of reading Job and Lamentations together. Though, he argues, the case for intentional allusion between the two books is "weak," pursuing this inevitable connection focuses attention on the often-overlooked theme of mourning in Job, revealing his friends' failure to provide appropriate comfort, leaving Job devastated and alone like the besieged city in Lamentations. Employing a strict criteria for identifying verbal parallels, Richard Schultz also claims some of the arguments for verbal dependence between Job and Ecclesiastes are difficult to sustain. Even so, his analysis of these parallels, along with broader conceptual links indicated by shared key words, still yields insight into the "solidarity" of the messages of the two texts, as they together oppose, "overly optimistic views of the benefits of wisdom and wise living."

All of the essays in this volume demonstrate, therefore, that "the distinction between author-oriented and reader-oriented perspectives is a difficult and slippery one," as Hilary Marlow observes in her exploration of the intertextual relationship between creation imagery in Job and Amos. Perhaps this explains why the terms, such as "diachronic" and "synchronic," or even "author-oriented" and "reader-oriented," used to differentiate these approaches end up being so problematic, as Barton points out.[12] They are helpful heuristic devices for describing different reading emphases, but, ultimately, hermeneutics cannot be hermetically sealed off into one approach or the other. As Ferdinand de Saussure said of the "diachronic" and "synchronic" approaches to semiotics when he coined the terms, they are both autonomous *and* interdependent.[13]

This brings us to a final point Barton makes in his opening essay. He observes that both diachronic and synchronic versions of intertextuality as commonly practiced by biblical scholars are used as methods to provide insight into texts. Intertextual theory, however, as it was developed by Kristeva and her fellow post-structuralists, is not an interpretive method but more of a mindset, a way to think about texts. He calls this theoretical form of intertextuality the "hard" version, as opposed to the methodological "soft" varieties. According to "hard" intertextuality, Barton remarks, "Studies of intertextuality in Job, as in this volume, will not be important because they tell us anything about Job, but because they illustrate the truth of intertextuality in general." The essays which follow provide a wealth of new insight into the "soft" intertextuality of Job, as the meaning of this (perhaps deliberately) enigmatic book is illuminated and enhanced by teasing out and analyzing the intertextual threads with which it is woven into a variegated tapestry of texts extending across both the canon and history. Placed in their own intertextual relationship between the covers of this book, these essays also shed light

---

12. Even the helpful temporal–spatial distinction, he suggests, breaks down if pushed too hard.

13. Saussure 1983, 87. See also Barr 1995, 2–3.

on current trends in "intertextual method" in the study of the Hebrew Bible. Finally, from a "hard" intertextual perspective, this volume suggests that "the truth of intertextuality" may be that the intersection of texts is also one of authors and readers.[14]

14.   Thus Kristeva (1980b, 86–87) claims, "The one who writes is the same as the one who reads." She goes on to deny personality to the writer/reader ("he himself is no more than a text rereading itself as it rewrites itself"), but the contributors to the present volume do not take intertextuality to that radical conclusion.

DÉJÀ LU:
INTERTEXTUALITY, METHOD OR THEORY?

John Barton

Not everyone likes the term "intertextuality." Witness the literary critic William Irwin: "...*intertextuality* is a term that should be shaved off by 'Dutton's Razor,' the principle that jargon that does not illuminate or elucidate but rather mystifies and obscures should be stricken from the lexicon of sincere and intelligent humanists."[1] Jay Clayton and Eric Rothstein, in 1991, were already writing, "...the new and voguish 'intertextuality' has served as a generational marker for younger critics who end up doing very much what their elders do with influence and its partners, like 'context,' 'allusion,' and 'tradition'."[2] In biblical studies, intertextuality, seen as the study of all kinds of interrelations between texts, often similarly strikes more traditional scholars as a vogue word for what has been done for centuries. Thus Johannes de Moor, in his Introduction to the Proceedings of the 1997 joint meeting of the British and Dutch Old Testament Societies, writes: "To the Bible scholar, intertextuality is nothing new. The way in which Jewish works of the Second Temple period and the New Testament used the Old Testament forced exegetes to address the issue of intertextuality long before this postmodern shibboleth was created."[3] Indeed, as Anthony Thiselton comments, the third-century Origen is a pre-eminent example of a scholar in whose work "scripture is interpreted by scripture,"[4] and this to many seems a clear case of intertextuality—reading one text in the light

---

1. Irwin 2004, 240. The reference is to the Californian scholar Denis Dutton (1944–2010), Professor of Philosophy at the University of Canterbury, Christ Church, New Zealand.
2. Clayton and Rothstein 1991, 3.
3. De Moor 1998, ix, cited in Moore and Sherwood 2011, 34.
4. Thiselton 1992, 171.

of another. In biblical studies today the term is widely used to cover all cases of interrelation between texts in the Bible, and hence to include what has more traditionally been referred to as "Scripture citing Scripture," "inner-biblical interpretation," and the "reception" of earlier biblical texts in later ones. Though the term is certainly seen by some scholars as modish, its use is now widespread, and the present book testifies to its attractiveness to many biblical specialists. Important contributions, already in the 1980s, can be found in the work of Richard B. Hays[5] on Paul, and in a collection edited by Sipke Draisma.[6] A working definition of intertextuality in the sense most biblical specialists have adopted is provided by Peter D. Miscall: "'Intertextuality' is a covering term for all the possible relations that can be established between texts."[7] As we shall see, this is by no means what the term meant when it was first introduced into literary theory by Julia Kristeva, but it does correspond to what many biblical specialists have come to mean by it.

There is also widespread agreement among biblical scholars that intertextuality, so defined, comes in two varieties, which (again using terms that have become popular in the last couple of decades) can be called "diachronic" and "synchronic." In other words, the focus can be on either the historical development of texts, in which a later one draws on an earlier one, or on a possible interrelation between texts that can be discerned by someone who reads them together, especially when, as in the case of the Bible, they form part of a defined corpus (or canon). Along these lines Geoffrey D. Miller, in an influential recent survey of intertextuality in Old Testament study,[8] notes that Patricia Tull[9] contrasts these two approaches as characteristic respectively of "traditionalist" critics, who are interested in historical development, and "radical intertextualists," who simply see all the texts in the Bible as mutually illuminating on a "synchronic" level. He himself prefers to call them "author-oriented" and "reader-oriented." But this may be misleading if it implies that "diachronic" study insists on authorial intention. Allusion or quotation of earlier texts is indeed often seen as a matter of deliberate decision by the later author, but this is not essential—earlier texts may be simply "in the air." Equally, a "synchronic" approach is not necessarily the same as a "reader-response" theory, even though the two are often

5. R.B. Hays 1989; see also Hays, Alkier and Huizenga 2009.
6. Draisma 1989.
7. Miscall 1992, 44.
8. G. D. Miller 2011, 283–309.
9. See Tull 2000a.

linked, because it is possible to postulate that links between two texts are somehow "objectively" present, and not simply generated by the reader—I think that Robert Alter, discussed below, may believe something like this. The terminology can thus get confusing, with expressions that overlap, and do not describe precisely the same contrasts in approach or method, even though they are meant to.

The contrast is perhaps best captured, from outside biblical studies, by Clayton and Rothstein, who introduce some helpful additional nuances:

> One may see intertextuality either as the enlargement of a familiar idea or as an entirely new concept to replace the outmoded notion of influence. In the former case, intertextuality might be taken as a general term, working out from the broad definition of influence to encompass unconscious, socially prompted types of text formation (for example, by archetypes or popular culture); modes of conception (such as ideas "in the air"); styles (such as genres); and other prior constraints and opportunities for the writer. In the latter case, intertextuality might be used to oust and replace the kinds of issues that influence addressees, and in particular its central concern with the author and more or less conscious authorial intentions and skills. Theoretical treatments of intertextuality have all leaned heavily toward the model of substitution, though many practicing critics, perhaps especially in America, have used the term "intertextuality" in a context of enlargement.[10]

It seems clear that biblical interpreters commonly use the term in both senses. For the latter sense, there is no other term readily available; for the former, "intertextuality" has the advantage, as Clayton and Rothstein make clear, that even in the case of diachronic development of one text from another it does not imply, as "influence" or even "allusion" may do, that the author is working consciously or deliberately with the earlier text. So, in both cases there does seem to be a good case for using the term, helpful though it would be if we had two terms that were widely accepted to distinguish the two broad senses.

Where the first type of intertextuality is concerned, critics scornful of the term in both literary and biblical studies are in principle correct that what it identifies is not new. Literary history has long been concerned with the influence of writer upon writer ("intersubjectivity"), but also of text on text in a wider sense. The influence of one writer on another may produce a text that is a deliberate imitation of another (as Vergil's *Aeneid* was a kind of "tribute" to the works of Homer), and there are probable examples of this in the Bible, where one could argue that Sirach is a sort

---

10. Clayton and Rothstein 1991, 3–4.

of "new Proverbs." For the influence of text on text, an example might be the laws of Deuteronomy, which may well be an update of the laws in Exod 21–23 (the "Book of the Covenant"),[11] but this development is not very comfortably described in terms of *authorial* influence—we are probably faced here with the work of schools of "tradents" whose identity will always elude us.[12] But identifying even this less intersubjective, more anonymous type of influence still falls easily within the bounds of traditional "historical"/"diachronic" criticism and interpretation. In this sense, the biblical text has long been treated "intertextually" even though the term is modern, and interpreters use it simply to point to a phenomenon that has long been known.

Nevertheless, recent decades have seen a great increase in interest in such intertextuality from a historical perspective, and a much more systematic attempt to study it in a rigorous way. A milestone was Michael Fishbane's *Biblical Interpretation in Ancient Israel*,[13] which offered a highly sophisticated discussion of cases of "inner-biblical interpretation," showing how later texts reflected a kind of proto-midrashic exegesis of earlier ones. Sometimes this is obvious and explicit, as with the reference in Dan 9:2 to the prophecy "in the books" by the prophet Jeremiah that the Exile would last seventy years, reinterpreted to mean seventy "weeks of years," that is, 490 years. But Fishbane showed that in a huge number of other examples the same type of thinking is operating, but the inner-biblical reference is implicit, requiring a reader to have an intimate and detailed memory of the wording of older biblical texts. H. G. M. Williamson's study of the composition of the book of Isaiah could similarly be seen as an example of intertextuality (though it is not a word he uses much, thereby showing that it is not essential): he argues that the author of what we call Deutero-Isaiah worked over the text of Isa 1–39 to make it match his own work, and so produce an integrated book by slanting the (supposed) words of the prophet Isaiah to speak to his own later, exilic, situation.[14] There is now a large literature on inner-biblical exegesis in this historical mode, some of which connects with the current interest in the "reception" of biblical texts. Where what is being studied is reception by later writers (or in art or music), this would

---

11. Cf. Levinson 1998.

12. There are literary critics who restrict the term "intertextuality" rigidly to cases of deliberate use of an older text by a later writer—see Pfister 1985. But this is unusual in the English-speaking world.

13. Fishbane 1985.

14. See Williamson 1994.

normally be called reception history; but where the reception is of one biblical text by another, later, one, we might well call it intertextuality. The term is indeed not absolutely essential, since "inner-biblical interpretation/exegesis" will often do just as well; but, as we have seen, "intertextuality" has the advantage of not emphasizing authorial intention so strongly as that seems to do.[15] We could get by without it, but it does have a definite usefulness.

For non-historical, synchronic, completely non-intentional links between texts, however, there is really no other term available. This style of intertextuality is very largely a recent development, and cannot be safely dismissed by saying "we've seen it all before." Often it depends, as will be argued later, on the world of literary theory, from which the term ultimately derives. But even in studies that are relatively uninterested in "Theory," there is a concern for possible connections between texts that is wholly uninterested in questions of historical dependence or influence, indifferent to "sources" and to the whole business of what Robert Alter calls textual "archaeology."[16] One helpful way of putting this is to say that it identifies relations between texts in space rather than in time.[17] This may well be a happier metaphor than the two kinds of time—punctiliar versus ongoing—captured by the synchronic/diachronic distinction.

Although the language of intertextuality derives from Francophone (and ultimately Slavonic) literary criticism, much modern exploration of intertextual relations in the Bible (and, indeed, in literature more generally) has been conducted in North America. Alter himself set the study of the Hebrew Bible on a new path with his theory of "type-scenes" in the biblical narrative. Though this has affinities with some form criticism, it was original in approaching the phenomenon of "stock" episodes (the hero at the well, the patriarch's wife in danger) not with an interest in the oral roots of such a "form" or how it developed over time, but with how it helps to texture the narrative in its present form. There are

15. Thus Clayton and Rothstein (1991, 4) observe that "influence has to do with agency, whereas intertextuality has to do with a much more impersonal field of crossing texts."

16. See Alter 1981.

17. Thus Granowski 1992, 182. At the same time, Granowski's comment "[t]his novel perspective…proves very valuable to the critic who is interested in discussing—unimpeded by questions of historical development and influence—the various elements within one text that derive an extra dash of significance from their allusion to another text" is likely to annoy more theory-focused critics, who might well see the phrase "an extra dash of significance" as rather trivializing.

obvious parallels here with "final form" exegesis of the biblical text, and with "pre-critical," especially midrashic, interpretation of the Bible as a tapestry of interwoven threads, meant to be read as the work of a single author [God]. Alter does not deny that the biblical text developed historically, but he is not interested in that: his concern is with how the parts are interrelated in the Bible as we now have it. A later text may illuminate an earlier one just as much as the other way around—for interpretation, the rabbinic dictum "there is no before and after in scripture" is strongly productive of good and powerful readings. The interrelations are indeed "spatial" rather than temporal. "No text is an island."[18]

It is not unusual now to read interpretations of biblical texts in which one text is read through or next to another, without any implication of temporal sequence or knowledge of one by the author of the other. Peter Miscall's article, already cited, reads Genesis and Isaiah as "intertexts" for each other: both, he argues, will be understood better if they are juxtaposed, even though there was no "historical" readership for which both stood together in a single corpus until the formation of the biblical canon, a long time after both books were already complete.[19] And an intertextual reading is in any case not a "canonical" reading; though there are similarities in practice, there is no common theoretical base.[20] Reading intertextually has nothing to do with the religious authority of the texts, and there is no assumption that the "best" or "correct" intertext will be another book in the canon. One can perfectly well read Genesis and the Epic of Gilgamesh as intertexts, or indeed Genesis and Darwin's *Origin of Species*—which would be an interesting experiment! It remains true, however, that when biblical scholars pursue intertextuality, they generally do limit themselves to books in the canon. Danna Nolan Fewell, for example, suggests that reading Esther and Ruth together will result in the reader's being able to "challenge" the sexist assumptions in the opening chapters of Esther more readily.[21] Here the intertext subverts the text in a way, relativizing its more repellent themes. There is no suggestion here that the author of Esther had read Ruth, or vice versa, or that there is some kind of "canonical intentionality" to correct one through the other. It is simply that putting them side by side, as a "readerly" approach, will modify the abhorrent impression the book of Esther otherwise makes when it apparently endorses Ahasuerus's rejection of

18. Miscall 1992, 45.
19. Ibid.
20. Though see the quotation from Hays in n. 25 below.
21. Fewell 1992, 17.

Vashti for not being willing to be shown off to his courtiers, and his subsequent edict that men must rule over their wives.

Thus there is no doubt that intertextual interpretation can be practised in two different modes, which in the present volume tend to be distinguished as synchronic and diachronic, but which, I have suggested following Granowski, might better be described as spatial and temporal. However the difference is formulated, it is not difficult to see that there is one. There is undoubtedly some correlation with the difference between what are usually called a "historical-critical" and a "literary" approach to interpretation respectively, with the literary approach partaking to a greater or lesser degree in a "postmodern" style of thought that sits very lightly to authorial intention and to the historical context of texts, and is interested in what texts can be *taken to mean* rather than in hypotheses about what they "really" mean. As I have argued elsewhere, the absolute polarization of these two approaches is probably exaggerated,[22] but very few biblical scholars are equally happy with both. (The same is true in wider literary studies, as illustrated in the quotation from Clayton and Rothstein above.[23])

This discussion has shown, however, that for all their differences the two kinds of critic that practise an intertextual interpretation are nevertheless agreed on one thing, and that is that intertextuality is a *method* or *approach* to the *interpretation* of texts. Especially in biblical studies, this tends to be taken for granted. We read texts, after all, to get something from them; in the case of biblical texts, it is still the case that a majority of interpreters read them to get religious truth from them. An intertextual approach often appeals to such interpreters because it may improve the quality of the religious "information" that can be extracted—as in Fewell's suggestion that reading Ruth and Esther intertextually will mitigate the appalling sexism in Esther. Stefan Alkier argues that intertextual interpretation has potential spin-offs for Jewish–Christian dialogue: "Isaiah, in an intertextual connection to a Jewish textual world, motivates other productions of meaning than Isaiah in an intertextual connection to a Christian textual world."[24] This, he argues, encourages pluralism and wards off both an illegitimate attempt to fuse Judaism and Christianity into a shared "Judaeo-Christian tradition" that does justice to neither, as also a fundamentalist insistence on some fixed sense in the scriptural text that excludes readers from other backgrounds. Intertextual

22. See Barton 1995.
23. See n. 10 above.
24. Alkier 2009, 13.

interpretation (here of the "spatial" kind) thus produces better (more theologically acceptable and fruitful) readings, and opens up the biblical text in religiously valuable ways.[25]

It is not only biblical scholars who assume that intertextuality is a method of interpretation. Even in France, the land of its birth, intertextuality often came to be seen as a method for better interpretation of texts. This was at least partly true for both Michael Riffaterre and Gérard Genette, working in the 1960s and 1970s, who used intertextuality to improve the understanding of the texts they interpreted. "Intertextuality is a mode of the perception of texts, the true mechanism of literary reading."[26] Julia Kristeva herself, the inventor of the term intertextuality, practised not only what I have been calling "spatial" (synchronic) intertextual interpretation, but also considered the "temporal" (historical, diachronic) questions of sources and influences: Jonathan Culler notes that she even asks which editions of particular source texts a given author might have been familiar with, which would strike many biblical intertextualists as a very fusty "historical-critical" question.[27] The use of "intertextuality" to mean a particular way of reading texts in order to understand them better, and get more out of them, is thus common across the spectrum of textual study.

In spite of all this, Stephen D. Moore and Yvonne Sherwood convincingly argue that intertextuality was not in origin, and is not in its central concerns, a method for interpreting texts. It is a *theory* about textual meaning, which is something quite different. As they put it, "Biblical scholarship seems to turn everything it touches into a method, even concepts as methodologically unpromising as 'intertextuality'"[28] All the applications of intertextuality discussed so far are attempts to produce a methodology or "approach" which will generate a particular way of reading and interpreting texts, so as to learn more about, and from, those texts. This is obviously true of the "temporal"/diachronic approach, which is a way of discovering more about a text's background and

---

25. Cf. Hays, Alkier and Huizenga 2009, xii: "The project of discerning intra-canonical echoes…has provided an easy methodological justification for the long-established Christian interpretive strategy of reading the canon synchronically as a witness to the gospel and of discovering a literary continuity within the diversity of the biblical texts."

26. "L'intertextualité est un mode de perception du texte, c'est le mécanisme propre de la lecture littéraire" (Riffaterre 1979, 496).

27. Culler 1981, 105–6.

28. Moore and Sherwood 2011, 33. I made a similar point myself in 1984: "Biblical 'methods' are *theories* rather than methods" (Barton 1984, 244).

influences. But it is also true of the "spatial"/synchronic approach, in which ideas deriving from various "postmodern" worlds of thought are turned into a set of interpretative methods by which texts are read in new ways, with attention to their relation to other texts, in the absence of historical connections. Either way, the goal is to understand the texts better. Many, perhaps most, practising biblical scholars might regard this point as completely banal: what else is a scholar doing, if not trying to understand the biblical text? Seen from the world that gave birth to the idea of intertextuality, however, this is a misunderstanding. Applications of intertextuality as an interpretative method amount to what we might call a "soft" understanding of the concept—simply adding another method to the toolbox of the biblical critic. But the original idea is a "hard" one: a theory about texts in general, and indeed about how human beings understand the world as a whole, for which intertextual "readings" of specific texts are merely evidence or illustration.

I will not set out here an account of the origins of the term "intertextuality," which seems to have been coined by Julia Kristeva in the 1960s.[29] She developed it out of a reading of Bakhtin and his notion of "dialogism," and it was in turn developed and extended further by Roland Barthes and Jacques Derrida. The idea as it has entered the lexicon of poststructuralist discourse is an idea about the interrelationship of *all* texts—not simply of certain specific texts—which are seen as forming an interlocking mesh. As Kristeva put it in describing one of Bakhtin's ideas, it is "conception of the 'literary word' as an *intersection of textual surfaces* rather than a *point* (a fixed meaning), as a dialogue among several writings."[30] Or again, "in the space of a given text, several utterances, taken from other texts, intersect and neutralize one another."[31] The task of the philosopher of intertextuality is not to reconstruct the "intertexts," except as illustrating the truth of these definitions, but to reflect on what the whole concept implies about human culture in general.[32]

---

29. It can be found in her doctoral thesis (Kristeva 1969b).
30. Kristeva 1980b, 65.
31. Kristeva 1980a, 36.
32. Kristeva herself quickly saw that "intertextuality" was turning into a method of identifying allusion rather than, as she had intended, a theory about culture: "since this term has often been understood in the banal sense of 'study of sources' we prefer the term *transposition* because it specifies that the passage from one signifying system to another demands a new articulation of the thetic—of enunciative and denotative positionality" (Kristeva 1984, 59–60). This suggests she would see a lot of what is called intertextuality in biblical studies as "banal."

A useful way of describing the difference between intertextuality in a soft, methodological sense and intertextuality as a "hard" theory of culture is offered by Clayton and Rothstein, who use the anthropological contrast of "emic" and "etic": "while influence prefers what the anthropologists call 'emic' explanations, those in keeping with patterns of thought that would make sense to the men and women being written about, the critics who practice intertextuality often prefer 'etic' explanations, those geared for the analyst and not for the ideologically blinded analysand."[33] Intertextuality in its "hard" sense is not interested in establishing what are the actual influences on an author, such as could be included in the notes to a critical edition, and on which the author might well agree with the critic. It is interested in seeing the text at the centre of many other texts, many of which the author may well be unaware of. Indeed, in Derrida "text" is defined much more broadly than "words on paper": the whole world is in some sense a "text," and a given piece of writing exists as one cultural artefact among all the products of human culture, with all of which it is more or less intertwined. Intertextuality is indeed in this sense an "etic" theory, which does not appeal to how the creators of cultural artefacts see their own works, but observes the whole cultural scene as it were from outside. At the same time, anyone interested in the theory of intertextuality is likely to say that the impression that one is really "outside" the culture being studied is itself an illusion!

The point is that no literary (or musical or artistic) creation ever starts from scratch. In Barthes' phrase, it always depends on the *déjà lu*, what has already been read. Paradoxically, the "system" of literature to which a work belongs has to exist before the individual work, otherwise we cannot understand the work—if no novels existed, we would have no idea how to read a novel, and all the past novelists jostle behind the new novelist's back; yet on the other hand there can only be a phenomenon called "the novel" because individual novelists have written this or that novel, one of which was the first (some say it was *Robinson Crusoe*). Perceptions of genre are, indeed, a particularly good illustration of the truth in this idea. Genres are conventional schemas that provide a set of expectations within which we read any given work, once we have assigned it to some particular genre. We have great trouble in reading a piece of writing if we are unable to identify its genre. Yet a genre exists only as a generalization from the various actual works that belong to it.[34]

33. Clayton and Rothstein 1991, 17.
34. That genre-recognition is a kind of intertextuality is suggested in Frow 1990, 46, in the very useful introduction to intertextuality by Michael Worton and Judith Still.

Jonathan Culler makes the point by referring to an analogy with Ferdinand de Saussure's theories about the relation between *langue* and *parole*, the total system of a given language as against individual utterances in that language:

> Discourse conventions can only originate in discourse; everything in *la langue*, as Saussure says, must have been first in *parole*. But *parole* is made possible by *la langue*, and if one attempts to identify any utterance or text as a moment of origin one finds that they depend upon prior codes. A codification, one might say, can only originate or be originated if it is already encoded in a prior code; more simply, it is the nature of codes to be always already in existence, to have lost origins.[35]

As Culler goes on to say,

> Intertextuality thus becomes less a name for a work's relation to particular prior texts than a designation of its participation in the discursive space of a culture... The study of intertextuality is thus not the investigation of sources and influences as traditionally conceived, it casts its net wider to include anonymous discursive practices, codes whose origins are lost, that make possible the signifying practices of later texts.[36]

Thus Kristeva "defines intertextuality as the sum of knowledge that makes it possible for texts to have meaning."[37] Reality is a "texte générale." This is not far in practice from the proposal by Harold Bloom, from the (apparently) vastly different American tradition, to the effect that there are no texts, only relations between texts.[38] There are strange affinities here with T. S. Eliot's theory that the literary works in a "canon" form an order among themselves, and when a new (important) work is written, it both derives its meaning from the rest of the canon and yet changes the overall meaning of that canon.[39] Except that in Kristeva's theory there is no question of "great" works, as there was for Eliot (and is for Bloom). In Kristeva, the matter is understood much more democratically, and the "intertexts" of any given piece of writing reach beyond the world of "high" literature to encompass all the products of human culture, with all the texts ever written and all the social conventions ever established. Bloom thinks that major writers rebel against

---

35. Culler 1981, 103.
36. Ibid. Cf. Orr (2003, 28): "Prior text materials lose special status by permutation with others in the intertextual exchange because all intertexts are of equal importance in the intertextual *process*."
37. Culler 1981, 104.
38. Bloom 1975, 3.
39. See, classically, Eliot 1934.

their own "belatedness,"[40] which supposes an author with intentions in a very pre-postmodern way. Yet he goes on, in an idiom closer to Kristeva, "belatedness seems to me not a historical condition at all, but one that belongs to the literary situation as such." This leads him at once to mention Jorge Luis Borges, who observed, paradoxically, but from this point of view truly, that writers "create their own predecessors."[41]

The individual human subject, indeed, is not immune from this analysis. It is not only writings that take the meanings they can have from the web of other writings and cultural conventions in which they are embedded. So do authors and readers. "This 'I' which approaches the text is already itself a plurality of other texts, of codes which are infinite or, more precisely, lost."[42] Writers bring to the act of writing everything they have previously read (heard, seen); readers bring the same baggage to the act of reading. No two readings will be the same, any more than any two pieces of writing will be the same, because everyone is "situated" at a particular place within the environing culture and its history.

Biblical scholars who embrace intertextuality are perhaps not always aware of the general intellectual background I have just sketched briefly. If they are, they may deliberately choose to concentrate on the "soft," methodological version, and ignore the background in post-structuralism and deconstruction that originally animated the ("hard") theory. This is not necessarily illegitimate, but may lead to misunderstanding in any attempted dialogue with critics outside the biblical world, who may treat biblical scholars' work as naïve and inconsequential, thinking that it is meant to relate to areas of literary theory of which it is in fact innocent.

A further danger is that biblical scholars may not fully appreciate the political background of intertextuality, formed as it was in Paris in the 1960s.[43] The question of how texts have meaning looks harmless enough, and the suggestion that the meaning depends not simply on the author, but on the other texts to which the author alludes (perhaps even unconsciously), can also be accommodated within the world of humanistic literary criticism—as we have seen, a number of critics see nothing much new in the idea, and wonder why we need a new and portentous term for

---

40. Bloom 1973, xxv.

41. As Bloom observes, Borges himself "made a career out of exploiting his secondariness," often adopting (and adapting) the ancient literary tradition of pretending that his original work was really an ancient document he had discovered—thereby subverting the idea of "originality."

42. Barthes 1970, 10.

43. Irwin's "Against Intertextuality" (2004), is informative on this, from a very unsympathetic point of view.

it. Even when we note that intertextuality gives the *reader* a considerable role in the text's meaning, on the grounds that the reader too has been formed by texts previously read, traditional biblical critics may not be scared off too badly. As I have argued elsewhere, "reader-response" criticism also comes in a soft as well as a hard variety, and can be seen as merely accentuating something we are all dimly aware of: that texts are not entities with absolutely fixed meanings that the reader has merely to decode "objectively."[44] But the critics who invented intertextuality were not interested in who gives meaning to texts from a purely "literary" perspective. They were interested in questions of *control* in a political sense. Who owns texts? Who decides what they are to mean? For these critics in Paris this was a highly political question, and it has remained so for many who have adopted the varied package of post-structuralist theory to which the idea of intertextuality properly belongs.[45]

One background issue was certainly the dominance of the *Académie Française* in French discourse about literature. The obscure style cultivated by almost all the figures we have been considering, and by their current Anglo-American heirs, infuriates many literary critics, as well as many in the world of biblical studies: see the comments of Irwin, cited above, about even the term "intertextuality" itself. But it is important to see that this, too, was originally a political statement. Clear, measured sentences conforming to classical models and conveying an unambiguous message were the ideal of the *Académie*. The circles around Kristeva, Barthes, and their associates, of course believed that this (purported) clarity was a front for political dominance by a ruling elite: a studied "neutrality" of style that was in reality anything but neutral. The clotted sentences, plays on words, and misspelt terms in post-structuralist writing (all too easy to parody) are not deliberate perversity, but deliberate protest. The supposed control of authors over the meaning of their texts was not seen as an interesting question in philosophical aesthetics, but as part of the ruling class's dominion over the oppressed. The idea that the intertexts of a text comprise not only earlier, equally "classical" works (as in T. S. Eliot), but also (and chiefly) popular writing, and even artefacts in other media and in "low" culture, was an expression of revolt. As Irwin (no friend of such movements!) writes, "Capitalism was justified by precisely the kind of false and misleading clear communication that the intertextualists opposed."[46]

---

44. See Barton 2002.
45. This is seen clearly by Beal (1992b).
46. Irwin 2004, 232.

Of course, from an intertextual perspective, "clarity" is an illusion anyway. The most "neutral" piece of writing contains what everyone nowadays has learned to call a "subtext": what is really being said in what is being said. The present essay is a case in point. Overtly, I am trying to explain the background of the concept "intertextuality" as clearly as I can. But covertly, the reader may suspect, I am trying to dissuade people from it, because I am a leisured member of the English establishment and am not going to relinquish my sense of control over the meaning of the texts I read without a fight. Even in saying that, however, I am probably trying to draw the sting of my underlying intentions by a tone of light mockery and a pretence of candour. If I write "clearly," it is because people are more easily deceived by "clear" writing. The reader must decide on this (and that is an insincere offer). And so on, *ad infinitum*.

A really pure intertextuality might well refuse to undertake any empirical interpretation of actual texts, seeing that as a sell-out to supposed "objectivity." In practice, this has not been the case. As we saw above, Kristeva herself studied a number of texts and asked "soft" questions about what had influenced them: what specific other texts had been, for their authors, the *déjà lu*.[47] In a similar way, since intertextuality is a theory about *all* texts without exception (and indeed about other cultural artefacts), it does not apply only to works written since the rise of modern literary theory. In principle it applies equally to ancient texts, and in using it in the study of the Bible no violence is being done to its original programme. Indeed, there has been considerable interest in biblical texts among some of the exponents of literary theory: Barthes famously wrote an essay on Gen 32, which has become a classic.[48] However, most theories about literature as such tend in practice to prefer working with one kind of text rather than another. Romantic theories of poetry tended to be applied to Romantic poets rather than to, say, early modern ones; Eliot's neo-classicism did not lead him to reread the Romantics "classically," but to rediscover, for example, the "Metaphysicals."[49] This is human nature. It is not surprising, therefore, that Kristeva and others tended to concentrate on the modern novel, especially as Bakhtin had launched his theory of "dialogism" by analyzing the novels of Dostoevsky. Kristeva even suggested—surely undermining her own

---

47. See, e.g., Kristeva 1970, which is an analysis of Antoine de la Sale's novel *Jehan de Saintré*.

48. Barthes 1971.

49. See my comments on this tendency in Barton 1987.

position here—that dialogism *increased* after the end of the nineteenth century, whereas according to the theory dialogism would be a feature of texts as such, not susceptible to increasing or decreasing.[50] The temptation to turn the theory into a set of empirical observations could thus appear even in the theory's founder.[51]

But, as we have seen, empirical work on texts is not an end in itself in a strict intertextual theory. It serves only to illustrate the truth of the theory, rather than to provide new "insight" into the specific text being analyzed. We cannot even say that the empirical work *demonstrates* this truth, though, since it is not a "scientific" hypothesis about texts, but more a kind of mindset with which to approach culture, and indeed life. One could even argue, with Culler, that the quest for evidence for intertextuality actually *undermines* the theory,[52] by treating it as though it were verifiable (and hence also falsifiable). Intertextuality is a way of looking at things, not an idea one can prove or disprove.[53] The whole world of postmodernist thought is one in which the idea of "proof" is, as they say, "problematized."

50.   See Clayton and Rothstein 1991, 20.

51.   In fact the route from Bakhtinian dialogism to Kristevan intertextuality is not crystal-clear. Dialogism notes that in some genres of literature many different points of view are in dialogue, and the text finally comes to rest in none of them. One could well illustrate this from Job, where some readers think there is, as it were, no authorial voice, but the interpretations of just and unjust suffering simply jostle with each other without resolution (see, e.g., Newsom 2003). Applied to literature as such, this can certainly lead to the conclusion that texts have no fixed and certain meaning, but always remain a medley of voices. The idea that the meaning the text does come to have for a given reader depends on its relation to other texts, either actually read or culturally presupposed, represents a further step, and gives the lie to the suggestion sometimes made that there is really nothing in Kristeva that was not already there in Bakhtin. On the other hand, it has also been suggested that a properly worked-out theory of intertextuality did not really arrive until the work of Barthes, so that Kristeva is only a kind of bridge between the two (male) critics—whereas in fact the idea does seem to be already well developed in Kristeva. Mary Orr suspects (and I suspect rightly) that both suggestions are ways of sidelining Kristeva, who, as a woman, is seen as unlikely to have discovered and developed a genuinely new idea (see Orr 2003, 28).

52.   Culler 1981, 111.

53.   Miller criticizes Fewell for not illuminating the biblical text by intertextual reading: "Instead of explaining how one might read the Bible intertextually, she simply notes how some literary scholars have understood what intertextuality is" (G. D. Miller 2011, 288). But to me it seems that this shows a true understanding of intertextuality on Fewell's part!

Thus if biblical scholars are to practise what I have called "hard" intertextuality, they will have to treat the detailed and painstaking work of searching out allusions, quotations, and echoes of one biblical text in another as simply a way of drawing a number of pictures of a universal truth (an odd term to use in a poststructuralist context, but justified by Theory's global claims). Studies of intertextuality in Job, as in this volume, will not be important because they tell us anything about Job, but because they illustrate the truth of intertextuality in general. It is obvious that the "softer" form, in which intertextuality is an exciting new method, is likely to appeal more to most working biblical scholars, and most of the essays presented in the present volume will be construed, and are intended to be construed, in that way. This still leaves plenty of room for the recognition of "non-intentional" cross-reference and allusion, and does not mean that only allusions that can be ascribed to authorial intention "count." But—and here I agree with Moore and Sherwood—it would be good if biblical scholars sometimes avoided "domesticating" ideas that come from Theory, and did not at once turn them into "helpful" ways of deriving theological insight from the Bible. Intertextuality as a theory, along with other products of postmodernist thought, is highly challenging to any idea of the fixity, canonicity, and inspiration of the biblical text. In the biblical "guild" we should face up to that, either accepting it or contesting it, rather than seeing it as one more handy tool to put in our exegetical kit.

Part I

JOB IN DIALOGUE WITH THE PENTATEUCH

To Be Adam or Not to Be Adam: The Hidden Fundamental Anthropological Discourse Revealed in an Intertextual Reading of אדם in Job and Genesis

Manfred Oeming

1. *Methodological Problems and Implications*

The book of Job contains a plenitude of fundamental statements about the essence of human beings. Among them we read some short and mostly enigmatic, though interpretively significant, assertions about the primal man, the "Urmensch" (Job 15:7; 20:4; 31:35). But what kind of methodological framework is adequate for illuminating these dark statements? We find here an intensive controversy among scholars.

Many assume that we do not find the clues for a correct understanding of these anthropological testimonials in the Hebrew Bible itself; they postulate that the best interpretive resource is the wealth of mythological stories from the peoples surrounding Israel—even if these mythologies are only badly preserved, requiring more or less fanciful additions and completions. In such an approach, many of the relations are quite unclear, and thus ripe for further discussion.[1]

Others assume that searching for inner-biblical relations and intertextual connections inside the well-known Hebrew literature will better enable us to understand these passages. This "intertextuality" comes in two different forms: "diachronic" and "synchronic."[2] This means the focus can be on either the historical development of texts, in which a later one draws on an earlier one, or on a possible interrelation between texts that can be discerned by someone who reads them together, especially when, as in the case of the Hebrew Bible, they form part of a defined

1. See pp. 24–26 below.
2. See G. D. Miller 2011.

corpus (or canon).[3] A quotation or allusion is never just a repetition, but a variation with more or less new interpretations. In an extreme form we have to take into account the possibility that a "quotation" can be a cynical bitter parody of the traditional text by the author(s) of Job, a kind of "antithetical allusion," in which the earlier text may be the "target" of a subversive attack (Kynes 2011). Searching for textual candidates capable of shedding light on dark verses in the book of Job, we find special connections in the Psalms (esp. Ps 8),[4] and, in particular, the primeval history of Genesis. According to my understanding, the book of Job was written after Gen 1–11[5] and therefore, in light of the evidence to follow, it is not only probable but nearly sure that Job is quoting or intentionally alluding to Genesis. The intertextual relation of Job and Genesis is not just a synchronic connection (one available to be found by every reader—or not) but also, and first of all, a diachronic allusion. By using the term "allusion," I am committing myself to a diachronic reading of the relationship between the two texts in contrast to a synchronic "intertextual" reading. For me the most influential works on intertextuality, which I attempt to follow, are Benjamin Sommer's exegesis of the book of Isaiah[6] and Will Kynes's interpretation of the book of Job.[7]

In this sense, the statements about the "Urmensch" in the book of Job are an excellent example of the general methodological problems associated with intertextuality, tradition history, history of reception and history of religion in reading Job.[8]

2. The Plurality of Anthropological Concepts in the Book of Job and Their Backgrounds

Konrad Schmid is right: "The fact that the book of Job is a learned book is beyond question. Since it is a book of the Hebrew Bible, it can be readily assumed that this learning can be detected as a scribal scholarliness."[9] In the study of inner-biblical exegesis in Job,[10] its relationship

---

3. See John Barton's article in the present volume: "*Déjà lu*: Intertextuality, Method or Theory?"
4. Dell 1991, 127–35; Frevel 2004.
5. See Gertz (2012), who argues that P and non-P material in Gen 1:1–8:22 (Gen 6:1–4 excluded) existed in the early Persian period.
6. Sommer 1996a, 1996b, 1998.
7. Kynes 2011 and 2012.
8. Cf. Pyeon 2003; Wilson 2006.
9. Schmid 2011, 243–44.
10. Fishbane 1992; Mettinger 1993.

with Genesis has always played a special role. In particular, the proximity to the genaology from the patriarchal period in Gen 36:9–43 has
been often observed, with the book of Job interpreted as a gigantic
midrash on this chapter (cf., e.g., Gen 36:11, 15–16, 28, 34). Certainly
Job is immersed in the general colouring of the patriarchal times, but the
message of the book is arguably less shaped by a specific person at a
certain historical moment, but rather by "the existence of man in
general." Therefore, intertextual references should lead us to an analysis
of the *theologically* "fundamental" texts of Genesis, especially Gen 18,
which brings us closer to the actual center of the book of Job. In
Abraham's dialogue with Yahweh on the justice of the deity's action, he
famously declares, "Far be it from you to do such a thing, to slay the
righteous with the wicked, so that the righteous fare as the wicked! Far
be that from you! Shall not the Judge of all the earth do what is just?" If
only ten righteous lived in Sodom, God eventually agrees, for these ten
just people the whole city will be spared.[11]

This dispute about the *justice of God* is one side of the book of Job;
the other main aspect of the dialogues between Job and his four friends is
a question of anthropology, the issue of the *justice of human beings*:
"What are mortals, that they can be clean? Or those born of woman, that
they can be righteous?" (Job 15:14). It is clear that the core of the book
presents a fundamental *anthropological* dispute, and this is what I want
to focus on in the present study, ultimately in relation to intertextual
connections with Genesis. The concordance confirms the anthropological
emphasis of Job; the word אדם ("human"/"Adam") occurs in the *BHS*
554 times, and the books with the most occurrences are as follows:

1.	Ezekiel	132×
2.	Ecclesiastes	49×
3.	Gen 1–11	46×
4.	Proverbs	45×
5.	Jeremiah	30×
6.	Isaiah	27×
7.	Job	27×
8.	Numbers	24×
9.	Leviticus	15×
10.	Exodus	14×

In every other book, the word appears fewer than ten times. The twenty-
seven appearances in the book of Job demonstrate the significance of the

---

11. Schmidt 1976, 131–64.

term אדם in the book.[12] It is used to express a notable plurality of anthropological concepts:[13]

(a) Often it is used for a general description of the nature of human beings, with special emphasis on *human dignity* because אדם is a creature of God:

> Remember that you fashioned me like clay; and will you turn me to dust again? (Job 10:9)[14]

As in the garden of Eden, God is constantly looking for humans. "Adam where are you?" asked God in Gen 3; in the book of Job, God is called נצר האדם ("watcher of humanity," Job 7:20).

(b) Many texts emphasize the *lowliness of man*:[15]

> Can mortals be righteous before God? Can human beings be pure before their Maker? (Job 4:17)

Markus Witte has suggested that all these verses (4:12–21; 15:11–16; 25:1–6; 40:3–5; 42:2, 3*, 5–6) belong to a special redactional layer—dating from the third century B.C.E. and close to the piety of the *hodayot* in Qumran—which explains the suffering of Job by the idea of the natural sinfulness and impurity of all human beings. Witte calls this the "Niedrigkeitsredaktion" (redaction of anthropological lowliness).

(c) A third group of thoughts is concentrated on the *coherence of doing and receiving*:

> For according to their deeds he will repay them, and according to their ways he will make it befall them. (Job 34:11)

This worldview is already true for Adam, the first man, as for Job, the "perfect" (תם) man (Job 1:1).

(d) *The destiny of Adam is to work very hard.* This involves texts with possible allusions: Job 5:7 to Gen 2:15 and 3:17:

---

12. Cf. Remus 1993.
13. Cf. Sir 33:10–11: "Every human being was made from the earth, just as Adam was. But the LORD, in his deep wisdom, made them all different and gave them different tasks."
14. Cf. Frevel 2007.
15. Witte 1994. See especially the synopsis (190–92) and the summary (223–28).

כי־אדם לעמל יולד

Yet Adam (man?) is born to labor (Job 5:7)

ויקח יהוה אלהים את־האדם וינחהו בגן־עדן לעבדה ולשמרה

The LORD God took the man and put him in the garden of Eden to till it and keep it. (Gen 2:15)

בעצבון תאכלנה כל ימי חייך

in toil you shall eat of it all the days of your life. (Gen 3:17)

הלא־צבא לאנוש על־ארץ וכימי שכיר ימיו

Do not human beings have a hard service on earth, and are not their days like the days of a laborer? (Job 7:1)

(e) *Adam should not be alone* but in constant proximity to his wife. There are certain parallels between Eve in Genesis and Job's wife.[16] Usually, according to a long-lasting tradition, Job's wife is interpreted as a helper of Satan ("adiutrix diaboli"), attempting to deceive Job into forsaking YHWH:

ותאמר לו אשתו עדך מחזיק בתמתך ברך אלהים ומת

Then his wife said to him, "Do you still persist in your integrity? Curse God and die." (Job 2:9).

However, I am skeptical of this interpretation because Job's wife has, according to my analysis (developed from the Septuagint where she prays a whole psalm of lament), a very positive function and the parallel reading of these texts must include a positive reevaluation of Eve.[17] Thus, according to Gen 2:

לא־טוב היות האדם לבדו

It is not good that the man should be alone. (Gen 2:18)[18]

16. Gen 3:11–13: "He said, 'Who told you that you were naked? Have you eaten from the tree of which I commanded you not to eat?' The man said, 'The woman whom you gave to be with me, she gave me fruit from the tree, and I ate.' Then the LORD God said to the woman, 'What is this that you have done?' The woman said, 'The serpent tricked me, and I ate'." Cf. 1 Tim 2:14: "and Adam was not deceived, but the woman was deceived and became a transgressor."

17. Cf. Tob 8:8(6) σὺ ἐποίησας Αδαμ καὶ ἔδωκας αὐτῷ βοηθὸν Ευαν στήριγμα τὴν γυναῖκα αὐτοῦ, "You created Adam and gave him his wife Eve to be his helper and support." See Seow 2007; Oeming 2007.

18. This is the reason why William Blake never portrays Job without his wife in his illustrations of the book.

(f) The crucial question is *whether a human can be sinless before God or not*. Job's friends argue that no human is without sin, but Job consistently claims to be free from any sin.

Direct quotations from Gen 1–3 are not evident in the discussion so far. Even allusions are uncertain and the assumption of an interrelation is—especially in isolation—dangerous, and it is no wonder that in scholarly research the interrelation is disputed in a highly controversial manner. The following analysis, however, tries to explore as a test case what happens when we read the "fundamental anthropological" statements of the book of Job in an intertextual connection with the image of Adam in Gen 1–3.

3. *Job in Relation to Adam: The Relevant Texts in Genesis*

The three main relevant texts to focus on Adam, the first man, are Job 15:7; 20:4 and 31:35. I will consider them each in turn.

3.1. *Job 15:7*
Eliphaz asks Job:

הראישון אדם תולד

Are you the firstborn of the human race? (Job 15:7a)

There is a widespread tradition in the exegesis of this text of combining it with a mythical ancient Near Eastern or Greek tradition of a so-called Urmensch. Gisela Fuchs offers an investigation of the idea of a "Primitive man" in ancient literature:

> This refers to a 'heavenly entity' with royal features, in which the boundaries between man and God are fluid, as with Gilgamesh, Enkidu and Adapa. Primitive man is honored with a special wisdom—a characteristic to which also Ezek 28:1–10 alludes—he has beauty or fame. The particular closeness of primitive man with God has an intrinsic, but also a local component. His whereabouts are therefore often associated with "God's garden" or "God's mountain."

Fuchs suggests that Job 15:7 is alluding specifically to an offense of primitive man, specifically the robbery of wisdom. She paraphrases accordingly: "Have you (Job) robbed wisdom to which you are not entitled?"[19]

---

19. Fuchs 1993, 101–4 (101, 103).

According to Dexter Callendar, the text belongs—like the myth of Adapa—in the context of some conflicts between the primal human figure and the deity and "explores the relationship between God and Job; or better, perhaps, Job and deity. What is at stake is Job's right to challenge the actions of God; and the validity of that right."[20] Is Job like God/deity? Since it seems to be a competition between humanity and the divine, this suggests a mythical context. Many scholars read Job in the light of these *extra-biblical* mythical traditions. The imagination of commentators in the depiction of the "original man" can be far-reaching. Fohrer, for example, sees a whole chain of myths in the background. The purpose of all the allusions is clear: "They should devastatingly crush the gigantic hybris of Job" (Fohrer 1963).

But this interpretation is problematic. One has to read a great deal between the lines. Fuchs herself notes: "The motif of primitive man is in Job 15 completely isolated." Instead of assuming an erratic fragment of a myth—unknown elsewhere in the canon—I prefer to read it together with biblical traditions like that in Gen 2. According to this text Adam has had *direct communication* with God. YHWH gave him the privilege of a face-to-face conversation. So N. H. Tur-Sinai is nearly right in his intertextual reading:

> The meaning of this question is at once clear by v. 8: "Hast thou listened in God's circle…and stolen wisdom for thyself?" If you were Adam, who had converse with God, we might indeed believe that you have heard God's secret and guiltily carried off with you the true wisdom thus acquired… The whole passage is thus a most fitting retort to Job's words about the divine voice which allegedly spoke to him in a dream.[21]

We find the (cynically expressed) tradition that Adam was a perfect primal creature in Job 38:21:

ידעת כי־אז תולד ומספר ימיך רבים

You do know, because you were born when they were, you must be very old by now![22]

But Job is not, this text suggests, as perfect as the first man was (in the beginning).

20. Callender 2000, esp. "Is Job the Primal Human? (Job 15:7–16)," 137–78.

21. Tur-Sinai 1981, 248. Tur-Sinai is here referring to his attribution of the nocturnal vision in Job 4:12–21 to Job, and not Eliphaz as it is presented in the MT.

22. Similarly, in Sir 49:16, a text that probably belongs to the same period or not much later that the book of Job: Σημ καὶ Σηθ ἐν ἀνθρώποις ἐδοξάσθησαν, καὶ ὑπὲρ πᾶν ζῷον ἐν τῇ κτίσει Αδαμ ("Shem and Seth and Enosh were honored, but above every other created living being was Adam").

In the end the interpretations of scholars arguing from the mythical background and scholars emphasizing the canonical parallels are quite similar. The result is in any case that Eliphaz is mocking the hypertrophic self-understanding of Job. He is not as wise as he thinks.

3.2. *Job 20:4*
Zophar asks Job:

הזאת ידעת מני־עד מני שים אדם עלי־ארץ

> Have you *not* known these things of old, from the time that Adam was set upon the earth?

Even Zophar seems to be aware of the idea that Adam enjoyed a special closeness to God at the beginning of the history of humankind and thus had a rich treasure of knowledge. At the same time it becomes clear that this early knowledge (through the expulsion from paradise?) was lost. One does not need to seek any extra-biblical myths, for one can better draw on inner-biblical ideas. Fuchs (1993, 115–18) assumes that Job 20:4 is alluding to the myth of a world of giants, a variant of a battle with chaos in the shape of the monster growing to the sky.

As an alternative I would prefer—in an intertextual networking with Gen 3—to see here a description of the Fall. When Adam wants "to be like God," or if humankind is building a tower that reaches "up to heaven," then this hybris is without long-lasting success. Even the primeval history teaches that the happiness of the wicked, the success of the ungodly act, is of short duration. Adam's transgression is uncovered by God and he is convicted of disobedience. Perhaps Job 20:7, "Where is he?" (איו), is an allusion to Gen 3:9: "Adam, where are you (איכה)?" Zophar may therefore ascertain—full of mockery—that it is impossible for Job to be as smart as the original Adam.

3.3. *Job 31:33*
Job himself gives a kind of a summary of his ethical behavior:

אם־כסיתי כאדם פשעי לטמון בחבי עוני

> (If I covered =) I never covered my transgressions as Adam by hiding my iniquity in my bosom.

The text is debated philologically. According to Fohrer,[23] כאדם is a scribal error and it has to be changed into מאדם: to hide the sin "*before other human beings*"; others would like to change it into באדם, "*among*

---

23. Fohrer 1963, 426.

human beings" (Duhm). But all these changes are arbitrary because they are without manuscript evidence. Also, the interpretation *"according to the human habit"* (Ewald, Dillmann, Davidson) is not convincing because it fails to realize the intertextual resonances surrounding the verse in Job 31:34–40 and takes Adam as a general expression, not as a personal name. However, as Tur-Sinai (1981, 446) observes, "Despite all doubts כאדם refers to Adam of the story of the Creation… More specifically, this is an allusion to Adam and his wife, of whom it is expressly stated that after sinning they 'hid themselves' (Gen. III,8)."

The LXX reads εἰ δὲ καὶ ἁμαρτὼν ἀκουσίως ἔκρυψα τὴν ἁμαρτίαν μου ("or if too having sinned unintentionally, I hid my sin"). ἀκουσίως means "involuntarily" and implies a theory of sin according to Lev 5, where שׁגג, "to sin without knowledge," is used (in contrast to "to sin with elevated arms").

Daniela Opel offers a mediating view:

> The theme of the first two verses appears universally human (כאדם), because Job denies having concealed his crimes for fear of other people, as it is in human nature (cf. Ps 32:5; Prov 28:13). It was only because of the later added content in Job 31:38–40 that…v. 33 receives the character of an allusion to Gen 3:8—the first man and his wife tried to hide from God, after eating the forbidden fruit from the tree of knowledge, to have a judgment which is similar to God's, and the result is that human beings develop not only shame but also a sense of guilt that caused them to hide themselves from God, but that is ultimately not possible. This contrasts Job with the behavior of primitive man. Job did not try to conceal his guilt before the omnipresent God, impossible in any case (Job 31:14), especially not before the fear of the mob.[24]

4. *Significance of the Results*

When we work in a canonical context (this means according to the canon formulated in the late Persian/early Hellenistic periods) and consider the three references in Job to Gen 2–3, which are admittedly not quite clear in isolation but convincing in their accumulation, we find that the book of Job belongs to the history of reception and interpretation of the primeval history. This means especially three things:

- The friends deny that Job is like Adam. The author(s) apparently know and emphasize (already in the pre-Christian Jewish exegesis of the fourth to second century B.C.E.!) the difference, later spelt out by commentators, between the "prelapsarian" Adam

24. Opel 2010, 126.

(before the fall of humanity) and the "postlapsarian" Adam (after the fall of humanity). They negatively emphasize that Job is not as wise and prudent as (the original) Adam was based on his nearness to God. Job is much less than the prelapsarian Adam. They allude to the vast knowledge of the original Adam in regard to Job only, ironically, to deny it to him and with emphatic cynicism. If Job claims to be as knowledgeable as the (prelapsarian) Adam, this can only be the expression of a sinful hybris and failure, a fall, and punishment ("expulsion from paradise" cf. Job 29) is expected.

- The friends positively affirm Job as a "postlapsarian Adam." Fallen low, east of Eden, Adam (= Job as a human being) is in the sphere of sin and justly under God's distrust, anger, and punishment. Only through humility and repentance may he hope that God will forgive him.

- Job, in contrast, wants to maintain a positive affirmation that he is not like the disobedient and evasive Adam, committing sins and trying to hide them before the people. Job is different from the usual "postlapsarian Adam." One might even say Job claims to be "the better Adam": "I'm more than Adam; I have the knowledge of the 'postlapsarian Adam' and in spite of this I'm still innocent!" Job sees himself as the perfect Adam. Is the will of God realized in any creature more fully than in Job? It is not Adam that is perfect but Job! (See God's judgment in Job 1:8.)

The question is if we are capable of realizing the context of this extraordinary anthropology. According to Konrad Schmid, we can see here the inner-Jewish debate[25] in the Persian period: "A human being can and should be righteous before God, and thus the Book of Job confirms the basic condition of the Deuteronomic thinking against the anthropological skepticism, for example, of the primeval history and Qohelet."[26] I am not sure that the intention of the book as a whole is to support such an anthropological ethical optimism. I think on the contrary that the prevailing position is that of the friends: an anthropological pessimism, which also occurs in Elihu's and God's speeches. Also the final judgment in Job 42:7 ("You have not spoken rightly to me") is not an anthropological statement but a criticism of the wrong direction of the argumentation of

25. Wilson (2006) also understands Job as a document of an inner-Jewish dispute in the second century B.C.E. For him, Job was written with a strong anti-messianic intention, especially opposing the idea of a priestly messiah. The Adam traditions are not at all in Wilson's focus.

26. Schmid 2011, cf. 254 n. 1.

the friends—they have spoken *of* God, not *to* him.[27] On the other side are the speeches of Job and the judgment of God in the prose introduction. So the book as a whole takes us into a lively discourse with no clear decision. Both sides are quoting earlier biblical texts, both perceptions have arguments (e.g. experience against tradition). It is the hidden fight of an inner-biblical exegesis: "to be Adam" against "not to be Adam." In the end, in ch. 42, Job is a real wise man, not because of his closeness to God, like Adam, but because he suffered evil from God (42:11).

27. For further details, see Oeming 2000.

THE "REVERSAL" OF *HEILSGESCHICHTE* IN JOB 3

John Burnight

In an oft-cited 1971 *Vetus Testamentum* article, Michael Fishbane proposed that the malediction with which Job begins ch. 3 represents a "counter-cosmic incantation" that "reverses" the creation in Gen 1 and brings about—at least for the day of Job's birth—the return of primordial chaos and darkness.[1] The first of the "darkness" invocations (יְהִי חֹשֶׁךְ in 3:4a), for example, can be viewed as a negation—Clines (1989, 84) calls it a "parodic reversal"—of the *fiat lux* in Gen 1:3.[2] Points of contact between Job 3 and other biblical passages have also been widely acknowledged. Many commentators, for example, have compared elements of Job 3 to Jeremiah's imprecation in Jer 20:14–18. Habel (1985, 103), among others, observed that Job's paraphrase of Jeremiah forms an *inclusio* around his curse, with Job 3:3 echoing Jer 20:14–15, and Job 3:10–11 echoing Jer 20:17–18.[3]

But while the similarity of the two passages has frequently been noted, the context of Jeremiah's curse seldom has: it is set during the impending invasion of Jerusalem by the Babylonians (cf. Jer 20:4–6). Job, then, in cursing the day of his birth, is alluding to a prophetic speech set during the events which would ultimately lead to Judah's "death." In this essay I will argue that Job's opening *cri de coeur* in ch. 3 also makes use of other motifs and terminology that are evocative of key periods in the nation's history: in particular, the period of Egyptian bondage and the Exodus, as well as the Exile and restoration. In effect, many of Job's

---

1. Fishbane 1971; see also Perdue 1986.

2. See also, e.g., Dhorme, Terrien, Gordis, Habel, Newsom, and others. Dell (1991) has proposed that the genre of the book of Job as a whole can be classified as a "parody."

3. The similarity of the two passages was remarked upon over a millennium ago by Saadiah Gaon; see also Dhorme, Gordis, and many others.

utterances in ch. 3 can be viewed as a "reversal" of traditional *Heils-geschichte* themes,[4] including those of God's deliverance from slavery in a foreign land, and his promises to give "rest" to his people.[5] In several cases, Job makes what can plausibly be viewed as direct allusions to other biblical texts related to these events, both within the book of Exodus and elsewhere in the biblical corpus (specifically, in Numbers, Psalms, and Isaiah). Recognition of this strategy can help to account for some of the poet's seemingly peculiar thematic and rhetorical choices. Michael Riffaterre argues that intertextual markers "are both the problem, when seen from the text, and the solution when their other, intertextual side is revealed."[6] In this essay, I will argue that Israel's *Heilsgeschichte* can serve as the solution to some of the exegetical "problems" in Job 3.

One example can be found in the first stich of 3:5.

Job 3:5a

May darkness and deep shadow claim it　　　יגאלהו חשך וצלמות

Opinions differ as to whether יגאלהו is derived from the root גאל I, which BDB glosses as "redeem, act as kinsman," or the less common גאל II, "defile." A number of interpreters prefer the latter, viewing "redeem" as inapposite given the subject(s) and context.[7]

The majority of modern commentators and translations, however, interpret the verb as a form of גאל I, translating it as "claim" or similarly, with a variety of explanations being offered as to the underlying meaning of the expression. Driver and Gray (1921, 32–33), for example, write that גאל here means:

---

4. *Heilsgeschichte* is used here as a term of convenience to refer to two of God's principal salvific acts toward Israel/Judah: the liberations from "foreign bondage" effected during not only the Exodus but also during the restoration from the Exile. The biblical descriptions of these events, as well as the captivities preceding them, frequently utilize common terminology and motifs; see below.

5. The term "reversal" here is borrowed from Robert Alter (1985, 76), who makes a compelling argument that Job 3 can itself be viewed as the object of a "grand reversal" in God's first answer from the whirlwind in ch. 38. Benjamin Sommer (1998, see esp. 36–46 and 75–78) also applies this term to Deutero-Isaiah's reuse of words and images from earlier "negative" prophetic oracles to console, rather than to rebuke, the people.

6. Riffaterre 1991, 58.

7. E.g. Dhorme ("pollute"), Tur-Sinai, Horst, Perdue; cf. the Targum's יטנפון, and the opinions of Rashi, Ibn Ezra, and Gersonides.

properly to claim effectively property the possession of which has lapsed
(i.e. to redeem it); the right, or duty, of doing this devolved commonly
upon the owner's nearest relation…hence the idea is, as soon as the day
appears, let darkness, as its nearest relation, at once assert [its] rights, and
take possession of it.

Two terms are used to describe this "redeeming" darkness: חשך וצלמות.
Though the meaning and etymology of צלמות have been much debated,
less attention has been paid to the actual phrase that forms the compound
subject, which outside of Job is found in the Bible only in Ps 107. It
occurs there twice in connection with the divine redemption of the nation
from foreign bondage (cf. vv. 10, 14). Forms of גאל also occur twice in
this passage to describe this "redeeming" (107:2):

Let the redeemed of the LORD proclaim,	יאמרו גאולי יהוה
Whom He has redeemed from the hand of the adversary	אשר גאלם מיד־צר

The people's previous state of bondage is described in v. 10:

Those who dwelt in darkness and deep shadow,	ישבי חשך וצלמות
Prisoners in misery and iron (chains).	אסירי עני וברזל

The phrase is repeated in v. 14, which describes their rescue:

He brought them out of darkness and deep shadow	יוציאם מחשך וצלמות
And broke their bonds apart.	ומוסרותיהם ינתק

חשך and צלמות are also used in prophetic literature to describe the
suffering of the nation in foreign bondage. The terms occur in near
parallelism in Isa 9:1 in a description of the conditions from which the
exiled Israelites are to be restored, while Jer 13:16 contains צלמות and a
verbal form of חשך in a warning regarding the coming fall of Jerusalem
and the Exile. Each term is also used individually as a metaphor for the
nation's bondage, both in Egypt (e.g. Jer 2:6) and Babylon (e.g. Isa
42:7).

In addition, both the Exodus and restoration from the Exile are
frequently characterized as God "redeeming" (using forms of גאל) his
people. Along with the examples in Ps 107, the term—both as a finite
verb and a participle—is used this way in Exodus, the Psalms, Jeremiah,
Micah, and especially Deutero-Isaiah.[8] Job's language thus subverts

---

8. Exod 6:6; 15:13; Pss 74:2; 77:15; 78:35; 106:10; Isa 41:14; 43:1, 14; 44:6, 22,
23, 24; 47:4; 48:17, 20; 49:7, 26; 51:10; 52:3, 9; 54:5, 8; 59:20; 60:16; 62:12; 63:3,
9, 16; Jer 31:11; 50:34; Mic 4:10.

the traditional motif of God's redemptive acts: rather than the deity redeeming *out of* חשך and צלמות, these "darknesses" are themselves called upon to carry out the "redeeming."

The next colon continues the poet's strategy of "reversal" in an ingenious way:

Job 3:5b

May a cloud dwell upon it   תשכן־עליו עננה

Many commentators have found this expression curious; Jacobsen and Nielsen (1992, 196–97), for example, write,

> Beginning with verse 5 the wish that a cloud descend over the day seems rather anticlimactic after the day in the preceding section has already been consigned to darkness and blackness… Since in the Book of Job we are dealing with a great poet, one cannot but wonder whether his original text did not have a stronger expression here and, in fact, whether he would ever have dwelled so monotonously and repititiously [*sic*] on the one theme of darkness as the present version of the text has him do.

Some interpreters have proposed that the *hapax legomenon* עננה denotes something more than a typical "cloud." Gordis (1978, 33) writes that the term is "a collective noun, the force of which is not transmitted by the English 'clouds,' but by the German *Gewölke*." Michel, Hartley, and Perdue ("thick cloud") offer similar translations. None of these interpreters, however, offers any evidence that עננה is a "stronger" or "more intense" cloud than that denoted by ענן.[9] Though this possibility cannot be ruled out, Greenstein (2003) has more recently offered a compelling argument that such forms are a literary conceit by which the poet intends to give Job's speech a "foreign" flavor.

But the seeming banality of the expression remains puzzling. As above, however, an intertextual reading may provide an explanation. Several commentators have noted that the expression שכן ענן על occurs several times in the Exodus-wandering narrative, when the theophonic cloud rests on the tabernacle. In fact, this is the *only* context in the biblical corpus—apart from the example in Job 3:5—in which this verbal idiom occurs with a form of ענן. The first instance is found in the closing verses of the book of Exodus (40:34); after the tabernacle is completed, the theophanic "cloud" (ענן) "settles upon it" (שכן עליו הענן), preventing

---

9. In Arabic, *ʿanān* is the collective ("clouds"), while the form with *tāʾ marbūṭa* is the *nomen unitatis*.

Moses from entering. This event also would prevent the Israelites from continuing their journey until the cloud was "taken up" (יסעו, cf. vv. 36–37).

All of the other biblical occurrences of the expression שכן ענן על are found in Num 9–10. In every case, it is used to convey the idea of the divine "cloud" "settling" upon the tabernacle (ישכן הענן על־המשכן, cf. 9:17–18); as long as the cloud is "settled," the Israelites remain camped. A lengthy description of this process, with multiple occurrences of the phrase, is found in 9:17–23. The final occurrence of the idiom describes an example of such a stoppage, that in the Wilderness of Paran in 10:12.

With these intertextual considerations in mind, Job 3:5b can be viewed as a continuation of the "reversal" of the traditional biblical motif of divine redemption in which God frees his people from bondage and brings them to the Promised Land. The poet accomplishes this in an exceedingly clever fashion: while maintaining the "darkening" imagery begun in 3:4, in 3:5b he also evokes these passages describing the Israelites' "wandering." In every other passage where this expression occurs, the cloud "settling" means that the Exodus—the central redemptive act in the nation's history—is brought to a halt. Seen in this light, Job's seemingly banal wish for what is essentially a "cloudy day" becomes, like the previous cola, a repudiation of an important motif from Israel's national history: Job curses the day of his birth with an expression that metaphorically stopped the "birth" of the nation.

Job 3:10

Another feature of Job 3 that has been viewed as puzzling is Job's emphasis on the themes of exhaustion and a lack of "rest."[10] The idea is introduced in 3:10, where Job states that the reason for his curse is that he has been made to see עמל:

For he shut not the portals of my belly,	כי לא סגר דלתי בטני
Hiding travail from my eyes.	ויסתר עמל מעיני

Modern versions and commentaries typically translate עמל here as "sorrow," "trouble," "misery," or similarly. But these translations, while perfectly reasonable, do not adequately capture the term's other connotations: it frequently designates "labour" or "toil."[11] Habel (1985, 109)

---

10. E.g. Saadiah (1988, 101), and modern commentators such as Clines (1989, 105).

11. Cf., e.g., Pss 105:44; 107:12; Eccl 2:10 (*bis*), 21, 24; 3:13; 4:4, 6, 8, 9; 5:14, 18.

notes that עָמָל is used to describe the hardships of the Israelites in Egypt (cf. Deut 26:17), and it also occurs in the Ps 107 passage discussed above (v. 12). The connotation of labour is also present in the other forms of the root in Biblical Hebrew,[12] and numerous examples are attested with this meaning in a number of cognate languages.[13] In light of these considerations, a translation such as Driver and Gray's (1921, 35) "travail"—with its connotations of both labour and suffering—may be preferable in this verse.

This reading also serves as an appropriate introduction to the "rest" themes that will be prominent in Job's "lament" (vv. 11–26). Habel (1985, 104) calls these verses an *Ichklage*: they are modeled after the "individual lament" psalms, but differ in form in that they do not address God in the second person.[14] But there is also another difference: the *content* of Job's lament departs significantly from that of its psalmic counterparts. Job does not speak here in the language of individual suffering; instead, he utilizes terminology and motifs that are used elsewhere in the biblical corpus to characterize periods of *national* crisis. Job's lament contains a number of motifs and images that describe the freedom of the grave in terms that are evocative of Israel's bondage in a foreign land, both before the Exodus and during the Exile. Verses 17–19 provide vivid examples of this:

Job 3:17–19

There the wicked cease their raging,	שם רשעים חדלו רגז
There rest those whose strength is spent.	ושם ינוחו יגיעי כח
Captives are at ease together,	יחד אסירים שאננו
They hear not the slave-driver's voice;	לא שמעו קול נגש
Whether small or great, he is there,	קטן וגדול שם הוא
And the slave is free of his master.	ועבד חפשי מאדניו

12.   The qal verb derived from this root denotes the act of "labouring, toiling" in all of its biblical attestations, and this is the basic meaning of the nominal form עָמָל ("labourer, sufferer"; cf. the notes to 3:20 below; also Job 20:22; Judg 5:26; Prov 16:26) and the verbal adjective עָמֵל ("toiling," Eccl 2:18, 22; 3:9; 4:8; 9:9) as well.

13.   Cf. e.g., Old, Imperial, and Jewish Aramaic, Syriac, Sabean, and Arabic (ʿamal, "doing, acting action, activity; work, labour"). The lone attestation in Ugaritic (*KTU* 5.11.8) appears in a context that appears to involve either work or compensation for work. The LXX translates the occurrence in 3:10 with πόνος (related to πένομαι, "to work for one's living"), which seems to have a similar semantic range to that of עָמָל; though its most basic sense is "hard work, toil," it can also denote the suffering caused by toil, or anything produced by such toil.

14.   Dell (1991, 125) writes that these verses contain a "misuse" of a lament form, thus fitting her classification of Job as a "parody."

The poet's use of אסירים and נגש in v. 18 makes the "foreign bondage" theme explicit. The first of these terms occurs just 12 times in the Hebrew Bible; though it is traditionally translated as "prisoner," several scholars have argued that this is misleading. Clines (1989, 96), for example, writes that the "image here is of captives, prisoners-of-war (not criminal or civil 'prisoners'…), who by long custom formed the forced labor gangs of the ancient Near East."[15] Indeed the word is used in Ps 68:7 to describe the Hebrew slaves in Egypt. In at least five of its other biblical occurrences, it refers to the Judeans in Babylonian captivity.[16]

The participle נֹגֵשׂ (normally glossed as "slave-driver, taskmaster"), as many commentators have observed, is evocative of Israel's slavery in Egypt. Habel (1985, 111) writes:

> The term "taskmaster" (*nōgēś*) is used of the Egyptian overseers who harassed the Israelites in bondage. These allusions to liberation from oppression suggest that initially Job identifies strongly with the oppressed.

It is noteworthy, though, that Job is not here talking about "widows" or "orphans" (the typical victims of oppression in Israelite religious literature). He instead focuses on a very specific type of the "oppressed": those in hard labour and bondage, themes that are prevalent in Egypt and the Exile, but receive little attention during the period of the Judges or the monarchy. Like אסיר, the term נגש is quite rare: outside of Job, it is found only 13 times. Five of these are in Exodus, referring to the Hebrews' Egyptian oppressors (Exod 3:7; 5:6, 10, 13, 14). The first of these occurs in God's initial statement to Moses that he has heard of the Israelites' suffering in Egypt, and "given heed to their cry because of their taskmasters (נֹגְשָׂיו)," while the four occurrences in Exod 5 are concerned with the slave-drivers pressing the slaves to fill their quota of bricks even though they are no longer being given straw. The chapter ends with the people blaming Moses (v. 21), and Moses in turn blaming God (vv. 22–23) for making the slaves' lot worse, despite promising to deliver them.

---

15. See also Rowley, Driver and Gray, Tur-Sinai, and others. The term occurs in semantic parallelism with *ʿbd* in the Baal Cycle from Ugarit: *ʿbdk . bʿl . y ymm . / ʿbdk . bʿl* [nhr]m . / *bn. dgn. ʾasrkm* (*KTU* 1.2 I 36–37).

16. Pss 79:11 (cf. v. 1), 107:10 (which, as noted above, some scholars view as referring to both the Exodus and the Exile), Isa 14:17, and Zech 9:11–12. In the other three instances (Pss 69:33; 102:20; Lam 3:34), the exact identity of the "captives" is unclear, though Ps 102:20 does discuss the restoration of Zion and Lamentations has the Exile as its backdrop.

נֹגֵשׂ is also used to describe the nation's Babylonian "oppressors" during the Exile. Like רֹגֶז from v. 17, it occurs in Isaiah's "Oracle against Babylon" (Isa 14:1–4; see the discussion of v. 26 below). The themes of bondage and oppression are thus associated not only with the Exodus, but also the Exile. Again in this verse, the terms and imagery are reminiscent of biblical passages that describe the suffering of the nation in Egypt and Babylon: both the period before Israel's "birth" and during the Exile are viewed as times of hard labour, imprisonment, and oppression.

The appearance in 3:19 of עבד following the "captives" and "slave-driver" of v. 18 again calls to mind the theme of national bondage. Egypt is frequently given the appellation "house of slaves" (בית עבדים), as in the prologue to the Ten Commandments (Exod 20:2).[17] This idea is also expressed in the Deuteronomic version of the sabbath commandment (Deut 5:15), in which Israel is reminded that they were (collectively) a slave (וזכרת כי־עבד היית), and it is a recurring theme in Deuteronomy (cf. 6:21; 15:15; 16:12; 24:18, 22) and Exodus (1:13, 14; 2:23; 5:9, 11; 6:6, 9).

Forms of עבד are also used to describe the plight of the nation during the Exile. Indeed, the Exile itself is described poetically as a return to the slavery of Egypt in the last of the curses in Deut 28:68 ("The LORD will bring you back to Egypt in ships…"). Lamentations 1:3 also discusses the "servitude" (עבדה) inflicted on the exiles, indicating that Judah—like Job—can find no "rest" (מנוח). These and other passages indicate that, in the biblical tradition, the Exile is seen as a return to bondage, a "negation" of God's redemptive acts during the Exodus.[18]

The last word of v. 19, אדניו, has been viewed by some scholars as a subtle jab at the deity, as well. Balentine (2006, 91–92), for example, has suggested that "his lord" here may be an oblique reference to God. He notes that God refers, in his dialogue with the Satan, to Job as "my servant" (עבדי) in 1:8 and 2:3; the next occurrence of the term is here in 3:19, after Job's calamity. He then observes that the poet's use of אדניו is ambiguous:

> When used with reference to God, this word is normally translated "Lord." When used of humans who exercise power, the word may be translated as "lord" or "master." Like a slave, Job longs to be free from his "master." Given the way suffering has eroded Job's former certainties, he is no longer clear whether his oppressor is human or divine.[19]

---

17. Other examples include Exod 13:3, 14; Deut 5:6; 7:8; 8:14; 13:10; Josh 24:17; Judg 6:8; Jer 34:13; Mic 6:4.

18. See also, e.g., 2 Kgs 25:24; Isa 14:3; Jer 17:4.

19. Perdue (1991, 144) makes a similar argument for נגשׂ in 3:18.

If Job is obliquely referring to God here, then he introduces already in this chapter a theme to which he will return frequently later in the dialogue: that God is a harsh overlord who oppresses rather than protects. In any case, the theme of vv. 17–19—that death is a "sure thing" where rest and peace can be obtained—can be viewed as a tacit accusation that God's promises of "rest" to his people have failed. In 3:23, Job expands upon this tacit critique with an ironic allusion to Isa 40:

Job 3:23

| To the man whose path is hidden, | לגבר אשר־דרכו נסתרה |
| Whom God has fenced about? | ויסך אלוה בעדו |

It has frequently been observed that the second colon of this verse can be read as an ironic commentary on the Satan's words in the prologue (1:10), in which he claims that Job "fears God" because God has "fenced him in" protectively. But while a number of commentators have noted that the phrase דרכו נסתרה in the first colon is identical to an expression in Isa 40:27, the implications of this connection have not received sufficient attention. The Isaiah passage reads:

Why do you say, O Jacob,	למה תאמר יעקב
And assert, O Israel,	ותדבר ישראל
"My way is hidden from the LORD,	נסתרה דרכי מיהוה
And the justice due me escapes the notice of my God?"	ומאלהי משפטי יעבור

This verse, in fact, is the only other occurrence of the phrase דרך נסתרה in the biblical corpus. Job's use of the phrase provides yet another example of the poet offering an ironic twist on a "positive" biblical passage: in Isaiah, the prophet is reassuring the skeptical nation that God does indeed take note of their conduct, and that he will provide them with "rest" from their troubles (cf. 40:28–31) by restoring them from the Exile. Job's words, however, echo the nation's question without providing an answer, implicitly rejecting Isaiah's comforting words.

Job 3:13, 26

Job's emphasis on his lack of rest is most apparent in 3:13 and 3:26. In the first of these, he describes what his fate would have been if he had died at birth:

| Yea, I would have lain down and been silent, | כי־עתה שכבתי ואשקוט |
| Slept, then I would have had rest | ישנתי אז ינוח לי |

In 3:26, Job finishes his speech with a lament about what his life has become, using similar language:

I am not at ease, I am not quiet,	לא שלותי ולא שקטתי
I have no rest, but turmoil comes.	ולא־נחתי ויבא רגז

This emphasis on "exhaustion" and "turmoil" in the poem is curious: given the nature of his troubles, why is he lamenting the lack of peace and quiet? Job might be expected to lament his poor health, or perhaps the loss of his family and property. "Rest" and "quiet" do not appear to be the issue, as the prologue notes that he has just sat in silence for a full week (2:13).[20] In the first speech cycle, however, Job makes no specific mention of his loss of family and property, and little mention of his physical ailments, while his desire for rest is noted many times. Clines (1989, 105) is among those noting the peculiarity:

> (Turmoil) is not self-evidently the emotion people in Job's position would feel about their suffering: self-pity, anger, disgust, hopelessness, yes; but anxiety and turmoil, hardly.

In addition, a desire for "rest" is not typical of the psalms classified as "individual laments," though they often address similar questions of theodicy. In fact, no form of נוח or שקט occurs in any of the 48 psalms either fully or partially classified as such,[21] and while forms of שכב and ישן (from 3:13) do occur (five and three times, respectively), they describe the actual circumstances of the lamenter rather than something which is lacking and desired.[22]

The desire for and attainment of "rest" is, however, a motif that is found in the biblical stories of critical moments in Israel's national history. Dhorme (1984, 34), for example, compares the use of the idiom נוח ל in v. 13b to that in Neh 9:28, where it describes the rest enjoyed by the nation after God delivers them from their oppressors. It is also used in the hiphil in Exod 33:14, in which God promises to "give rest to" the people (והנחתי לך) and accompany them on their journey to the Promised Land, as well as in the assurances that they will find safety in their new home, which use the Deuteronomic formula "the LORD gives (you) rest" (Deut 3:20; 12:10; 25:19; Josh 1:13, 15; 22:4; 23:1; cf. also

---

20. As noted long ago by Saadiah Gaon, who cites Job 2:13 in his commentary to 3:26: "I qualified Job's words *I have no respite*, giving 'It is though I have no respite.' For the text says clearly that Job had rested and taken respite (2:13)"; see Saadiah (trans. Goodman) (1988, 181).

21. See Limburg (1992, 532) for a complete list.

22. E.g. Ps 3:5: "I lay down and slept; I awoke, for the LORD sustains me."

Isa 14:3 and 1 Chr 23:25). The act of taking possession of the land is characterized as entering into God's "rest" (Ps 95:11).

Verse 26 concludes with another instance of the rare term רֹגֶז (cf. 3:17). A variety of translations have been offered for this word, including "troubling," "raging," "strife," and "turmoil." Outside of Job, it occurs only twice in Biblical Hebrew: in Isa 14:3 and Hab 3:2. In the latter, Habakkuk asks that God "remember mercy in (his) wrath" (ברגז רחם תזכור). He may be pleading for a reprieve from the Babylonian oppression, since the first two chapters of his book are concerned with the imminent arrival of the Chaldeans. The context of the Isaiah passage, in any case, is clear: it is part of the "Oracle against Babylon," which as previously discussed shares a number of other thematic and terminological correspondences with Job's lament (see the discussion of 3:17–19 above). רגז occurs in Isa 14:3 in near parallelism with עצב ("pain") and עבדה קשה ("hard labour") as part of a discussion of the suffering of the nation during the Exile:

And it will be in the day when the	והיה ביום הניח יהוה לך
LORD gives you rest from your pain	מעצבך ומרגזך ומן־העבדה
and turmoil and harsh service in which	הקשה אשר עבד־בך
you have been enslaved...	

Verse 7 describes the results of God's actions, also utilizing two of the terms (נוח and שקט) found in both 3:13 and 3:26:

The whole earth is at rest *and* is quiet;	נחה שקטה כל־הארץ
They break forth into shouts of joy...	פצחו רנה

Job's words, though, mock this hopeful assurance: he himself has no "rest" or "quiet," but only turmoil. Once again, Job's complaint—when taken literally—seems ill-suited to his personal circumstances. But like that of the previous verses, Job's language in 3:26 does make sense when viewed as a cynical commentary on the biblical traditions concerning God's promises to his chosen people: the assurances of "rest" are empty, and only רגז comes. Job's words in 3:11–19 indicate that he believes the grave to be the only place where true rest can be found.

Concluding Remarks

Job's opening speech thus effects a series of rhetorical "reversals" of traditional biblical themes. The recognition that Job is making use of—and subverting—traditional terminology and motifs can help to illuminate a number of individual statements that have been viewed as puzzling. The idea of "darkness" and "death-shadow" being the agents of "redemption" (גאל) in 3:5a, for example, is understandable if Job's subversion of the traditions of "foreign bondage" (the only other context in which the phrase חשך וצלמות is found) is recognized. His otherwise tepid wish for what appears to be a "cloudy day" in the next colon takes on a new significance when the allusion to the "cloud" over the tabernacle is perceived. His reference to the "hidden path" (דרכו נסתרה) in 3:23 tacitly counters Isa 40:27 (the only other occurrence of this phrase), in which the prophet reassures the people that God has taken notice of their suffering. His emphasis on "rest" and freedom from bondage, seemingly irrelevant to his personal circumstances, are similarly illuminated.

I do not mean to suggest that the book of Job is primarily allegorical; such a view would do an injustice to the sophistication and complexity of the poet's work. His point is not merely to tell the history of Israel in poetic form, and his concerns are not limited to the experiences of the nation. He is indeed, as has often been argued, dealing with the problem of evil and suffering on a universal scale. But he is writing for an audience familiar with biblical traditions, and he makes use of this familiarity in the pursuit of his rhetorical ends. As many scholars have noted, in treating these themes the author of Job makes intertextual use of a wide variety of motifs drawn from a number of sources, such as the creation myths, Psalms, Proverbs, and prophetic literature. Until now, however, the poet's use of Israel's central myths—those of the nation's *Heilsgeschichte*—have largely been overlooked.

JOB AND THE PRIESTS:
"HE LEADS PRIESTS AWAY STRIPPED" (JOB 12:19)

Samuel E. Balentine

The title for this essay references the only occurrence of the word "priest(s)" (כהן) in Job or in any other wisdom book in the Old Testament. The context for this occurrence conveys a negative assessment. In this last response to the friends in the first cycle of dialogues (Job 4–14), Job argues that priests and temple officials, along with other leaders—"counsellors," "judges," "kings," "elders," and "princes"—have lost their status and power in society (12:17–21). The image of priests being led away naked underscores the humiliation that comes with the loss of their authority. In short, as David Clines notes, the priests' "cultic office has lost its efficacy."[1]

This lone reference to "priests" in Job invites several questions:

- What was the Joban author's understanding of the priests and the priestly traditions that convey their roles in society?[2] Are priests only part of a generic list of once powerful but now diminished political and religious leaders in communal life, or does their inclusion in this list have import for understanding the complex Joban story?
- Why does the author attribute the diminishment of the priests and other leaders to God (the implied referent for the pronoun "he")? Is there some specific reason God divests priests of authority, some real or imagined failure on their part in relation to Job that merits God's ire? Or, is the author's objective simply to demonstrate that, from Job's perspective at least, God has

---

1. Clines 1989, 301.

2. For the purpose of this essay, the term "priestly traditions" refers broadly and primarily to the following corpus of Pentateuchal texts: Gen 1:1–2:4a; Exod 25–31; 35–40; Leviticus; and Num 1–10; 26–36. Other texts clearly identified with priestly traditions, for example, Ezekiel, also contribute to this corpus.

incomprehensible "wisdom" and incontestable "strength" to tear down what God wills (Job 12:13–14, 16), in sum, to "strip understanding from the leaders of the earth" (12:24)?

- These and other such questions invite reflection on the relative dating of the book of Job in relation to Old Testament Priestly traditions. For the purpose of this essay the question can be sharpened by asking whether possible connections between Job and Priestly traditions are the result of the Joban author reading backwards, from Job to Priestly traditions, which assumes the chronological priority of the Priestly traditions, or whether the connections result from readers who place Job and Priestly writings in conversation with each other, irrespective of their chronological relationship.

  From a methodological perspective, the two approaches may be categorized as "diachronic"/"author-oriented" or "synchronic"/"reader-oriented." The former typically relies on authorial intent, which may be demonstrated by the density of identifiable lexical and thematic parallels that are shared by two or more texts. As such, one may argue that "an author has intentionally borrowed from other texts" for the purposes of either revision or polemic. The latter typically relies on a synchronic approach to texts, in which readers, not authors, recognize the inherent dialogical nature of all texts and thus construct connections that are meaningful. "If a reader recognizes a link between two or more texts, then that link is legitimate *ipso facto*."[3]

I concede at the outset that these questions currently exceed definitive answers. Critical assessment of the possible connections between Job and Priestly traditions has only just begun. Most scholars who have addressed this issue thus far have either assumed or simply asserted the chronological priority of Priestly traditions, and thus, concomitantly, attribute any connections with Job to authorial intent.[4] My own work to

---

3. For a cogent summary and critique of the two methodological approaches, see G. D. Miller 2011; for the citations here, see 285, 294, respectively.

4. In addition to mostly random observations in commentaries on Job, the following studies should be singled out. In a seminal study, Leo Perdue (1977) demonstrates that Job, and wisdom literature in general, both embraces and adapts cultic genres and priestly rituals. Commenting on numerous connections between Job and Leviticus, especially their respective views of retribution, Mary Douglas (1999, 212) suggests that "Leviticus' general reflection on God's justice *reaches forward* to the Book of Job" (emphasis added). Similarly, William Scott Green and Israel Knohl have argued, from different perspectives, that Job either "stretches" or

date falls broadly within the limitations of the current discussion.[5] In thinking about the trajectory of my work, however, I find it instructive that my first probes into Job and the priests were the unexpected result of colliding deadlines that forced me to work on two seemingly very different texts at the same time. Approximately halfway through writing a book-length commentary on Job, I had to suspend the work in order to write a commentary on Leviticus.[6] I have no doubt that my simultaneous immersion in both Job and Leviticus heightened my awareness of the ways in which they are connected, but it is also the case that my first discernments were mostly synchronic. In retrospect, I did assume that the Joban writer was dependent on and reacting to an existent Priestly tradition. While I still suspect this is highly likely, it is now clear to me that in the absence of a full-scale investigation of the demonstrable use of specifically Priestly language in the book of the Job, the question of the chronological relationship between Job and Priestly traditions must remain open. To date, no such study has been done, although with good reason we may expect this situation will be corrected in the future. If it could be demonstrated that the Joban author was intentionally employing specifically Priestly language and themes, then a solid foundation could be laid for arguing that he was deliberately responding to and critiquing an existing Priestly tradition. Without a thorough analysis of Priestly language and themes in Job, however, the question of "provenance, influence, and authorial intent"[7] cannot be resolved.

A Framing Perspective: The Priestly Profile of Job in the Prologue and Epilogue

An overview of scholarly work to date indicates that readers have seen connections with Priestly traditions in all major sections of the book of Job. The narrative construal of Job and his world in the Prologue–Epilogue (Job 1–2 + 42:7–17), which provides the structural frame for

---

"transforms" conventional Priestly understandings of retributive justice (Green 2002; Knohl 1995, 165–67; 2003, 115–22). Konrad Schmid argues that Job's attitude toward conventional Priestly representations of sacrifice confirms that "the Book of Job does not repudiate Priestly theology, but rather takes an ambivalent position towards its fundamental precepts" (2008, 147; cf. 2007, 241–61).

5. Balentine 2002a, 29–52; 2002c, 502–18; 2003, 349–69; 2006; 2007, 63–79.
6. Balentine 2002b.
7. Cf. Miller 2011, 286–87. The issue could be explicated in terms of Benjamin Sommer's (1998) delineation of four types/categories of intertextuality: exegetical function, influence (revisionary or polemical), allusion, and echo.

the book, has evoked comparison with the Priestly creation account in Gen 1, with the primordial couple in the Garden of Eden recast as Job and his wife in the "garden of Uz."[8] The poetic dialogues between Job and his friends, which comprise the middle of the book (Job 3–31), have invited reflection on the efficacy of cultic remedies for affliction and suffering. The friends advocate Job's submission to conventional expectations—confession, sacrifice, and repentance (e.g. Job 8:5–7; 11:13–20; 22:21–27; 33:23–28). Job counters that cultic options provide no remedy for those whom God wounds "for no reason" (חנם, Job 9:17; cf. 1:9; 2:3).[9] God's speeches (Job 38:1–41:34), which seem intended to resolve the debate between Job and his friends, evoke consideration of Priestly construals of both creation (Gen 1) and the tabernacle/temple (Exod 25–31; 35–40),[10] now transposed to convince Job that the administration of divine justice is a cosmic matter that exceeds every spatially limited conception, whether tied to memories of Sinai or Jerusalem.

Of these proposed connections, the profile of a "priestly Job" in the Prologue–Epilogue is perhaps the most intriguing, and, from the perspective of reception history, clearly the most influential.[11] The opening of the book locates Job in "the land of Uz," an indefinable place somewhere in "the east" (1:1, 3) where, according to Hebraic geography, the primeval Garden of Eden was planted (Gen 2:8). Readers are thereby invited to imagine that when we enter into the world of Uz, we are simultaneously entering into a distinctly theological conception of primordial beginnings that marks the first place on earth where human beings were introduced to God's cosmic design and charged with the responsibility to "till it and keep it" (Gen 2:15). In Eden, God's summons is directed to Adam and Eve; in Uz, it is directed to Job and his wife. Read as "The Creation Story: Part Two," the Joban prologue invites consideration of this question: How will Job's life in the "Garden of Uz" compare to life in Eden's paradise?

The ensuing drama in Uz unfolds in six narrative scenes, replete with creation imagery that alternates between heaven and earth, which invites a comparison between the "genesis" of Job and the "genesis" of the world.

---

8. E.g. Meier 1989, 183–93; Balentine 2006, 41–78.

9. E.g. Green 2002, 574–75; cf. Balentine 2003, 358–63; 2007, 66–67; 2006, 58–60; 2008, 213–28.

10. E.g. W. P. Brown 1999, 341–42; Balentine 2006, 645–49.

11. In what follows, I reprise and expand my observations in Balentine 2002a and 2006, 41–78.

Gen 1:1–2:4a	Job 1–2	
(Day 1)	1:1–5	On *Earth*: Job's unparalleled piety
(Day 2)	1:6–12	In *Heaven:* God's first dialogue with the Satan
(Day 3)	1:13–22	On *Earth*: The destruction of Job's family and possessions
(Day 4)	2:1–7a	In *Heaven*: God's second dialogue with the Satan
(Day 5)	2:7b–10	On *Earth:* Job's personal affliction
(Day 6)	2:11–13	On *Earth*: The friends arrive to "console" and "comfort" Job
(Day 7)		[No parallel]

These structural parallels call attention to the absence in Job 1–2 of a seventh scene. In the Priestly creation account, God "blesses" (ברך, Gen 2:3) the seventh day and calls it holy. The Joban Prologue ends instead in a protracted seven days and seven nights of silence. No one can speak a word it seems, not Job, not the friends, and not God, "for they saw that [Job's] suffering was very great" (Job 2:13). The silence serves to heighten the drama by raising the reader's expectations. When the seven days and nights of silence end, will Job image God by declaring that his world is "very good" (Gen 1:31)? Will Job punctuate his last words to this point—"Should we accept only good from God and not accept evil?" (Job 2:10 NJPS)—by blessing the Creator for the life he has been given?

Two hermeneutical moves may be considered when thinking about these questions. The first is to follow the conventional understanding of the compositional history of the book of Job, which treats the Prologue–Epilogue as originally a set prose piece, now fragmented by a later insertion of the poetic dialogues in the middle. From this perspective, the Epilogue provides the missing seventh scene; it is God who breaks the silence that ends the sixth scene by "blessing" Job and restoring his fortunes. There are seven total occurrences of the verb "bless" (ברך) in Job. Six are located in the Prologue (1:5, 10, 11, 21; 2:5, 9); the seventh occurs in the Epilogue (42:12). The six Prologue occurrences are widely understood as intentionally ambiguous; two are routinely understood with the normal meaning "bless" (1:10, 21); four are widely taken as a scribal substitute for "curse" (presumably the verb קלל; cf. Job 3:1; Job 1:5, 11; 2:5, 9), on the assumption that the author considered it unacceptable to transmit a text that mentioned cursing God. Whether or not this argument can be sustained,[12] what "blessing" God or being "blessed by" God means in the Prologue is unclear, until, perhaps, the Epilogue

---

12. Linafelt 1996. For my assessment of this argument, see Balentine 2006, 49.

provides the seventh and final occurrence of the term, which indicates unequivocally that "God blessed the latter days of Job more than the beginning" (42:12). Lest there be any doubt, the narrator quantifies the blessing by reporting that God doubled the possessions Job had lost.

A second option is to read the final form of the text sequentially, moving directly from the end of ch. 2 to the beginning of ch. 3. This places the prose and poetry in immediate and tensive juxtaposition, irrespective of the compositional history. From this perspective, Job 3 "completes" the Prologue by attributing the first words that break the sabbatical silence that hovers over the ash heap to Job, not God. With this reading, the seventh scene reports that instead of blessing his "very good" world (טוב מאד, Gen 1:31), despite undeserved suffering that was "very great" (הכאב מאד, Job 2:13), Job "curses" his life (3:1–10; note the use of קלל in 3:1) and laments his destiny (3:11–26) in a world where God consigns him to nothing more than "trouble" and "turmoil" (רגז, 3:26). Beyond the clear parallels with Jer 20:14–18, multiple commentators have noted that Job's seven curses in 3:1–10 can be read as a "counter-cosmic incantation"[13] that has the rhetorical effect of nullifying the hopes and promises attached to each day of the Priestly seven-day creation schema. The clearest example is Job's opening curse of "that day" when he was born—"let that day be darkness" (יהי חשך, 3:4)—which rhetorically reverses God's first creative act, "let there be light" (יהי אור, Gen 1:3). The remaining parallels are not exact, as indicated below, but they are sufficient to suggest that Job's first words from the ash heap offer a direct challenge to each aspect of God's primordial design for human life:

Genesis 1: "And God said…"		Job 3: And Job said…	
v. 3	Let there be light	v. 3	Let there be darkness
v. 7	[Let there be] waters *above* the firmament	v. 4	Let not God *above* seek it…
v. 2	darkness was upon the face	v. 5	Let gloom and deep darkness claim it…
v. 14	[Let there be] lights to separate day and night…for seasons and for years	vv. 6–7	Let thick darkness seize that night Let it not rejoice among the days of the year Let it not come into the number of months Let that night be barren

13. Fishbane 1971, 153.

v. 21	[Let there be] great sea monsters	v. 8	Let those whose curse it curse the Sea those who are skilled to raise up Leviathan
v. 15	[Let there be] lights to give light upon earth	v. 9	Let the stars of the dawn be dark Let it hope for light, but have none
		v. 15	Let it not see the eyelids of the morning[14]

Both hermeneutical options discussed above underscore the importance of reading the narrative frame of Job (Job 1–2 + 42:7–17) not only as a set piece that advocates an uncontested all's-well-that-ends-well conclusion but also as presenting an issue, framed in terms of Priestly theology, that invites serious dissent. Are Priestly assertions of God's primordial design for a "very good" world that is worthy of blessing vulnerable to a different assessment? When canonized texts like the final form of the book of Job suggest that God is complicit in suffering that happens "for no reason," when such texts advocate that the faithful respond to God's primordial designs with curses and laments rather than blessing and praise, what should readers conclude? Such is the drama created by the structural frame of the book of Job.

The structural connections between Job 1–2 + 42:7–17 and Priestly affirmations of God's designs for a "very good" world are augmented by close attention to specific linguistic links between the two. The Prologue identifies Job as "blameless" (תם, 1:1, 8; 2:3; cf. 8:20; 9:20, 21, 22). The word occurs in a variety of contexts, but given the story that unfolds, especially Job's complaint that God intends to "slash open" his body and pour out his blood (16:13, 18), it is hard to overlook the fact that one of the principal referents for תמים, a derivative from the same root as תם, is the sacrificial victim that must be "unblemished" when presented on the altar.[15] The drama of the story rests on the presenting report that

14. The generative work on this issue has been done by Fishbane (1971). Others have appropriated and expanded Fishbane's observations; see especially, Perdue 1986, 295–315; 1991, 96–98; 1994, 131–37. The parallels above are adapted from Balentine 2006, 84.

15. The word תמים, "unblemished," occurs approximately 40 times in Priestly texts, predominantly in cultic regulations concerning sacrifices (e.g. Lev 22:19; Num 19:2; Ezek 43:22–23). I am instructed and cautioned by D. R. Magary's observation that the semantic association between תם and תמים is more suggestive than exact (Magary 2002, 54).

Job's "blamelessness"—morally, ethically, and perhaps also ritually construed—inexplicably targets him as a victim suitable for sacrifice.

The Prologue and Epilogue frame the story by reporting that Job offers sacrifice. Job 1:5 describes his presentation of "burnt offerings" (עֹלוֹת) as a preemptive propitiation for any inadvertent sins his children may have committed. Job 42:8 reports that Job receives the "burnt offering" (עוֹלָה) presented by his friends, who require his prayer of intercession, if God is to forgive their wrongdoings.[16] Commentators rightly note that these reports of sacrifice do not envision Job as a cultic official in a formal ritual setting;[17] he acts instead in accord with conventional patriarchal practice, as head of the family (cf. Gen 8:20; 22:2, 13; 31:54; 46:1). N. Habel, has noted, however, that in his role as a devout mediator for the household, Job "plays the part of the perfect priest."[18]

The Prologue describes two scenes in the heavenly council that involve conversations between God and the Satan concerning Job's fate (1:6–12; 2:1–6).[19] The first scene, which reports the destruction of Job's

---

16. On the Priestly regulations for the "burnt offering" (עוֹלָה), see Lev 1:1–17.

17. Note, e.g., Clines (1989, 16): "the story's setting in time and place lies beyond the horizon of priestly law." For a more categorical dismissal of any connection between Job and Priestly rituals, see the comment of J. Fichtner (1933, 42): "Der Kult spielt...für das Hiobbuch keine Rolle."

18. Habel 1985, 88; cf. Hartley 1988, 69–70. The *Testament of Job* embellishes Job's concern for proper sacrifice. *T. Job* 2–5 reports that Job was concerned about the burnt offerings being offered at a nearby "idol's temple." When he learns from an angel that the temple belongs to Satan, Job asks for permission to destroy it. The angel grants permission but warns Job in advance that if he does so, then he will have to endure Satan's wrath as the price for his ultimate victory. According to this account, Job's afflictions are a direct result of his having put an end to idolatrous sacrifice.

19. The dialogue between God and the Satan in Job 1–2 is the only recorded conversation between these two in the Old Testament. The report in Zech 3:1–10 invites close comparison (for the conceptual parallels with Job 1–2, see Tidwell 1975, 343–55). When Zechariah looks into the heavenly council, he sees three figures: an angel of the Lord, Satan, and Joshua, the high priest. Joshua's presence indicates that on this occasion it is *the priest's* piety that merits scrutiny. The Satan has evidently raised charges against the priest. The charges are not recorded here, but we may speculate that they concern Joshua's fitness as a priest, perhaps including the accusation that because Joshua was born and has lived in an unclean land (Babylon), he is unclean, thus unworthy of administering priestly rituals (cf. Petersen 1984, 195). That Joshua stands in the council "dressed with filthy clothes" (Zech 3:3), suggests that whatever the specific cause of concern, he is associated with uncleanness.

God rejects the Satan's allegations against Joshua and replaces his filthy clothes with ornate robes that evoke the regalia worn by the high priest in his ordination

property and his children, culminates in Job's initial response. He tears his clothes and shaves his head (1:20), the latter, especially, a ritual gesture of mourning[20] (cf. Isa 15:2; 22:12; Jer 7:29; 16:6; Ezek 7:18; Amos 8:10; Mic 1:16), then gives audible expression to his worship by using a conventional liturgical formula of blessing: "Blessed be the name of the Lord" (1:21; cf. Ps 113:2).[21] Job's friends enact similar rituals in Job 2:12, although in this case the seven days and seven nights of silence evoke the traditional time for mourning the dead, not the living (cf. Gen 50:10; 1 Sam 31:3; Sir 22:12).

The second heavenly council scene concludes with God permitting the Satan to afflict Job with "loathsome sores" (2:7) that cover his body from head to toe. The term that describes Job's condition is שׁחין, one of the terms Leviticus uses to describe the seven skin diseases the priest is empowered to address (Lev 13:18–23). Job's affliction thus suggestively identifies him with those whose uncleanness requires priestly rituals for relief and restoration. Levitical instructions for the priest are typically quite detailed and complex (Lev 13–14), but one salient issue merits attention. Leviticus 13–14 repeatedly locates skin disease on a spectrum of what makes a person ritually "clean" (טהר) or "unclean" (טמא). To be "clean" is to be whole, without bodily blemish, thus to be holy and acceptable for communion with God. To be "unclean" is to be ritually unfit for participating in the cult. Leviticus 13–14 does not, however, use the word "sin" to describe physical blemishes, nor does it stipulate confession of sin as a prerequisite for the afflicted person's restoration to full participation in the cultic activities of the community. Instead,

---

ceremony (see Exod 29 and Lev 8) and on the Day of Atonement (Lev 16). One item of Joshua's apparel—his turban (צניף)—is singled out for special mention. The term is not the usual one for a priestly turban (מצנפת, e.g. Exod 39:28; Lev 8:9), although it comes from the same root and is clearly related to this garment. It is instructive to consider that the only other occurrence of this term is with reference to Job. In his final speech before God appears, Job reasserts his "integrity" (תמה; cf. Job 2:3, 9; 27:5; 31:6), by claiming that he has faithfully responded to the cries for help from the poor and afflicted by clothing himself with righteousness and justice, "like a robe and turban" (צניף, Job 29:14). For the details in support of this argument, see Balentine 2002a, 34–35, 37–38; 2006, 441–42.

20. See, e.g., Anderson 1991; Pham 1999; Olyan 2004. In an unpublished paper ("The Meaning of Mourning in the Book of Job," presented at the Society of Biblical Literature International Meeting 2011, London), H. Thomas suggests that understanding the function of mourning rituals is an important hermeneutical lens for interpreting all major sections of the book of Job. I am grateful to Professor Thomas for sharing with me a copy of this paper.

21. Clines 1989, 39.

Lev 14 outlines an eight-day process by which the afflicted can be ritually cleansed and declared ready to reenter the sanctuary. Outside Leviticus, it is true that skin disease is associated with God's wrath and punishment. The parade examples are Miriam (Num 12:1–5), Gehazi (2 Kgs 5:25–27), and Uzziah (2 Chr 26:16–21), which likely reflect the view, widespread in the ancient Near East and in Israel, that skin disease can be a telling indicator that God is punishing a sinful person. Given the entrenchment of this perspective, it is reasonable to speculate that the author of the Joban dialogues (Job 4–31) strategically portrays Job's friends as staunch advocates of the view that disease equates to divine punishment. Zophar's counsel in Job 11:13–20 is but one telling case in point. *If* Job repents of his iniquity, *then*, Zophar assures him, he "will lift up [his] face [to God] without blemish" (11:15). The word "blemish" (מום) occurs only here in Job. Elsewhere, it is predominantly a Priestly term for physical defects that render a priest unfit for approaching the altar (Lev 21:17, 18, 21, 23) or an animal unsuitable for sacrifice (Lev 20:20, 21, 25). One might argue that Zophar uses the term "blemish" in the general sense of moral "shame" or "disgrace" (note Zophar's emphasis on "sin" words, "iniquity" [און] and "wickedness" [עולה], in Job 11:14); nonetheless, his use of this distinctively Priestly term for "blemish" invites reflection on the possibility that he understands Job's putative "sin" to have disfigured him both morally and physically, thus rendering him unfit for entry into the presence of God.

Intertextual studies do not typically concern themselves with reception history issues. In this case, however, it is instructive to note that Job has often been depicted as a priest in art and iconography. S. Terrien notes that more than forty statues of "Saint Job the Priest" have been preserved in Belgium, Luxembourg, and the Netherlands.[22] One sixteenth-century statue in the Mayer van der Bergh Museum in Antwerp, for example, shows a seated Job wearing the four-cornered biretta of Roman Catholic priests. Job's right hand is raised in blessing; in his left hand, he holds a chalice, perhaps representing the offering of the Eucharist.[23] A fourteenth-century statue located in the Church of Saint Martin in Wezemaal, a small village in the former duchy of Brabant that became the center for the "Cult of Saint Job," merits special attention. From the mid-fifteenth to the mid-sixteenth centuries, pilgrims made the journey to the Church of Saint Martin, where the main object of devotion was a statue depicting Job, dressed in a full-length robe and wearing a hat with earflaps, perhaps, as Terrien speculates, resembling the Phrygian cap

22. Terrien 1996, 149–56.
23. For the image and discussion, see ibid., 149–50, 151 Fig. 82.

worn by the priests of Mithras, the Persian god of light and wisdom.[24] In his right hand, Job holds a placard that says in Flemish "The Lord gives and the Lord takes away" (Job 1:21); in his left hand, he holds what appears to be a fiery chalice or the Host of the Eucharist.[25] From 1450–1550 pilgrim badges were struck for those making the journey to Wezemaal. Of the 25 extant badges, the oldest (c.1450) represents a priestly Job offering the sacrament of communion by which all those afflicted may be healed and reunited in the fellowship of the saints.

Concluding Reflections: "He leads priests away stripped"

I linger over Job's complaint, referenced at the beginning of this essay (Job 12:19). Setting aside the question of whether the Joban author is intentionally engaging with antecedent Priestly traditions, which I argue must be suspended until further evidence is available, important hermeneutical issues continue to press my thinking. On a first reading, Job is clearly protesting God's banishment of the priests from his world. A world stripped of the understanding and wisdom conveyed by its leaders is a world in which a "just and blameless man" becomes a "laughingstock" (12:4). It is a world where chaos reigns, where the wise are mocked, and the innocent condemned; where the strong become weak and the weak become weaker. In short, it is a world where there is no difference between light and darkness (Job 12:22). Worst still, from Job's perspective, the agent of such caprice in his world is none other than God. For reasons beyond Job's comprehension, God has decided that the priests no longer serve a sufficiently useful purpose to remain in his world. On a first reading, Job laments and protests the removal of the priests, presumably because he believes his world is the poorer without them.

On second reading, one may wonder whether the priests in Job's world have in fact failed, not only in God's estimation but also perhaps in Job's, and thus have brought their demise upon themselves. The "priestly" Job in the Prologue–Epilogue seems resolutely committed to

---

24. Ibid., 149. For the image, see 150 Fig. 81.

25. Minnen 2007, 603–9. A comprehensive, two-volume, multidisciplinary study of the "Cult of Saint Job" at Wezemaal is not yet published (Minnen forthcoming), including an English summary by Minnen ("'Den heyligen Sant al in Brabant.' The Church of St. Martin in Wezemaal and the Devotion to St. Job 1000–2000. Retrospective: The Fluctuations of Devotion"). I am grateful to be able to draw upon personal correspondence with Bart Minnen over many years and to have been able to review an advance copy of his contribution to this publication.

the efficacy of the sacrifices, prayers, and rituals that define religious behaviour from a cultic perspective. The Job of the dialogues, however, seems equally resolute in rejecting the counsel of his friends, erstwhile advocates for the cultic system that has now failed him, and perhaps, also betrayed God. On this reading, one wonders if Job's words in 12:19 are freighted with irony. Job's protests against God's abusive power, here and throughout the dialogues, cannot be effectively muted; nonetheless, it is fair to say that the friends are portrayed, minimally, as exceedingly poor representatives of a Priestly system that may, nonetheless, be worth saving. The intertextual connections between Job and Priestly traditions accentuate these issues by complicating them.

Whether reading backwards from Job to Priestly antecedents, reading Job and Priestly traditions synchronically, or reading forward, toward post-biblical interpretation by "common" readers,[26] such as artists, there are substantial reasons for considering Job's priestly profile. The cumulative evidence, based not only on the Prologue–Epilogue, which has been accented here, but also on the emerging work on the poetic dialogues and the divine speeches, suggests that investigation of the book of Job's interaction with, its critique and transformation of, "the Priestly theodicy"[27] is a project awaiting full exposition.

26. I borrow the term "common" reader from C. Ozick (2000, 59–73). She writes: "[T]he striking discoveries of scholars—whether through philological evidences or through the detection of infusion from surrounding cultures—will not deeply unsettle the common reader. We are driven—we common readers—to approach Job's story with tremulous palms held upward and unladen" (59).

27. J. Milgrom (1991, 260) argues that one of the pillars of "Priestly theodicy" is the belief that humans need have no fear of demonic deities that create evil. There is but one creature in the world with "demonic" power, and that is the human being, whose God-given free will has the capacity for evil that not only defies God but also potentially drives God out of the sanctuary. The proposed Priestly remedy for this situation is the cultic procedure, specifically the sacrificial offerings that atone for people's sinful behaviour. A cultic remedy for suffering that God permits "for no reason" is unavailable to Job. Whether sacrifice, repentance, or other cultic remedies can be stretched or sufficiently transformed to address innocent suffering, or whether the entire Priestly system of thought will collapse like a house of cards under its weight, is a major question raised by an intertextual reading of Job and Priestly traditions.

DOES THE TORAH KEEP ITS PROMISE?
JOB'S CRITICAL INTERTEXTUAL DIALOGUE WITH DEUTERONOMY*

Markus Witte

I

In the prologue of his commentary on the book of Job, Polychronios of Apamea (who died in 430 C.E.) reports the thesis that Job lived, because of his law-abiding way of life, after Israel was given the law at Sinai.[1] This patristic opinion conforms both to the Talmud Babli (*b. B. Bat.* 14b) and to the persuasion of many church fathers that Moses authored the book of Job. The placement of the book of Job after the Pentateuch in the Peshitta and the rabbinic opinion that Job belonged to the exiles who returned from Babylonia and possessed a *beth midrash* (*b. B. Bat.* 15a), is reinforced by a clear literary and theological relationship between the book of Job and Deuteronomy. Finally, the explicit mention of the Torah in the early-medieval targum of Job belongs to this context. As a matter of course these interpolations in the targum of Job based on equating the word אור with תורה (cf. Prov 6:23)[2] stand in the context of a hermeneutic of the perfection and self-interpretation of the Scriptures. However, in spite of the absence of typical terms from Deuteronomy and the apparently non-Israelite setting of the prose tale, the interpolations in the targum prove the perception of the relation between the books in early biblical exegesis.

Recently, in the context of intertextual and redaction-critical studies, the dissociation of wisdom literature and Torah, more specifically wisdom literature and Deuteronomy, which dominated critical research for a long time, has been overcome.[3] We assume Job was written by

* I warmly thank Dr. Kent A. Reynolds (Berlin) and Dr. Will Kynes (Oxford) for correcting the English version of this article.
1. Hagedorn and Hagedorn 2004, 37.
2. Cf. *Tg. Job* 3:16; 5:7; 11:8; 22:22; 24:13; 30:4; 36:33; 37:21 (*varia lectio*).
3. See, regarding the book of Job, Fishbane 1992; Braulik 1996; Oeming 2001; Schmid 2007; Heckl 2010b.

various authors between the fifth and third centuries B.C.E., thus after the presumed conclusion of Deuteronomy, in a circle of Jewish wisdom teachers as a dialogue about the basic questions of the character of God and human beings and as an appropriate presentation of the relation between God and human beings. Therefore the question of available literary and theological resources is self-evident. As Braulik (1996) showed using the example of Job 24, the book of Job presumes Deuteronomy has an almost canonical status. In the following I am going to take up Braulik's suggestions about Job 24, along with Oeming's (2001) about Job 31, and apply them to the question of the literary and theological function of the allusions to Deuteronomy in Job as a whole. Methodologically, in contrast to many other intertextual studies, the present essay incorporates elements of traditio-historical and redaction-historical approaches to trace references to Deuteronomy in each literary layer in Job in order to show how Deuteronomy is repeatedly alluded to in the multiple redactional layers of Job as the book developed. In so doing, I will focus on the different authors of Job and inquire into the purpose of their references to Deuteronomy. Categorically, this approach is largely equivalent to Miller's (2011) "diachronic" model of intertextuality. However, like Miller, I would prefer to consider this "inner-biblical exegesis" or "interpreting *Fortschreibung.*" In view of the different forms of intertextual marking, a structural intertextuality should be considered, following Braulik (1996), as the direct literal and linguistic relations between Job and Deuteronomy are not so obvious.

Within the literary formation of Job I take into account a basic layer consisting of the macro-text of the poetry (Job 3–39*), in which the motif of the creaturely lowness of humanity (Job 4:12–21; 15:11–16; 25:1–6; 40:3–5; 42:1–6) was inserted with the so-called Niedrigkeits-redaktion ("lowness-redaction"). After that, a connection with the originally independently transmitted Job-novel (Job 1:1–5, 13–21; 42:11aα, b, 12–17) followed, whereby Job 1:6–12, 22; 2:1–13; 3:1; 42:7–10, 11aβ was added by a first book-redaction ("Buchredaktion"). In this first book of Job the speech of Elihu (Job 32–37) and the second speech of God (Job 40:6–41:26) may have been inserted. As a reaction to Elihu's positive theology of creation and the conclusion that nobody seeks out God the creator (35:10), Job finally has hymns of creation[4] and confessions to God's righteousness[5] explicitly put into his mouth.

4. Cf. Job 9:2–14; 12:4–13:2; 26:5–14; 27:11–12; 28:1–14, 20–28.

5. Cf. Job 24:5–8, 13–25; 27:7–10, 13–23; 30:1b–8; 31:1–3, 11–12, 23, 28, 33–34, 38–40; 40:1–2; 42:3a, 4 (Witte 1994, 192). Certain stylistic differences between 9:2–14 and 26:1–14 as well as between 12:4–6 and 12:7–13:2 could indicate a

II

The basic layer of the book of Job raises the question of the character of God as the creator as a central theme. At the same time, it unfolds the collapse of a theology that tries to interpret the relation between God and humans by means of the terms and categories of law and justice.

Job, with whose name (אִיּוֹב, which could be taken as אֵי אָב—"where is the [divine] father")[6] the book plays in all its literary layers, challenges radically the meaning of life and by this the power of the creator. This challenge is made both with the call "let darkness" (Job 3:4 vs. Gen 1:3) and by means of a lamentation that asks why God gave humans a life shaped by suffering (Job 3:20 vs. Ps 36:10). On the part of the friends, this provokes the interpretation of suffering as a consequence of conscious or unconscious sin, thus as a punishment or an instrument of education (Job 5:17), and in all cases as an appropriate reaction of the justly reciprocating God, who does not warp the law (Job 8:3). The friends, not Job, are the first ones who establish explicitly and terminologically the correspondence between law and justice and the question of suffering (Job 4:7).

Job's situation is characterized by a deep horror and torturous disturbance, nevertheless he receives the juridical offer of an explanation based on both wisdom and deuteronomic–deuteronomistic tradition (Job 3:25–26; cf. Deut 28:60, 65–67). Once brought into play, the idea that justice brings fulfilled life and that religious, moral and social integrity brings blessing cannot just be pushed away (Deut 30:16). The one like Job, who tries this, and for whom the equation of deuteronomic theology is no longer a solution, falls into a double trap: if he denies the association between God's justice and the fate of the human being, he appears as an evildoer, who is threatened by a bad life (Job 15; 18; 20; cf. Deut 28:15–67), but if he follows these thoughts further, he gets into a maelstrom of self-justifications, which end with the conviction that God is not just. The poet lets Job fall into both traps—and eventually lets him break free through God's intervention. By this means the poet shows the borders, if not the dead-end paths, of a one-dimensional theology of justice.

---

differentiation of a "Majestätsredaktion" (majesty-redaction), responsible for the input of the hymns, and a "Gerechtigkeitsredaktion" (justice-redaction), responsible for the confessions of justice. Here both levels are summed up as the latest layers of the book. They can also be called the "final redaction."

6. Cf. Hartley 1988, 66 n. 11.

The pillars of this theology of justice, which are questioned in the book of Job, are, first, a wisdom based on common experience and passed on for generations and, second, the ancient Near Eastern (and old Greek) conception of a cosmic order combined with the thinking of a deed-consequence connection. But, third, the foundation of this criticized theology of justice is also the commandments of Deuteronomy mediated by Moses and written by God himself.[7] This is most evident in Job's detailed avowal of innocence in ch. 31. However, this is also shown both in the speeches of the friends, preceding this confession of innocence and preparing Job's dispute with the Torah, and in Job 24, which Braulik (1996, 67) described correctly as the "Negativfolie" of Job 31. Since the theology of this law has failed Job, the question is raised whether the theology of Deuteronomy is finished at last.

In his "oath of purgation" in ch. 31 Job includes the ethical and religious areas in which he proved himself. The ethical and religious ideal presented in ch. 31 corresponds, apart from its anchorage in wisdom, by and large to the Decalogue.[8] The prohibition of idols (Deut 5:8) and the prohibition "to worship sun and moon" (Deut 4:19; 17:2–3) find their analogy in Job 31:24–27(28). The prohibition against misusing the name of God (Deut 5:11) possesses its counterpart in Job 31:5. Job 31:18 connects with the commandment to honour parents (Deut 5:16).[9] The prohibition to commit adultery (Deut 5:18) corresponds to the explanations of sexual ethics in Job 31:(1), 7–10. The proper handling of property (Deut 5:19, 21) is unfolded in Job 31:13–18, 29–32. The prohibition against false testimony (Deut 5:20) corresponds with Job's commitment to the claim of slaves and poor (Job 31:13–14, 21–22, 30).[10] The prohibition against coveting (Deut 5:21) sets the trend for the whole avowal of innocence. The lack of mention of the prohibition against killing can be explained in view of the subtle ethical stylization of Job 31 (cf. v. 15 and vv. 29–30). The absence of a counterpart to the genuinely Jewish Sabbath commandment (Deut 5:12–15) is typical for sapiential confessions of innocence.[11]

---

7. Braulik 1996, 85.

8. Oeming 2001, 66–73; Opel 2010, 79–156.

9. This understanding assumes the following translation: "Because from my adolescence onwards he [namely the יתום mentioned in v. 17] was great [i.e. important] like [my] father / and from the womb onwards I conducted her [the עלמנה mentioned in v. 16] like a mother."

10. Cf. also the common use of the term שוא in Deut 5:11, 20 and Job 31:5.

11. Cf. Pss 15; 24; 26; 101; 119:101–102; Isa 33:14–16; Mic 6:6–8; *T. Iss.* 4; *T. Benj.* 6. Even in the ethics of Ben Sira, which are based on the Torah, the Sabbath is missing as a central theme.

The climax of this declaration of innocence patterned on the Decalogue is Job's reference to the "sign" (תו) of his belonging to Yhwh (31:35–37). This "sign" is identical to the book (ספר) mentioned in v. 35c, written by Job's legal opponent (איש ריבי), who is God.[12] Accordingly, Job's "sign" is a cipher for the Torah authored by God (cf. Exod 24:12; 34:1; Deut 4:13; 5:22; 10:2–4; as well as, in view of the whole Torah, 2 Kgs 17:37).[13] These "signs" with words of the Torah stand vicariously for Job's commitment to the exclusive adoration of Yhwh and therefore as an analogy for the first commandment (Deut 5:6–7).[14] However, Job does not only affirm the *unique* God in 31:35–37. In Job 23:13 and 31:15 the poet already puts the term אחד ("the only One," Deut 6:4) into the mouth of the suffering righteous one and so has Job appear as a witness to the *Shema Israel*.[15] Likewise, the closest parallel to the use of the divine epithets in Isa 44:6 shows that Job makes a strong confession in Yhwh as the only God (Job 19:25; cf. also Isa 63:16). The first designation of God as הוא, "He" (cf. Job 23:6; Deut 32:6), in the original opening of his confession of innocence (31:4)[16] can be explained against this background. Job confesses to exactly this God, whom Moses sings about as creator and father (אב) of Israel (Deut 1:31; 32:6; cf. Isa 63:16). Job is precisely in search of this father, so that he will not have to call death his "father" (Job 17:14). Between Deut 32 and the individual, secondary sections of Job 31, there are further conceptual and thematic intersections, suggesting an intended contention with Deut 32 by the poets standing behind Job 31. First, the salutation of the earth, opening the song of Moses (Deut 32:1), echoes in the concluding confession of Job that he did not devour its yield (Job 31:38–40). Second, the motif of the devouring fire (of God) is shared by Deut 32:22 and Job 31:12. Third, in Deut 32:31 and Job 31:11, 28 the rare term פָּלִיל is used, which appears elsewhere only in Exod 21:22.[17] Interestingly in the fragment of a phylactery from Qumran (4Q141 with fragments of Deut 32:14–20,

---

12. Cf. ריב in Job 10:2; 13:19; 23:6.

13. Witte 2004, 723–24.

14. For the thesis that Job's "sign" (תו) can be identified with an early sort of tephillim, see Witte 2004, 730–33.

15. In Job 23:13 (הוא־באחד) we have to reinterpret the introductory *beth* as *beth-essentiae*. For אחד as a title of God, see furthermore Zech 14:9.

16. Job 31:1–3, 38–40 are a secondary framing of the avowal of innocence (cf. Witte 1994, 184).

17. Cf. also the use of the divine name אלוה, which appears 41 times in the book of Job and in the Torah only in Deut 32:15, 17. Braulik (1996, 79) lists further connections between Deut 32 and Job, which I consider to be less compelling.

32–33) we find evidence that Deut 32 (at least partly) was used as a part of the early tephillim.

The Decalogue in Deut 5 is framed by a reflection on an encounter with God (cf. vv. 4, 22). Job 31:35–37 thematizes exactly such a meeting with God, whereupon the poet, as in Deut 5:27, uses the verb קרב (Job 31:37). In Job 31:37, Job announces that he wants to convey his moral and religious integrity to God (נגד, hiphil). This line of communication from human to God is accompanied by the speech of God addressed to humans when Deut 5:5 reports how God communicated (נגד, hiphil) his words by Moses to Israel. The moral conduct (הלך, דרך) of the pious demanded in Deut 5:32–33 is exactly the subject of Job 31.[18] The aim of a just life in Deut 5:33 is fulfilled life. The search for such a life is found not only in Job 31, but also throughout the poetry of the whole book.[19] In the closing of the book (42:16), the search explicitly finds its aim according to Deut 5:16, 29, 33; 6:2.

Deuteronomy 10:17–19a refers to God as the power who secures the right of the poor. In the focus of the theological reasoning of the social ethics of Job 31 one finds exactly this *theologoumenon* (Job 31:14). In Deut 11:16, Israel is warned by means of a singular formulation not to get entrapped (פתה לב) into a betrayal of confidence in Yhwh. In Job 31:27, Job confesses with the same words that he was not misled (פתה) into idolatry.

Job's confession of his fidelity to God culminates in his self-appellation as a "prince" (נגיד, 31:37). This corresponds with the semantics of bearing the "sign" of Torah observance as a "crown" (עטרה, 31:36). Generally the appellation נגיד stands for the kings of Israel installed by Yhwh, and most often for David.[20] Following the expression of the confession of innocence in ch. 31 with the reference to the "scripture of God" worn emblematically on the body, the use of the title נגיד suggests Job feels promoted to a royal rank through his fidelity to the commandments of God. It is the Torah which lets Job appear as a royal wise man (cf. Job 29) and as an heir of David. On the one hand, Job 31:36–37 illustrates something related to the aphorism in Sir 11:1 (H[A]), which promises the wise man, according to a transmitted variant of the Talmud Yerushalmi (*y. Ber.* 7.2), will be enthroned under

---

18. Cf. the use of "way" as a metaphor in 31:4–5 and 31:37 as well as in 13:15 and 23:10–12, a prolepsis and summary of the declaration of integrity in Job 31.

19. Cf. Job 3:20; 7:16; 14:14; 19:25–27; 21:7.

20. 1 Sam 13:14; 25:30; 2 Sam 5:2 (*par.* 1 Chr 11:2); 6:21; 7:8 (*par.* 1 Chr 17:7); Isa 55:4; 1 Chr 5:2; 4Q504 frg. 1 IV.6–7; 11QPsa 28:11.

"princes" (נגדים).[21] On the other hand, Job 31:36–37 stands beside the statement of R. Schim'on in *Pirke Avoth* 4.13: "There are three crowns (כתרים): the crown of the Torah, the crown of the priesthood, and the crown of the kingdom, but the crown of good name is best of them all."[22]

Job's calling on the deuteronomic commandments in ch. 31 as the last instrument to make God respond and justify himself is well founded. Thus a direct line leads from Job's wish for new hope (6:8) through the wishes of a God-given respite from his suffering (14:13), the transcription of his words (19:23), the direct encounter with God (23:3), his accusation that God is not observing the deuteronomic law (24:1–12),[23] the wish for restoration of the earlier circumstances of his life (29:2), and the hope for an audience (שמע) and answer (ענה) from God (31:35). The usage of the word-pair ענה–שמע in the psalms[24] shows that Job aims at his cries to God being heard (cf. Ps 65:3). In Job 5:8 and 8:5, the friends advise Job explicitly that he should turn to God in his prayer. Job does this perpetually,[25] although he is afraid that God does not answer prayers because his suffering continues (Job 24:12;[26] 30:20). But finally Job is not afraid of the darkness that surrounded Yhwh at the mountain of God (Job 23:17 vs. Deut 4:11; Sir 45:5 [H[B]]). In 31:35–37, Job expresses his hope that God will hear him and answer his prayers.[27] His "sign," his observance of the Torah, must move God eventually to exhibit his glory, like he did at Sinai, and to give new life to Job (cf. Deut 5:24).

Against this background, Eliphaz's admonition that Job should accept תורה from the mouth of God and lay God's words in his heart (22:22) is more than general sapiential advice. This is Eliphaz's ultimate attempt to bring Job to the path of the deuteronomic commandments (cf. Deut 6:6). Here Eliphaz finally and now explicitly returns to his macarism, articulated in 5:17. The parallels to Job 5:17 in Ps 94:12 and Prov 3:11–12, as well as Ps 1, show the Mosaic torah as the source of education (Ps 94:12). Without mentioning the term תורה in Job 5:17, Eliphaz calls on Job to

---

21. Cf. Vattioni 1968, 55, and for the dominion of the righteous/sages, see Job 36:7; Isa 60:21; Ps 37:9, 22, 29–30; Wis 3:8; 5:16; *Sib. Or.* 3:767–71; *1 En.* 5:7; 96:1; 108:12.

22. Cf. *b. Yoma* 72b (the Torah serves the commendable one as a crown [זיר] and demotes him in a royal rank) and the later association of the three crowns in *T. Abr.* B 10:8 and passim.

23. See in detail Braulik 1996, 66–90.

24. Pss 4:2; 27:7; 102:2–3; cf. also 119:26, 145+149; 143:1.

25. Job 7:7–21; 10:9–22; 13:23–27; 17:3–4; 30:20–23.

26. Instead of תִּפְלָה ("tastelessness" cf. Job 1:22) read תְּפִילָה.

27. Job 9:35–10:2; 16:19–21; 19:23–25.

learn from the torah of Moses (cf. Ps 1:2; Deut 4:29–40).[28] So Eliphaz plays, besides the role of the wise man, the prophet, and the priest, that of the teacher of the Torah, as well. The vision of a salutary future that Eliphaz offers Job in his last speech (22:26–30; cf. 5:19–26) corresponds to the announcement of salvation in Deut 28:3–8. Job, however, has already kept (שמר)[29] the way of God presented in Deuteronomy; he has not departed from the commandments (מצות)[30] and has the words from God's mouth in his breast (23:12;[31] cf. Deut 30:14; Ps 37:31). Job is on the search for God, as advised by Eliphaz in 22:22. He is, figuratively speaking, just like Elijah on the way to the central sites of the theophany, to the mountain of God in the north (23:9a; cf. Pss 48:3; 89:13) and to the mountain of God in the south (23:9b; cf. Ps 89:13; Hab 3:3).[32] He also has the deuteronomic principles of the Torah on his lips, which is obvious in the protest that he never uttered (הגה, 27:4, cf. Ps 1:2) deceit (רמיה).[33] He lays the Torah around his neck (Exod 13:9; Deut 6:8–9; 11:18) and considers his faithfulness to the Torah to be his righteousness (27:6 vs. Deut 6:25).

So Job not only rejects the accusations of the last speech of the friends (22:6–9) by his avowal of innocence in ch. 31 and hence creates the basis for an assumed answer to his prayer, he also approaches God, praying with the Torah on his forehead, expecting God's light to shine on him again (cf. 29:2–3), as Eliphaz predicted (22:28) and the Torah declares (Num 6:24–26). The one who is heavily marked by God (13:26–27) throws the "sign" of his loyalty to God into the scale of the desired just judgment (31:6). After God has removed the crown of human dignity from Job's head (19:9),[34] the Torah remained his crown (31:36). It shall turn him into a kingly counterpart (נגיד) with God (נֶגֶד, 31:37). A transcription of Job's words into a rock and therefore the perpetuation of his call is still outstanding (19:23). However, he already carries with him God's word carved in stone (Deut 5:22; 9:10; 10:1–5) if he approaches God relying on his loyalty to the Torah to receive blessing.

---

28.   Cf. Job 5:18 with Deut 32:39.

29.   Cf. Deut 30:16 and furthermore Deut 5:10; 8:2, 11; 28:9, 45; 30:10.

30.   מצוה is a central term of deuteronomic–deuteronomistic theology and occurs 46 times in Deuteronomy; cf. also with regard to Job 23:11–12; Deut 4:2, 40; 6:17; 28:1.

31.   Instead of מֵחֻקִּי ("more than my own law") read בְּחֵקִי.

32.   Cf. Hartley 1988, 340.

33.   For the contrast of רמיה and תורה, cf. 1QS VIII.22.

34.   As counterpart to this see also Job 29:14, 20 and 40:9–10 and as a contrast Ps 8:6 (which the poet perverts in Job 7:17 and 19:9) and Ps 103:4.

In the original poetry there follows *one* speech of Yhwh from the storm (Job 38–39) as a direct reaction to Job's last wish. Job's appeal to the Torah makes an impact: God answers (ענה, 38:1; cf. 31:35b) the man Job (גבר; cf. 3:3, 23; 16:21). The one whom Job wants to approach crowned by the Torah (31:37) approaches Job (38:1).[35]

However this God, whom Job wants to notify (נגד, hiphil, 31:37) of his integrity and his own character, instead ironically demands this information (נגד, hiphil, 38:4, 18) about the creation and also about his own divine character. Deuteronomy does not occur in the whole first (and original) speech of Yhwh, which is concentrated on the creation. Vice versa the theme of "creation" does not play a role in Deuteronomy[36]—and Job falls silent. The demand for blessing, found in Job 31:35–37 and patterned on forms of speech and motifs from the Psalms and Deuteronomy, is rejected in the speech of God.

If Job, in spite of his loyalty to the deuteronomic commandments, suffers under the curse (Deut 28:15–69), if the evildoers go out without punishment and live in peace (Job 21:6–33 in contrast to Deut 30:9), if Yhwh in his epiphany (Job 38:1) does not even mention Deuteronomy with a single word, then this indicates a relativization of Deuteronomy and its theology in the progression of the poetry. The speech of Yhwh from the storm to Job corresponds to God's revelation to Moses at Horeb. The climax of a three-fold revelation of God inaugurated by the Priestly Writer, as *elohim* to the world, as *el shadday* to the patriarchs and as *Yhwh* to Moses and Israel (cf. Exod 6:3), comes across again in the poetry of Job, though modified. Thus the lesson that Job, who held to the torah of Moses, receives from Yhwh is different from and more than the one in Deuteronomy. Job seems from this point of view to be a critic of this torah, for it does not live up to its promise, as he knows from his own experience and as God acknowledges, and because Job's God differs from and exceeds the deity described in Deuteronomy.

III

The critical reception of Deuteronomy occurs throughout all the editorial layers of the book of Job. So in the process of Job's literary formation, each new layer redetermines the tendency of Job as it refers to Deuteronomy with a distinctive focus. This shall be briefly outlined by four examples.

---

35. As Ezra 1:4 and Nah 1:3 show, the poet of Job indicates a theophany with the term סערה.

36. The exceptions are marginal; cf. Deut 4:32.

The "Niedrigkeitsredaktion" presents in the first Eliphaz speech the motif that humans as God's creatures cannot be righteous before God as an additional interpretation of Job's fate (Job 4:17–19). Behind this motif we find, compared to the original poetry of Job, but also to Deut 9, a radicalized conception of sin and also a negative anthropology. The human is characterized, as a human being, by a fundamental, creaturely conditioned injustice and inferiority in contrast to God (cf. 15:14–16; 25:4–6). To stress the relevance of this motif, the author integrated it into a nocturnal scene of revelation (4:12–21). The terms of this scene are redolent of Deut 4 and Num 12, as well as of 1 Kgs 19.[37] Eliphaz appears similar to Moses by means of his vision of a תמונה. In addition to the torah of Moses, the revelation granted to Eliphaz comes like the prophetic torah of Habakkuk (cf. Hab 2:3–4).[38] In the closing words of Job tracing back to the same editorial level as Job 4:12–21; 15:11–16 and 25:2–6 we find again an allusion to the special view of God (Job 42:5). Job even sees here more than Moses (cf. Exod 33:18) and, in his remorse (Job 42:6), reacts the way he had expected God to respond.[39] Behind Job 4:12–21 and 42:5–6 the conception of a *revelatio continua* becomes apparent, extending the content of the unique "historical" revelation of the Torah (cf. Deut 3:24; 4:10) by adding the motif of the absolute injustice of humanity. The criticism of Deuteronomy that appears here is less severe than in the basic layer of the poetry in Job. But a critical discussion with Deuteronomy does appear here, which is supplemented by the theology of creation and hamartiology.

The "*Buch-Redaktion*" features the clearest overlapping in its terms and motifs with Deuteronomy.[40] The extensive blessing of Job before his visitation (Job 1:2–3, 10) is tinted by the promises in Deut 28:12 and 30:9.[41] Job's disease (2:7) is described with the term שחין רע, which only occurs elsewhere in Deut 28:45. Thus Job is portrayed as someone standing under the curse of the Torah.[42] Similarly, the annotation that God changes Job's fate at the end (שוב שבות, 42:10) has a near parallel in Deut 30:3.[43] Furthermore, Job is described uniquely as עבד יהוה in this

37. Cf. Schmid 2007, 255–58.

38. Cf. Witte 2009, 74–77.

39. See, to the contrary, Exod 32:14; Deut 32:36; Isa 52:9; Jer 18:8, 10; 26:3; Jonah 3:9–10 and on this Fishbane (1992, 98).

40. For the deuteronomism of the prose tale, see also Heckl (2010b, 263–72).

41. Cf. Deut 2:7; 14:29.

42. Cf. Schmid 2007, 251–52.

43. Cf. Jer 29:14; 30:3; 33:7; Hos 6:11; Amos 9:14; Ps 14:7. The verse offers a central connecting factor for the collective comprehension of Job as a cipher for Israel, suffering from the exile (cf. Heckl 2010b, 301–3, 381, 439, etc.).

redactional level (1:8; 2:3; 42:7–8), by which he even seems to exceed Moses (Num 12:7–8; Josh 1:2). The closeness of Job to Moses is also stressed in this redactional stage of the book by his role as an intercessor for his friends (42:8; cf. Deut 9:20). With the double reimbursement of Job's loss (42:10), this redaction emphasizes the validity of the theologoumenon of the justice of God.[44] Insofar as this redaction notes explicitly that Job, as the exemplary pious one, spoke about God what was "right" (נכונה, 42:7), in contrast to his friends, the critical character of the poetry of Job is conserved: Job has correctly ascribed his suffering to God himself; God acts unpredictably.

The speeches of Elihu, secondarily added to an earlier book of Job, tend to stand as close as possible to a genuine and affirming theology based on Deuteronomy. Already the name of its protagonist can be understood as an interpretation of the *Shema Israel*: "Elihu—He (יהוה) is my God" (cf. Deut 32:39).[45] This self-image is underlined by the name of his father ברכאל ("God has blessed"), in which a key-word (ברך) of the prose tale as well as a central term from Deut 28 is used.[46] The fact that the author of the Elihu speeches has his hero appear because of the "self-righteousness of Job" (Job 32:2) is in line with Deut 9:4–6. There Israel does not stay alive because of its own righteousness but because of God's. The basic theological ideas of the Elihu speeches, that God educates with suffering (33:16; cf. Deut 8:5; 11:2), that God is an incomparable teacher (36:22; cf. Deut 6:1) and that God is of incomprehensible greatness and justice (37:23; cf. Deut 10:17), converge on the theology of Deuteronomy (cf. Deut 32:4). Nevertheless, the Elihu-redaction exceeds Deuteronomy when alluding to the specific inspiration of Elihu as a source of knowledge (32:8–10, 18–22). This knowledge exceeds the inspiration claimed by Eliphaz (4:12–21) and Zophar (20:4). It also goes beyond Deuteronomy by specifying the figure of the interceding angel, the group of the בני האלהים in Deut 32:8 (*varia lectio* cf. 4QDeut^j; LXX). The fact that Elihu is explicitly omitted from the verdict against Eliphaz and his two friends (42:7) suggests that, in the eyes of the transmitters of this shape of the book, Elihu represented the "correct" theology.[47] Thereby, the tendency of the original poetry is completely inverted, and the justice of God appears unconditionally valid (34:5–7; 37:23; 40:8;

---

44. Cf. Schmid 2007, 251–52.
45. Cf. Isa 43:10, 13; 48:12; Ps 102:28.
46. Cf. Job 1:5, 10, 11, 21; 2:5, 9; 42:12.
47. Nevertheless, there is the contrary line in the oldest history of the book's interpretation, when, in the *Testament of Job*, Elihu is regarded as the incarnation of (the) Satan.

cf. Deut 32:4). Even if Elihu does not bear the title of a נביא, he seems on this redactional level a legitimate prophetic successor to Moses (cf. Deut 18:15–18).

The hymns of creation put into Job's mouth by the final-redaction appear mainly to describe God's destructive action in the creation (Job 9:2–14; 12:7–13:2; 26:5–14), however they cannot be constrained to this, as the insertion of the song of wisdom in Job 28, tracing back to this redaction, shows. They serve as evidence, like the secondary explicit confessions of Job to the justice of God, that Job is indeed (as introduced in 1:1) the exemplary righteous and pious one as well as the expansive teacher of his friends. Job 28, compared with the characterization of Torah obedience as wisdom in Deut 4:6, still has a sceptical tendency: insight in cosmic wisdom is hidden from humans (Job 26:14; 28:12–14, 20–22). The form of wisdom appropriate to humans is the fear of God (28:28).

Conclusion

Combining intertextual analysis with elements of traditio-historical and redaction-historical approaches demonstrates how the inner-biblical relationship between Job and Deuteronomy involves an intratextual clash between the different redactional layers of the book of Job. The manifold inner-biblical critical debate about Deuteronomy in Job's literary layers varies from a sharp challenge of the deuteronomic theology of the justice of God and the association of a successful life with obedience to the commandments of the Torah in the basic layer of the poetry of Job to the attempted reconciliation in the Elihu-redaction and in the final redaction. So, the book of Job may be read as a critical commentary on Deuteronomy and on its foundation of the righteousness of God and humanity.

From the perspective of the history of theology in ancient Israel, the critical discussion of Deuteronomy in Job seems to be a precursor, possibly even a precondition, to an identification of Torah and cosmic wisdom in the book of Jesus Sirach (24:23), which is only slightly later than the last redactional layer of Job. So Job belongs to the diverse history of the critical adoption of Deuteronomy into the sphere of wisdom[48] and is therefore also evidence that the theology of Deuteronomy was a significant theological influence for Judaism in Hellenistic times.

---

48. Cf. Prov 13:13; 19:16; 28:4, 7, 9; 29:18; Pss 19; 119.

PARODY AS A CHALLENGE TO TRADITION: THE USE OF DEUTERONOMY 32 IN THE BOOK OF JOB

Edward L. Greenstein

The meaning of the book of Job is often made by way of parody.[1] While Job parodies a number of passages known to us from elsewhere in the Hebrew Bible (e.g. Ps 8:5 in Job 7:17–18; Gen 11:6 in Job 42:2),[2] the present study will examine the particular intertextuality of Job and the classic poem known as *Ha'azinu* or the Song of Moses (Deut 32), and especially the ironic and parodic use of the poem in Job. The Song of Moses is a classic work that every Israelite was meant to learn by heart (see Deut 31:19). Its imprint can be discerned in many later passages.[3] I intend to show that the poet of Job not only adapts lines from Deut 32 as the building blocks of his discourse but also that he makes pointed use of this classic repository of ancient teaching for the purposes of parody— by placing paraphrases of the Song of Moses in the mouths of Job's interlocutors and by having Job parody the very same font of wisdom. This rhetorical trope is of a piece with one of Job's major contentions:

---

1. See, e.g., Dell 1991, 147–53; Zuckerman 1991, Chapter 10; Greenstein 2011b.

2. See, e.g., Fishbane 1992; but for the former see also Schmid 2007, 258–59 and for the latter see also Greenstein 2009, 358–59.

3. In addition to the twenty-odd passages enumerated in Rappel 1996, 35–39, compare also, e.g., Deut 32:2a with Prov 3:20b; Deut 32:30a with Josh 23:10. See below for parallels to Job. This is not the place to elaborate my theory that the Song of Moses is the poem that gives its name to the Book of Yashar, an ancient collection of poems cited in Josh 10:13 and 2 Sam 1:18 and apparently lying behind the LXX reading of 1 Kgs 8:12. I have made preliminary presentations of this thesis at the annual meeting of the SBL in November 2006 ("From Oral Epic to Writerly Verse and Some of the States in Between") and at a conference on "The Biblical Literary" at the Hebrew University of Jerusalem in June 2010 ("Signs of Poetry Past: Literariness in Pre-Biblical Hebrew Literature"). I hope to publish a full presentation of my arguments.

that traditional wisdom is bankrupt, at least in dealing with a situation like his, and that one would do better to draw insights from one's experience (see Greenstein 2007a; 2011b).

Intertextuality and Parody

Before proceeding to delineate the intertextual connections on the linguistic and thematic levels between Deut 32 and Job, it will be helpful to discuss, in brief, some of the ways that I am using the term "intertextuality" and how I understand parody and regard it as a form of intertextuality.

As is often remarked, intertextuality is understood in very diverse ways.[4] It is a way of looking at texts in relation to one another, bringing to bear the fact that just as all discourse incorporates, comprises, already made discourse, so do all texts incorporate, comprise, already made texts. As one of the first theoreticians of intertextuality, Roland Barthes (1977, 146), has famously put it: "The text is a tissue of quotations drawn from the innumerable centers of culture." Readers typically pause in order to think of another text, so that the flow of reading involves a series of fluid intertextual associations (cf. Barthes 1986). Meaning will accordingly be made by readers reading texts in the light of one another.

From a more diachronic perspective,[5] neither authors nor readers can operate without relating their texts to earlier texts and traditions. As Harold Bloom (1975, 32) has explained it: "You cannot write or teach or think or even read without imitation, and what you imitate is what another person has done... Your relation to what informs that person *is* tradition, for tradition is influence that extends past one generation, a carrying-over of influence."

In biblical studies there is a marked tendency to distinguish and separate synchronic and diachronic perspectives (see, e.g., Greenstein 1989, Part 1). The same tendency obtains in distinguishing a synchronic approach to intertextual reading, which is ordinarily informed by the postmodernist view that one writes (inscribes meaning) in what one reads (see, e.g., Derrida 1973; cf. Greenstein 1996: esp. 31),[6] and a diachronic

---

4. For an exemplary history of intertextuality and its diverse understandings, see Allen 2000. For a brief bibliographic survey, see Hebel 1989, 9–16.

5. For the contrast between intertextuality as a synchronic mode of reading and influence as a more historical understanding of how texts can be interrelated, see Clayton and Rothstein 1991.

6. For a similar point concerning a group of readers sharing a set of conventions and reading strategies, see Fish 1980, esp. 171.

approach, in which a later text is taken to relate to a source, more directly by quotation or more indirectly by allusion (see, e.g., G. D. Miller 2011; cf. Sommer 1998, Chapter 1).

G. D. Miller (2011, 286–87) contrasts a reader-oriented (synchronic) perspective with an author-oriented (diachronic) one. Readers must decide, insists Miller (288), whether they are taking a readerly or authorly orientation. The latter, historically minded, perspective should be separated from the synchronic one and called something else (305), perhaps "influence." Vassar (2007), on the other hand, makes use of literary allusion as a synchronic guide to intertexts. Reading one text before another is a reader's choice, and not an author's determination (17): "From the reader's perspective, it is not the sequence of writing that determines influence, but rather the sequence of the reading" (cf. van Wolde 1989, 43; Beal 1992b, 30–31). Miller (293) criticizes Vassar for seeing what for him is a diachronic phenomenon (influence) in a synchronic perspective (intertextuality), pointing out some lapses of consistency in Vassar's rhetoric.[7] However, there is no reason that one cannot read texts one before the other rather than side by side if one chooses to, without committing oneself to a historical claim of chronological precedence.

Intertextual reading—which is in effect all reading—can therefore be understood as a mode of reading that may or may not entail a diachronic perspective (cf. Ben-Porat 1976). A textual allusion may be understood, from an author-oriented point of view, as a marker of intertextual relationship by a later author to an earlier one; but it may also be understood, from a readerly orientation, as a reader's textual observation that may be used to warrant or simply make one feel more comfortable in bringing two particular (inter)texts into one's consideration.

Parody is accordingly regarded by many as an intertextual phenomenon (e.g. Hutcheon 1985, 22; Rose 1993, 1 and passim; Dentith 2000, 5–6). Conventionally, parody is understood as the imitation of an artistic work, an artist (or author), a genre, or a tradition in an ironic fashion, for the purpose of criticism or mockery (cf., e.g., Dentith 2000, 9). While most critics, like Rose, underscore the lampooning aspects of (some)

---

7. I, too, have discerned such lapses. For example, in relating Deut 30 and Ps 1 to each other, Vassar (2007, 41) writes of "similarities [that] guide the reader back to the Pentateuch in general and specifically to the book of Deuteronomy." In all fairness to Vassar, however, it is very difficult to find or mint the appropriate vocabulary to transform what has conventionally been formulated diachronically in a synchronic mode.

parody, others, like Hutcheon, point out that parodic imitation may equally express admiration. In that case, parody is the evident use of another work or tradition without respect to any positive or negative valuation. What is involved is the transference of a work or style into a new context (Hutcheon 1985, Introduction).

Parody would appear, then, to be diachronic in orientation—the parody and the work or convention it is parodying bear a relationship of precedence and belatedness. Nevertheless, the term "influence" is also clearly inappropriate, and, as I have explained above, there is no reason not to characterize the relationship between a parody and its object as intertextual. One may even claim that parody is no more than a reader's interpretation of intertextual relations, and that, in spite of the chrono-logical priority of one text over the other, the relative importance of the two intertexts is equal. There can be no parody without both the parodic work and the object of the parody. Theoretically, then, neither the Song of Moses nor the book of Job has priority. However, for the purposes of the present treatment, and on the basis of my conviction that Job is a much later composition, I shall be speaking of the influence of Deut 32 on Job and of the latter's (often parodic) use of the former.

In the relationship between the Song of Moses and Job the intertextual connections are diverse. Sometimes the uses of the Song in the discourse of Job are simply "echoes" (see Beal 1992a, 21; Sommer 1998, 15–17), and some may best be characterized as linguistic-poetic influence. My argument will be that the density of the Song's use in Job enhances the power and significance of the instances of parody. For that reason, I turn first to a survey of the intertextual relations between the Song and Job.

The Intertextuality of the Song of Moses and the Book of Job

The poet of Job draws on many classics of Hebrew literature (see, e.g., Dhorme 1967, clii–clxxiv; Segal 1949; Pyeon 2003; Greenstein 2004; Wilson 2006; Schmid 2007)—it is a virtual "echo chamber for earlier texts" (Mettinger 1997, 6).[8] I find nearly a dozen passages in Deut 32 for which there is a distinct parallel in Job. In some cases it would seem that the poet of Job, who customarily draws language from other texts (as well as other languages; Greenstein 2007b), picks up archaic expressions

---

8. Margalioth (1981, 43–64) compares parallels between Job and a variety of other biblical texts in order to establish the priority of Job. The more evolved quality of the poetic usages in Job can be adduced to make the opposite contention. One is disappointed to find no reference to the Song of Moses in Rohde 2007.

from the classical source. Examples are: יעיר, "he watches over, protects" (Deut 32:11; Job 8:6);[9] the verb כשה, "grow fat" (Deut 32:15; Job 15:27 in the piel); נבר, "deny" (piel; Deut 32:27; Job 21:29); the poetic word-pair נזל–רעף/ערף, "distill, precipitate" (Deut 32:2; Job 36:28 and cf. the expression נטף מלה, "cause words to fall" [hiphil; Job 29:22]).[10] The phrase נכון למועדי רגל, "he is firm when the foot might stumble" (Job 12:5) shows the apparent influence of the phrase לעת תמוט רגלם, "when their feet collapse" (Deut 32:35), especially if one understands that the phrase in Job follows the word לעת "in a time of" in the preceding colon. That word can be reconstructed by reading the unintelligible string לעשתות as לעת שית, "in time of catastrophe."[11]

Even the celebrated verse Job 38:7 would seem to be inspired by the Song of Moses. The verse reads:

ברן־יחד כוכבי בקר / ויריעו כל־בני אלהים:

When the morning stars sang out as one,
And all the Sons of God exulted.

Adhering to the Masoretic text of Deut 32:43a, where there is an orphaned line (הרנינו גוים עמו), there is barely any resemblance to the verse in Job. The verb הרנין seems related to רון/רנן, "to sing out," in Job, but that is all. However, a version of Deuteronomy found at Qumran (4QDeut[q]) presents a remarkably similar text to the couplet in Job: הרנינו שמים עמו / והשתחוו לו כל אלהים, "Sing of his people, all ye

---

9. That the rare verb עיר, which is probably related somehow to Ugaritic *nǵr*, "to watch over, protect" (= Heb. נצר, Aram. נטר), has the sense of "protect" in this context can be supported by adducing the same figure of a bird's circling its young in the context of a promise of protection—using the apparently cognate Akkadian verb *naṣāru* in an Assyrian oracle (Parpola 1997, 15, lines ii 4'–8'; cf. Tawil 2009, 326).

10. The term אכזר, "cruel," appears only in Deut 32:33 and Job 30:21; 41:2. Elsewhere it attaches the adjectival suffix *-y*; see, e.g., Isa 13:9; Jer 6:23; 30:14; 50:42; Prov 5:9; 11:17; 12:10; 17:11; 27:4; Lam 4:3.

11. I develop this reading based on an insight of my teacher Professor H. L. Ginsberg (see Greenstein forthcoming). Here are some salient points: the emendation involves no more than a metathesis and repointing; the term I read שית for the received שות would ordinarily be spelled with aleph instead of yod (see Lam 3:47). However, in Job one often finds exceptional orthography; compare רישון for expected ראשון in Job 8:8. The term שאת is paired in the verse from Lamentations with שבר, "ruin," and שבר is often paired with שד, "destruction" (e.g. Isa 51:9; 59:7; 60:18; Jer 48:3), which is a most apt parallel to פיד, which occurs in the preceding colon.

heavens![12] / Pay homage to him, all ye gods!" (Skehan and Ulrich in Ulrich et al. 1995, 141, lines 6–7). Although the second line might seem to be influenced by the almost identical Ps 97:7b, the relative originality of the Qumran reading would seem to be assured by its double invocation of other gods than YHWH to sing praises at his bidding (in the MT version, monotheistically questionable references were removed; cf., e.g., Tigay 1996, 516–18; Rofé 2002). If that is the case, then the replacement of "gods" by "stars" in Job 38:7 can be readily explained. In Job "the gods" are interpreted as "Sons of God," that is, the angels. "The stars" and "the heavens" are used as poetic synonyms for the angels in Job 25:5 and 15:15, respectively (compare 4:17–18). There is accordingly a basis for suggesting that Job 38:7 has been influenced by Deut 32:43 (in a version different from MT). In keeping with the emphasis on nature in the God speeches, it is not the angels but their celestial doppelgangers that sing.

A more extensive literary allusion to the Song of Moses may be found in Job 29:6. Since I have treated this instance in detail elsewhere (Greenstein 2011a, 191–92), here I shall only summarize the most salient points. In the surrounding chapter Job recalls the era of his prime, before catastrophe struck, "when Shaddai was still with me" (v. 5). One of a variety of images by which Job describes that time is this (v. 6):

בְּרְחֹץ הֲלִיכַי בְּחֵמָה / וְצוּר יָצוּק עִמָּדִי פַּלְגֵי־שָׁמֶן׃

When my feet were washed in cream (or curds),
and the rock poured streams of oil over me.

Clearly in parallelism with "streams of oil" the word written חמה, ordinarily "wrath" or "venom," should be read חמאה, "cream, curds" (thus the ancient versions and see already Rashi and Ibn Ezra; cf. BDB, 237, 326). The word הליכי is a unique but transparent term for "feet" (so, e.g., Rashi). The figurative meaning of the verse would also be plain but for its intertextual association with the Song of Moses. The pouring out of "streams of oil" by a rock evokes the account of how the Israelites in the wilderness were provided with drinking water from a rock (Exod 17:1–7; Num 20:7–13; cf. Pss 78:15; 114:8).

A poetic evocation of this event is found in Deut 32:13b–14a:

וַיֵּנִקֵהוּ דְבַשׁ מִסֶּלַע / וְשֶׁמֶן מֵחַלְמִישׁ צוּר׃
חֶמְאַת בָּקָר וַחֲלֵב צֹאן עִם־חֵלֶב כָּרִים וְאֵילִים...

---

12. "Heavens" here refers to the celestial beings; see Rofé (2002, 50), citing Jer 14:22 and Ps 89:6. As Rofé points out in his study (48), the LXX supports the Qumran reading.

> He (YHWH) suckled him (Israel) with honey from a boulder,
> And with oil from a flinty rock;
> With curds from cattle and milk from goats,
> With milk from lambs and rams...

The identical words for "curds," "oil," and "rock," together with the similar image itself, make the intertextual association clear. However, the use of the term "rock," in the context of the Song of Moses, is ambiguous. "On one level, the nourishing liquid comes from a rock, from a צור. But on another level, the one who causes the liquid to burst forth from the rock is God. The term צור is, of course, a widespread metaphor for God: God is a 'rock'" (צור; see Greenstein 2011a, 192). "Rock" is a metaphorical epithet for the deity several times within the Song itself (Deut 32:4, 15, 18, 31). Accordingly, as a striking intertext of Deut 32:13b–14a, Job 29:6 elicits a strong association with the episodes of the divine nourishment of Israel in the wilderness. The "rock" that bathed Job in cream and oil is also understood to be the deity, who had provided him with the good life, as he recounts in the preceding verses.

Having surveyed several instances of the linguistic and literary use of Deut 32 in the poetry of Job, I shall proceed to show how the Song of Moses serves as both a source of wisdom and the object of critical parody in Job.

The Song of Moses as a Source of Wisdom

Wisdom in general, and wisdom in Job in particular, often appeals to ancient tradition (see esp. Habel 1976; Balentine 2006, 152–53). The parade example is found in Bildad's first discourse (Job 8:8–22; see Greenstein 2007a, 64):

> Just ask the former generation,
> And consider[13] the deep-wisdom of their ancestors,
> For we are only yesterday and have no knowledge,
> For our days on earth are but a (fleeting) shadow.
> They will instruct you, they will tell you...

And there follows a series of quoted wisdom sayings, basically until the end of the chapter. The phrase "They will instruct you, they will tell you" (הלא־הם יורוך יאמרו לך) echoes the sentiment and language of Deut 32:7b: "Ask your father, and he will tell you; / your elders, and they will

---

13. Reading בונן for בונן with the support of the Peshitta; see Dhorme 1967, 115–16.

instruct you (ויאמרו לך)." Turning to one's forebears for instruction is a classic tenet of wisdom.

Eliphaz draws directly on the wisdom embedded in the Song of Moses, along with other sources, in proffering to Job an explanation of his suffering—that his afflictions are not a punishment for sin but rather an admonition that he had better cling to his erstwhile piety (Job 5:17–18; see Greenstein 2009, 345; 2011b, 47):

> Happy is the mortal whom God reproves (יוכחנו)—
> Do not reject (אל־תמאם) Shaddai's discipline (מוסר).
> For once he inflicts pain, he binds up;
> Once he strikes (ימחץ), his own hands heal (תרפינה).[14]

The first part of this counsel derives from a wisdom source like Prov 3:11–12 (cf. Deut 8:5; Ps 94:12):

> The Lord's discipline (מוסר), O my son, do not reject (אל־תמאם);
> And do not despise his reproof (תוכחתו).
> For it is the one he loves the Lord reproves (יוכיח),
> Like a father (reproves) the son he favors.

The second part of Eliphaz's advice elaborates a line from the Song of Moses (Deut 32:39b):

> I make die, but (also) make live;
> I strike (מחצתי), but I (also) heal (ארפא).[15]

That the Joban poet is drawing on this verse finds support in the fact that the following line "and no one can rescue from my hand" (ואין מידי מציל) is parodied in Job 10:7 "and no one can rescue from your hand" (ואין מידך מציל).[16] There Job typically takes a statement about God's power from a positive context (YHWH characterizing himself) and presents it ironically in a negative one (Job's helplessness in the face of God's injustice; cf. Newsom 1996, 414). In the Song of Moses, YHWH explains to Israel that after he punishes them for their unfaithfulness, he

---

14. The spelling of רפא, "to heal," with yod rather than aleph is unusual; but see the same phenomenon in Jer 8:11, 15 (מרפה); 19:11; 51:9 (נרפתה). For the reverse phenomenon, see, e.g., Job 4:14 (קראני).

15. The verse from Deut 32 would also appear to serve as a resource for Isa 30:26b. Perhaps the Isaian verse is the immediate source of Job 5:18. However, whereas in Isaiah we have the verbs מחץ and רפא, as well as חבש, "to bind," which also appears in Job 5:18, in Deut 32:39b we find a similar syntactic structure to what we find in Job along with the shared verbs.

16. See also Isa 43:13. The verse from Deuteronomy, in its several parts, has a number of parallels in biblical and post-biblical literature; see Driver 1916, 378.

will restore them. Eliphaz connects the divine affliction of Job to no more than a disciplinary reproach, transforming the punitive context of the source to the benevolence inherent in his theology. Compare the continuation of the passage: God will protect Job from as many as seven possible disasters (5:19–23) and replenish his estate (v. 24) and his family (v. 25).

Using the Song of Moses to Parody Wisdom

In the course of the first cycle of dialogue among Job and his companions, the friends repeatedly throw traditional wisdom in Job's face (see Greenstein 2007a). Bildad and Zophar conclude their disquisitions by rehearsing a theme adumbrated by Eliphaz, to the effect that God will support the innocent and restore Job his fortunes (8:20–22; 11:18–19). Job, in his response in ch. 12, reminds his friends that he, too, has wisdom—no less than they (see v. 3)—and proceeds to demonstrate this fact by quoting a series of pseudo-proverbs that mimic their advice.[17] The battery of pseudo-wisdom begins in v. 4 and continues until the end of the chapter, but it is interrupted by an aside by Job to his would-be sage companions in vv. 7–8. Commentators tend to jumble these verses together with the pseudo-quotation of wisdom lore (see, e.g., Clines 1989, 292–93). However, the introductory word ואולם, "however," is generally used in Job to introduce a request or wish.[18] Here Job reacts to Bildad's suggestion in 8:8–22 that Job seek the wisdom of the ancients (see above), and, using ואולם the way it is ordinarily employed, proffers his own counter-advice (cf., e.g.. Good 1990, 234–35; Newsom 1996, 427; contrast Clines 1989, 293).

Nevertheless, the language in which Job formulates his advice echoes not only the words of Bildad but also the "original" source of this wisdom—the Song of Moses. Job's opening mimics Bildad, using the

---

17. The phrase ואת־מי־אין כמו־אלה, "and who does not have such (wise sayings) as these," with its deictic pronoun, is a technique for introducing direct discourse or quotations; see Greenstein 2005, esp. 253. Verses 4–6 are philologically challenging, but I have treated them in Greenstein forthcoming. Their gist mimics the advice of Eliphaz and Zophar: the righteous will remain safe and secure in times of catastrophe.

18. The term (ו)אולם in the function of an adversative occurs 19 times in the Bible, ten of them in Job. In nine of these attestations it belongs to direct discourse, and in eight (including our instance) it accompanies a request (from the addressee), a wish (from a third party), or a cohortative; see Job 1:11; 2:5; 5:8; 11:5; 12:7 (here); 13:3; 17:10; 33:1.

phrase "Pray ask" (שְׁאַל־נָא) of 8:8; and he employs the verb "instruct" (הוֹרָה) of 8:10 as well. The overall structure of Job's address in 12:7, however, is clearly patterned on Deut 32:7b:

שאל אביך ויגדך / זקניך ויאמרו לך:

Ask your father, and he will tell you;
Your elders, and they will instruct you.

Whereas Moses counsels the Israelites to inquire of their elders, Job (12:7–8) advises his friends to seek the wisdom of the dumb animals of the field:

ואולם שאל־נא בהמות ותרך ועוף השמים ויגד־לך:
או שיח לארץ ותרך / ויספרו לך דגי הים:

Rather, ask of the behemoth—and it will instruct you.
Or of the fowl of the sky—and it will tell you.
Or converse with the earth[19]—and it will instruct you;
And the fish of the sea will recount to you.

Most commentators interpret Job's words as an earnest expression of the wisdom notion that "all earthly creatures…are able to instruct man" (Hartley 1988, 209), that Job finds wisdom throughout creation. Such exegesis ascribes to Job the theology that many attribute to the divine speeches from the whirlwind—as though Job had not already disparaged creation and fulminated against the destructive powers of the deity (see, e.g., Perdue 2007, 98–102, 107–10; cf. Perdue 1991). If, however, one understands that the entire discourse in which this aside to the companions is embedded is a parody of conventional wisdom, and that Job, in substituting dumb animals for the people's elders, is aping Moses in a grotesque fashion, then Job is not promoting wisdom but savaging it (Greenstein 2011b, 45).

It is characteristic of Job that he parodies traditional wisdom, especially that cited by his companions. An unambiguous example is the following (Greenstein 2011b, 42). Proverbs 13:9 conveys the principle of just retribution using this image:

The light of the righteous shines, / but the lamp of the wicked wanes.

---

19. Some emend this perfectly good Hebrew phrase so that it conforms strictly to the parallel lines and refers to the *animals* of the earth; see, e.g., Dhorme 1967, 172; Hartley 1988, 208; Gray 2010, 217. It is more plausible that we have an ellipsis of the fuller expression "animals of the earth" (Gordis 1978, 138).

Bildad, in a response to Job in which he insists that the wicked receive
their just deserts, elaborates the second line of this verse (Job 18:5–6; cf.
Dhorme 1967, clxv):

> So does the light of the wicked wane,
> And the flame of his fire fails to glow;
> The light goes dark in his habitation,
> And his lamp wanes on him.

Job (21:17) objects to such a piety, proved flagrantly false by his
particular case, and challenges the truth of its claims:

> How often does the lamp of the wicked wane,
> Does catastrophe fall upon them?

In a way similar to his parody of the traditional wisdom mindlessly
repeated by his friends, Job parodies the wisdom of the ancients as it is
showcased in the Song of Moses. By having Job's companions rely on
Deut 32 for some of their wisdom, and by having Job ridicule that
wisdom by grotesquely parodying it, the poet depicts Job's rhetorical
agenda as one of undermining wisdom through mockery (and other
means; see Greenstein 2011b). Job's use of the Song of Moses for the
purpose of parodying it is emblematic of the parodic character of the
book as a whole, in which not only the words of Moses but even the
words of God are mimicked and mocked (see Greenstein 2009, 358–59).

The Most Subversive Cut of All

One of the companions' main grievances against Job is that he accuses
God of injustice (see esp. ch. 9). Both Bildad and Zophar in their first
discourses defend the deity's character in this regard—God would not
corrupt justice (8:3; 11:2–6). The belated interlocutor, Elihu, insists
on the same claim: "And so, people of mind, listen to me: Far be any
wickedness from God, and corruption from Shaddai!" (34:10). In this
they depend on the tradition of divine justice that one finds in such
passages as Deut 32:4 (cf. Balentine 2006, 149):

הצור תמים פעלו / כי כל־דרכיו משפט
אל אמונה ואין עול / צדיק וישר הוא:

> The Rock—his acts are whole, / Yea, all his ways are just.
> A trustworthy God, without corruption. / Right and straight is he.

This catechism leaves its imprint on several doxological passages, for
example, Ps 25:8 ("Good and straight is YHWH…"), Ps 92:16 ("Relating
that YHWH is straight, / My Rock in whom there is no corruption"). The

terms (חמ(ים, "whole, having integrity," and ישר, "straight, upright," are found together in various forms in a number of (primarily wisdom) contexts (e.g. 1 Kgs 9:4; Pss 25:21; 37:37; Prov 2:7, 21; 11:3–6; 28:10; 29:10; cf. Syring 2004, 59–60).

However, there are only two places in the Hebrew Bible in which this pair of terms takes the form of modifiers characterizing the same individual. The one is the excerpt from the Song of Moses quoted above. The other is the well-known introduction of Job, first by the narrator and then by YHWH. Job is said to be תם וישר (1:1, 8; 2:3)—"whole and straight." Whereas in the Hebrew tradition it is the deity who is held up as the paragon of justice and integrity, in the book of Job it is Job who is the paragon of virtue. Job himself takes special pride in his integrity (see Greenstein 2006). In 6:25, he refers to his pronouncements as אמרי ישר ("honest speech").[20] He twice suggests that he is תם ("whole, innocent," 9:20–21). He indicates his own צדק ("rightness, justice," 6:29) and swears there is no עולה ("corruption, deceit") in anything he says (6:30; 27:4). In fact, he begs his friends to refrain from speaking עולה, even if it is in defense of the deity (13:7). It will be recalled that in Deut 32:4 the divine "Rock" is called a צדיק ("righteous one") in whom there is no עול ("corruption"). Through a radical intertextual trope, the God who would do only justice in the Song of Moses is refigured in the book of Job as a man who has suffered intolerable divine injustice and who is himself absolutely committed to doing and speaking the right.

Conclusion

The final example demonstrates that the intertextual interplay between Job and Deut 32 can be understood to extend throughout the book, encompassing the frame tale as well as the dialogues. Even if the book of Job in its present form is the result of a literary process involving several stages, in which an earlier form of the prose narrative was not yet combined with the poetic discourses, there is, in my view, an integrating structure, informed by an all-encompassing poetics, that shapes and provides a unified character to the whole (see Greenstein 2009, 338–39). The issue of how to speak about God, for example, is, I have tried to show (Greenstein 2006), a concern that embraces the entire book, from beginning to end. The poetics of the book can be similarly found to pervade the work. Parody, as has been seen (e.g. Dell 1991, 147–53; Greenstein 2007c), characterizes the frame tale of Job no less than the poetic core.

20. For this verse, see Greenstein 2008, 60–62.

What I have endeavored to show in the present study is that the use of the classic poem in Deut 32 in the book of Job is crucially parodic. Because that poem provides wisdom to Job's friends, and Job sets out to challenge traditional wisdom, Job parodies that text. One can compare the way that Job parodies Ps 8:5 in Job 7:17–18 (cf. Fishbane 1992). In contrast to the conventional theological view, known especially from Psalms, that the deity's attentiveness is essential for the survival of the righteous, Job makes the opposite claim: that divine attention is over-bearing, reflected not in compassion but in excessively punitive behavior. The parody of tradition in Job is characteristic of the entire work; our examination of the use of the Song of Moses in Job is, therefore, only one case in point.

Part II

JOB IN DIALOGUE WITH THE PROPHETS

THE RELATIONSHIP BETWEEN JOB 1–2, 42 AND 1 SAMUEL 1–4 AS INTERTEXTUAL GUIDANCE FOR READING

Raik Heckl

1. *Introduction: Intertextual Method*

The title of this article indicates that it considers a particular function of a relationship between texts: the literary function of textual references. So, the approach is author-oriented and aims at an analysis. Methodologically there is an affinity to recent concepts that consider intentionality and the perspective of the author. According to these approaches, it is possible to formulate plausible hypotheses of interpretation and to limit the possible contexts of the text.[1]

In this essay I will employ the terminology of G. Genette, who uses the philosophical approach of J. Kristeva in his concept.[2] Genette differentiates between several relations established by the author, ranging from direct references like allusion or quotation[3] to complex structural connections, which he terms "hypertextuality."[4]

---

1. Cf. Jannidis et al. 1999, 25: "Die Bezugnahme auf die Äußerungen des empirischen Autors—seien es Aussagen oder Handlungen—dient dann dazu, Interpretationshypothesen zu belegen beziehungsweise zu plausibilisieren und die Vielzahl potentiell einbeziehbarer Kontexte zu begrenzen." This development depends on the interest in intentionality, newly awakened since the end of the twentieth century. See, for instance, the articles in Iseminger 1992.

2. Steins tried to use this postmodern approach to explain the origin of the biblical canon and to find an adequate canonical exegesis. See Steins 2003, 187–90. As a critique of this approach, which Steins had developed earlier (1999, 69–83), see Willmes 2002, 68–84.

3. Cf. Genette 1997, 2.

4. Cf. ibid., 9

It is possible, however, to connect the Kristevan concept of inter-textuality with the recent discoveries about the origin of ancient scribal cultures. Connected with the education of the elites in ancient cultures, a proper curriculum of texts arose,[5] which was passed on from generation to generation. Thus, the intertextual connections between biblical texts could be a result of the growing curriculum in the postexilic period and the dominant role of some early Jewish texts.[6] Intertextual references are first of all an expression of an emerging scribal culture and its developments and changes.

There are different kinds of relations between texts. On the one hand, there are some relations between the poem and the prayer and Wisdom literature. The differences between the versions and the similarities between different psalms led to the assumption that the world of poetic texts was much more varied than what survives in the biblical poetic books. This rich tradition could influence the production of other literature only because the psalms would have been used by many people. On the other hand, there are more intended relations that result from literary discourses.[7] We find these relations especially in the narrative literature of the Hebrew Bible, which, as I have argued elsewhere, arose mostly as literature with a religious programmatic usage during the religious conflicts of the exilic and postexilic period.[8] This can be seen in the special role of the intertextuality in these texts. Diachronically the intertextual connections are present on different levels, because the relations between the texts often changed during their literary development. Fortunately, this kind of literature has a particular pragmatic function. Based on a tradition-historical analysis it is possible to describe the discourses in which the texts were used as well as to identify their contexts.

The present study deals with one of these complex relationships between texts that results from a discourse about literature that was religiously authoritative, or at least claimed authority. I have described the details of this literary connection between the book of Job and Samuel–Kings elsewhere,[9] so here I will only outline the primary intertextual

5. Cf. Carr 2005, 9–10, 112–42; van der Toorn 2007, 2, 96–104, 236.
6. The two authoritative texts that in my opinion are the first, Deuteronomy and, later on, the Pentateuch, had a huge influence on the emergence of other literature. Cf. Heckl 2010a. This leads to many instances of intertextuality.
7. Cf. G. D. Miller 2011 and the literature mentioned there.
8. Cf. Heckl 2007, 200–202. Blum 2005, 30, speaks of addressee-oriented literature ("adressatenorientierte Mitteilungsliteratur") with the purpose to inform.
9. Cf. Heckl 2010b. My monograph deals with the last phases of the development of the book of Job. It argues that the composition of Job as a poem framed by a

connections. The main interest of this study is the discourse behind them, which inspired these intertextual links. The discussion of this process enables a description of how the biblical literature came into being in the late postexilic period.

2. *The Relationship with 1 Samuel*

A literary connection exists between the beginning of 1 Samuel and the prose frame of Job that is formed by two motifs.[10] The first is Eli's rebuke of his sons in which he proclaims the impossibility of interceding for somebody who has sinned against God (1 Sam 2:25a), which is directly countered in the epilogue of Job. There Job successfully pleads with God for his friends, with whom *Yhwh* was angry (Job 42:7–9). The second deals with a curse against God. This topic is connected to the death of Job's children in Job 1[11] and to Job himself through his wife's speech.[12] The equivalent in 1 Samuel is the sacrilegious behaviour of Eli's sons, which is used as a reason for their death.[13]

Both motifs occur relatively seldom in the Hebrew Bible.[14] Their connection in the prose frame of Job suggests a literary relationship between the book of Job and the beginning of 1 Samuel. Both motifs, the intercession and the curse against God, are main subjects in the prose frame of Job. They are important in 1 Sam 1–4 as well, but they are not

---

prose text has been developed by adding the prose frame to an earlier independent poem. The intertextual connections with the books of Samuel and Kings played an important role in the final composition of Job. For a summary, see Heckl 2010b, 470–78. The thesis of secondary framing of the poem has already been held by Eerdmans (1939) (because of the supposed age of the theology in the poem) and by Hurvitz (1974), and Schniedewind (2004, 179) (because of the language). Syring (2004, 169) tends also to support this view. However, he supposes an original prose story without a special intention ("Die ursprüngliche Hioberzählung enthält ausschließlich descriptive Elemente" [154]) later connected with the poem by three redactions (see 166–67).

10. In the present study I can only show the basic connections. For a comprehensive account, see my monograph (Heckl 2010b). Concerning these two main motifs, see 392–97.

11. Cf. Job 1:5, 13, 19, 22. The scenes in heaven aim at Moses' curse against God. The death of his children together with Job's preceding fear that the children might have cursed God in their hearts (Job 1:5: אולי חטאו בני וברכו אלהים בלבבם) create the background for the plot.

12. Cf. Job 2:9b.

13. Cf. the LXX to 1 Sam 3:13 and my following argumentation.

14. Cf. for the examples and their evaluation Heckl 2010b, 243–44, 298–301.

emphasized as in Job. This increase in emphasis suggests the prose tale of Job depends on the beginning of the books of Samuel. The parallel openings of 1 Samuel and Job as well as other parallels concerning structure and content confirm that there is an intended intertextual link between these two books.

The beginnings of the texts reveal how they are connected:

1 Sam 1:1

וַיְהִי אִישׁ אֶחָד מִן־הָרָמָתַיִם צוֹפִים מֵהַר אֶפְרָיִם וּשְׁמוֹ אֶלְקָנָה
בֶּן־יְרֹחָם... (MT)

Ἄνθρωπος ἦν ἐξ Αρμαθαιμ Σιφα ἐξ ὄρους Εφραιμ, καὶ ὄνομα αὐτῷ Ελκανα
υἱὸς Ιερεμεηλ (LXX)

אישׁ היה מן הרמתים ציפה מהר אפרים
ושמו אלקנה בן ירחמאל... (*Vorlage* of LXX[15])

Job 1:1

אישׁ היה בארץ עוץ איוב שמו והיה האישׁ ההוא...

Already in the opening verse, as in other parts of the exposition, there is a particular affinity between Job and the reconstructed *Vorlage* to the LXX of 1 Samuel.[16] The books similarly give basic information about what happened to the main characters before the actual events start. The structuring phrases ויהי היום (1 Sam 1:4; Job 1:6) and וכן יעשה שנה בשנה (1 Sam 1:7); ככה יעשה איוב כל הימים (Job 1:5b) are parallel in form. There is a parallel use of the verb tenses as well. The waw-perfect serves in both contexts to give the basic information before the story starts. The use of the tenses even attracted attention in previous exegesis.[17] Interestingly, its use has the same function in both expositions.[18]

In content there is an affinity between the roles of Eli's and Job's children and also the relationship between the father himself and his children. The prologue of Job uses the explanation of the rejection of the Elides in 1 Sam 3:13 as its main subject, namely, the curse against God. This also influenced the emphasis on the fate of Job's children.[19] The

15. Shelly 1983, 45.

16. Cf. Heckl 2010b, 398–404.

17. Interestingly, Dietrich (2003–2006, 21–22) sees the use of the waw-perfect in the exposition of 1 Samuel as a stylistic device, while for instance Schwienhorst-Schönberger and Steins (1989, 13) interpret the parallel phrases as literary additions because of the tenses used.

18. Cf. the analysis in Heckl 2010b, 326–27.

19. The connection between the prose-frame of Job and 1 Sam 1–4 explains the peculiarity of the story of Job that the sin of Job's children is only present in Job's fears, and later on their sin is only suggested as a possible cause for their death. It

subject of the curse against God is present in the assumed sin of Job's children and in the fact that the Satan and Job's wife bring it up in connection with Job. It is derived from the phrase כי מקללים אלהים בניו, the (reconstructed) phrase from the LXX of 1 Sam 3:13.[20]

Moreover, there are similarities in the bad news brought to Job in Job 1:13–19 and to Eli in 1 Sam 4 both in form and in content. Both consist of four messages. The rapid change of scenery in Job 1:13–19 could be influenced by a textual feature of the *Vorlage* of the LXX of Samuel as well. There we find the dittography of the sentence והאיש מהר ויבא אל עלי. The stereotypical repetition of the going and coming of the messenger could be based on this.[21]

The second, already mentioned, important parallel in the prose frame is Job's plea to God for his friends (42:8–10). This seems to depend on 1 Sam 2:25. There Eli uses a rhetorical question to convey to his sons that there is no intercession for those who have sinned against God. The character of Job in the frame seems to be an answer to this rhetorical question.[22] This suffering pious man who holds on to his relationship with God is able to perform the intercession that was expected by God according to, or better, against Eli's rhetorical question. Job is paralleled with Eli as well as Samuel, but he excels Eli, and, if we take the entire story of Samuel (1 Sam 8) into account, also Samuel himself, because of Job's obedience throughout his suffering. This makes his intercession effective for others and enables him to save his friends from the wrath of God.[23]

A special influence of those aspects related to the character of Hannah seems to be likely as well. According to the other connections between the two stories, Hannah's first prayer spoken in her sorrow (1 Sam 1:10) that reaches God could also have played a role by prefiguring the effective intercession of Job. Some possible connections with the so-called

---

is the mentioning of the consumption of wine in Job 1:13, 18 that has negative connotations in wisdom literature (cf. Prov 20:1; 21:17; 23:20; 31:4) and this casts a shadow on them.

20. In the MT we have a so-called Tiqqun Soferim. The Masoretes omitted the א of אלהים to level the original formulation that the LXX still witnesses.

21. καὶ ὁ ἄνθρωπος σπεύσας εἰσῆλθεν καὶ ἀπήγγειλεν τῷ Ηλι (1 Sam 4:14) // καὶ ὁ ἀνὴρ σπεύσας προσῆλθεν πρὸς Ηλι καὶ εἶπεν αὐτῷ (1 Sam 4:16). See Shelly's (1983, 48) reconstruction.

22. Cf. Heckl 2010b, 408.

23. There might be another connection due to the fact that Samuel is already known as an exemplary intercessor. Cf. 1 Sam 7:5; Jer 15:1. Jer 15:1 is of particular importance because there the speech of Yhwh to Jeremiah excludes even an effective intercession by Samuel and Moses.

Song of Hannah confirm the importance of Hannah in the figuration of Job as well.[24]

Therefore, the functions, as well as some peculiarities, of the characters Eli, Samuel and Hannah culminate in the character of Job. The reasons for the concentration of these various characteristics in one person are that the prose frame of Job could follow on the exemplary importance of some special literary characters in the postexilic period[25] and that Job was already shaped as the example of suffering piety in the older poem of Job.[26] The prose frame emphasized this character and stimulated the comparison between Job and other exemplary characters in the literature of Israelite and Jewish tradition.

The existence of this intertextual interface explains most of the important features of the prose frame of Job. This suggests that, despite common scholarly assumption, an older independent Job story never existed.

Job as an Imitation and a Counter-story to the Books of Samuel and Kings

As has just been shown, an examination of the exact reception of the opening line and of connections in form and content reveals the intended intertextual links between the book of Job and 1 Samuel. The special connections between the content of the books lead the reader to the assumption of a deeper connection. Because Job depends on the text of 1 Samuel, it was intended that the ancient reader should read the prologue of Job in the light of 1 Sam 1–4.[27] However, 1 Sam 1–4 is not only the beginning of the story of the Elides, of Samuel or of Saul, who is indeed implicitly mentioned in Hannah's naming (1 Sam 1:20, cf. 1:17, 27); the four chapters are also the beginning of the history of Israel's kingdom from its introduction mediated by Samuel until the destruction of Jerusalem. The parallel beginnings of the two books are first of all a signal for the reader to read both books as related to each other and to

---

24. It is not possible to pursue this point in the present study. Considering the connections already pointed out it is, however, possible to show that these connections are intended. Cf. Heckl 2010b, 409–19.

25. As previously noted, Moses and Samuel appear in Jer 15:1. In a similar way, Job is mentioned together with Noah and Daniel in Ezek 14:13–21.

26. Cf. summarizing Heckl 2010b, 473–74.

27. The reception of the version of the *Vorlage* of the LXX in Job seems to have concealed this intertextual connection. The affinities between 1 Samuel (in MT) and Job are less obvious.

compare the framed book of Job with the books of Samuel and Kings. The subsequent connection between the death of the Elides and Job's loss shows that this parallel reading is intended.

What, however, is the aim of a parallel reading of a story focussed on one individual character and of an entire historical book? First of all, the similarities in form and content can only point to a wider connection of the content of both books. In the epilogue of Job we find the crucial indication that the books of Samuel and Kings are indeed referred to as a whole in the prose frame of Job. There the restoration of Job is mentioned by using the formula ויהוה שב את שבית איוב, which describes the change of Job's fate. Originally this phrase might have had nothing to do with the exile,[28] but in other texts its use is always connected to an exile's change of fate.[29] Apart from Job 42:10 it is only used collectively.[30] In the Bible it always describes national catastrophes that are changed into salvation. Because the prologue of Job reflects the deuteronomistic theology,[31] the author of the prose frame of Job could not use the formula free from these associations with the exile. There is also a possible relation to Deut 30:3, where the formula is also used. The context of this verse speaks about the exile as a result of the curses in Deut 28 and about the compassion of Yhwh. The curses of Deuteronomy and the compassion of Yhwh are taken up by the prose frame of Job and are unfolded by the narration.[32] Since the connection between the prologue and 1 Sam 1–4 is so clear, the formula שוב שבית in the epilogue shows that the prose frame of Job refers to the exile, and the end of Samuel–Kings in 2 Kgs 25:27–30 with the possible restoration of Jehoiachin

---

28. Willi-Plein (2002, 201–2), assumes that in Job the formula has only its original meaning of a turn of one's fate.

29. "For Israel specifically, the idiom is tied to God's prior promise of a land to the ancestors" (Ngwa 2005, 125).

30. We find the formula related to Israel, Judah and Jerusalem in Deut 30:3; Jer 29:14; 30:3, 18; 31:23; 32:44; 33:7, 11, 26; Pss 14:7; 53:7; 85:3; 126:4; Lam 2:14; Ezek 39:25; Hos 6:11; Jonah 4:1; Amos 9:11; Zeph 2:7; 3:20. In Jer 48:47 it appears related to Moab, in Jer 49:6 to the Ammonites and in Jer 49:39 to the Elamites. Ezek 16:53 speaks of the fate of Samaria compared to the fate of Sodom. Of particular interest is a very late entry in Ezek 29:14, where the formula is used in relation to Egypt. There the verse explains the formula by the sentence והשבתי אתם ארץ פתרוס על ארץ מכורתם, which constructs a fictional exile of Egypt.

31. Cf. Schmid 2010c, 42–43; Lang 2006, 68–69.

32. The curse in Deut 28:35 is cited in Job 2:7. This creates the expectation for the reader that Job will answer the supposed curse of God by cursing God himself. The compassion of Yhwh is mentioned in Job's successful intercession in Job 42:8–9. For the possible relation to Deut 30:3, see Heckl 2010b, 302.

provides a hint for the use of the formula שוב שבית in Job. Therefore the prose frame is not only related to the beginning of the deuteronomistic books of Samuel and Kings but to Samuel–Kings as a whole. Job's connections stretch from the fate of the Elides to the end of the kingship and the destruction of Jerusalem. So Job reflects the deuteronomistic theology of blame and punishment that interprets the exile as a consequence of apostasy from Yhwh. According to the deuteronomistic concept, the restitution after the exile depends on the return of the people to their God.[33] Against this historical theological concept the book of Job develops its own concept.

With this in mind we have to take the following features of Job seriously: Job is set in the milieu of the patriarchs. Being over 140 years old he is even older than Abraham,[34] but at the same time he stays "anonymous". Job is the only character in the book whose genealogical origin and nationality are unknown. Significantly, the book does not give his age in spite of that mention of 140 years. However, he uses the tetragrammaton in particular theological phrases and God calls Job his servant and praises him in the heavenly counsel as incomparable on earth.[35] Hence, the pious sufferer of the frame narrative can only be intended to represent Israel as the partner of Yhwh.[36] Job as an ideal representative of Israel becomes a character who contradicts the deuteronomistic history of blame and punishment. The existence of Job as a representative of Israel in suffering indicates that innocent suffering does exist in history. The survival of the ideal representative character reflects the ongoing existence of Israel under foreign rule after the end of national independence. The paradigm of the exile as a consequence of Yhwh's judgment is replaced by the view that the innocently suffering Israel bears its fate in patience. According to the terminology of Genette, the intertextual link between the texts can then be described as one of imitation. This means that a hypertext is created according to a model of the hypotext. The

33. Cf. for instance 1 Kgs 8:33–36, 50. Wolff (1964, 315–21) indicated that the deuteronomistic theology aims at repentance and recommencement.

34. Cf. Heckl 2010b, 311, 344.

35. It is of particular interest that we find the formula of comparison not only related to God in the Song of Hannah in 1 Sam 2:2, but also related to Israel in the blessing of Moses in Deut 33:29: אשריך ישראל מי כמוך עם נושע ביהוה, "Blessed are you, Israel! Who is like you, a people saved by Yhwh?" Cf. also Deut 4:6.

36. Brenner (1989, 40) asks why Job is depicted as pious when in the Hebrew Bible foreigners are nowhere characterized in this way, but she concludes that the frame is meant to be ironic (46). Kellett (1940, 250) suggests that "Job stands for Israel." The philosophy of Margarethe Susman also refers to this view. Cf. Susman 1968, 71–77.

"model…introduces between the imitated text and the imitative one a supplementary stage and a mediation that are not to be found in the simple or direct type of transformation."[37] Thus, Samuel served as the hypotext for the composition of Job.

Thus, the deuteronomistic theology of history (from Samuel to Kings) becomes connected with the character of the pious sufferer. Relocating the story of Job before the history of Israel and thus defamiliarizing the topic emphasizes the representative character of Job and makes it possible to present an alternative ending.[38]

Like the deuteronomistic conception of Samuel–Kings, the finished (framed) book of Job presents a kind of theology of history. The canonical book of Job is therefore a witness to the critical reception and interpretation of deuteronomistic theology.

In my opinion, the song of Hannah played an important role in developing this theological conception of the book of Job. The song was eschatologically supplemented in the late Persian period and found its place in 1 Sam 2 and, at the same time, in 2 Sam 22, in order to reinterpret messianically the origins of Israelite kingship.[39] Thus, Job's theology of history is not only critically directed against deuteronomism, but it also opens new perspectives: the restoration of Job who represents Israel follows the reconciliation between God and the pagan world, represented by Job's friends. There is an underlying hope for a categorical turn to the salvation of Israel and of the pagan world. In my view, it is possible to label the theology of Job eschatological because the prose frame of Job, likely influenced by the messianic implications of the song of Hannah, is created as a counter-history against the deuteronomistic theology of history.

The Relevance of the Reception of Samuel–Kings for the View of Biblical Literature and Tradition

The framing of the book of Job is a literary enterprise which could look back upon already existing literary works of narration, which came into being as religious texts. The concluding narrative framing pursues the aim of associating the former independent poem of Job, which had a very specific form and content, with the postexilic narrative books. The

---

37. Genette 1997, 6.
38. For more, see the next section.
39. With reference to the two psalms and their function in the book of Samuel, cf. Bartelmus 1987, 32–33.

connection of Job with Samuel–Kings shows the argumentative character of the authorship behind it. It attempts to establish an interpretive discourse about different concepts of the history of Israel.

Though we do not have biblical texts comparable to the poem of Job, affinities between the poem of Job and some ancient Near Eastern texts[40] suggest that the poem was originally a text of scholarly wisdom.[41] The narrative framing makes the poem accessible to a new audience, an audience who knows narrative books like Samuel–Kings and the Pentateuch and who accepts them as authoritative religious texts.[42]

The relations between these texts make other conclusions about the literary discourses possible:

1. That the original poem of Job becomes situated in the time of the patriarchs in order to turn the sufferer into a representative of Israel by juxtaposing his story with the book of Samuel–Kings is a discourse understandable only in a developed scribal culture.

2. That the authoritative texts Samuel–Kings and Deuteronomy are not merely harmonized, supplemented or commentated on presupposes a plurality of thinking about relationship to God, so theological discourses were open to revise theological answers in spite of the acceptance of authoritative books like the Pentateuch and Samuel–Kings.

3. At the same time, it is possible to conclude from the existence of this interaction with Deuteronomy, the Pentateuch and Samuel–Kings that the Pentateuch and Samuel–Kings were indeed already an integral part of the scribal culture of Israel in the postexilic time when the composition of Job was finished. Thus, 1 Sam 1:1 can be seen as the starting point of the narrative that leads to the exile. This is an important contribution to answering the question about the beginning of the Deuteronomistic History. The author of Job had a work in mind that started with 1 Sam 1. The book of Ruth indirectly confirms the testimony of Job because its author tried to close the obvious gap between Judges and Samuel by creating a prehistory of the kingdom of David in the time of the Judges. In a similar way,

---

40. Cf. Uehlinger 2007. Particularly close to the poem of Job are *Ludlul bēl nēmeqi* and the so-called Babylonian Theodicy. Cf. Uehlinger 2007, 137–46; Schmid 2010b, 57–62.

41. Cf. van der Toorn 2007, 116; Heckl 2010b, 358, 311.

42. Cf. Heckl 2010b, 473. This happens also outside of the Bible in the prophecy of Nefertiti (e.g. Blumenthal 1982, 21–22).

the Chronicler also confirms the witness of Job. In 1 Chr 1–9 the time of the kings is strongly connected with the Pentateuch and with the book of Joshua but more loosely with the book of Judges.[43]

4. That it is possible to make an individual character a representative of Israel also presupposes a theological reflection on the individual's relationship to God. Because of Job's age of more than 140 years, it is very likely that Job, who was not classified exactly genealogically, should be located directly before the stories of the patriarchs.[44] Indeed, the representative function of Job follows the representative relevance of the patriarchs in the stories in Genesis. However, while the representative relevance of the patriarchs for the later history exists only at certain points, and Abraham, Isaac and Jacob are primarily the individual beginning of the history of Israel, Job represents the whole history until the exile, contrasting with an existing historical concept.

The Discourse about Deuteronomistic Theology as a Root of Jewish Eschatology in the Late Postexilic Period

The narrative frame of the book of Job creates a new unit, in which the poem is assigned a new meaning. The contradiction of the frame with the deuteronomistic concept of history[45] leads to the assumption that the speeches of Job's friends directed against him in the centre of the book also support the critical stance toward deuteronomistic theology. The radical application of the act-consequence relationship on the situation of the suffering pious Job further suggests a deuteronomistic influence on these speeches. The friends' speeches and Job's accusations against God[46] must have contributed by creating a critique of deuteronomistic theology. That the author of the frame used the strict form of the act–consequence relationship from the friends' speeches and at the same time made Job plead with God on behalf of his friends as representatives of the pagan nations can be seen as a side effect of an only partial reception

---

43. Important characters in Judges, such as Deborah, Gideon, Jephthah, and Samson, are not mentioned in the genealogies of the Chronicles.

44. Job 42:16 mentions that Job lived 140 more years after the birth of ten more children. This clearly indicates that he exceeds Abraham's 175 years.

45. Cf. Heckl 2010b, 429–30.

46. In my analysis of the poem I follow the thesis of Sitzler (1995, 216, 219, 232). Sitzler identified the accusation against God as a common motif in Mesopotamian and Egyptian literature. Cf. Heckl 2010b, 212–16.

of the poem by the frame.[47] The new theological decisions, however, are important. It is not only a plain universalism that brings Israel and the pagan world together. Instead, the turn to salvation takes place for the friends and for Job in a different way: it is Israel represented by the character of Job who plays the crucial role.

At the same time, the book of Job emphasizes the close relationship between Israel and God by using Job as a representative. The suffering pious man who has the right to be supported by his God replaces the concept that Israel's suffering is justified as the result of divine punishment. Job becomes the representative of the innocently suffering nation that nevertheless holds onto its relationship to God. The ideal of the non-utilitarian relationship to God is the theologically crucial point.[48] The book of Job realizes this form of a relationship with God in the shape of a theology of history.[49] It expresses Israel's hope for an eschatological turn to salvation while living in diaspora.[50]

The book of Job uses traditional answers to formulate this turn to salvation. It receives the hope awakened during and after the exile of a close relationship between Yhwh and his elected king by using the messianism contained in 1 Sam 2. It connects, however, the hope for a future king with the individual relationship of the suffering pious. Hence, it shapes a new concept of the relationship between Israel as a whole and God.

Though we hardly find eschatological ideas in the Pentateuch, it does share the ideal of the book of Job about the relationship between God and Israel. The Pentateuch and the framed book of Job try to bring different theological concepts together using traditional material and older theological ideas in a new work. The Pentateuch revises the deuteronomistic theology from a cultic concept of religion. The core of this concept is the cultically mediated closeness of God, which already exists in the story of creation in Gen 1. We find this in particular in Deut 31, one of the last texts in the Pentateuch. There we encounter a concept of history that leads to a future salvation. While there the embrace of the Pentateuch

47. Cf. Heckl 2010b, 373–76.

48. Cf. Heckl 2010b, 242, 257, 475.

49. This is the reason why the typical deuteronom(ist)ic theologoumena of the worship of Yhwh alone, the prohibition of images and the observation of the commandments are not mentioned. The prologue, however, presupposes obedience to the commandments when God designates Job as his servant, as blameless and upright and as a man who fears God (Job 1:8).

50. Though Job is not an eschatological book, its preoccupation with the deuteronomistic theology of history sets the stage for Jewish eschatology.

as a constitution leads to a permanent stay in the land,[51] the close relationship between God and Israel according to the book of Job brings salvation not only for Israel but also for the nations.[52]

51. Cf. Otto 2000, 257–61; Heckl 2011, 239–42. Concerning the affinity between the last stages of the Pentateuch and Job, cf. Otto 2007, 203.

52.   Another discourse related to the framing of the book of Job can be seen in the reception of the vague hope of an end of the exile of 2 Kgs 25 by Chronicles. In 2 Chr 36 this vague hope is replaced by awakening the mind of Cyrus to command the exiles to return from their land of exile. The programmatics of the ending of Chronicles in 2 Chr 36:23 can be seen well if compared with the longer account of Cyrus's decree in Ezra 1:1–4.

JOB AND ISAIAH 40–55:
INTERTEXTUALITIES IN DIALOGUE

Will Kynes

In this essay I will put diachronic and synchronic approaches to inter-textuality into dialogue in order to demonstrate how they can together contribute to pushing beyond a scholarly impasse and providing new exegetical insight. At least in biblical studies, the concept of intertextuality, despite the objections of some,[1] has developed into an umbrella term encompassing any connection between texts.[2] Within this broader under-standing, two approaches have developed, one primarily interested in the intentions of authors, and therefore attending to the relative dates of texts, and the other largely unconcerned with these questions since it considers texts part of an infinite web of meaning to be untangled by the reader.[3] Whereas diachronic approaches read texts in a historical sequence, synchronic ones enable the reader to interpret texts simultane-ously, irrespective of their relative places in history. The two approaches have been set in direct opposition to one another so that, in the words of one scholar, they are "separated by an unbridgeable chasm."[4] That may be true of their most extreme forms, but, in fact, synchronic and dia-chronic concerns have always intertwined in critical reading of the Bible,[5] and the same can be the case in intertextuality.[6]

---

1. E.g. G. D. Miller 2011, 305; Carr 2012.
2. Miscall 1992, 44; Moyise 2002, 39–40.
3. Plett 1991, 3; Clayton and Rothstein 1991, 3–4.
4. Hatina 1999, 41.
5. Barton 2007a, 188. For example, elsewhere, Barton (2000, 36) observes that the diachronic search for sources underlying biblical texts was motivated by incon-sistencies perceived when it was read synchronically.
6. For recent studies of intertextuality in the Hebrew Bible that explicitly integrate diachronic and synchronic concerns, see Schultz (1999), Pyeon (2003), and Stead (2009), though none of them present a clear method for how this is to be done.

Using the two approaches together, in this essay I aim to answer three questions: first, are the connections between Job and Isa 40–55 the result of literary dependence? Second, if so, which text is referring to the other? And, third, what is the purpose of those allusions? I believe the answers to these questions are interdependent, each contributing to solving the others. A statement like that, of course, raises the specter of circularity. However, with the answer to the first question as a foundation supported by external evidence, such as the rarity of the shared words and phrases and their recognition by previous scholars,[7] the latter two questions, like sides of an arch, can be built simultaneously to meet at the capstone, which will then offer structural integrity to the entire argument.

There has been thorough though not extensive work done on the first question of possible literary dependence, stretching from the late nineteenth century[8] through two articles arguing for the dependence of Isa 40–55 on Job by Robert Pfeiffer (1927; cf. 1941, 467–76) and Samuel Terrien (1966) to a recent Ph.D. thesis by Christina Brinks-Rea (2010), who has produced a thorough treatment of the thematic, stylistic, and verbal similarities between the texts. Terrien claimed there were more than forty verbal affinities between the texts, which were too numerous and close to allow the hypothesis of independence to be seriously entertained (309), and Brinks-Rea concludes that, though much previous work has exaggerated the evidence for literary dependence (165), in several select passages Job is likely alluding to Isa 40–55: Job 9:2–12 (cf. Isa 40:26; 44:24); 12:7–25 (cf. Isa 41:20); and 16:17 (cf. Isa 53:9) (167–78, 185, 237).

Altogether, more than a century of research has yielded strong indications of some kind of literary dependence between the texts, but the extent and direction of that dependence are still open to debate. This raises the second question: can the direction of dependence be determined? For some, the scholarly consensus on the dates of these two texts is enough to resolve this question, with a sixth-century "Deutero-Isaiah" clearly preceding the postexilic (fifth- to third-century) book of Job.

I have attempted to rectify that in Kynes 2012. The method taken in this essay is an abbreviated form of the one there, which involves eight steps alternating between synchronic and diachronic concerns.

7.   For criteria for recognizing allusions, see R. B. Hays 1989, 29–32; Leonard 2008, 246.

8.   See Kuenen 1873, 492–542; Cheyne 1880–81, 2:226, 235–44; 1887, 84–85; Dillmann 1891, xxxiv; Budde 1896, xlii; Peake 1904, 38–39; Strahan 1913, 19. Cheyne and Dillmann argued Isa 40–55 was dependent on Job. Kuenen, Budde, Peake, and Strahan argued Job was dependent on Isa 40–55.

However, the date of Job is by no means a fixed point, which allows some scholars to continue to dispute this conclusion.[9] As a result, other factors have been incorporated into the discussion, most often a possible chronological development between the respective theological messages of the two texts. However, this has proved inconclusive, open to interpretation in either direction.[10]

Synchronic Approaches to a Diachronic Question

Facing the lack of conclusive diachronic evidence, two scholars have introduced different approaches that may be considered synchronic because they interpret the texts simultaneously, considering the meaning and likelihood of both possible directions of dependence, before suggesting a sequential relationship. In so doing, they are imagining at least one relationship between the texts that could not have historically existed, since both texts cannot be dependent on each other in a single parallel. Terrien (1966), who wrote before the terms "diachronic" and "synchronic" or even "intertextuality" were applied to these questions, devotes most of his article to comparing the respective purposes to which the two authors put the distinctive language they share. This synchronic comparison contributes to his diachronic conclusion that Deutero-Isaiah is attempting to answer the questions raised by Job (309).[11]

---

9.   Hartley 1988, 13–15; Nurmela 2006, 8, 13, 42, 102. Though Nurmela does not discuss the date of Job in detail, Hartley (1988, 20) is joined by Pope (1973, xl) in suggesting a seventh-century date for Job.

10.   For example, those who argue for the dependence of Isa 40–55 on Job often point to the lack of explicit mention of vicarious suffering in Job as an answer to the problem of innocent affliction prominent in both texts (see, e.g., Terrien 1966, 309; Hartley 1988, 15), assuming that if the author of Job had known Isa 40–55, he would have incorporated this solution more prominently into his work. In response, however, some have argued that the author of Job has applied the nationalistic view of suffering in Isa 40–55 to the individual (e.g. Gordis 1965, 216). Naish (1925, 41) claims Job omits vicarious suffering because he does not find it comforting. Peake (1904, 38–39) similarly observes, "Israel may suffer for the nations, but what would Job's vicarious suffering avail?" Discussing Wisdom texts, Dell (1997) questions the entire undertaking of identifying a chronological development of ideas in the Hebrew Bible.

11.   Terrien also mentions the absence in Job of the technical term בָּרָא for creation common in Isa 40–55 and observes that the parallel phrases addressing the shared theme of divine transcendence are concentrated in Job 9–10 but spread out over the whole of Isa 40–55 (e.g. Job 9:4//Isa 40:26; Job 9:12//Isa 45:9). However, against the latter argument, this phenomenon occurs in the reverse for the themes of the agony and mortality of human existence, which, according to Terrien, are spread

Risto Nurmela's (2006; cf. 1996, 32–37) synchronic approach to the issue puts the two possible allusions next to one another and asks, primarily, which one fits more naturally into its context. This text, he argues, is more likely the original, with the awkwardness in the later text resulting from the allusion. So, for example, for the connection between Job 12:9 and Isa 41:20, in which both texts share the same phrase "that the hand of the Lord has done this" (כִּי יַד־יְהוָה עָשְׂתָה זֹּאת), he concludes that Isa 41:20 is referring to Job because the expression "links up perfectly with the context in Job, but in Isaiah its function remains somewhat obscure" (13).[12] He also argues, along the lines of *lectio difficilior*, that the text with the more peculiar vocabulary is more likely original since later allusions are more likely to use more common words. These two criteria are somewhat contradictory, in that the first claims the text that reads more awkwardly is likely later, while the latter claims the more awkward text is likely earlier. If later authors can smooth out vocabulary, then they could also adapt allusions to new contexts.

Given the subjectivity of identifying awkwardness in ancient texts[13] and the demonstrated ability of biblical authors to adapt allusions to their surrounding context,[14] in my view, Terrien's approach holds more promise. If Nurmela is addressing the *internal* coherence of the allusion, how the shared language fits in its two respective contexts, Terrien is addressing the *external* coherence of the allusion, how it relates to the context from which it came.[15] However, Terrien has not taken this

---

across Job, but concentrated in the initial poem of Isa 40–55 (40:1–41:4) (309), and for the parallels between Job and the description of the Suffering Servant in Isa 53 (308). For a detailed study of intertextual connections between Job and the Suffering Servant, see Bastiaens 1997.

12. However, given that this is the only use of יהוה in the dialogue section of Job, the shared phrase actually seems to fit more awkwardly in Job. See Gordis 1978, 138. The fact that those who do not see this as an allusion to Isa 40–55 have to contrive arguments to attempt to explain this away supports its awkwardness in Job. See Nurmela 2006, 13; cf. Clines 1989, 294.

13. In fact, when Brinks-Rea (2010, 171, 175) addresses the Job 12:9//Isa 41:20 parallel, she argues that the phrase actually is more awkward in Job, where it is ambiguous, than in Isa 40–55, where its meaning in context is "straightforward."

14. See, e.g., the intratextual allusions within the book of Job (e.g. 21:17// 18:5–6).

15. This accords with the helpful principle provided by Richard Schultz, who uses the word "quotation" where many would use "allusion": "One should seek in quotation such a use of the borrowed phrase that a knowledge of the *quoted* context is essential in order to properly understand the *quoting* context" (Schultz 1999, 227; emphasis original).

approach far enough, and I would argue that this leads him to a faulty conclusion on the relationship between Job and Isa 40–55.

Considering the external coherence of the possible allusions between Job and Isa 40–55 brings us to the third question about the purpose of those allusions, which will enable a fresh evaluation of the second question of direction. Terrien claims that Isa 40–55 is responding to the questions of existence posed by Job. This is a possible explanation, but is it really the most probable? Most of these parallels occur, on the one hand, in Isa 40–55, in the midst of praise of God as sovereign creator and sure redeemer of his people, and, on the other, in Job's complaints that God's sovereignty has become threatening, as the deity's comfort has turned to affliction. It is precisely because Job's redemption is in doubt that he vehemently appeals to God. Thus, instead of answering Job's questions, allusions to Job's speeches would undercut the message of Isa 40–55 altogether.

It is, of course, possible that the author of Isa 40–55 is unconcerned with the context of the Joban passages to which he is purportedly alluding, but, given the careful attention to context in his allusions to a wide range of other texts as demonstrated in a number of recent studies, this seems unlikely.[16] My argument here is that there is a more cogent explanation for the antithetical relationship between the respective meanings of the parallels in their contexts: parody. While the negative meaning of Job's accusations would linger and spoil the confident praise in Isa 40–55 were the author of the latter text alluding to them, it is precisely the contrast between the positive message of Isa 40–55 and Job's reversal of it that would give his use of the parallel language its bite.

Parody and Dialogical Interpretation in Job

Not only does this explanation make better sense of the purposes of the purported allusions, it also agrees with Job's use of other biblical passages. Consider the parallel between Ps 8:5 and Job 7:17–18, which has earned nearly universal acceptance as Job's "bitter parody" of the psalm. Job twists the humble adoration of the psalmist's question, "What are human beings that (מה־אנוש כי) you are mindful of them, mortals that you care (פקד) for them?," into accusation: "What are human beings, that (מה־אנוש כי) you make so much of them, that you set your mind on them, visit (פקד) them every morning, test them every moment?" This

---

16. See Tull Willey 1997; Sommer 1998; Schultz 1999. None of these studies address possible connections with Job, likely because they all consider Job to be later.

parody is not alone in the book. Parodies of the Psalms are widespread.[17] Job appears to be employing a similar technique in his allusions to Isa 40–55. For example, Brinks-Rea (2010, 170–75) observes that whereas the shared phrase in Job 12:9 and Isa 41:20 mentioned above contributes to a description of God's redemption in Isa 40–55, in Job a cynical hymn to God's destructive power follows, which leads her to conclude that an allusion to Job's sarcastic parody in Isa 40–55 "seems unlikely," while Job's parody of Isa 41:20 would fit the context well and accord with his use of other texts. So, based on the analogy of Job's "bitter parody" of Ps 8 in Job 7, a synchronic comparison of the external coherence of the possible allusions between Job and Isa 40–55 strongly suggests the diachronic conclusion that Job is the later text. Thus, Job attacks the message of Isa 40–55 in light of his experience, unremitting and unexplained affliction that does not accord with the prophet's confident proclamations of God's goodness. Often discussions of allusions in Job, including the discussion of the parody of Ps 8, stop here, but there is more to be said.

First, Job 7:17–18 is not the only allusion to Ps 8 in the book. In fact, Job's parody initiates a dialogical interpretive debate between the characters in which they return to the psalm several more times, but for the purposes of the present study, I will only attend to Eliphaz's initial response:[18]

> 14 What are mortals, that (מָה־אֱנוֹשׁ כִּי) they can be clean?
>   Or those born of woman, that they can be righteous?
> 15 God puts no trust even in his holy ones (קְדֹשָׁיו[19]),
>   and the heavens (שָׁמַיִם) are not clean in his sight;
> 16 how much less one who is abominable and corrupt,
>   one who drinks iniquity like water!

Here, he repeats the same opening question and basic structure found in both Job's allusion and the psalm, and adds allusions to the psalmist's mentions of the "heavens" (שָׁמַיִם) and "heavenly beings"[20] (אֱלֹהִים) in vv. 4 and 6 of the psalm.

Second, considering these repeated allusions to the same text not only strengthens the case for the allusion in the first place,[21] it also sheds light on the purpose of the initial allusion in Job 7. Eliphaz responds by taking the ambiguity at the heart of the psalm and emphasizing its negative

---

17. Kynes 2012. For parody as a widespread technique in Job, see Dell 1991.

18. For a discussion of the use of the psalm across the Job dialogue, including the following allusions in Job 19:9 and 25:5–6, see Kynes 2012.

19. This is the *qere*. The *kethib* is קְדֹשׁו.

20. For this translation, see Kraus 1993, 1:183.

21. For the cumulative nature of the case for allusions, see Sommer 1998, 35.

potential, denigrating human value as insignificant and immoral in relation to the heavens. But if Job's parody was intended to reject the undoubtedly positive message of the psalm as a whole, then how is Eliphaz's response actually a repudiation of Job's sentiment? If Job were to reject the psalm, then he would agree with Eliphaz that humanity is unworthy of God's loving care, and would thereby undercut his case against God by removing the basis for arguing that God should treat him differently. It is more reasonable to argue that, though Job parodies the psalm, he does so not to ridicule or reject it but to appeal more powerfully to the paradigm of divine–human relationship it presents in order to strengthen his appeal against God.[22] If his parody creates a "rivalry" between the view of God he depicts and the one given in the psalm, it is a contest he hopes the psalm will win.[23]

Allusions to Isaiah 40–55 in Job

This same dialogical interpretation occurs in allusions to other psalms in Job,[24] as well as to Isa 40–55, though with this text the technique is not quite as pronounced. Here, briefly, are four examples. These possible allusions are not the strongest between the two texts, and, in fact, it must be admitted that they could be coincidental or even shared references to a common source. However, if one concedes that Job is alluding to Isa 40–55 in the stronger cases (e.g. Job 12:9//Isa 41:20 and the group of parallels concentrated in Job 9:2–12[25]), as does even Brinks-Rea, who believes such claims are often exaggerated, then the Job poet's evident knowledge of some form of Isa 40–55 legitimates the search for further allusions which may be weaker.[26] As Robert Alter (1996, 118) observes, "allusions often radiate out to contiguous allusions." The rarity of the shared language in these examples, the thematic interplay between its use

22. Frevel 2004, 261–62. For the possibility that a parody may appeal to an earlier text as a paradigm instead of rejecting or ridiculing it, see Kynes 2011.

23. Brinks-Rea (2010, 176–77), who describes the parody's effect as a "rivalry," argues that through Job's parodies of Isa 40–55, "2 Isaiah's message has been 'smeared,'" creating a "dialectical" relationship between the texts in which they criticize one another (see Greene 1982, 45). However, it better fits Job's argument for him to use Ps 8 to criticize God than to criticize the psalm.

24. See Kynes 2012, where recurrent allusions to Pss 1, 39, 73, 107, and 139 are also discussed, with both Job and the friends alluding to the same psalms in every case but Ps 39.

25. Job 9:4//Isa 40:26; Job 9:8//Isa 44:24; Job 9:10//Isa 40:28; Job 9:12//Isa 43:13; 45:9.

26. See Brinks-Rea 2010, 179.

in the two sources, and its repetition in both the speeches of Job and the friends in line with the dialogical technique demonstrated above all suggest that the author of Job is drawing widely on Isa 40–55 to inform the dialogue between Job and his friends.

Job 9:10; 5:9; and Isaiah 40:28

First, Terrien observes a parallel between Job 9:10 and Isa 40:28, in which both texts describe God's greatness as "unsearchable" (אֵין חֵקֶר).[27] In Job's speech in 9:2–12, this "praise," along with several other parallels with Isa 40–55,[28] contributes to his complaint that one cannot contend with the transcendent God (9:3). Terrien (1966, 303) claims that Isa 40–55 is responding by affirming the grace of the creator. But it is more likely that Job, as in his parody of Ps 8, has once again taken praise and turned it into accusation.

Supporting this understanding of the parallel as well as its status as an allusion from Job to Isa 40–55 is the earlier use of the same rare phrase in Eliphaz's first speech (5:9). However, Eliphaz, like Isa 40–55, uses the phrase to entreat Job to "seek God" (5:8) in his distress.[29]

Job 9:12; 25:2–4; and Isaiah 45:9

Second, Job, continuing to lament God's transcendent imperviousness to complaint in ch. 9, says, "He snatches away; who can stop him? (מִי יְשִׁיבֶנּוּ) Who will say (יֹאמַר) to him, 'What are you doing? (מַה־תַּעֲשֶׂה)'" (9:12). The first of Job's questions appears in Isa 43:13[30] and the second in Isa 45:9.[31] Terrien (1966, 303) does not address the former parallel, but he notes that Job, by denying the second question ("what are you

---

27. This phrase only occurs elsewhere in Job 5:9 (see below); Ps 145:3; Prov 25:3.

28. See n. 25.

29. Nurmela (2006, 8), who claims Isa 40:28 is alluding to Job 9:10, faces the difficulty of distinguishing that allusion from the same shared phrase in 5:9, particularly because the addresses of Job's friends are rejected in the book (Job 42:7). He claims Isa 40:28 is referring only to 9:10, but having two different characters interpret the same phrase in different ways better explains this repetition.

30. "I am God, and also henceforth I am He; there is no one who can deliver from my hand; I work and who can hinder it (מִי יְשִׁיבֶנָּה)?" (Isa 43:13). This verse also has a close parallel in Job 10:7 ("although you know that I am not guilty, and there is no one to deliver out of your hand?"), which further suggests literary dependence.

31. "Woe to you who strive with your Maker, earthen vessels with the potter! Does the clay say (יֹאמַר) to the one who fashions it, 'What are you making'? (מַה־תַּעֲשֶׂה) or 'Your work has no handles'?" (Isa 45:9).

doing?") evidently considers inquiring into God's behavior futile, as he here associates God's transcendence with malevolence. However, in Isa 45:9, Terrien claims, the question is considered legitimate as an inquiry into the highly moral quality of God's providence with respect to the nations. But if the intent of Isa 45:9 is to inspire trust in God, an allusion to Job's complaint is an inappropriate resource. Through parodying this verse, however, Job would display the ambiguity of human inability to question God and entreat the deity to turn his oppression to the type of comfort promised to Israel in Isa 40–55.

The ambiguity of this text in Isa 40–55 is reinforced when Bildad alludes to the same passage in his third speech. He declares,

> Dominion and fear are with God;
> he makes peace (עשה שלום) in his high heaven (במרומיו)...
> How then can a mortal be righteous (יצדק) before God?
> How can one born of woman (ילוד אשה) be pure? (Job 25:2, 4)

The phrase עשה שלום appears only here and in Isa 45:7,[32] where God declares absolute sovereignty over all things, including "making weal" (עשה שלום) and "creating woe" (בורא רע).[33] God continues in the next verse, commanding the "heavens" (שמים) to shower "righteousness" (צדק) so that "righteousness" (צדקה) may sprout on the earth. Additionally, in v. 10, after the verse to which Job alludes, the passage in Isa 40–55 continues, "Woe to anyone who says to a father, 'What are you begetting (תוליד)?' or to a woman (אשה), 'With what are you in labor?'" (cf. Job 25:4, though these words imitate Job 15:14) and, in v. 12 refers to God's command over the "host" (צבא) of heaven (cf. "his armies," גדודיו, in Job 25:3). Thus, Bildad adds to the repetition of the distinctive phrase עשה שלום several more verbal and thematic resonances with the same passage in Isa 45 to which Job alluded. He, like Job, twists its meaning, but his intent is not to accuse God of falling short of the comfort it is meant to provide, but to use its vision of a transcendent unquestionable God to silence Job's complaint.

---

32. With עשה in the imperfect it also appears in Isa 27:5.

33. Nurmela (2006, 42), who affirms dependence here, argues that שלום and רע compose "a more or less unique pair of opposites," whose awkwardness is underscored by a variant in 1QIsaᵃ, where the more common parallel term טוב replaces שלום. However, though this may indicate that the MT is the *lectio difficilior* and therefore earlier than the Qumran variant, it does not support Nurmela's claim that it is earlier than Job 25:2. In fact, generally in Nurmela's approach the *lectio difficilior* is the *earlier* text, not the later one.

Job 9:12; 11:10; and Isaiah 43:13

Third, Job uses the first of the questions he shares with Isa 40–55 in 9:12 ("who can hinder it?") for the same purpose as the second, to present God's transcendence, as he is currently experiencing it, as threatening. In Isa 40–55, however, it communicates God's saving intention, as the proclamation of salvation in the previous verse (43:12) indicates.

This type of intervention for good is exactly what Job is denying. It would make little sense for the author of Isa 40–55 to allude to Job. However, Job could be using this phrase from Isa 40–55 to accuse God of not acting in such a way in his life.[34] Zophar's use of the same phrase in the next speech indicates that this is the case. Zophar says, "If he passes through, and imprisons, and assembles for judgment, who can hinder him (מִי יְשִׁיבֶנּוּ)?" (11:10). Zophar has taken the promise in Isa 40–55, which Job transformed into a complaint, and turned it into a threat.

Job 5:12–13; 12:17; and Isaiah 44:25

Fourth, in the context of his earlier allusion to Isa 40:28 in ch. 5, Eliphaz also appears to allude to Isa 44:25. That text proclaims that God "frustrates (מֵפֵר) the omens of liars, and makes fools (יְהוֹלֵל) of diviners (בַּדִּים); who turns back the wise (חֲכָמִים), and makes their knowledge foolish." Eliphaz, similarly declares, "He frustrates (מֵפֵר) the devices of the crafty, so that their hands achieve no success. He takes the wise (חֲכָמִים) in their own craftiness; and the schemes of the wily are brought to a quick end" (5:12–13). These are the only two places where the verb פָּרַר appears as a hiphil participle.[35] Though previously overlooked in the discussion of this parallel, the recurrence of "the wise" adds to the allusion. For both Eliphaz and Isa 40–55, this image is intended to express God's power and justice, though Isa 44:25 offers it as comfort, while Eliphaz implicitly threatens Job.

Job, however, returns to the same verse in ch. 12, in which he parodies other aspects of Eliphaz's speech in ch. 5 (e.g. 12:15//5:10). He says that God "leads counselors away stripped, and makes fools (יְהוֹלֵל) of judges" (12:17), which repeats the rare polel form of the verb הלל found in Isa 44:25,[36] and, along with that verse, uniquely applies it to God, while

---

34. See Job's similar use of the same phrase in 23:13.

35. Terrien (1966, 308) claims it also occurs in Ps 33:10, but that the verb הֵפִיר is a hiphil perfect of פּוּר (Delitzsch 1887–89, 1:485).

36. The only other occurrence is Eccl 7:7.

following a similar syntactical structure.[37] However, in contrast to Isa 40–55 and Eliphaz, Job describes God's power not as just, but as arbitrary, without the indications found in the other passages that those whom God afflicts deserve this fate. This accords with Job's experience, though it is an experience he hopes will end, which suggests he actually hopes the just God will return to oust the unjust one he is now experiencing.

Conclusion

This study has demonstrated how synchronic and diachronic concerns may be mutually beneficial in the discussion of intertextual connections in the HB. In these four examples, a synchronic comparison, which takes the parallel language and envisions how it would relate to the respective contexts from which it would have come were it an allusion, leads to the diachronic conclusion that Job is much more likely to be the later text. Job's parody of the praise and promise in Isa 40–55 make more sense than Isa 40–55 incorporating Job's complaint and accusation into its message. Also, by inserting this shared language into the dispute between Job and the friends, the author of Job unsettles it, giving it to different characters who use it for different purposes in their debate. If Job is the later text, this accords with the dialogical interpretation of other texts in Job, such as the psalms, but complicates matters if Isa 40–55 is later. The most pressing problem would be the passages in Isa 40–55 that would then have to incorporate language from the divergent messages of the speeches of both Job and the friends (Isa 45:9//Job 9:12; 25:2–4; Isa 44:25//Job 5:12–13; 12:17). But even when the same language appears in different speeches in Job (Isa 40:28//Job 5:9; 9:10; Isa 43:13//Job 9:12; 11:10), the reader would face the difficulty of determining to which speech Isa 40–55 was referring.[38]

---

37. Note also the synonym for "wisdom," as well as the play on the word בד in Isa 44:25, which could mean "diviner" or "deceiver," as Job proclaims "With him are strength and wisdom (תושיה); the deceived and the deceiver are his (לו שגג ומשגה)" (Job 12:16).

38. See n. 29. The only case where a phrase in Job is repeated twice in Isa 40–55 is in Job 13:28//Isa 50:9; 51:8, where the simile of a moth-eaten garment is used. However, unlike the debate between Job and his friends, both times in Isa 40–55 this image has a similar context, so Job could be referring to either or both occurrences. A comparison of the contexts in Isa 40–55 and Job again suggests that Job is the later text, taking the proclamation against enemies in Isa 40–55 and applying it to God's treatment of humanity in general and himself particularly by implication.

Beyond strongly suggesting the author of Job was familiar with Isa 40–55, exegetically, these examples demonstrate the contrasting ways Job and his friends use earlier texts. While Job parodies passages, using them as a paradigm to accuse God, the friends use them more directly. But their wooden interpretation often either twists the earlier promises into threats or empties them of their force by not taking into account Job's situation.

This diachronic conclusion then aids the synchronic comparison of the passages, as the allusions reflect back on Isa 40–55, revealing an ambiguity in the presentation of God there. Though each of the affirmations from Isa 40–55 discussed above may offer comfort when placed in the soteriological context of that text, all carry a threatening aspect, which Job experiences and complains of and the friends use to silence his complaints. And yet, if Job does indeed use his parodies to try and convince God to change God's ways, then the positive side of that imagery must inform his interpretation, as well. He feels the threat but longs for the comfort Isa 40–55 offers, and so this text is an ideal resource to express his frustration.

"CURSED BE THE DAY I WAS BORN!":
JOB AND JEREMIAH REVISITED

Katharine Dell

Alone among the prophetic books, that of Jeremiah contains impassioned pleas to God from the depths of human despair, sections of the text that are known as the "confessions" or "complaints" of Jeremiah.[1] These are found in Jer 11:18–23; 12:1–6; 15:10–21; 20:7–12 (or 13) and 20:14–18, although this selection is debated with some scholars adding 17:14–18 and 18:18–23.[2] They are often perceived as rather different from other parts of the book, to such an extent that they have been seen as later redaction, not the original complaints of the historical Jeremiah.[3] They have been viewed as stylized pieces from an existing lament tradition,[4] be that a prophetic complaint genre or from wider psalmic and even ancient Near Eastern lament traditions. Links with the lamenting sentiments of the book of Job have long been noted and particularly the verbal overlap between Jer 20:14–18 and Job 3 in the violent cursing of the day of birth.[5] While Job is traditionally classified as wisdom literature, a breaking out of the boundaries of the usual genres of that literature is noted in the case of Job's laments. I and others have argued for a wider set of genre traditions employed by the author of Job and often with subversive or parodic intent.[6] However, it is arguable that the classification

---

    1.   A seminal article is von Rad 1983. One wonders whether "the confessions of Jeremiah" was coined as a parallel to the title of Lamentations—"the lamentations of Jeremiah," also traditionally attributed to this prophet.

    2.   Lundbom (1999) writes that the category "confessions" is "well established if not entirely satisfactory" (634).

    3.   Most famously Carroll (1986) denied the existence of the historical Jeremiah, arguing that these were literary redactions. His position is supported by Clines and Gunn (1976). On the other side of the debate are older scholars, notably Bright (1970). Also Blank 1950–51; Davidson 1983; Crenshaw 1984; and Polk 1984.

    4.   Argued in particular by Baumgartner (1988).

    5.   This is noted by commentators both on Job and on Jeremiah. See Vinton 1978.

    6.   Dell 1991; cf. Zuckerman 1991.

of one text as "prophecy" and another as "wisdom" has hindered a close study of the relationship between the two texts. I would also suggest that the predominant form-critical "genre" angle on the lament tradition has also muddied the waters of comparison.[7] The classification of the laments of both Jeremiah and Job as part of a wider lament tradition that is shared with the psalms of lament[8] has led to hesitation in considering there to be any direct link, and both Jeremiah and Job have been seen as "types" within a tradition[9] rather than individual lamenters or protesters in a potentially related historical and literary context.

The use of intertextual method in recent times has perhaps opened our eyes more clearly to these methodological problems.[10] A move away from common genres to actual textual connections has been a welcome development. This has been prompted in large part by the departure from necessarily having to posit historical connections and a method that on one level simply asks how does this text read in the light of another. Thus texts may speak to each other, and to us, regardless of whether any author intended a connection or any situation gave rise to the connection. This is what I understand by a synchronic reading—a moment of interpretation that allows quite unrelated ideas or texts or both to impact one on another.[11] In this instance, however, there is a chance that the lament texts found in Jeremiah and Job could be linked historically and on a literary-historical level as well as being two texts ripe for inter-action. This is clear by the closeness in historical time of the two productions, Jeremiah being essentially a product of the sixth-century Exile even if redacted into the next century and Job being at the latest from the fourth century B.C.E. but with some possibility of a date closer to the Exile itself. However disputed the dates are, the historical time period is close, and there are also clear verbal and thematic overtones one with another, as I shall go on to discuss. That Job is imitating and progressing the sentiments of Jeremiah is the most natural literary and historical conclusion, even if they do both owe something to a wider lament tradition. Thus I make no apology for a more diachronic intertex-tual approach that seeks to explore connections between texts within a

---

7. The isolation of the confessions in the first place was on form-critical grounds and so one might ask whether in fact it is right to isolate them at all.

8. For example Pss 20:10; 31:13. The form-critical category of lament was given prominence in Hermann Gunkel's seminal work on the Psalms.

9. E.g. Hölscher (1937) who thought the "confessions" to be essentially misplaced psalms.

10. On Job in particular, see Pyeon 2003.

11. As Jonathan Culler (1981, 118) observes, "One can often produce heat and light by rubbing two texts together."

viable historical and literary biblical world. And yet, in putting together such a set of parallels, a synchronic element is apparent in the very choice of two sets of texts where some parallels exist, though none are strong enough to be obvious on a purely diachronic reading. Therefore, like several recent studies on intertextuality in the Hebrew Bible,[12] my approach incorporates aspects of both diachronic and synchronic intertextuality. In addition, unlike a more form-critical approach, this method is untrammeled by the genre classification issues that have set up fences between the two texts, boundaries that have hindered appreciation of their demonstrable intertextual connections.

I have argued elsewhere that the figure of Jeremiah is a clear inspiration to the unknown prophet of the Exile, Deutero-Isaiah, as he formulates his servant idea.[13] This provides an interesting parallel to these possible connections with Job. If the figure of Jeremiah was remembered in the tradition as one who suffered undeservedly, this would have been a clear paradigm for the author of Job. Edward Greenstein has argued this case for Jeremiah and Job in his article "Jeremiah as an Inspiration to the Poet of Job."[14] He concludes, "[T]he poet of Job…found inspiration in the figure and literature of Jeremiah, an earlier personality who felt betrayed and abandoned by God and by humans in spite of his outstanding loyalty to God and his ways" (107). He argues that it is not just a matter of isolated passages or expressions but it is the entire character of Jeremiah that was an inspiration to the Job poet. He also argues that the author of Job transforms the Jeremiah material into sentiments that go even beyond the radical towards the surreal or absurd.

The confessions of Jeremiah provide the best starting point for this discussion and it is perhaps most instructive to start with the most widely noted and closest parallel, that of Jer 20:14–18 (the last confession) with Job 3:1–12.

1. *Jeremiah 20:14–18*

Jer 20:14:

אָרוּר הַיּוֹם אֲשֶׁר יֻלַּדְתִּי בּוֹ	Cursed be the day on which I was
יוֹם אֲשֶׁר־יְלָדַתְנִי אִמִּי אַל־יְהִי בָרוּךְ:	born! The day when my mother bore me, let it not be blessed. (NRSV)

---

12. Schultz 1999; Pyeon 2003; Stead 2009.
13. Dell 2010.
14. Greenstein 2004.

Parts of Job 3:1, 3, 4, 8:

Job 3:1b:

ויקלל את־יומו

and he [Job] cursed the day of his birth.

Job 3:3a:

יאבד יום אולד בו

Let the day perish in which I was born.

Job 3:4a:

היום ההוא יהי חשך

Let that day be darkness!

Job 3:8a:

יקבהו אררי־יום

Let those curse it who curse the Sea

The clear parallel here is in the cursing of the day of birth—Job 3:1 is a third-person description, but then 3:3a is Job's own complaint. In 3:4a the "darkness" of the day forms a parallel to the day not being blessed in Jer 20:14. Job 3:8a uses two words for "curse"—קבב and ארר. The Jeremiah passage favours the root ארר—another curse word used in Job is קלל.

Jer 20:15:

ארור האיש אשר בשר את־אבי
לאמר ילד־לך בן זכר שמח
שמחהו:

Cursed be the man who brought the news to my father saying, "A child is born to you, a son," making him very glad.

Job 3:3b:

והלילה אמר הרה גבר

…and the night that said, "A man-child is conceived."

Here the main connection is the specific mention of the birth of a male child. In Jeremiah it is a man bringing the news, in Job it is a more poetic personified night who says the words.

Jer 20:17–18:

אשר לא־מותתני מרחם
ותהי־לי אמי קברי ורחמה הרת
עולם:
למה זה מרחם יצאתי לראות
עמל ויגון ויכלו בבשת ימי:

because he did not kill me in the womb; so my mother would have been my grave, and her womb forever great.
Why did I come forth from the womb to see toil and sorrow and spend my days in shame?

Job 3:10–11:

כִּי לֹא סָגַר דַּלְתֵי בִטְנִי	because it did not shut the doors of
וַיַּסְתֵּר עָמָל מֵעֵינָי׃	my mother's womb and hide trouble
לָמָּה לֹּא מֵרֶחֶם אָמוּת	from my eyes.
מִבֶּטֶן יָצָאתִי וְאֶגְוָע׃	Why did I not die at birth, come
	forth from the womb and expire?

Common features here include the "Why" question (also in Job 3:20, 23); giving a reason for their plight—"because" and mention of the mother and her womb. Also there is the idea in both of shutting the doors of the womb—that is, a blocked birth that would have resulted in death (Jer 20:17; Job 3:10). There is the further idea of dying after appearing from the womb in Job 3:11, put slightly differently in Jer 20:18 in terms of asking why the prophet did in fact come out of the womb safely when all his future life was to hold in store was "shame."

Another important intertext to the Jeremiah passage is Job 10:18–19, a parallel not often mentioned by scholars.

Job 10:18–19:

וְלָמָּה מֵרֶחֶם הֹצֵאתָנִי אֶגְוָע	Why did you bring me forth from the
וְעַיִן לֹא־תִרְאֵנִי׃	womb?
כַּאֲשֶׁר לֹא־הָיִיתִי אֶהְיֶה	Would that I had died before any eye
מִבֶּטֶן לַקֶּבֶר אוּבָל׃	had seen me,
	and were as though I had not been,
	carried from the womb to the
	grave.

Job puts the responsibility for his birth here directly on God, using metaphorical language that suggests God's direct involvement even in the act of birth itself. Prior to this Job's audience was unspecified—it could have been the friends or possibly God indirectly, but here it is specific. In Jeremiah God is ultimately to blame for the change in their relationship from positive to negative, but this is only implied, not directly stated.

2. Jeremiah 20:7–12

Going further back into Jer 20, in vv. 7–12 (v. 13 not included on my scheme), another confession section, there are a few parallels with Job.

Jer 20:7b:

הָיִיתִי לִשְׂחוֹק כָּל־הַיּוֹם כֻּלֹּה	I have become a laughingstock all
לֹעֵג לִי׃	day long; everyone mocks me.

Job 30:1a:

ועתה שחקו עלי צעירים ממני
לימים

But now they make sport of me,
those who are younger than I

Job 30:9:

ועתה נגינתם הייתי ואהי להם
למלה:

And now they mock me in song; I
am a byword to them.

Job 12:4a:

שחק לרעהו

I am a laughingstock to my friends

There is a clear link in the use of "laughingstock" (שחק) and related
sense in "mock" (לעג, Jeremiah)/נגן ("mocking song," Job).

Jer 20:8:

כי־מדי אדבר אזעק חמס ושד
אקרא כי־היה דבר־יהוה לי
לחרפה ולקלס כל־היום:

For whenever I speak, I must cry
out, I must shout, "Violence and
destruction!" For the word of the
LORD has become for me a
reproach and derision all day long.

Job 19:7:

הן אצעק חמס ולא אענה
אשוע ואין משפט:

Even when I cry out "Violence!" I
am not answered; I call aloud, but
there is no justice.

There are clear links in the use of "I cry out" with slightly different
choice of root, אזעק (Jeremiah; also used in Job, cf. Job 35:9), אצעק
(Job) and "violence" (חמס). Both have the context of God being to blame
(as is made clear in Job 19:6).

However, I would suggest that the intertextual tapestry is close here on
a thematic level, if not on a verbal one. The Jeremiah passage has usually
been likened to lament psalms and other prophetic outpourings,[15] but in
fact it echoes many of Job's sentiments in the dialogue speeches. Feeling
the force of God's power to the point of being almost overpowered is a
frequent sentiment in Job (Jer 20:7; cf. Job 9:17; 23:6; 26:14; 27:22); the
idea of God prevailing over one as in Jer 20:7a is found, for example, in
Job 6:4; 19:21. The concept of the word of the Lord as a reproach and
derision all day long is also mirrored in Job's reproach in Job 19:3; and
the idea of no let-up is found in both—in Jer 20:8 (cf. Job 10:20) where
he asks to be left alone and in Job 19:8 where Job is "walled up" and
cannot pass by. In both, trying not to think about affliction but being

15. See McKane 1986.

unable to (Jer 20:9; cf. Job 9:27–28) is accompanied by physical manifestations of inner feelings (Job 15:15–16). Further connections appear in
the characters hearing whisperings and being fearful of unknown terrors
(Jer 20:9; Job 6:4; 30:15); their friends becoming suspicious (Jer 20:10;
cf. Job 19:13–19); God's power on Jeremiah's behalf (Jer 20:11) to
overcome enemies (cf. Job 5:20); also testing the righteous (Jer 20:12; cf.
Job 7:18) and finally a more positive note of renewed commitment (Jer
20:12; cf. Jer 11:20; Job 19:25–26).

3. *Jeremiah 15:10–21*

Moving back in the book of Jeremiah to Jer 15:10–21, another "confession," parallels with Job 6 are particularly evident, as Greenstein has
noted. However, they go beyond simply that chapter.

Jer 15:10:

אוי־לי אמי כי ילדתני	Woe is me, my mother, that you
איש ריב ואיש מדון לכל־הארץ	ever bore me, a man of strife and
לא־נשיתי ולא־נשו־בי כלה מקללוני:	contention to the whole land! I
	have not lent, nor have I borrowed,
	yet all of them curse me.

Job 6:22–23:

הכי־אמרתי הבו לי ומכחכם	Have I said, "Make me a gift"? Or,
שחדו בעדי:	"From your wealth offer a bribe for
ומלטוני מיד־צר ומיד עריצים	me"? Or, "Save me from an
תפדוני:	opponent's hand"? Or, "Ransom
	me from the hand of oppressors"?

Clearly the other intertext to the first part of Jer 15:10 is Job 3:1–3 and
10:18 with regard to wishing that he had not been born. Greenstein notes
here in Jer 15:10 and Job 6:22–23 a shared theme of "economic depend-
ency" but goes further and suggests that the Job text is a "rhetorical take-
off on Jeremiah" (101), the idea that well-to-do Job might need a bribe
from his friends being "absurd."

Jer 15:18:

למה היה כאבי נצח ומכתי אנושה	Why is my pain unceasing, my
מאנה הרפא היו תהיה לי כמו	wound incurable refusing to be
אכזב מים לא נאמנו:	healed?
	Truly, you are to me like a deceitful
	brook, like waters that fail.

Job 6:15:

אחי בגדו כמו־נחל כאפיק   My companions are treacherous
נחלים יעברו: like a torrent-bed, like freshets that
   pass away.

In relation to Jer 15:18b, as Greenstein notes, Job takes the same image and applies it to his friends, extending it as an image through vv. 15–20 in the story of caravans being turned from their course by a treacherous torrent. אַכְזָב—a rare term for wadi found in Jeremiah echoed in Job 6:28. Greenstein suggests a translation "I would not betray you like a wadi" or "I would not be a wadi for you." He writes, "The pointed use of אכזב in Job 6:28 in a context concerning personal disappointment would seem to depend on its source in Jer 15:17. The image of the wadi as a metaphor for disappointment is therefore taken from Jeremiah by the poet of Job" (101).

Jeremiah 15:18a is also paralleled in Job 34:6b.

Job 34:6:

על־משפטי אכזב אנוש חצי   In spite of being right I am counted
בלי־פשע: a liar; my wound is incurable,
   though I am without transgression.

Job 34:6a links up with the frustration of being treated badly and distrusted by former friends, as found in both texts.

Jer 15:19:

לכן כה־אמר יהוה   Therefore thus says the LORD: "If
אם־תשוב ואשיבך לפני תעמד   you turn back, I will take you back,
ואם־תוציא יקר מזולל כפי תהיה   and you shall stand before me. If
ישבו המה אליך ואתה לא־תשוב   you utter what is precious, and not
אליהם: what is worthless, you shall serve
   as my mouth. It is they who will
   turn to you, not you who will turn
   to them."

Job 13:22:

וקרא ואנכי אענה או־אדבר   Then call, and I will answer; or let
והשיבני: me speak, and you reply to me.

Job 31:35a:

מי יתן־לי   Oh that I had one to hear me!

In Jer 15:19 the prophet recalls his relationship with God—these verses are cited in Job, on the other hand, as a desire to have a closer relationship with God.[16] One is clearly an oracle from God while Job is asking for such a word from God. However, formulation of the bargaining language is similar and does provide a parallel.

4. *Jeremiah 12:1–6*

Jer 12:1a:

צדיק אתה יהוה כי אריב אליך
אך משפטים אדבר אותך

You will be in the right, O LORD, when I lay charges against you; but let me put my case to you.

Job 9:2:

אמנם ידעתי כי־כן
ומה־יצדק אנוש עם־אל׃

Indeed I know that this is so: but how can a mortal be just before God?

Job 9:3:

אם־יחפץ לריב עמו
לא־יעננו אחת מני־אלף׃

If one wished to contend with him, one could not answer him once in a thousand

Legal language in the attempt to argue with God seems to originate here in Jeremiah. So too does the idea that in fact disputing with God does not necessarily get you anywhere (cf. Job 9:4, 14–20, 27–35—indeed a quite considerable thematic interaction with ch. 9 of Job on this point can be found here, cf. Job 23:2–17). The Job text could arguably be seen as an expansion of Jeremiah's sentiment.

Jer 12:1b:

מדוע דרך רשעים צלחה
שלו כל־בגדי בגד׃

Why does the way of the guilty prosper? Why do all who are treacherous thrive?

Job 21:7:

מדוע רשעים יחיו עתקו
גם־גברו חיל׃

Why should the wicked live on, reach old age, and grow mighty in power?

---

16. Greenstein denies this link.

The perennial question of the prosperity of the wicked/guilty arises here. There are many examples of this theme, too many to number here, in the dialogue of Job.[17]

Jer 12:4c:

כי אמרו לא יראה את־אחריתנו׃   And because people said, "He is blind to our ways"

Job 22:14a:

עבים סתר־לו ולא יראה   Thick clouds enwrap him, so that he does not see

There is a shared perception here that Yahweh does not see what is happening, both on a physical level and on a deeper personal level of interrelationships.

5. *Jeremiah 11:18–23*

Jer 11:20a:

ויהוה צבאות שפט צדק בחן   But you, O LORD of hosts, who
כליות ולב   judge righteously, who try the heart and the mind

Job 19:27b:

כלו כליתי בחקי   My heart faints within me.

Finally, there are very few verbal connections with Job in Jer 11:20. One shared term is כְּלָיוֹת (Jer 11:20a). In Job 19:27b Job uses this word to indicate "heart" or "innermost being." There are, however, some thematic links—enemies devising schemes (Job 21:27, where he accuses God; otherwise he describes the "schemes" of the wicked); one's name no longer being remembered (cf. Job 18:17) and pleas for God's retribution (e.g. Job 19:28–29).

Conclusion

Certain chapters of Job resonate with Jeremiah's words in the confessions. Lexical connections exist and thematic parallels are close. These kinds of connection are not exclusive to these two texts of Jeremiah's confessions and Job, but as "intertexts" key lexical and thematic parallels are highlighted. The use of a combined diachronic and synchronic method

17. Greenstein finds verbal links with Job 21:8 and 23 as well as v. 7.

helps to draw these themes to the fore, the diachronic approach being entirely viable given the historical closeness in time of these two texts, and the synchronic method adding an element of lateral comparison that the diachronic approach alone does not have the flexibility to allow. Of course this is only a sample—there are quite a few references in Job that echo Jeremiah but from other parts than the confessions.[18] Jeremiah's own sentiments are intensified when we come to the confessions and this process continues with further intensification and extension in Job. This is not quite a parody *ad absurdum*, as Greenstein would have us believe, but certainly particular themes are filled out in Job (see Pyeon 2003). Despite the author's proclivity for parody, I would classify this particular set of examples as a re-use of known tradition rather than as a misuse with parodic intent, a re-use of forms being the placing of a common form with its usual content into a new context rather than involving a content change (see the discussion in Dell 1991). On this model the content can be expanded or contracted but the essential sense is the same, while in a misuse of a form the content is deliberately changed, usually for parodic effect.

Finally, there are signs of the Jeremiah figure, or tradition, having influenced the author of Job, quite possibly in literary-historical terms. A diachronic approach to these texts invites us not simply to draw textual comparisons between the words and sentiments of the text but to consider links between Jeremiah and Job as characters. Whether or not they actually existed in a historical sense does not detract from their literary historicity and proximity in time as contemporary figures. It is permissible to surmise that the author of Job was aware of the character of Jeremiah on some level, whether that be by reputation or by personal experience. As an important figure of recent exilic times, Jeremiah was likely to have continued to be a figure of inspiration (as he was to Deutero-Isaiah, see Dell 2010). The close lexical and thematic links I have isolated also suggest a literary connection between the two texts, probably an authorial link on the part of the Job text, although redactional reshaping of texts in relation to one another within the canon of Scripture may also be a possibility. The fact that both are part of a wider lament tradition may also account for some of the textual similarities, leading one to exercise caution when speaking in terms of authorial dependence. A diachronic approach then opens up afresh more literary-historical questions relating to intertextual connections between the two. This trajectory indicates a deeper connection than simply a synchronic

---

18. Greenstein lists many examples in his contribution to the present volume.

meeting of the two texts would imply. And yet, it is a synchronic approach that has highlighted these very links that have otherwise been less noticed than they might have been in the scholarship and that therefore adds freshness and vitality to a broader intertextual approach to these ancient texts.

"Even if Noah, Daniel, and Job were in it…" (Ezekiel 14:14): The Case of Job and Ezekiel

Paul M. Joyce

A consideration of Job's intertextual interaction with the other books of the Hebrew Bible would be incomplete without grappling with the many questions surrounding the only explicit mention of Job in its pages. The sole reference to Job outside the book that bears his name is in Ezek 14.[1] Verse 14 reads "even if Noah, Daniel, and Job, these three, were in it, they would save only their own lives by their righteousness (צדקה), says the Lord GOD," and v. 20, "even if Noah, Daniel, and Job were in it, as I live, says the Lord GOD, they would save neither son nor daughter; they would save only their own lives by their righteousness."

Ezekiel 14

First, these Ezekiel references to Job should be considered in their own context. Ezekiel 14 falls into two parts, vv. 1–11 and vv. 12–23. Although both seem to reflect the influence of the priestly case-law format and also manifest a strong emphasis on Israel's responsibility for the national fate, there is otherwise little continuity in content. Verses 12–20 at first appear to lay down a general principle according to which YHWH deals with any land that sins against him. Verse 13 reads "When a land sins against

---

1. Among the apocryphal/deuterocanonical books of the Old Testament, Ecclesiasticus (Sirach) makes explicit reference to Job in the survey of great figures of Jewish tradition in ch. 49, and there may also be a connection between Job and Ezekiel there. Sir 49:8 reads, "It was Ezekiel who saw the vision of glory, which he showed him above the chariot of the cherubim." The following verse reads, "For he also mentioned Job who held fast to all the ways of justice." The NRSV reasonably represents the "he" in the Greek of v. 8 as "God," and then proceeds also to represent the "he" in the Greek of v. 9 as "God." It is interesting to note that the latter case could be construed to say that Ezekiel mentioned Job, which would presumably be an allusion to Ezek 14:14, 20, expanding the intertextual network.

me..." There follows reference to four forms of punishment: "famine" (v. 13), "wild animals" (v. 15), "sword" (v. 17) and "pestilence" (v. 19). In each of the four cases, it is said that even if figures of exemplary righteousness were present, they would save only their own lives (vv. 14, 16, 18, 20). Three paragons of virtue are cited (named explicitly only in the first and last cases, vv. 14, 20). First we are told that these "would save only their own lives by their righteousness" (v. 14). Verses 16, 18 and 20 then elaborate upon v. 14 to say that these good men would not deliver sons and daughters. Though the Hebrew does not employ possessives here, it is likely that this means "their own sons and daughters." These, being among the closest relatives, represent those one would think most likely to be spared, if anyone at all were to be spared with the righteous. This is very similar to Ezek 9:6, where even "little children" who do not bear a designated mark on the forehead are to be slain.

In v. 21, the general principle is then related specifically to the fate of Jerusalem in particular: "How much more (כִּי אַף) when I send upon Jerusalem my four deadly acts of judgment!" This passage has often been understood to be strongly individualistic but this is a misreading. The basic ideal that the righteous should be spared in a general punishment seems to be taken for granted here, as in Ezek 9. It seems to be assumed that Noah, Daniel and Job would deliver their own lives by their righteousness if they were present (for fuller exegesis of the passage, see Joyce 2007, 125–28). The passage asserts that the old principle of individual responsibility is to be operated with unprecedented rigour. The prophet anticipates an imminent judgment that will "cut off man and beast" (RSV; 14:13, 17, 19, 21). His purpose is to stress the thoroughness of judgment; there will certainly be no place for what Daube called "Communal Merit" (Daube 1947, 157–58), not even on the basis of family solidarity. It is important to recognize that we are dealing here with rhetoric. Ezekiel does not envisage segregation between paragons of virtue and their unrighteous offspring actually taking place; rather, the motif is a forceful way of saying to the wicked that justice will be thorough and absolute. The priestly case-law format in which Ezek 14:12–20 is presented must not be allowed to obscure this fact. It might at first sight seem that the rigour of YHWH's application of the principle of individual responsibility when punishing lands is presented as a general rule, which is only related specifically to Jerusalem at v. 21, but the theoretical appearance of Ezek 14:12–20 is to be attributed to Ezekiel's adaptation of the test-case format. The purpose of Ezekiel here is an *ad hoc* one; he addresses a specific and desperate situation. This is an example of prophetic hyperbole: the sins of Israel are so great (the situation is even worse, it is implied, than at the time of the Flood) that an overwhelming punishment is now imminent, so thorough that the most righteous people who can be imagined would not be able to deliver even their closest relatives.

Noah, Daniel and Job

The three named paragons of Ezek 14 are Noah, Daniel and Job (cf. Spiegel 1945; Noth 1951). Though they cannot be pursued far in this context, Noah and Daniel here provide interesting comparators for Job, since figures bearing these names too appear elsewhere in the Hebrew Bible. It is to be noted that all three are in some sense international figures; this fits with the priestly test-case format, appearing, as it does, to lay down a general principle according to which YHWH deals with sinful lands. Noah is the righteous hero in the Genesis flood story; there Noah's close family are spared (Gen 6:18; 7:1, 7), even though it seems to be Noah alone who had found favour with God (Gen 6:8, 9; 7:1). Noah lives before the call of Israel through Abram (Gen 12:1–3) and so is non-Israelite; also there are affinities between Noah and several ancient Near Eastern traditional figures, including the Babylonian Atrahasis and Utnapishtim (cf. Wahl 1992). Turning to "Daniel," he could be the hero of the biblical book of Daniel, who is presented as among the sixth-century Judahite exiles in Babylonia (so Block 1997, 449). But given the "if they were here now" format, it would be surprising if Daniel were effectively a contemporary of Ezekiel (if indeed one grants a sixth-century context for Daniel), and moreover in such a case one might expect him to come third in the list. In any case, an earlier figure is more probable (cf. Day 1980). The spelling of the name Daniel here, as in Ezek 28:3, lacks the middle letter yod (unlike the fuller spelling found in the book of Daniel). This suggests that the allusion in Ezek 14 is probably to the legendary king Dan'el (*dnil*), as found in the Epic of Aqhat from the Ras Shamra tablets from twelfth-century B.C.E. Ugarit.[2] Given that Noah and Daniel are thus arguably in some sense international figures, it is significant to note that the righteous hero of the biblical book of Job is said to be of the land of Uz (Job 1:1), probably Edom and so non-Israelite (cf. Goshen-Gottstein 1972).

The significance of the sequence of the three paragons of Ezek 14:14, 20 might be considered. Does the sequence move from the earliest to the latest figure? We noted earlier that such considerations have featured in

2.   This is not to rule out the possibility that the book of Daniel is itself indebted in some way to the ancient tradition of this legendary king (in spite of the fact that the book of Daniel uses the fuller spelling of the name).

attempts to identify the Daniel figure. Why is Job placed third in the list of virtuous heroes? Is it because he was the latest figure historically, an exilic contemporary of Ezekiel's or perhaps a post-exilic figure referred to by an even later redactor of Ezekiel? Such arguments seem rather unpromising. Or is it more likely that the three saints are placed in descending order of success, considered from the point of view of whom the particular virtuous hero had saved with him? Noah took his sons into the ark with him (Gen 7:7). Daniel's three young companions were delivered alongside him (Dan 1–3). But Job, though righteous, could save neither son nor daughter, even if he was later granted more sons and daughters (Job 1:19; cf. 42:13). This too seems somewhat strained, and it is best to regard the sequence as either unexplained or insignificant.

At this point let us review in more detail what is said about Job in relation to his sons and daughters in the book that bears his name. Job had "seven sons and three daughters" (1:2). Job "would send and sanctify them, and he would rise early in the morning and offer burnt offerings according to the number of them all; for Job said, 'It may be that my children have sinned, and cursed God in their hearts'" (1:5). However, in spite of Job's righteousness (1:1), and indeed this special piety with regard to his sons and daughters, he loses them all: "...another came and said, 'Your sons and daughters were eating and drinking wine in their eldest brother's house, and suddenly a great wind came across the desert, struck the four corners of the house, and it fell on the young people, and they are dead...'" (Job 1:18–19). After the speeches of God and Job's vindication, such as it is, Job regains sons and daughters: "He also had seven sons and three daughters" (42:13)—the same number he is said to have lost in ch. 1. The new daughters, though not the new sons, are named, and we are told that they were especially beautiful and that their father gave them an inheritance along with their brothers (42:14–15). We may note in passing that also in this final chapter, Job's three so-called friends are spared, through his intercession. God says to Eliphaz the Temanite: "...go to my servant Job, and offer up for yourselves a burnt offering; and my servant Job shall pray for you, for I will accept his prayer not to deal with you according to your folly..." (42:8). And, we are told, "...the LORD accepted Job's prayer" (42:9).

By referring to Noah, Daniel, and Job as a trio, Ezekiel creates a relationship between the three figures, which cannot but encourage a comparison of their stories with one another. This sets up an intertextual network, broader than Ezek 14 and the book of Job. There are clear affinities between Noah and Job, both of whom are described as "righteous and blameless" (צדיק תמים, Gen 6:9; Job 12:4). As indicated earlier, the name Daniel (with short-form spelling, as in Ezek 14:14, 20) also occurs in Ezekiel at 28:3, in the context of an oracle against the prince of Tyre, where he features as a paragon of wisdom: "You are indeed wiser than Daniel." Affinities between Ugaritic Dan'el and biblical Job are intriguing. In the Epic of Aqhat from Ras Shamra, Dan'el is granted a son, Aqhat. Like Job, Dan'el, though righteous, is unable to deliver his son from divine harm and Aqhat is destroyed. However, it is widely surmised by scholars that in the missing ending of the epic Aqhat, the son of Dan'el, is revived or replaced, a motif that invites comparison with the granting of new children to Job in Job 42:13.

Rhetorically, the point of the reference to the three righteous men in Ezek 14 is, however, not about the details of how their sons and daughters fared in their own day or in their own stories. Rather the implication (as in the reference to Moses and Samuel in Jer 15:1) is that one would naturally assume that the most righteous people who can be imagined would be able to deliver their sons and daughters, but the present situation is so bad that such assumptions have no place. An overwhelming punishment is now imminent, such as not even Noah, Daniel or Job would be able to moderate.

Intertextuality

Our particular focus is the intertextual relationship between Job and Ezekiel. The references in Ezek 14 share with the book of Job not only the name Job but also his designation as a person of special virtue (cf. Job 1:1, where Job is described as "blameless and upright, one who feared God and turned away from evil"). It does not seem plausible therefore to regard the occurrence of the name as merely a matter of coincidence. So, this is a significant parallel—but beyond that, what is to be said? The notion of intertextuality calls for closer examination.

In a recent overview of intertextuality in Hebrew Bible research Geoffrey Miller (2011) distinguishes helpfully between reader-oriented and author-oriented approaches to intertextuality (see also the earlier valuable discussion in Tull 2000a). The reader-oriented approach is indebted to poststructuralist thought (in which context the term "intertextuality" has its primary home) and relies on a purely synchronic analysis of texts. The focus is solely on the reader and the connections that he or she draws between two or more texts. A text has meaning only when it is read in conjunction with other texts, and it is irrelevant whether these texts were intentionally alluded to by the original author, or even available to the author. The author-oriented approach, on the other hand, while placing significant importance on the role of the reader, incorporates a diachronic perspective as well. Here the focus is on identifying the specific connections that the author wants readers to perceive, as well as determining which text predates the others and has influenced them. Scholars adopting this more diachronic approach debate whether perceived connections between texts can be attributed to authorial intent or are merely coincidental. In order to prove the former, some scholars have articulated criteria for identifying intentional allusions. Miller argues that the more diachronic, author-oriented approach (indebted to traditional methods of biblical criticism) should not be called "intertextual" at all, but should be given a different name, as some scholars have indeed tried to do. Although none of these alternatives has achieved consensus, the two with the widest support seem to be "inner-biblical exegesis" (e.g. Fishbane 1985) and "inner-biblical allusion" (e.g. Eslinger 1992).

As for the method I adopt in this essay (expressed in general terms first, without reference to the case of Job and Ezekiel), I regard both author-oriented and reader-oriented approaches as legitimate, so long as they are carefully distinguished and there is clarity about one's interpretative purpose. A pluralism of distinct legitimate "interpretative interests" has been championed effectively by Brett (1990; 1991, 5–6, 11–26). Moreover, many of the contributors to *Synchronic or Diachronic?* (de Moor 1995) attempted to give both diachronic and synchronic approaches their place while carefully distinguishing them.[3] I welcome Miller's proposal that the term "intertextual" be reserved for reader-oriented approaches as helpful in achieving such clarity. With Eslinger I favour "inner-biblical allusion" as a good term for the main subject of the author-oriented approach. However, in the context of the author-oriented approach, I wish also to find room for the possibility that texts may sometimes carry features that influence later texts without authors or redactors necessarily being conscious of this. The concept of authorial intention was rigorously critiqued in the twentieth century (cf. Barton 1996). We need to remember that texts may have features that are neither intended by authors nor projected onto the texts by readers, but are intrinsic to the texts themselves.

An Author-Oriented Approach

I shall next consider in turn what might be said about our topic in author-oriented terms and then in reader-oriented terms. First the author-oriented, diachronic approach. The references to Job in Ezekiel were

---

3. The focus of *Synchronic or Diachronic?* was not on intertextuality, but its treatment of the synchronic/diachronic issue is informative for the present discussion.

long considered an indicator of the latest possible date for the book of Job; if the exilic prophet referred to Job then the book that told Job's story must be earlier. The dating of Ezekiel has remained a fixed point for the most part (even if some scholars posit extensive redactional development of the exilic book). However, over the course of the twentieth century there was a trend to later dating of the book of Job. If this were correct, it might be that Ezekiel's references to Job inspired the author of Job, much as the isolated reference to the prophet Jonah in 2 Kgs 14:25 may have inspired another Hebrew book. (For an overview of the book of Job in historical perspective, see Clines 1989, lvi–lxii.)

It is important to make more nuanced distinctions here, since this is not a simple matter of which book is the earlier, Job or Ezekiel. It could be that the figure of Job is early, even if the present book of Job is not. Indeed, since Job shares some features with the Patriarchs he might be thought to fit well enough in the so-called pre-exilic age. (This is not the place for a debate over the historicity of the Patriarchs.) There may have been an early folktale about him that formed the foundation of the prose prologue of the book of Job (in chs. 1–2) and possibly also the prose epilogue (42:7–17). One or both of these could predate the long poetic section of the book (3:1–42:6) and indeed be earlier than sixth-century Ezekiel.

It is possible that some details in the frame narrative of Job were derived from Ezekiel. Perhaps the mention of sons and daughters in Ezek 14 inspired the author of Job to include them in the story. In the poetic dialogue, there are verses where it appears that Job has not lost his children (e.g. Job 19:13–14, 17; though see also 8:4; 29:5). It may be that the poetic dialogue does not know of this feature of the story, and that the framing narrative (which might, contrary to other suggestions, be later than the poetic dialogue) has picked up, and transformed, the "sons and daughters" motif of Ezek 14. On an author-oriented, diachronic approach, many such possibilities can be discussed in detail. The relative historical order of materials can be considered and then questions of possible dependence judged in the light of this—recognizing, of course, that the mere fact that one text or tradition may be earlier than another does not require that there be a relationship of dependence between them. This is not the place for a full discussion, but the probability would seem to be that Job, at least in its final form, is later than Ezekiel (though, as we have seen, even if this is the case, many detailed hypotheses merit serious consideration). Moreover, another very plausible diachronic theory is that both Ezek 14 and Job depend upon the same folktale motif, that of the virtuous hero Job. This is an option to which I shall return.

A Reader-Oriented Approach

I turn now, more briefly, to the approach Miller terms "reader-oriented." Here the focus is solely on the reader and the connections that he or she draws between two or more texts. The texts lie before us on the pages of the Bible and questions of relative antiquity and of dependence of texts, one upon another, do not arise. Within a poststructuralist intertextual approach, as we have noted, a text has meaning only when it is read in conjunction with other texts, and it is irrelevant whether these texts were intentionally alluded to by the author, or even available to the author. A text can have multiple meanings, especially as new intertexts are read and as new readers engage with them. The reader is thus sovereign. The charge of the traditional scholar that this amounts to mere subjectivism is judged irrelevant; indeed it attracts the counter-charge that the claimed objectivity of traditional scholarship is illusory. Such an approach can accommodate playful exercise of the imagination—not unlike the flights of fancy undertaken by the targumists in elaborating each of our books for an Aramaic audience!

Parallels Between the Books of Job and Ezekiel

At this point it should be asked whether there are other parallels between the two books. The answer to this question will be of relevance both to an author-oriented approach and to a reader-oriented approach. Although there are various links between Job and prophetic tradition (Altheim and Stiehl 1970), common ground with Ezekiel is limited. Let us review the parallels, such as they are, starting with those bearing on Ezek 14. In addition to the appearance of the name of Job in Ezek 14:14, 20, and his presentation as a person of particular virtue, there would seem to be two shared features between the book of Job and Ezek 14, neither of them substantial. First, in Job 1:13–19, four messengers arrive reporting disasters that have befallen Job's offspring, servants and animals. This can be likened, in its fourfold pattern but not in its details, to the punishments of Ezek 14:13–19. And then, second, in Job 22:27–30 Eliphaz anticipates that when Job makes peace with God, even the guilty may be delivered on account of Job. This can obviously be compared, or rather contrasted, with the Ezek 14 theme that Job and his peers, if they were present, would save neither son nor daughter, but only their own lives by their righteousness.

Other parallels between the books (not bearing directly on Ezek 14) may now be reviewed. In Job 2:13 we read, "They sat with him on the ground seven days and seven nights, and no one spoke a word to him, for they saw that his suffering was very great." This can be compared with Ezek 3:15, "I came to the exiles at Tel-abib, who lived by the River Chebar. And I sat there among them, stunned, for seven days." In Job 10:11–12, we read, "You clothed me with skin and flesh, and knit me together with bones and sinews. You have granted me life and steadfast love, and your care has preserved my spirit." This can be compared with Ezek 37:7–10, "…suddenly there was a noise, a rattling, and the bones came together, bone to its bone. I looked, and there were sinews on them, and flesh had come upon them, and skin had covered them; but there was no breath in them… I prophesied as he commanded me, and the breath came into them, and they lived…" In Job 22:13–14, we read, "Therefore you say, 'What does God know? Can he judge through the deep darkness? Thick clouds enwrap him, so that he does not see, and he walks on the dome of heaven'." With this may be compared Ezek 8:12, "Then he said to me, 'Mortal, have you seen what the elders of the house of Israel are doing in the dark, each in his room of images? For they say, "The LORD does not see us, the LORD has forsaken the land"'." A three-fold pattern of punishment is shared by Job 27:14–15 ("If their children are multiplied, it is for the sword; and their offspring have not enough to eat. Those who survive them the pestilence buries…") and Ezek 5:12 ("One third of you shall die of pestilence or be consumed by famine among you; one third shall fall by the sword around you; and one third I will scatter to every wind and will unsheathe the sword after them") and also Ezek 6:12 ("Those far off shall die of pestilence; those nearby shall fall by the sword; and any who are left and are spared shall die of famine…"). Some language of theophany is shared between the books: in Job 38:1 we are told, "Then the LORD answered Job out of the whirlwind," while in Ezek 1:4 we read, "As I looked, a stormy wind came out of the north: a great cloud with brightness around it and fire flashing forth continually, and in the middle of the fire, something like gleaming amber." Though the formulations differ, they have the Hebrew word סערה, "whirlwind, stormy wind," in common. Nonetheless the similarity is slender.

A more thematic potential parallel to be highlighted is in the language of responsibility. In a speech of Job in ch. 21 we read, "You say, 'God stores up their iniquity for their children.' Let it be paid back to them, so that they may know it. Let their own eyes see their destruction, and let them drink of the wrath of the Almighty" (Job 21:19–20). The Hebrew is elliptical; the English NRSV, cited here, supplies the words "You say," places speech marks around the words "God stores up their iniquity for their children," and also translates the verbs that follow as jussives

("Let...") rather than indicatives. Nonetheless, the NRSV does here offer a very plausible rendering, in which case Job 21 is not dissimilar from Ezek 18 in its protest against the traditional notion that the sins of the ancestors are visited upon subsequent generations. But if there is a significant similarity here, this could simply reflect Ezekiel's general influence on the post-exilic age. The issue of individualism is often, rightly or wrongly, brought into discussions of such material. While some have suggested that Job represents the communal suffering of Israel, many see Job, especially if post-exilic, as an attempt to apply the problem of suffering to the situation of the individual. This might be thought to be like Ezekiel, often interpreted as an innovator in matters of individualism. But such an interpretation is based on a misunderstanding, both of Ezekiel and of the supposed evolution of individualism in ancient Israel (cf. Joyce 2007, 23–26).

I have attempted here a thorough listing of parallels between Job and Ezekiel, since this would be essential to any more developed exploration in either author-oriented or reader-oriented terms. The outcome would seem to be that there is relatively little in common between these two works. The relative paucity of parallels is the more significant given the large scale of both books. When Hartley singles out four books of the Old Testament as having particular affinities with the book of Job, these are Proverbs, Psalms, Lamentations and Isaiah (especially Isa 40–55); Ezekiel has no place in his list (Hartley 1988, 11–15). The contrast between the major prophetic books of Isaiah and Ezekiel in this regard is striking. Morgan (1981, 109–12) considers the relationship between Ezekiel and the wisdom tradition more generally. While noting that it is less apparent than in the cases of Isaiah of Jerusalem and Jeremiah, he does find in Ezekiel evidence of "definite contact with and use of the tradition," particularly in Ezekiel's citation of proverbial sayings (albeit sometimes then refuted) and use of allegory; however, he makes no reference to Job in his discussion.

Conclusion

As indicated earlier, I wish to find a place for both author-oriented and reader-oriented questions. As for an author-oriented approach, while all historical judgments fall short of certainty, it seems likely that the book of Job, in its final form, is later than the book of Ezekiel. But given the paucity of parallels between the two books, it is by no means clear that the author of Job is dependent on Ezekiel. The reference to the three paragons in Ezek 14 is proverbial in tone, and it is likely that Ezekiel is alluding to an old tradition including a virtuous hero Job. It is, moreover, quite possible that the book of Job takes the same early tradition as its starting point. There seems to be no conclusive indication that the author of Job is aware of how Ezekiel has used the motif, and they should probably be deemed independent in this regard as in others. On a reader-oriented approach, the relatively small number of parallels between these two large books must in some ways limit the scope for intertextual reading. But the trio of saints that Ezekiel puts together opens up, as we have seen, a broader intertextual network that proves both fascinating and fertile. Moreover, in readerly terms, historical hypotheses can be played with heuristically: although the balance of the evidence may favour a later date for the final form of Job than for that of Ezekiel, as a reader I can (if I wish to think in historical terms at all) reflect on how it might be if the book of Job, even in its final form, were earlier than Ezekiel. After all, Ezekiel himself is exercising his imagination ("If Job were here now…") and as readers we might choose to exercise our liberty to do likewise!

JOB AND JOEL:
DIVERGENT VOICES ON A COMMON THEME

James D. Nogalski

Method and Task

The current essay will utilize a synchronic, reader-oriented intertextual approach to enter into a comparative analysis of the ways in which the verb שוב functions differently within Job 8–10 and Joel. For an excellent summary of the backgrounds and difficulties associated with the term intertextuality, see Geoffrey D. Miller's 2011 study. Miller surveys the use of the term in Old Testament scholarship and offers descriptive categories (reader-oriented and author-oriented) to avoid pejorative connotations and long-standing debates when talking about the methods as diachronic or synchronic. His calls for clarity and transparency should be heeded, but his preference stated at the end of the article (303–5) that "intertextuality" should be reserved for the synchronic, reader-oriented approach appears short-sighted. Many diachronic, author-oriented studies will continue to use the term intertextuality because ancient composers were also readers and re-readers of precursor texts (see Ben Zvi 1996, 3–6). In many respects, attempts to document, characterize, and interpret ancient authors' use of existing texts parallel the synchronic, reader-oriented task (e.g. Bautch 2007). Diachronic, author-oriented studies may attempt to describe an *ancient* reader's intertextual reading (as well as to extrapolate historical implications from this reading). For this reason, scholars will continue to use "intertextuality" for both tasks.[1]

My approach, however, exhibits no interest in the intentions of the author, but is rooted in two convictions of postmodern literary studies: (1) no text has meaning until it is read in relationship to other texts; and (2) every text holds a plurality of meanings based upon the texts with and

---

1. In shedding light on the thought world of ancient authors, a diachronic, author-oriented approach to intertextuality overlaps considerably with the tasks of tradition history and redaction history as defined in comprehensive treatments of exegetical methodology (see Steck 1998, 15–20).

against which it is read.[2] This reader-oriented approach thus decries reading a text in isolation and resists any attempt to find *the* definitive meaning for a text. By reading Job 8–10 and Joel together, the rhetorical function of the verb שוב will generate an exploration of literary and theological implications for interpreting the claims of Job, Bildad, and Joel in their respective contexts and in "response" to one another. In so doing, the conversation that arises from this synchronic approach puts into relief the theological claims of these three characters.

This essay will evaluate the first Bildad speech (Job 8) and Job's response (Job 9–10) for their intertextual echoes with the book of Joel, especially chs. 1 and 2. Six times (9:12, 13, 18; 10:9, 16, 21) Job's response to Bildad draws upon the verb שוב, the same verb that forms the interpretive crux of Joel's extended call to repentance that culminates in Joel 2:12–14. Re-reading the Bildad speech heightens other motifs that resonate with the imagery of Joel. And yet, the ideological perspectives of these three characters hardly fit neatly with one another. Nevertheless, this trialectic reading (from Bildad to Job, to Joel, and back) offers a fresh venue for hearing the broad range of voices as comments upon one another. These three voices continually raise points of contrast as they move between the language of the individual vs. the community, between calls for accommodation vs. protest, and between voices of wisdom vs. prophets. Joel (a prophetic voice) and Bildad (the "wise friend" of Job) deliver calls for changes in action and attitude to enable God to act beneficently. The community's silence in Joel creates ambiguity while Job's rejection of Bildad's critique challenges the easy answers of orthodoxy. To understand the dynamics involved in reading these passages intertextually, it will be necessary to situate Job 8–10 in its larger context, to compare the use of the verb שוב between Job 9–10 and Joel, and to create a conversation between Job, Joel, and Bildad.

The Literary Context of Job 8–10

Bildad's Response (Job 8) to Job's Speech (Job 6–7): A Literary Dilemma

The response of Bildad to Job creates a dilemma for the reader. The narrator/editor gives strong signals of connectedness to push the reader to relate the speeches of Job and Bildad to one another (chs. 6–7, 8, 9–10) using ויען ("and he answered") in 8:1 and 9:1 and in the characters' initial references to something that has gone before at the beginning of

2. See Fewell 1992.

both speeches.[3] However, the relative dearth of lexical commonalities between these passages and the lack of specific references to the argumentation from the preceding speech force the reader to create some kind of thematic coherence to fill in the gaps. When the reader seeks to understand *how* these speeches respond to one another, the task quickly becomes complicated because the "responses" lack specific lexical or rhetorical links and because the few lexical similarities that are present tend to push the reader to other parts of Job than the immediate context.

Consider the following illustrative examples. First, the phrase "How long?" represents the first of only three occurrences in Job (8:2; 18:2; 19:2), and all three relate to Bildad/Job interchanges.[4] Second, the topic of the punishment of the children in 8:4 evokes the Job narrative to many readers, but this association does not respond directly to the speech of Job in chs. 6–7 since "children" are not mentioned there. Instead, any invocation of the punishment of the children motif relates to the narrative frame. Third, and similarly, the terms "pure" (זַךְ) and "upright" (יָשָׁר) applied to Job in 8:6, evoke the narrative introduction which characterizes Job three times (1:1, 8; 2:3) as "blameless" (תָּם) and "upright" (יָשָׁר). Hence, the phrase is similar, but the words used for "pure" and "blameless" are different.[5] Finally, "sin" and "transgression" appear at the end of Job's speech (7:20–21) and near the beginning of Bildad's response (8:4), but even these key words are not readily linked since Job asks rhetorical questions that presume *he* does not sin or transgress, while Bildad refers to the sin and transgression of *someone's* children. The situation which Bildad's speech addresses is so different from Job's situation that most commentators treat Bildad's speech as sarcastic or ironic.[6] Bildad's speech condemns the children (8:4), but the narrative indicated no sin of which the children were guilty. Rather, Job acted on their behalf to make certain that they had not inadvertently sinned (1:5).

---

3. Bildad, in Job 8:2, asks, "How long will you say *such things*?"; and Job responds to Bildad in 9:2, "Indeed, I know that *this* is so."

4. The first two references appear at the beginning of Bildad's first two speeches while the third one appears at the beginning of Job's second response to Bildad's second speech. This phrase suggests that impatience characterizes the interaction between Bildad and Job.

5. Even the word "upright" is not typical for the poetic sections of Job, appearing once more (23:7) in the singular and twice in the plural form (4:7; 17:8). The noun "uprightness" (יֹשֶׁר) also appears three times in the speech of Elihu (33:3, 23, 27).

6. See the irony described in Habel (1985, 174), or the sarcasm as interpreted by Course (1994, 53). Others see the "if" clauses as signs of hypothetical formulations that suggest Bildad is sincere but indirect. See Crenshaw 2011, 71; Clines 1989, 202–3.

The Message of the Bildad Speech

Despite the lack of verbal connections between Job's speech in chs. 6–7 and Bildad's response in ch. 8, scholars find creative ways to link the two speeches, frequently supplying Bildad with motives that would help account for the shift in topics. For example, Habel and Crenshaw portray Bildad as a defender of divine justice motivated by the incompatibility of God's very nature and the implications of Job's claim to innocence.[7] Consequently, Bildad's speech functions largely as a new thematic chapter in the larger drama. The rhetorical flow of Bildad's speech begins with a defense of divine justice (8:2–7) that assumes calamity must derive from sin. The opening salvo (8:2) makes the transition by dismissing the words of Job as "a great wind" who has spoken for too long. The following rhetorical question (8:3) brusquely rejects any notion that God could act in a manner that was not just and righteous. The second half of this defense, though, conveys the impression that Bildad offers Job a way to resolve the dilemma by suggesting the children's demise was caused by their own behavior (8:4) while Job has the option of making supplication to God (8:5) and living uprightly (8:6) so that the future will bring a greatness that makes the problems of the past seem trivial (8:7).

The logic of the second portion (8:8–22) turns from the theoretical to the illustrative as Bildad underscores his conviction by drawing upon ancestral tradition (8:8–10) and a series of botanical metaphors (8:11–19) before returning to the two motifs of 8:2–7 with which the speech began: (1) God's justice involves rewarding the righteous and punishing the wicked (8:20); and (2) a blameless life offers hope for a better future (8:21–22).

The logic of the illustrations may not always be easy to follow, but their essential function reflects the twin themes that surround them. Moreover, precisely these two themes convey the inherent logic that makes Bildad's speech understandable as a "response" to Job since chs. 6–7 convey numerous examples where Job implies his life has been above reproach but the consequences of his righteous behavior have left him in despair, not with hope. The unstated implications of Job's extended recitation of good behavior are left to the reader to deduce: if good behavior does *not* result in reward, then God has not played fair. By supplying these implications, the reader can make sense of Bildad's thematic shift. Job has not said that God is unjust, but Bildad's response assumes this accusation and comes to God's defense.

---

7. Habel 1985, 174; Crenshaw 2011, 71.

Job's Response to Bildad: More Monologue than Retort

Also, Job's response (chs. 9–10) hardly displays an integral connection to the statements of Bildad, even though the narratival/editorial frame invites the reader to see Job's speech as a response (9:1). Further, 9:2 cannot begin an entirely independent poem since it refers back to something: "Truly, I know that *such is the case*, but how can a man be right with God?" Functionally, Job 9:1–2a creates a narrative transition to the following poetic monologue (whether originally independent or not).[8]

Scholars have put forth various proposals concerning the structure and unity of these two chapters as a response to Bildad. They argue the chapters contain between two and seven sections, whose interrelatedness to and independence from one another likewise varies from scholar to scholar.[9] Those opting for two main units see the primary breaking point between 9:2–24 and 9:25–10:22 based upon form-critical criteria. The former speaks about God in the third person while the dominant form of address in the latter speaks directly to God (with the exception of 9:32–35). Debate exists concerning the addressees of 9:2–24 because the text never addresses anyone directly. Hence, 9:2–24 functions like a mono-logue—in context, a text spoken by Job to Job—placed here to function as Job's response to Bildad. Since God does not respond to Job's address in 9:25–10:22, the second half of this response essentially remains a monologue even though it uses the style of a prayer.

The content of this speech, when read in relation to the twin themes of Bildad's speech (divine justice and righteous living), functions meaning-fully as an extended reframing of Bildad's accusations. Job admits Bildad's first point and affirms God's just character (9:2) but rejects the accusation of guilt implied by Bildad. Job assumes his own innocence (9:20–21). He also rejects Bildad's argumentation that a blameless life

---

8. Job 9:1–2a, however, could serve as the introduction to a previously independent poem (9:2b–24) whose theme is "How can a man be right with God?" So also, Heckl 2010b, 69.

9. Those proposing three units (9:2–24; 9:25–35; 10:1–22) tend to explain the third masculine singular references to God in 9:32–35 as more consistent with the preceding verses (9:25–31) than with the verses that follow (10:1–22). A smaller number suggest four or more units make up this response. These scholars subdivide 9:2–24 into two sections (9:2–13, 14–24) and understand 10:1–6 as more closely related to the unit which precedes (9:25–35) than that which follows (10:7–22). Clines correctly refers to these distinctions as "more subtle and more debatable" than the form-critical differences related to speaking about God or speaking to God (Clines 1989, 223).

benefits the righteous (9:22–24). Similarly, Job's prayer implicitly challenges God to make good on the promises to reward the righteous rather
than turn a blind eye.

The Verb שׁוּב in Job and Joel

The role played by שׁוּב in Job's response to Bildad functions as a good
case study for an intertextual reading since the six examples in Job 9–10
(9:12, 13, 18; 10:9, 16, 21) appear in two different sections of the
speech's structure, no matter whether one divides the response into two
or more units. The verb שׁוּב appears more frequently in this speech than
in any other speech in Job. Virtually every Job speech contains the verb,
suggesting it functions as a kind of leitmotif for the character, but its
range of meanings is by no means uniform in the sixteen times that the
verb occurs in the mouth of Job.[10] Still, the use of שׁוּב in Job 9–10
coheres in one sense. The verb appears in support of the related motifs of
dire threat and death to the speaker. God's "restraint" in these three
instances threatens the speaker.

The first three examples of שׁוּב appear in the soliloquy (9:2b–22), and
the verb's meaning concerns "restraint" using hiphil forms in 9:12, 13
and 18. In the first two instances, no one can restrain God's wrath. In the
final instance, God "restrains my breath," making it difficult for the
speaker to breathe.

The verb שׁוּב also appears three times in the prayer (10:9, 16, 21).
These verbal forms use שׁוּב in three different ways: "to send back"
(10:9), "to repeat" (10:16), and "to return" (10:21). All three of these
nuances represent an expression of death for the speaker. In 10:9, the
speaker asks God whether God intends to *send* the speaker *back* to the
dust from which God created the human (a subtle allusion to the
Yahwistic creation story [Gen 2:7; 3:19]). Job 10:16 depicts God as a
lion who *repeatedly* (שׁוּב) hunts down its prey (the speaker) whenever
the prey steps out of line. Given the metaphor, the hunting lion can only
imply a recurring threat to the speaker's life. In 10:21, the speaker asks
God to leave him alone to find solace because the days of his life are few
before he goes to "the land of gloom and deep darkness" from which the
speaker will *not return* (a clear reference to the speaker's death).
Consequently, the verb שׁוּב consistently conveys a sense of threat and
death in Job's "response" to Bildad.

Unlike Job, Joel uses the verb שׁוּב (2:12–14; 4:1, 4, 7) in response to
calamity to convey hope. The use of שׁוּב in Joel functions as the primary

10. Job 6:29; 7:7, 10; 9:12, 13, 18; 10:9, 16, 21; 13:22; 14:13; 16:22; 17:10;
23:13; 30:23; 31:14.

concept in the major literary transition in Joel by calling the community to return to YHWH in hopes of turning from devastation to deliverance.

Joel 2:12–14 marks the turning point of the writing. Joel 1 calls the community to lament, addressing specific groups, including elders (1:2), drunkards (1:5), farmers (1:11), vintners (1:11), priests (1:13), and the land personified (1:8). In addition, the prophet prays to YHWH (1:19–20). Subsequently, 2:1–11 depicts the threat of the day of YHWH coming against Jerusalem. This depiction implies the arrival of a cosmic army, led by YHWH, to destroy the land. At this point 2:12–14 implores the people to change before it is too late:

> Yet even now, says the LORD, return (שׁוּב) to me with all your heart, with fasting, with weeping, and with mourning; rend your hearts and not your clothing. Return (שׁוּב) to the LORD, your God, for he is gracious and merciful, slow to anger, and abounding in steadfast love, and relents from punishing. Who knows whether he will not turn (שׁוּב) and relent, and leave a blessing behind him, a grain offering and a drink offering for the LORD, your God?

Joel 2:12–14 uses שׁוּב to depict a very different set of actions than Job 9–10. These verses employ שׁוּב positively, twice commanding the people to return to YHWH, and once holding out the prospects that YHWH will return to the people and bless them. These actions are contingent upon one another. Only if the people שׁוּב to YHWH is there a chance that YHWH will שׁוּב to them. YHWH responds by offering a series of blessings (2:18–27), contingent upon the response to the call to repent in 2:12–17.

The remaining uses of שׁוּב in Joel (4:1, 4, 7), though less pivotal, also offer promises to Judah and Jerusalem. The use of שׁוּב in Joel 4:1 is written as a qal, but the sense of the verb (as well as the spoken *qere* tradition) treats the verb as a hiphil form ("cause to return" or "bring back"). YHWH promises to "restore" or "return" the possessions of Judah and Jerusalem. Similarly, Joel 4:4 anticipates YHWH punishing those who have acted against Judah (i.e. returning their own deeds against them). Joel 4:7 also uses a hiphil form in this same way. Thus, the long-term promise to Judah and Jerusalem expressed in Joel 4 implies that possessions will be returned, and that the aggressive acts of enemies will be returned upon them, but only after (cf. 4:1) the people have returned to YHWH (2:12–17).

Using the verb שׁוּב in these two books as a starting point, one finds that Bildad, Job, and Joel provide some intriguing points of comparison and contrast. Observing these similarities and differences sheds new light on all three characters.

Creating a Conversation between Joel and Job 8–10

Joel and Job

Two realities deserve notice when comparing Joel and Job. First, the analysis of שוב in Joel and Job 9–10 exhibits quite a contrast of meanings, but, second, the underlying logic of Bildad's speech (Job 8) shows considerable affinity with assumptions about the rhetorical logic of Joel 1–2. These points of similarity help one to create a productive intertextual conversation between Joel 1–2 and Job 8–10 that helps shape one's understanding of each passage. Consider what has already been noted concerning the use of שוב in Job 9–10. The verb appears in contexts that threaten death for an individual, while the same verb in Joel promises relief and restoration for a collective group (Judah and Jerusalem).

The prophetic text in Joel 1–2 implores Judah and Jerusalem to return to YHWH in order to allow YHWH the chance to restore the nation. Joel 2:12–14, in particular, implies the guilt of the community can only be overcome by corporate repentance (in the sense of turning to God). As such, these verses tend to presuppose the same lines of argumentation implied in Bildad's speech, but the three-fold logic is applied to the people as a whole: (1) God is just and must punish the recalcitrant; (2) since the community has experienced (Joel 1) and is about to experience (Joel 2:1–11) disasters of epic proportions, then one must assume that the group has turned from God; (3) a return to God is the only means available to stop the deity's wrath.[11]

By contrast, the wisdom text in Job 9–10 uses the verb שוב to resist the application of cause and effect theology to the character Job. The verb שוב in Job appears, then, in the context of a *via negativa*. Job does not use the verb to express a desire to "return" to God. Rather, the character uses the verb to express YHWH's unrestrainable wrath (9:12, 13) and the refusal to "restore" breath to Job (9:18).

The context of Job's response (Job 9–10) undercuts the logic of Bildad. The first Bildad speech (Job 8), when re-read, strengthens the impression of the ineffectuality of Bildad, who represents traditional teachings. For the careful reader, the "pure and upright" formulations in Bildad's speech (8:6) challenge the reliability of Bildad to assess the issue of divine punishment since the reader of Job already knows that the calamities experienced by Job have nothing to do with punishment.

---

11. Crenshaw argues the case in light of justice and mercy: "For Joel…YHWH's repentance forms a bridge between divine wrath and mercy" (Crenshaw 1995a, 137). Crenshaw correctly observes that in the ancient world, Joel would have been heard as assuming guilt, but Joel does not indicate the nature of the guilt (146).

Rather, the reader knows that Job's plight results not from being punished for wickedness, but as a test because of his righteousness. From the very first verse of the book, the reader learns that Job is blameless and upright (1:1, 8; 2:3), which earns him the attention of the Satan. Consequently, Bildad's accusation (8:6) that Job's character has caused God to punish him, undercuts Bildad's authority as a wise counselor in the eyes of Job's readers. The subversion of Bildad's authority also creates suspicion for the reader when Bildad's speech implies that the sin of Job's children caused God to punish them (8:4), even though such a claim remains unstated in the narrative frame of the book.

The artist who composed Job, however, was not recounting a historical report of one righteous man. The role of Job serves as paradigm for a righteous man faced with the human condition. As often noted, Job protests against easy answers, but the power of these protests derives from the many ways in which Job makes his point by challenging accepted wisdom and traditional teachings. In a very real way, Job takes on religious orthodoxy as an insufficient means to express the complexity of life. Job protests against the reduction of tradition into simplistic cause and effect theology. By contrast, Joel starts from the calamities against the nation as the motivation for an orthodox response.

Joel and Bildad

What happens when one brings the dialectic of tradition and protests in Job 8–10 into conversation with the rhetoric of Joel 1–2? Job's protest and the undercutting of Bildad's authority created in Job 8–10 raise questions about the efficacy of Joel's pronouncements precisely because, as typically interpreted, Joel essentially presupposes the same cause and effect theology espoused by Bildad.

Joel 1 depicts a scenario of cataclysmic devastation by conveying a series of calls to lament the desolation of the land caused by locusts, drought, and military invasion. Cumulatively, these calls to the community portray a situation as dire as any situation faced by Judah and Jerusalem depicted in biblical texts. The rhetoric calls for a response from the community, but the devastation leaves the reader with a portrait of the land that makes Job's plight appear tame by comparison because of the corporate nature of the disasters. Whereas Job faces personal tragedy that affects him and his family, the devastation of Joel 1 affects everyone in the land: the elders, the children, the farmers, the priests, and all the inhabitants. This scenario magnifies exponentially the problems faced by Job individually. Following this extended call to different groups (1:2–18), the prophet petitions YHWH in 1:19–20 by summarizing the situation in which the fields, the trees, and the brooks have been devastated. They provide nothing in the way of sustenance for the animals, much less human society.

In addition to this devastation, the reader learns in 2:1–11 that the land faces an even greater threat. Joel 2:1 sounds the military alarm that the day of YHWH is at hand that will bring an attack from a cosmic army led by YHWH himself (2:11). Considering the plight of Judah and Jerusalem in Joel, one can hardly miss the parallels to Job in which calamity follows calamity to the point where it seems all hope is lost (Joel 1), and then even greater calamity threatens the land (Joel 2:1–11). Only then does the prophet use the language of repentance, calling for the people to return (שׁוּב) to YHWH (2:12–14). This action is followed by a call for a fast (2:15–16) that begins identically to 2:1 ("blow the trumpet"). Joel 2:17 then reports a plea for mercy from the priests. These responses in 2:12–17 are typically (and probably correctly) interpreted as presuming the same cause and effect theology that Bildad articulates in Job. Namely, the prophet issues a call for repentance and fasting *because* the prophet *assumes* that the devastation of the land reflects YHWH's punishment because of the guilt of the people.

The word "assumes" in the previous sentence is significant because nowhere does Joel 1–2 specify this guilt, a fact that has generated a great variety of explanations.[12] Rather, in a classic case of turning to God as one's last resort, Joel 2:12–14 and 2:15–17 call for a change of heart and acts of contrition. Hence, the prophet in Joel 1–2 asks of the community what Bildad asks of Job as an individual. Bildad does not need to convince Joel to follow Bildad's advice, because the prophet shares his perspective. The underlying logic can be described clearly enough. Calamity of this magnitude cannot have escaped the attention of YHWH, so it must come from YHWH. YHWH does not act arbitrarily; ergo this calamity must result from the sin of the people. Only by returning to YHWH can the people hope to persuade YHWH to remove the punishment. Repentance is the only choice left to the people in the rhetoric of Joel. Bildad would be pleased. Job, however, would protest.

Job and Joel

At the very least, Job would challenge Joel to make the case. Job would refuse to assume that the calamities afflicting the country resulted from sin. He would demand to know what he or his countrymen had done to

---

12. For discussion of these possibilities, see Crenshaw (1995a, 40–42), although Crenshaw's own assertion that Joel does not necessarily presume guilt appears rather forced despite his desire to take account of the innocent victims.

cause YHWH to make them suffer. He would likely intercede on behalf of the people in a very different way. If Job were a prophet, Job might speak past Joel in much the way that he speaks past Bildad and challenge YHWH directly. The words of Job's response in chs. 9–10 sound very different if read as a response to the calamities of Joel 1–2.

Job contends that no human can respond to God in a way that would justify humanity before God. Job avers that the power of the God who created the world makes it impossible for humans to contend with God (9:1–12). Job acknowledges God's power, but also argues that God's overwhelming judgment leaves the question of innocence out of the discussion (9:13–24). In Job's eyes, by sending devastation and calamity God destroys the wicked and the innocent. This charge is only magnified if read in light of the corporate catastrophes in Joel. Job recognizes the futility of challenging God if the battle concerns only power (9:25–35), and even wonders aloud why cleansing himself makes any sense at all if God is only going to plunge him into the muck of life (9:30–31). Job challenges God to take account of Job's own innocence since God created Job and Job's current plight makes God look bad (10:1–22). This last line of reasoning even finds its way into the priests' plea for mercy in Joel: "Spare your people, O Lord, and do not make your heritage a mockery, a byword among the nations. Why should it be said among the peoples, 'Where is their God?'" (Joel 2:17). Yet, Job offers no such plea. Rather, Job challenges God concerning the fate of the innocent and the pious. Joel does not take this bold step.

The rhetoric of Job's speech, as shown above, radically undercuts the reader's confidence in the reliability of Bildad through connections to the broader literary context. Bildad accuses Job of sin when the reader knows better. This undercutting is lacking, however, if one asks whether Joel's assumptions are supported in the broader literary context. When read as an isolated prophetic text, Joel presumes the guilt of the people, but never makes the case. At this point, if one asks about the broader literary context, Joel's presuppositions about the guilt of the people receive support when compared to the presumptions of Bildad.

Recent investigations into the Book of the Twelve have suggested that Joel—more than any other writing in the collection—was compiled from existing sources with the intention from the outset that it be read in its position between Hosea and Amos.[13] These investigations make the case that the book of Joel takes on new meaning when read in its location in the Book of the Twelve because of the intricacy of the connections to the

---

13. See Nogalski 2000; Schart 2007; see also the section labeled "Repentance, Guilt, and Punishment" in Nogalski 2011, 205–6.

writings on either side of Joel. These connections are created by catch-words, overlapping genres, explicit citations, and other constellations. These connections involve accusations of cultic abuse (such as Hos 2:7–8, 19[5–6, 17]; 4:7–9, 12–13) and ethical violations (as in 4:1–2) that threaten (2:10–11[8–9]; 4:3, 9–10) or make promises (2:14[12]) about the fertility of the land. Whereas both the threat and the promise in Hosea lie in the future, Joel 1 uses these images to portray the current reality. The agricultural symbols of a fertile land represent the images of the calamity facing the people.

Consequently, in the same way that Bildad's speech draws upon and presumes the narrative frame of Job, Joel presupposes Hosea and Amos. Specifically, Joel 1–2 contains connections to Hosea that invite the reader of the Book of the Twelve to read Joel as both a continuation of the message of Hosea and a reappropriation of that message for Judah and Jerusalem (whereas Hosea primarily concerns the northern king-dom).[14]

In short, the reader of Joel 1 who begins reading from Hosea receives a very different impression of the prophet's reliability than does the reader of Job who encounters the speech of Bildad. This reader of Joel does not experience the cognitive dissonance between what the prophet says and the larger context. To the contrary, Hosea describes behavior that would be punished by removing agricultural fertility. Joel describes a situation in terms quite similar to the threatened punishment of Hosea. The reader of the Twelve connects the punishment in Hosea with the current reality of Joel, and thus equates Joel's situation with the punish-ment of sin from Hosea. Thus, the reader of Joel would not immediately judge Job's questions concerning the innocence of the victims to have the same relevance as they do in the book of Job.

And yet, Job's protest against Bildad's assumptions cannot be ignored if one wishes to compare the two texts in order to deal seriously with the implications of cause and effect theology for the community of faith today. Bildad and Joel represent, in many respects, the dominant theo-logical perspective of Deuteronomy and Proverbs: do well and God will bless you. Nevertheless, Job's protest against the facile association of reward and a righteous life also resonates with other texts in the canon. Within the Book of the Twelve, Jonah portrays God as one who is eager to find ways to exercise compassion, even against the wicked (3:10; 4:2) and to protect the ignorant and innocent animals (4:11). Even this opposing position does not, however, do complete justice to Job's protest since Jonah still essentially presumes the same need for repentance in the

14. Schart 2007, 142–43.

face of divine wrath. Job, by contrast, wrestles at length with the problem of innocent suffering in ways that still work to subvert the notion that divine judgment offers adequate explanations for calamity on either the personal or the corporate level. Canonically, Job serves as an important corrective in this respect to the dominant theological voices in the Torah, the Prophets, and the Writings.

Conclusion

Reading and re-reading Job 8–10 in conversation with Joel 1–2 has illuminated several dynamics that underscore the difference between the wisdom of Job as protest literature and the function of Joel as prophetic literature. The verb שוב conveys messages of death in Job 9–10 but implies hope in Joel. Conversely, Job's "friend" has much in common with the presuppositions of Joel. Nevertheless, while connections to the broader literary context in Job cause the reader to mistrust the message of Bildad, the broader literary horizon of Joel conveys confidence to the reader of the Book of the Twelve that Joel's message can be trusted. Of course, this reading should not be terribly surprising in light of the purpose of the two books. Job is protest literature that seeks to make traditional theological paradigms problematic, while Joel anchors the major recurring themes of the Book of the Twelve and, as such, instructs its readers in corporate versions of the very traditions against which Job protests. Reading the two together displays how intricately the characters of the two books are tied to their own competing theologies.

CREATION THEMES IN JOB AND AMOS: AN INTERTEXTUAL RELATIONSHIP?

Hilary Marlow

Introduction

Both the growing interest in intertextuality among biblical scholars and the complexities surrounding its definition and application have been well documented in previous studies (Hibbard 2006, 10–20; G. D. Miller 2011) as well as by other contributors to this volume, so will not be revisited in detail here. Suffice it to say that in order for discussion of intertextuality to make a meaningful contribution to study of a biblical text or book, attention should be paid to the three distinct but overlapping features that typify intertextual approaches, which have been enumerated by Michael Stead—creation, meaning and hermeneutics (Stead 2009, 20). Textual creation recognizes that all texts, to a greater or lesser extent, comprise a "mosaic" of references to other texts, textual meaning suggests that meaning is created when one text comes into "dialogue" with another, and textual hermeneutics recognizes the role of the reader in determining meaning. Stead suggests that each of the above features covers a wide range of possibilities, giving rise to the diverse variety that characterizes intertextuality. So a text may contain anything from the merest trace of another to a direct citation of it; meaning may arise because two texts are clearly in contention with one another or, at the opposite end of the spectrum, because they nuance one another, and the reader's role may range from creating meaning to decoding it (Stead 2009, 20).

Stead's approach, which draws on the post-structuralism of Derrida and semiotics of Bakhtin, necessitates a different understanding of intertextuality than that proposed by others such as Benjamin Sommer, who posits a sharp dichotomy between the synchronic characteristic of "intertextuality" and the diachronic nature of "allusion" (Sommer 1998, 6–10). For him, intertextuality is the study of a wide range of correspondences among many different texts, while allusion "look[s] for specific connections between a limited number of texts" (8). He maintains that the latter approach is a more useful model for studying relations between biblical texts and particularly for the purposes of his study of Isa 40–66, which is clearly rooted in a specific time and context.

In a very helpful overview of intertextuality studies of the Hebrew Bible, Geoffrey Miller distinguishes two methodologies that he categorizes as "author-oriented" and "reader-oriented" (G. D. Miller 2011, 286). Sommer's approach falls firmly within the former category, since it is concerned with "how…a later biblical text connect[s] to a source from an earlier biblical text at a formal level" (Sommer 1998, 20). In Stead's work this is less clear cut—although he emphasizes the reader's role in attributing meaning, he merges reader-oriented insights with an author-oriented approach that attempts to understand Zech 1–8 by means of its *"dialogical discourse* with identified dialogue partners," namely, the former prophets (Stead 2009, 27, emphasis original).[1] Each approach has its limitations: Sommer narrows too far the potential for texts to be deemed intertextual and creates an artificial and perhaps arbitrary distinction between ways of reading texts. Stead's definition creates an impossibly broad range of possibilities, particularly since he includes in his computer-generated searches words from the same "semantic domain" (a classification determined by him) as well as those with the same lemma or word family. This results in connections that are, at best, tentative, and may mean that the significance of specific examples of intertextual quotation or allusion is missed. In this study of intertextuality between Job and Amos, both these approaches have been deemed problematic because they offer parameters that are either too restricted or too wide and because the distinction between author-oriented and reader-oriented perspectives is a difficult and slippery one, since it is based in most instances on interpretive decisions by readers themselves.

Having said this, the focus here will be to identify correspondences between the two texts that are sufficiently close and/or striking to suggest the possibility of intentionality at the authorial or transmission stages of the texts. Sommer's distinction between intertextuality and allusion will not be adopted; instead, such correspondences between texts will be referred to as intertextual connections or links between the texts under consideration. Within this category, the intensity of the connection may be described across a spectrum ranging from the clearly intentional to the perhaps unintentional or deliberately opaque:

1. An example of a fully developed reader-oriented approach is that of Ellen van Wolde, who states that the primary concern of intertextuality is not the chronology of the texts but "the logical and analogical reasoning of the reader in interaction with the text" (van Wolde 1989, 43).

quotation—reuse or reworking[2]—allusion—echo

This is a simplified version of Stead's "mosaic," which categorizes texts across a "spectrum of identifiability" from the certain to the unknown (Stead 2009, 21); although rather broad in its categories, it will suffice for the comparison being undertaken here.

Job and Amos

Questions over the dating and authorship of both Job and Amos have been subject to detailed analysis by commentators, and many theories concerning the redaction history of the latter have been proposed, none of which is entirely satisfactory (with regard to Job, see Pope 1973, xxxii–xlii; Dhorme 1967, lxi–cxi; Habel 1985, 35–42; with regard to Amos see Stuart 1971, 287–88; Wolff 1977 106–13; Andersen and Freedman 1989, 139–44). Given the difficulties in establishing when these two books reached their final form and in which order, it is not immediately obvious whether this study should explore Job's use of Amos or Amos's (in its final form) use of Job. Assumptions about which is the prior text would certainly influence, if not determine, interpretation of any intertextual links. An open mind will be kept on this question, at least in the first instance.

There are further complications to this study posed by the relative lengths of the texts being compared (Job, 42 chapters, 1070 verses; Amos, 9 chapters, 146 verses). It will not be possible here to do justice to the range and scope of Job's vocabulary and themes, nor to investigate more than a few instances of intertextual comparison—hence it is necessary to be selective. A key characteristic of Amos and Job is that both books make extensive reference to the non-human natural world, both earthly and cosmological. This exploration of intertextuality will therefore limit itself to considering texts that make reference to the natural world and its components.[3]

The starting point for this study will be a detailed examination of a notable connection between the two texts, namely, the references to Pleiades and Orion in Amos 5:8 and Job 9:9. From this, the exploration

---

2. Although the wording of this level of connection may suggest that the direction of dependence has already been established, this is by no means assumed in all cases.

3. Job's use of cosmic language and lengthy creation descriptions have been analyzed in numerous studies, by ecologists (McKibben 1994; DeWitt 2000) as well as biblical scholars (Gordis 1985; P. D. Miller 1987; Perdue 1986; see also Dell 2000); I have discussed Amos's nature language elsewhere (Marlow 2009, 120–57).

will be broadened to explore the immediate contexts of these texts and then to consider other intertextual links between references to the natural world in Amos and Job, ranging from shared phrases and vocabulary to common themes and motifs. Finally we shall discuss the direction of dependence of these connections, in relation to the form, content and tone of the respective texts.

Orion and the Pleiades

Job 9:9; 38:31–32; and Amos 5:8 are the only places in the Hebrew Bible to include the terms כסיל and כימה, generally translated as Orion and the Pleiades. Both the Job references add a third term, עש, usually considered to refer to the Bear, and 38:32 also refers uniquely in the Hebrew Bible to מזרות ("Mazzaroth"), the identity of which is unknown.[4] Although it is not immediately evident from either Job 9:9 or Amos 5:8 that כימה and כסיל are astronomical terms, the context of Job 38:31–33 establishes that heavenly bodies are in view. The terms have been subjected to extensive scholarly discussion, including comparison with Greek myths as well as other ancient versions, and although the exact identification remains uncertain, there is a long tradition that Orion and the Pleiades are most probably the constellations in view (Driver and Gray 1921, 86–88; see also Pope 1973, 71; Rowley 1970, 77).

Job chapters 9 and 10 comprise Job's third speech, and Job 9:9 forms part of a series of participial clauses spanning vv. 5–10 that describe the might of God's actions, particularly with regard to the natural world. Within this section vv. 5–7 concern the power of God to overturn the natural stability and rhythms of nature: removing mountains, shaking the earth, preventing the sun from rising. This is followed by two verses that portray God as the unique creator of the heavens and the seas (vv. 8–9), and then a summary sentence (v. 10) regarding the innumerable and incomprehensible nature of God's deeds. Verse 9 expands the statement in the preceding verse that God is the one "who alone stretched out the heavens" by adding greater detail: "who made the Bear and Orion, the Pleiades and the chambers of the south" (עשה־עש כסיל וכימה וחדרי תמן). Although חדר ("chamber") is used of the source of the wind in Job 37:8 (see also 38:22), here it probably refers to southern constellations in more general terms (Clines 1989, 231–32).[5] These verses juxtapose a sense of wonder at the marvels of God's wisdom (cf. v. 4) and power

---

4. It is suggested that the *hapax legomenon* מזרות may be a derivation from מזלות ("constellation") (BDB 561).

5. For an alternative perspective, see Pope 1973, 71.

(v. 10) as creator, with the recognition that the deity may also cause the created order to tremble and falter in the face of his anger (vv. 5–6).

The other reference to the Pleiades and Orion in Job 38:31–33 forms part of the first long speech addressed by God to Job (38:1–39:40). God poses a series of rhetorical questions concerning Job's inability to comprehend the workings of the physical universe. Job is asked if he can "bind the chains" of the Pleiades (התקשר מעדנות כימה) or "loose the cords" of Orion (משבות כסיל תפתח). As with Job's speech in ch. 9, the intent of this section is both to draw attention to God's supremacy as creator and sustainer of the universe and to highlight the trembling and faltering status of the creation (in this case Job himself) before the power of the deity (cf. 40:1–5; 42:5–6).

In Amos 5:8 the same names כימה וכסיל (the Pleiades and Orion) are included, in reverse order, in the second doxology or creation hymn.[6] The origin and purpose of these three fragmentary hymns in Amos (4:13; 5:8–9; and 9:5–6), which are widely regarded as later additions to the text, has been debated by scholarship, but without consensus (Marlow 2009, 139). A key characteristic of each of the hymns is the refrain יהוה שמו, "YHWH (is) his name."[7] This follows, in each case a series of participial phrases depicting both the creative activity of YHWH and his ability to overturn the secure workings of the natural world. At the start of 5:8 YHWH is described as creator: the one "who made the Pleiades and Orion" (עשה כימה וכסיל). But he is also known as destroyer of creation: the one who "pours [flood waters] out over the surface of the earth" (v. 8c).

The unique use in the Hebrew Bible by the author of Job and the author or final redactor of Amos of these two terms כימה and כסיל evokes comparison between the two texts. Moreover the use in both cases of participial phrases to describe God, while not unique to Job and Amos,[8] is suggestive, and the common theme of God as the one who creates but can also destroy his creation is surely not coincidental. The combination of unique vocabulary, shared syntax and thematic correspondence point to a close connection between the two texts and, I suggest, indicates the strong possibility of intentional intertextuality.

---

6. LXX Job 9:5 names these constellations in the same order as Amos 5:8. But it is open to question whether Gray is correct to assume that this is under the influence of the Amos text (2010, 195).

7. Amos 4:13 has the expanded version יהוה אלהי־צבאות שמו ("YHWH Lord of Hosts [is] his name").

8. Other notable examples are Isa 51:15 and Jer 36:35, which will be discussed below.

Although this is by far the clearest example of the re-use of vocabulary from one text by another, subsequent one, there are a number of other significant points of intertextual connection between Job and Amos to which we now turn. These range from exact phraseology through shared vocabulary and syntax to common themes. First, we will consider other links between Job 9:5–10 and Amos, before looking at some wider examples of shared vocabulary, themes and motifs.

Job 9:5–10 and Amos: Key Phrases

There are at least two phrases in Job 9:5–10 that are also found in Amos and in relatively few other places in the Hebrew Bible. In v. 8 God is described as the one who "treads on the high places [NRSV: waves] of the sea" (וְדוֹרֵךְ עַל־בָּמֳתֵי יָם). The expression "treading on the high places" also forms part of the first creation hymn of Amos: "who treads on the high places of the earth" (וְדֹרֵךְ עַל־בָּמֳתֵי אָרֶץ, 4:13), and a variation of it occurs in Mic 1:2(ET 3). These represent the only uses of the construction דרך עַל־בָּמֳתֵי in the Hebrew Bible. Both Job and Amos use the qal participle of דרך with Job favouring the *plene* spelling, which may be suggestive of a later date, although not conclusive. Once again vocabulary, syntax and theme come together to suggest an intentional connection between the two texts. However, given the uncertainty regarding the dating of Amos's creation hymns, as well as the possibility that both books may be drawing on pre-existing hymnic traditions, the question of degree and direction of dependence cannot yet be answered with certainty.

In Job 9:6 the hiphil participle of רגז is used to describe God's destructive action towards the earth: "who shakes the earth out of its place" (הַמַּרְגִּיז אֶרֶץ מִמְּקוֹמָהּ). The combination of the verb רגז with אֶרֶץ is only found in four other places, of which Amos 8:8 is one (the others are Ps 77:18; Prov 30:21; Joel 2:10). The Amos reference takes the form of a judgment oracle, with "earth" as subject of the qal verb: "On account of this will not the earth shake" (הַעַל זֹאת לֹא־תִרְגַּז הָאָרֶץ, 8:8), perhaps referring to the earthquake with which the book of Amos is associated (1:1). Although not one of the creation hymns, the similarity between this verse and the third hymn (Amos 9:5–6) has led scholars to posit a close connection between them, with debate over which takes precedence (see the discussion in Andersen and Freedman 1989, 809–10). In this example of shared phraseology between Job and Amos, although the syntax differs, the theme of God's wrath demonstrated in the natural world is shared. In Job the trembling earth is seen as a display of God's anger (9:5). In Amos 8 the anger of YHWH is not explicitly mentioned, but the context of indictment against Israel for unrighteous trading practices (vv. 4–6) makes clear that it is divine displeasure that causes the earth to shake.

Job and Amos: Shared Vocabulary and Themes

There are several notable examples of shared vocabulary between Job and Amos in texts that refer to the natural world. The first is the use of the verb הפך with reference to the created order in Job 9:5 and 12:5, and in Amos 5:8. In Job 9:5 the mountains are overthrown (הפך) in God's anger, while in 12:5 it is the waters that overwhelm (הפך) the land.[9] Elsewhere in the Hebrew Bible the combination of the verb הפך with some aspect of nature as its object is relatively unusual, comprising references to the Reed Sea crossing and the plagues of Egypt in Pss 66:6 and 78:44, God providing water from rock in Ps 114:8, soil degradation in Isa 34:9 and the darkening of the sun on the day of YHWH in Joel 2:31(ET 3:4).

The use of הפך with reference to creation is also found in Amos 5:8 and provides another connection between the Amos hymn and Job 9:5–10 to supplement that already noted.[10] YHWH is established as the one who governs the daily cycle of light and dark, who "turns (הפך) deep darkness into dawn, and darkens the day into night." Here, as in Job 9, the dividing line between YHWH as creator and guarantor of the earth's stability and YHWH as the one who disrupts those same rhythms is a fine one, and both texts move quickly from creation to its unmaking, from stability to crisis. In Amos 5:8 it is the outpouring of flood waters on the earth at YHWH's behest that heralds his displeasure, a judgment that is repeated in the final creation hymn (Amos 9:5–6) and echoed in 8:8.

The second important example of shared vocabulary concerns the use in both Job and Amos of the vocabulary of darkness: צלמות and חשׁך. In Amos 5:8, immediately following the verb הפך, the activities of YHWH include "turning the darkness (צלמות) into dawn and darkening (חשׁך) the day to night." A few verses later, in Amos 5:20, the day of YHWH is described as "darkness (חשׁך)...and not light (ולא־אור)." The noun צלמות occurs 18 times in the Hebrew Bible, of which ten instances are in the book of Job, where it appears alongside the noun חשׁך ("darkness" or

---

9. Although Job 28:9 uses similar vocabulary to 9:5 (הרים + הפך), the context is that of mining works destroying mountain peaks, and hence not within the same frame of meaning.

10. The verb הפך is also used in Amos of God overthrowing Israel (4:11) and bringing an end to her festivals (8:10), and of the Israelites' persistent disregard for God's justice and righteousness (4:11; 5:7; 6:12).

"gloom") five times.[11] Most of these 18 occurrences serve to illustrate the pessimistic outlook characteristic of Job, for example, 10:21: "before I go from where I shall not return, to a land of gloom and deep darkness" (אֶל־אֶרֶץ חֹשֶׁךְ וְצַלְמָוֶת; see also 3:5; 10:22; 24:17; 34:22).[12] However in Job 12:22 we find these terms used to describe God's action in creation, in a long sequence of participial phrases stretching from v. 17 to v. 25. While the majority of this section focuses on God's power over kings and rulers, in v. 22 God is acclaimed as "the one who uncovers the deeps from the darkness (חֹשֶׁךְ) and brings out deep darkness (צַלְמָוֶת) to light (אוֹר)."

The obvious disconnect between the subject matter of this verse and what surrounds it has led many to suggest a metaphorical rather than literal interpretation, such as God's ability to unmask conspiracies (Driver and Gray 1921, 119; Pope 1973, 94). Clines (1989, 301–3) proposes that the verse alludes to the revealing of the dark side of God. Others argue that it is a remnant of some cosmic myth that has been misplaced here (Pope 1973, 94). The overall impact of this section of Job's fourth speech is to draw a contrast between God's wisdom and might and the impotence of earthly rulers (Clines 1989, 302). Rather than being a metaphor for some aspect of God's activities in the human sphere, I suggest that the somewhat tangential reference to the creation of dawn and dusk has been added to stress the cosmic scope of God's rule and may indicate that the writer has drawn freely from a pre-existent tradition to give weight to his concluding remark that the leaders "fumble around in darkness and not light" (יְמַשְׁשׁוּ־חֹשֶׁךְ וְלֹא־אוֹר, v. 25). This disconnect combined with the striking resonances with Amos 5:8 and 5:20 in both vocabulary and theme make it plausible that not only is there an intertextual connection between the two but that Amos is the source text on which the author of Job drew for his description, rather than the other way round.

Job 11 and Amos 9: Shared Terminology and Theme

A slightly different example of correspondence between Job and Amos can be seen in a comparison between Job 11:7–11 and Amos 9:1–4. Here there is only a small amount of common vocabulary, but the combination of terminology and shared theme in the two texts suggests a connection between them. Job 11 is Zophar's first speech, in which he laments Job's

---

11. Job 3:5; 10:21; 12:22; 28:3; 34:22.

12. For a discussion of the meaning of צַלְמָוֶת and its relation to מוּת, "death," see Winton Thomas 1962.

lack of understanding (vv. 5–6) and encourages him to reach out to God (vv. 13–15). Verses 7–10 comprise a series of rhetorical questions on the impossibility of finding God and the boundless scope of his wisdom and power. This extends beyond the limits of the whole universe, physical and mythical, conveyed by the use of four inclusive phrases: "higher than the heavens," "deeper than Sheol," "longer than the earth" and "wider than the sea." Although this poem has some resonances with other Joban poems concerning God's wisdom, most notably 23:8–9, which also depicts the "undiscoverable" nature of God,[13] it has more in common with Ps 139:7–12, with which it is often compared. The extended search for wisdom in Job 28:13–28 also maintains that wisdom is beyond the realm of earth or sea (vv. 13–14), and that only God can find it (vv. 23–24), although arguably this wisdom is not equated with God as is the case in other wisdom poems (e.g. 9:4–10; 12:13–25).

In the judgment oracle following Amos's final vision (9:1–4), the impossibility of hiding from God's punishment is stressed by reference to the same four physical or mythical locations as are depicted in Job 11. Neither cosmic space—the depths of Sheol and the heavens (v. 2), nor the physical world—the heights of the earth, represented as ראש הכרמל ("the top of Carmel") and the bottom of the sea (v. 3), are able to conceal people from YHWH's eyes, set on them "for evil and not good" (v. 4). In both Amos and Job, this four-fold enumeration is intended to express the totality of the world: from the underworld to the heavens, from the far reaches of the earth to the depths of the sea. The only other comparable description of God's presence throughout the cosmos is Ps 139:8–9 which uses an almost identical set of four boundaries to delimit the range of YHWH's reach.[14]

The question of the relationship between these three texts (Job 11:8–9; Ps 139:8–9; and Amos 9:2–3) is a difficult one and there are points of similarity and difference between the three that resist confident assertions on extent and direction of influence. Surprisingly, few commentaries make more than a passing reference to the connections between the texts and, as already noted, comparative studies tend to focus on the connection between Job and Ps 139.[15] In addition to the stylized four-fold

13.   See also 9:4–10 and 12:13–25, already discussed.

14.   See also the depictions of the scope of YHWH's rule in Ps 135:6 and Hag 2:6. These more general descriptions perhaps draw on the creation narrative of Gen 1 (Clines 1989, 263–64).

15.   For an extended comparison between Job 11:7–12 and Ps 139, see Kynes 2012. Though considering Amos 9:2–3, Kynes maintains, based primarily on criteria of "external coherence," that Job (particularly chs. 10 and 11) parodies the positive meaning of Ps 139.

depiction of the world in Job 11:8–9 and Amos 9:2–3, two factors support the notion of an intertextual connection between the texts. The first arises from consideration of the wider context of the two texts. In both cases this concerns God's judgment, which cannot be hindered (Job 11:10) and from which there is no escape (Amos 9:4), and this contrasts with the positive message of Ps 139 that "I will praise you, for I am fearfully and wonderfully made" (v. 14). The second factor concerns the reversal of subject and object in the two texts. In Amos, God's relentless search for human beings is inevitably successful and *he* will find *them* wherever they have hidden, while in Job 11 Zophar adduces that, however much human beings search for God and his purposes, *they* can never find *him*. Here is an example of Stead's "textual meaning" whereby one text in dialogue with another creates meaning that the reader familiar with both may decode (Stead 2009, 20).

Shared Motifs of the Natural World

In addition to these instances of shared phraseology or vocabulary and thematic correspondence, a number of motifs of nature can be identified that are common to Job and Amos, but which do not necessarily employ the same vocabulary. On the spectrum of intertextuality these suggest echoes of one text in another. In Job 9:7 the sun is specifically depicted as under the command of God: "he speaks to the sun (חֶרֶס) and it does not rise." The same understanding of God as controller of the sun, and, implicitly, a re-assertion of the de-divinized nature of the latter, is behind the threatened judgment of Amos 8:9, albeit using different vocabulary: "I will make the sun (שֶׁמֶשׁ) go down at noon and darken the earth in broad daylight." This aspect of God directing the forces of nature is echoed elsewhere in both Amos and Job. For example, YHWH "calls for the waters of the sea" in Amos 5:8 and 9:5, while in Job 38:26 God "sends rain on the land with no people." The difference, if there is one, between the two books' use of the vocabulary of nature lies in the perspective from which each one speaks and the tone that is used in each case (see below).

A second motif common to both books is the notion that God's anger is manifest through the power of nature. Although never explicitly named in Amos, the anger of YHWH surfaces throughout the book, implicit behind much of the language of judgment, for example YHWH sending fire on the foreign nations in chs. 1 and 2, YHWH punishing (פָּקַד) Israel for its transgressions (3:2, 14) and YHWH flashing destruction against the strong (5:9). For Amos, the result of YHWH's anger is clearly seen in the physical world as well as in political threat, whether rising floodwaters (5:8; 8:8; 9:5), earthquake (8:8; 9:1), disruption of the earth's rhythms (8:9) or agricultural disaster (4:7–9).

In Job, God's anger is explicitly referred to in several places, including, as already noted, the destruction of mountains: "he overturns them in his anger (אַף)" (9:5), a notion that is further emphasized a few verses later in a reference to God's defeat of Rahab: "God will not turn back his anger (אַף)" (9:13). A more specific link with Amos 1 and 2 can be seen in the use here of the negative particle לֹא together with the hiphil of שׁוּב (see Amos 1:3, 6, 9, 13; 2:1, 4, 6). The allusion to the myth of conflict between YHWH and the sea monster resurfaces in Job 26 in an extended description of the power of God, which includes causing the sea to tremble (v. 5) and the heavens to shake at his rebuke (v. 11), as well as striking down Rahab and stilling the sea. According to Elihu in Job 36, the flashes of lightning and crashing of thunder in a storm demonstrate that "[God] is zealous with anger against unrighteousness" (36:33).[16] Whether or not it is explicitly mentioned, the notion that God's anger is pervasive, lying behind disruption of the earth and its rhythms as well as extreme weather events, is common to Amos and Job. Both books share the view that God's omnipotence lies in his ability not just to create, but also to overturn his own creation.

Direction of Dependence

The above survey has demonstrated significant connections between the books of Job and Amos in terms of a range of intertextual connections using the language of the natural world, from unequivocal examples of re-use to hints of echo, but with no direct quotations. Although it is not possible to determine conclusively the direction of dependence, we have drawn attention to some features that may support the traditional views on dating, namely, that Amos in its final form is the product of redaction in the later years of the exile and that Job should be dated to the post-exilic period. Furthermore, some of the Amos texts cited are regarded by many commentators as pre-exilic in date (most notably 9:2–3).[17] Two further points may be noted with regard to determining the direction of the intertextual connections explored above.

First, as already suggested, both Job (9:5–10; 12:22) and Amos (4:13; 5:8; 9:5–6) include a series of participles in their descriptions of God's activity in the world. The use of the participial format in this manner is

---

16. Reading קָנָה as קָנָא as per *BHS*'s critical apparatus.
17. Wolff 1977, 107.

not unique to Job and Amos, being found in at least two other prophetic texts: Isa 51:15 and Jer 31:35. These two texts each include the identical phrase "[the one who] stirs up the sea and its waves roar—YHWH of hosts his name" (רגע הים ויהמו גליו יהוה צבאות שמו). Here material very similar to the creation hymns in Amos is used in other prophetic texts, ones that are clearly situated in the exilic period.[18] It may be that Second Isaiah and Jeremiah are intentionally re-using material from Amos, an earlier prophet. Alternatively, these two texts as well as Job may be drawing on a pre-existent hymnic tradition that employs participial phrases together with the motif יהוה שמו to depict YHWH in conjunction with the natural order of the world.[19] Further evidence for a common prophetic tradition of phraseology and vocabulary used to describe YHWH is provided by the notion of YHWH as one who "treads the high places," which, as noted above, is shared by two of the written prophets, Amos (4:13) and Micah (1:2[ET 3]), as well as Job (9:8).

These examples of shared usage in texts from the written prophets suggest that it is much more likely that this phraseology originates in the prophetic tradition and thus helps to confirm the direction of intertextual dependence, namely, that Job intentionally draws on material from the prophets. However this does not invalidate the possibility of a specific intertextual relationship between Job and Amos. There is sufficient evidence in the examples given above to suggest that the author of Job re-uses, alludes to and echoes phrases, themes and motifs from the book of Amos.

Having posited the direction of intertextual connections, the second point concerns the way in which the language and themes of Amos are re-used or re-worked by the author of Job. This is not just the changes in word order or phraseology that have already been noted. It also concerns differences in tone between the two books, from the harsh strident oracles of the prophet to the questions and complaints of Job. Almost all of Amos is concerned with the judgment of YHWH against his people. The creation hymns with their refrain "YHWH is his name" do not function as a positive encouragement to faith in YHWH as creator. Rather, they are intended to provoke fear and awe at YHWH's capacity to

---

18. The complex issues surrounding the redaction and dating of Jeremiah, particularly the later chapters, are beyond the scope of the present study. With regard to Jer 31:35, those who opt for a fifth-century date suggest that the Jeremiah text draws directly from Isa 51:15 (e.g. W. L. Holladay 1986–89, 1:166).

19. If this is the case it is open to question whether each of the later authors introduce a quotation from an actual hymn or their own composition based on an earlier known format.

overturn his own creation in judgment for the people's wrongdoings. Although the book of Job also ends in awe at God's power over the universe (40:3–4), Job's speeches in chs. 9 and 12 stress God's wisdom (9:4; 12:13) and unknowability (9:10–12; 12:16), as well as his might. Job questions the traditional theologies of sin and retribution that are so evident in Amos. Even though Job's friends speak with great certainty, the rhetorical nature of Zophar's speech in Job 11, which asks whether God can be found in any part of the universe, stands in sharp contrast to the emphatic assertion in Amos 9 that it is impossible to hide from God. Again and again, the book of Job poses questions and invites reflection rather than offering confident proclamation on God's relationship to the world. The form of the text perhaps reflects the author's own questioning in the light of the theological crisis provoked by Judah's demise and the uncertainties of life in Yehud.

Conclusion

The examples of intertextuality that have been discussed above demonstrate a broad spectrum of intertextual links between Job and Amos, from re-working of texts through allusions to echoes. However, it is not always clear whether the dependence follows a direct linear sequence or is a mixture of theological traditions and phraseology common to prophetic texts. As other essays in this volume demonstrate, the author of Job seems to have drawn widely on various parts of the prophetic tradition. When it comes to references to the natural world, he may very well be doing so in direct dialogue with the book of Amos. It is striking that in these intertextual connections between the two books, the tone is what differs. Job moderates the proclamation of judgment found in Amos with a subtler understanding of God's character and actions in the world—one that reflects the questioning perspective of the book as a whole, and the post-exilic context in which it originated.

Part III

JOB IN DIALOGUE WITH THE WRITINGS

TELLING THE SECRETS OF WISDOM: THE USE OF PSALM 104 IN THE BOOK OF JOB*

Christian Frevel

The relation between the Psalms and the book of Job has often been dealt with in scholarly research, either arguing for a sub-genre of psalms or psalm genres in the book of Job (C. Westermann, H. P. Müller, G. I. Davies, A. Bentzen, K. Seybold and others), for the reception, allusion or reversal of particular psalms (esp. Ps 8: W. A. M. Beuken, T. N. D. Mettinger, M. Köhlmoos, C. Frevel, K. Schmid, and others), or more generally for common roots of both literary traditions in the sapiential tradition.[1] In analyzing the relations between the Psalms and the book of Job, more and more scholars explicitly employ concepts of intertextuality, while others operate with premises of intertextuality in a merely implicit way.[2] But this says everything and nothing at the same time, because "the term *intertextuality* is actually a 'grab bag' concept which embraces a broad range of literary phenomena, including genre, motif, formulae, type-scenes and parallel accounts, allusion, quotation and hypertextual commentary."[3] The concept is far from being a manageable toolbox for biblical exegesis,[4] and there are various types of intertextual devices which neither form a coherent concept nor a distinct method.[5] In its broadest understanding intertextuality relates to general assumptions about the nature of texts, the process of reception, the

---

*   I am grateful to Will Kynes for giving helpful comments on the topic and for improving the language of this essay.
    1. For the history of research see Mettinger 1993, 265–66; Köhlmoos 1999, 10–29; Pyeon 2003, 7–40; Heckl 2010b, 12–16.
    2. A phenomenon that can be traced in Old Testament exegesis in general, as Miller observes (2011, 284–85).
    3. Edenburg 2010, 137 (emphasis original).
    4. See the similar comments in the article in this volume by John Barton.
    5. See the recent overviews in G. D. Miller 2011; Edenburg 2010.

creation of meaning and the very structure of culture. In general, two conceptual approaches are usually differentiated. While poststructuralist concepts following J. Kristeva, R. Barthes, and/or J. Derrida et al. (which are based more or less on initial theories of the Russian structuralist M. Bakhtin) conceive intertextuality roughly as principally the unlimited relation of texts to other texts, others employ a more narrow understanding following G. Genette, U. Broich/M. Pfister et al. which limits intertextuality to methodologically verifiable relations between particular texts. Though the methodological discussion is much more complex, the role of the reader in the process of reception is crucial in both concepts, although the latter allows employing the intention of the author also, while in the former this is completely irrelevant. In the present study (besides some particular methodological remarks) my focus on distinct directions of impact ("palintextuality"[6]) should not be understood as the endorsement of an approach which prefers diachronic, author-oriented or intentional intertextuality only. My scope is a very limited and selective perspective which restricts the principally unlimited possibilities of intertextual relations to those which are considered heuristically to be based on pre-texts. The underlying assumption of this study is that the book of Job is to be understood as sapiential discourse and as part of a discourse in wisdom literature.[7] It presumes traditions and discusses them by allusion, quotation, echo, resonance, revision, parody, and so on. By focusing on its relationship with particular psalms as part of the sapiential tradition, the *heuristic* assumption is made that Job is the later text. This heuristic assumption is necessary for pragmatic reasons, because I can focus only on one text in the limits of this study. By searching for disintegrative textual signals which change the direction of reading for the (model and modern) reader, I will identify Ps 104 as one of the hypotexts[8] beneath the book of Job. This is accompanied by the assumption that the function of the textual relationship is to enhance and deepen the understanding of the argument of the book of Job.[9] While concentrating on the final form of the book of Job and of Ps 104, this by no means excludes their diachronic development.

The book of Job is not a unity in literary-historical respects, and it would be profitable to read the results of the following observations against a diachronic background. The same holds true for Ps 104, its

6. See Stocker 1998, 51–54.

7. See recently Saur 2011, 236–37.

8. For the terms "hypotext" and "hypertext," see Genette 1997, XI.5.25–26 passim; Mettinger 1993, 262; Heckl 2010b, 15.

9. For these two aspects, see Stocker 1998, 15.

growth and structure, its embedding into the fourth book of the Psalms, and so on, discussed in recent Psalms and Psalter-exegesis. Whether Ps 104 is literarily coherent (except for the contextual connectors in Ps 104:1aα, 35b), as Annette Krüger argues, or vv. 5–9, 19, 25–26, 29b, 31–32, 34–35 should be addressed as the multi-leveled reworking of the psalm, as Frank-Lothar Hossfeld assumes, is not decisive in our context.[10] Both agree that the psalm in its final form is post-exilic and precedes the book of Job in literary-historical respects.

Psalm 104 in the Book of Job: A Survey

When it comes to the reception of psalms in the book of Job beyond Ps 8, Ps 104 is often indicated especially in regard to the conception of creation not only in the speeches of God but in the whole book as well.[11] Thus it may be helpful to look at the suggested allusions, receptions, motif parallels, quotations, and implicit citations of Ps 104 in Job. These appear predominantly in the speeches of Job, the second speech of Elihu and the speeches of God from the whirlwind. In most of the references the sovereignty of God in his creation and preservation is expressed. However, explicit connections between the texts are scarce, with Job lacking verbatim quotations of the psalm which would exceed a word or a single phrase. On the other hand, there is little doubt that the author(s) of Job knew Ps 104. As will be seen, Ps 104 has to be considered unambiguously a hypotext or subtext in Job based on the accumulation of implicit allusions, catchwords and structural parallels.

For the Praise of God's Creational Power: Allusions in Job's First Speeches

There are motif parallels which may be interpreted more or less as allusions to Ps 104. First is the motif of the chaos waters which threaten the creation and which are repressed and restricted by God in Job 7:12 and Ps 104:6–9. However, the literal parallel to Job 7:12 is closer to Ps 74:13 where ם is personified and the monster תנין is mentioned, too.[12] Second, the hymn in Job 9 is often related to Ps 104. In Job 9:5 Job describes his divine adversary as the one who removes mountains (המעתיק הרים) and overturns them (הפך) in his anger (אף). Both motifs are present in Job in other chapters (Job 14:18; 18:4; 28:9). Job continues with the motif of primordial theophany accompanied by an earthquake or

---

10. See A. Krüger 2010, 62–64; Hossfeld and Zenger 2011, 42–61.
11. Cf. A. Krüger 2010, 442, 448; Köhlmoos 1999, 362.
12. For Job 7:12, see Mettinger 1993, 269.

a volcanic eruption, which is often used in the psalms.[13] But closely considered, the linguistic agreement with the passage in Job is modest: in contrast to Job 9:5, the verbal phrases עתק (hiphil) or הפך never have הרים as their object, and the verb פלץ in Job 9:6 appears uniquely in Job. In sum, Ps 104 shares some *motifs* with Job 9:5–6, but this does not establish a marked textual relation,[14] and may not be regarded as an (intentional) allusion to Ps 104.[15]

At first glance, the same holds true for Job 9:8, which shares the phrase נטע שמים, "to stretch out the heavens," with Ps 104:2. But if one compares the one "who speaks to the sun and it does not shine; who seals up the stars" in Job 9:7, which uses the common motif of heavenly eclipse in a distinctive way, to the one "who wraps himself in light as with a garment" in Ps 104:2, which is arranged in parallel to the one "who stretches out the heavens like a curtain," one may see a closer motif parallel to Ps 104.[16] If this is accepted, the allusions in Job 9:6–9 are in accordance with the praise of the creational power of God in Ps 104. Job 9:2–13 anticipates in some way the argument of Job 38–42. In sum, the allusions to Ps 104 in Job's first and second speech of the first cycle Job 4–14 are existent but rather marginal. The second cycle (Job 15–21) lacks references to Ps 104 completely, but a chain of references starts in the third cycle (Job 22–27[28]).

God's Creational Power as an Argument against God in Job 22–27
In Job's first speech in the third cycle (chs. 23–24) Job compares the needy (אביונים) and the poor of the land (עניי־ארץ) with wild asses in the desert (Job 24:5). On the one hand, judged from the subject matter, Job figures out the fate of the poor by referring back to Eliphaz's comment on the fate of the wicked, who "wanders abroad for bread" (נדד הוא ללחם, Job 15:23). On the other hand, seen from the literary point of view, he alludes to Ps 104:23. Annette Krüger considers this verse a clear reference to Ps 104:23 because of the combination of יצא and פעל which is limited to these two instances.[17] Though the linguistic clue is meager, there is a thematic affinity as regards the order of creation. While in Ps 104:23 humankind is sheltered against the wild beasts when

---

13. E.g. Pss 18:8; 46:3–4; 97:5; 144:5, and most relevant in this context, 104:8, 32.
14. For the term "marker," cf. Mettinger 1993, 263, 269.
15. *Pace* Köhlmoos 1999, 177.
16. Cf. ibid.
17. Cf. A. Krüger 2010, 443. For the various textual emendations in Job 24:5 which are inspired by Ps 104:23, see Witte 1995, 84–87.

the (divine and righteous) sun rises, the poor and needy of Job 24 have to range deserted, chaotic, and perilous areas to find their nourishing bread. While the wild asses in Ps 104:11 are watered by the springs and the brooks, the needy in Job 24:5 are threatened by the wilderness. In Job 24 there is no food in due season for the poor, whereas there is supply for all humankind in Ps 104:27. While humans in Ps 104:14–15 get their bread from the crop of the field, which God provides, and their hearts are made glad by the harvest of olives, grapes, and grain, or the products oil (שֶׁמֶן), wine (יַיִן), and bread (לֶחֶם), respectively, the poor depend on the permission to glean olives, grapes and grain after the work of the harvesters (Job 24:6; cf. vv. 10–11, 16–17). Further, prosperous daylight (Ps 104:23) contrasts the peril of night (Job 24:6–7; cf. 24:13–17). Although the linguistic clue is rather sophisticated, one is inclined to read the passage in Job 24 as a contrastive allusion to or reception of Ps 104 so that the disorder which is indicted in Job 24 is contrasted to the well-ordered creation of Ps 104 and God is accused of not being concerned for the poor (cf. Job 24:12, 25). It seems likely that the author(s) of Job 24 knew Ps 104 and its settled conviction of the creational wisdom. The argumentative use of Ps 104 in Job 24 is much less obvious than the use of Ps 8 in Job 7:17, but provided the acceptance of this textual connection, it runs in the same direction. The description of the sapiential order of creation in the psalm becomes an argument against God—he is urgently called to intervene. If not, he proves himself unjust, iniquitous and despotic. Job doubts the perfectness of the divine order of good and evil. Something is wrong if the righteous is needy and the wicked wealthy. The praise of the beauty of God's creation should not mask iniquities, Job argues challengingly but convincingly.

God's Creational Power as a Counter-argument in the Elihu Speeches
Strikingly, the next allusion to Ps 104 is in Elihu's second speech in Job 34:14, in which he tries to disprove Job's argument which is caricatured in v. 9. In contrast, says Elihu, "far be it from God that he should do wickedness" (Job 34:10; cf. v. 12). His (only) counter-argument is based on the primordial creation (v. 13; cf. Ps 24:1) and refers to Ps 104:29–30 in vv. 14–15: "If he plans in his heart (שִׂים אֶל לֵב) to gather his spirit (רוּחַ) and breath (נְשָׁמָה) to himself, all flesh (כָּל בָּשָׂר) expires (גָּוַע) at once and humankind turns to the dust (שׁוּב עַל־עָפָר)."[18] Thereby he intends to bring a humbled Job toward God again. The passage takes up Ps 104:29–30 and shares רוּחַ, אָסַף, גָּוַע, עָפָר, and שׁוּב with these verses. Although the preposition is different (עַל instead of אֶל), the allusion

---

18. Translation by Habel 1985, 473.

to Gen 3:19; Job 10:9; Eccl 3:20 and especially Ps 104:29 is obvious. גוע כל־בשר resembles Gen 6:17 and 7:21 but Ps 104:21 as well. אסף רוח as a metaphor for death is very rare and restricted to Job 34:14 (enlarged to נשמה) and Ps 104:29. Thus, the reference to Ps 104:21 is conclusive although it is no quotation. Elihu rather *uses* the psalm against Job, who has used Ps 104 with a different intention but in the same manner before. Psalm 104 forms the background of the argument of both; both positions relate to Scripture and are justified by it.

This may be corroborated with the second passage in Elihu's speech in ch. 36 that refers to Ps 104. Elihu argues scientifically for the majesty of God (Job 36:26) by pointing at the hydrologic cycle in Job 36:27–28 (cf. Ps 147:8, 16–18 and—although with less lexical accordance and only implicit reference to the hydrologic circle—Ps 104:13).[19] Is it sheer coincidence that Job had sneered at exactly that argument in Job 24:8 regarding the poor? Job had mocked further that wild goats and rock badgers have their shelter (מחסה in Ps 104:18), but the poor and needy have not (מחסה in Job 24:8). Elihu argues that the rain is unpredictable for human intellect (אף אם־יבין מפרשי־עב, Job 36:29) and thus Job does not have the comprehensive view to criticize the rainfall on the poorly dressed freezing poor. One may further compare the concept of God's booth (סכה) in the clouds in Job 36:29–30 to Ps 18:10–15 and Ps 104:2–3.[20] This would strengthen the allusion to Ps 104, though once again the linguistic connection is weak. The relation between Job 36:26–31 and the usage of Ps 104 by Job as it has been discussed above becomes striking within the context and course of argumentation. Elihu claims God's justice not only in nature and the *creatio, conservatio et gubernatio*, but rather combines this with the historical action of God in v. 31: he judges the peoples (דין עמים), which resembles Pss 7:9; 96:10. Because the claim of God's justice in the world order is not Job's problem, Elihu adds "he gives food in abundance" (יתן־אכל למכביר). To give food (נתן אכל) in due time was a crucial part of God's benevolent activity in Ps 104:27, along with giving rain (Ps 104:13). This was exactly the passage Job used to mock God in Job 24. Elihu, however, uses Ps 104 to argue that Job should accept the impenetrability of God's activity within the general presumption of his justice and that his benevolent activity is recognizable in his creation (cf. Job 37:7). In Job 37:8 he underlines God's provision of shelter by referring to the wild animals again. It was exactly this passage of Ps 104 which Job had contrasted subtly in

---

19. See Pilger 2010, 220 for further *loose* parallels: רעם/רע in Job 36:33; 37:4, 5 and Ps 104:7; cf. 104:21 (הכפירים שאגים).

20. Cf. A. Krüger 2010, 442.

Job 24:4. Hence, Elihu takes up the subtle argumentation of Job's disbelief which is used in the *argumentum ad deum* and contrasts it by the hymnic praise of God's graciousness and righteousness.[21]

God's Creational Power as God's Counter-argument in the Speeches from the Whirlwind

Psalm 104 plays a prominent part in the argument of the book of Job, as becomes clear in the speeches from the whirlwind in Job 38–42. The description of the creation in Job 38 resembles Ps 104 several times.[22] However, the start in Job 38 is faintly relevant. The reference to the foundation of the earth (אֶרֶץ יָסַד, Job 38:4) is not specific enough (cf. alongside Ps 104:5; e.g. Pss 78:69; 102:26), although it is striking that there is a reference to Ps 104 in the first sentences of God. Job 38:6 and Ps 104:5 share the lexeme אֶדֶן to denote a cosmological foundation.[23] The limitation of the sea in Job 38:8, 11 intersects more specifically with Ps 104:6–9 in lexical and thematic regards but as well with Jer 5:22 and Ps 65:8. More relevant is the reference to the nourishment of the young lions in Job 38:39, which is reminiscent of Ps 104:21–22. Both have טֶרֶף and כְּפִירִים in common and refer to God's welfare of the beasts. And again, as in Job 37:8, the refuge of the wild beasts is called מְעוֹנָה (Job 38:40). The term אֹכֶל which is used in Ps 104:21 to denote the prey of the wildlife—and, as Krüger has noticed, is used elsewhere in this sense only in Job 9:26 and 39:29—occurs in Job 38:41. Although the young ravens evoke Ps 147:9, this actually reinforces the connection to Ps 104. Another detail forms Ps 104:21 as the backdrop of Job 38:41: the young ravens cry to God (אֶל־אֵל יְשַׁוֵּעוּ) as the lions search for their food from God (לְבַקֵּשׁ מֵאֵל אָכְלָם). Strikingly, the ravens' food in v. 41 is called צַיִד, which denotes usually game or bigger hunted animals thereby fitting more likely into the prey pattern of lions rather than into that of ravens. Thus, the older suggestion of reading לָעֶרֶב as "in the evening" instead of "for the raven" has some merit.[24] This may be corroborated by the fact that Job 38 antedates Ps 147[25] so that the connection with Ps 104:21–22 outweighs that with Ps 147 in a diachronic perspective.

21. See Frevel 2009, 30, 39. Beside Ps 104, Pss 18; 29; 145; 147 play a greater role in the argumentation in Job 36–37, but that is another story.

22. Cf. Jamieson-Drake 1987, but he refrains from assuming a literary dependence.

23. Cf. A. Krüger 2010, 442, but compare Pss 24:2; 33:7; 65:8; 75:4; 89:10; 118:22 et al.

24. Cf. Duhm 1897, 188.

25. See Hossfeld and Zenger 2011, 624–25.

Significantly, as in Job's speech in Job 24:8 and in the Elihu speeches in Job 36:27–28, the passage is accompanied by a hydrological exhortation, which precedes in Job 38:37 the reference to the nourishment of the wildlife in Job 38:39–41 (and which uses שְׁחָקִים for the clouds as in Job 36:28!). Job is rhetorically rebuked once again: only God is master of the rain, and his pluvial gift irrigates the dried out land (Job 38:28). Hence, as in Ps 104:13, the giving of rain is an act of prosperity instead of humiliation for the poor as Job argued.

It is God not Job who is owed reverence and appreciation for maintaining and sustaining his creation. This is underlined in both speeches of God in Job 38–41. Both parts refer significantly to Ps 104, but the first speech refers in particular to the line of argumentation which was formed by the reference-chain Job—Elihu—God. The second speech refers to Ps 104 right in its beginning at Job 40:10, where God ironically prompts Job to attire himself with divine traits: "Deck yourself with majesty and dignity; clothe yourself with glory and splendor." Although the hendiadys הוֹד וְהָדָר is attested in 1 Chr 16:27; Pss 21:6; 45:4; 96:6; 111:3; 145:5, it is Ps 104:1 where it is combined with לָבֵשׁ. So the hymnic opening of Ps 104 and with it the whole psalm forms the antithesis to Job 40:10: God is the one who is clothed with honor and majesty because of his primordial creation and preservation. And only the one who controls the creation *and* the chaos is justified to do so.

The last allusion to Ps 104 is the widely noticed attestation of Leviathan in Job 40:29, where God asks Job whether he wants to play with the chaotic beast (הַתְשַׂחֶק־בּוֹ). This is conclusive because in Ps 104:26 YHWH has formed Leviathan to play with him (לְשַׂחֶק־בּוֹ).[26] In dominating the Leviathan, God demonstrates his majesty over the creation, which is far beyond Job's capability. God is not chaotic but rather forces back the chaos.

The Use of Psalm 104 in the Book of Job:
A Complex Sapiential Argument

To sum up: although Ps 104 is not cited extensively, this psalm acts as a relevant hypotext for the book of Job. Although the verbatim agreement is scarce throughout, indicating Ps 104 was not only alluded to by memorizing some of the phrases literally, it was the theology and the course of argumentation within this psalm which was engaged with. Assuming that the recipients of the book of Job had some literary

---

26. For discussion of the object referred to by the suffix, see A. Krüger 2010, 53–54.

competence and familiarity—be it in hearing, praying, reading or memorizing psalms—they will have recognized the aura or the echo of Ps 104
in Job's, Elihu's and God's speeches, where it is referred to. The authors
of Job were highly literate scribes who have written their discursive
literature for an audience or, better, reading public which was familiar
with the traditions too. The recipient of the book of Job was intended to
be able to recall Ps 104 as a hymnic praise of God's creation.

Strikingly, there are no direct or indisputable references to Ps 104
in the speeches of Eliphaz, Bildad and Zophar. This may reflect their
theology, which is less focused on the creation and its theological
function as rationale for God's actions. Rather, it is concentrated on the
wickedness of humankind, the relation of God to judgment, and the
correlation of divine justice and human sinfulness, respectively. Since
the argument of the book leads to an acceptance of God's sovereignty in
his creating and obtaining power, the theology of Ps 104 corresponds to
the proof of majesty in the speeches of God. Psalm 104 was particularly
relevant in the textual interplay between Job 24, the Elihu speeches and
the first answer of God. Job used the psalm to challenge God's providence
regarding the poor. Elihu does not disprove this empirical argument but
disputes its cogency as a counter-argument against the sapiential and
righteous order: the greater context of the divine order and providence
may produce ambivalences which remain inexplicable and should be
accepted for the sake of humility. This argument is followed in God's
speeches, once more with references to Ps 104. The book of Job uses the
psalms as part of the sapiential tradition in a highly intertextual manner.
The message is that Job may find the answer to his challenge within
(praying, reading or reflecting on) the psalms. It is striking that the argumentation in the book of Job relates especially to the interplay between
the *creatio prima* and the *conservatio et gubernatio* in Ps 104.[27]

"Usage" as Intertextual Pattern in Job:
Indicating Some Tentative Consequences

Miller has listed three ways of understanding intertextual relations by
means of a diachronic relationship: "intertextual connections contribute
to an enhanced understanding of the alluding text, especially vis-à-vis its
revision, abrogation or exegesis of the alluded text(s)."[28] The use of

27. This should be reflected against the background of the diachronic hypothesis
that especially Ps 104:5–9, 18, 25–26, 29b, 31–32, 34–35 are suggested to be redactional; see Hossfeld and Zenger 2011, 46–48.
28. G. D. Miller 2011, 284.

psalms in the book of Job fits into none of these categories entirely. In some instances it is revision, in some abrogation, but, in most of the reception of psalms discussed above, it is *usage* as wisdom literature which is presumed as a more or less familiar and authoritative tradition. This is more than just borrowing, recalling, alluding or echoing of the precursor text. As shown elsewhere for the use of Ps 8 in Job, and here for the use of Ps 104, the reception does not constitute a revision of the preceding text but rather an extension of its meaning in the process of reception. This reception, as part of inner-scriptural interpretation processes, may be a modifying or preserving of the "original," may be affirmative or negative, amplifying or curtailing the meaning or making it unequivocal or ambiguous. It may be traditionalistic, revolutionary or revisionary, sometimes even subversive, ironical, parodistic or polemical. By that it forms plurality rather than unambiguity but is by no means a suspension of meaning which is constituted in the interplay of texts. Discursivity and diversity are principles of composition in Old Testament wisdom literature as Markus Saur has underlined recently.[29] These intertextual relations form a concept which bridges the (false opposition) between the diametrical concepts of "author-centered" and "reader-oriented" methodologies because it takes seriously the fact that authors have always been readers. Considering this, the question of "authorial intent" (which is always guesswork) becomes much less decisive because the reading processes of the authors are established or (re-)constructed by (modern) readers again.[30] Or, in jeopardized abbreviation: between author and reader there is text. As regards Ps 104, the direction of impact was seemingly rather distinct, making the (final stage of the) book of Job the hypertext. There seemed to be no mutuality of impact between Ps 104 and Job. The influence on our reading of Ps 104 after having traced its usage in Job would be the subject of a study devoted to a second intertextual perspective, which was not intended here. Our observations were thus mostly based on the chronological priority of the hypotext, intertext or subtext Ps 104 (despite late redactional additions in the vast majority of its text). The authority (or perhaps better: authoritativity) of the hypotext is tied to its reception, which is based on memorization, recitation *and* reading.[31] Usage of texts intensifies their importance. The authors and "readers" of Job were intimately familiar with the psalms, especially, as we have seen, with Ps 104.

29. Saur 2011, 248.
30. Cf. G. D. Miller 2011, 287, 291, 298, 304.
31. See Carr 2005, 124–51; Edenburg 2010, 134.

Thus, generalizing the results regarding Ps 104, we can assume that the authors of Job were "readers" of the psalms within the growing Psalter (in whichever state). The "counsel of the wicked," which is favored by God (עצת רשעים in Job 10:3 *pace* Ps 1:1), who does *not* rise as God of vengeance against the wicked (יפע H-stem Job 10:3 and Ps 94:1) and many other passages may be seen as a clue that it is a post-exilic version of the Psalter at its almost greatest extent. But this aspect needs further discussion within a broader study. By referring to the "subversive" reception of Ps 8:5–7 in Job 7:17–18, Konrad Schmid has underlined the dialectical character of the relation between the book of Job and the Psalms: "Das Ijobbuch argumentiert also in dialektischer Weise mit dem Psalter gegen den Psalter."[32] While it is helpful to keep the dialectical, paradoxical and ambivalent character of the references in mind, one may doubt the direction and purpose of the dialectal discourse. With the reception of Pss 8, 104 and other psalms (especially Pss 1; 39; 73; 90; 94; 103; 107; 138–139; 143–144 et al.) in mind, one may wonder whether the book of Job argues really *against* the psalms or, whether it forms a scripturally based sapiential discourse that *uses* scripture to solve its "problems." The book of Job emerges from the "intellectual tradition," refers to it and develops it further.[33] By reflecting traditions, it modifies traditions and constitutes new traditions. While Job challenges positions of the psalms by his reflections on his experience and empirical knowledge, the book of Job also argues using the Psalter against Job's positions.[34] Overall, the theology of psalms is not refuted in the book of Job. It is quite the opposite, and more often the psalms form the rhetorical, sapiential and theological foundation of the argumentation in the book of Job.[35] It is neither acceptance nor rejection, rather dialogue and argumentation. Within this discourse, scripture (not only psalms, but torah and prophets too) is incorporated, known by heart as well as in written form. Some of the references are blatantly obvious by a direct quote; others are sophisticated and learned by subtle allusions. Both modes are combined and have the appreciation of the psalms in common.

One last remark should be made on the diachrony of the intertextual web as regards Ps 104 in the book of Job. If the assumption of Job 24:5–8 as secondary by Witte and others[36] is correct, the situation would be a

---

32. Schmid 2011, 260.
33. See with reference to Norman Whybray, Mettinger 1993, 258.
34. Cf. Frevel 2004, 268–70.
35. Cf. the similar conclusion for Lam 3 and Job 19 in Mettinger 1993, 274.
36. See Witte 1994, 122–23, 128–29.

bit more complex in diachronic respects. The broad reference to Ps 104 in the Elihu speeches would then bridge the speeches of God and the speeches of Job,[37] and this link would have been constituted in the speeches of Job redactionally. But this possibility would need further discussion because the secondary character of Job 24:5–8 is by no means beyond doubt, and—as has been shown above—there remain some allusions to Ps 104 besides the link with the Elihu passage.

37. Strikingly, the two references to Ps 104 discussed above (Job 34:14–15 and Job 36:27–28) are not considered to belong to the same layer in the most recent diachronic approach to the Elihu speeches by Pilger (2010, 80–81, 220, 246, 248).

"I ALSO COULD TALK AS YOU DO" (JOB 16:4): THE FUNCTION OF INTRATEXTUAL QUOTATION AND ALLUSION IN JOB

Michael A. Lyons

When we speak of "intertextuality," we often think of relationships between discrete literary works or references by the author of one literary work to a different literary work.[1] The book of Job, however, affords many opportunities for examining relationships or references between its own text-segments because of the differences (between speech cycles, between the narrative and the frame, between compositional layers) within the book itself. Yet even though the book is complex and composite, it is a single literary entity, so perhaps the term "intratextuality" or "innertextuality" would be a more appropriate label for the phenomena considered here.[2]

In this essay I will examine quotation and allusion as two kinds of text-referencing techniques that occur within the book of Job itself—that is, instances where the author refers (or creates the illusion of referring) to another text-segment within the book. These two techniques play a significant role in characterization, plot development, argument structure, and the creation of cohesion between sections of the book.

While "intertextuality" is typically not defined with reference to an author's deliberate interaction with another text, this notion is central to how I approach textual relationships in this essay. My methodology could be characterized as "author-oriented" insofar as I treat the book of Job as a literary product of a historical communication situation in which

---

1. For a definition of "intertextuality," see Kristeva 1980b, 65–66. As Kristeva and others use the term, it can refer to relationships between not just texts but any "signifying systems"; see Kristeva 1984, 60, and Culler 1981, 103.

2. For the term "intratextuality," see Carr 1998, 97; for "innertextuality," see Meyers and Meyers 1993, 33–34.

some textual phenomena (viz., quotation and allusion) can be attributed to the deliberate design of the author as part of a communicational strategy. The term "deliberate design" should not be taken to imply that we have access to the author's mental state, but simply that authors both ancient and modern intend to communicate and utilize certain techniques to further their goals. Yet my methodology could also be understood as "reader-oriented" inasmuch as all texts must be construed by readers: meanings do not "reside in" texts, but exist only in the heads of authors and readers. Of course, it is possible—under certain conditions—for the meaning construed by readers to closely approximate that of the author, if the two share the same linguistic and literary conventions.

Definitions

A quotation is a reference to an earlier text or utterance that replicates material from that source while calling attention to the *act* of referencing, to the *speaker or author* of the quoted material, or to the *source* being referenced.[3] It is this "calling attention" that constitutes the markedness of quotation.[4] Of course, the quoted source text or speech may be summarized or changed in various ways.[5]

It stands to reason that in the speeches of the book of Job the characters would appeal to traditional wisdom or take up each others' sentiments to dispute them. It is even possible that Job could (for various reasons) be made to utter statements that agree with positions taken by the friends. However, not all of these are instances of quotation. According to the definition I use here, quotation must be marked in some way.[6] Quotation

---

3. On the marking of quotation, see Plett 1988, 315, 321–22 and Helbig 1996, 17–57. In this essay I do not include a treatment of hypothetical reported speech (e.g. "if / lest [you / I] say": Job 7:13; 19:28–29; 22:29; 32:13) or quotations attributed to real or hypothetical characters not actually present in the story line of the book (Job 4:16–17; 9:12; 20:7; 21:14; 22:17, 19–20; 34:31–32, 34–37; 35:10–11; 36:23).

4. In the Hebrew Bible, the usual marker for quotations of a text is כככתוב בספר (e.g. 2 Kgs 14:6 → Deut 24:16). Quotations of speech are typically marked with a *verbum dicendi* (e.g. אמר, Gen 26:9 → 26:7); for other markers, see Fox 1980, 421–23, and Talstra 1994, 331–32. On the variety of verbs with which speech may be introduced, see C. L. Miller 1996, and Jacobson 2004.

5. See Clark and Gerrig 1990, 795–96.

6. Some have claimed that there are "unmarked" or "virtual" quotations in Job (e.g. Gordis 1939; 1949; 1965, 169–89; cf. the comments on Job 21:19 in Habel 1985, 321, 328; Hartley 1988, 316–17; Newsom 1996, 493). However, this claim has been strongly—and in my view, rightly—disputed; see Fox 1980; Talstra 1994; Ho 2009.

has a rhetorical function that is different from allusion or from simply taking up and interacting with the sentiments of another: it invokes (and can therefore subvert) notions of authority and testimony, and allows the quoter to frame another character in a particular way.[7]

A textual allusion is a kind of referencing in which an author uses material from another source (or from another text-segment in the same literary work), but without mention of the act of referencing, of the speaker or author of the quoted material, or of the source used.[8] It is this feature that distinguishes allusion from quotation; allusion lacks the marking present in quotation, and presumes the reader's knowledge of the source referred to.[9] In the book of Job, most allusions occur in the speeches (though they may also be found in the narrative sections),[10] and they display great diversity in both form[11] and function.

Allusion may consist of the repetition of a single word,[12] a cluster of words,[13] or an entire locution. Obviously it is easier to identify allusions that replicate large amounts of the source material. In the case of Job the detection of allusion is simplified by the fact that the author is utilizing repetition in dialogues created within a single literary work,

7. On the evidential and evaluative functions of quotation, see Galatolo 2007, 207–20; on quotation as distortion and manipulation, see Sternberg 1982, 108–9, 130–31 and Lane-Mercier 1991.

8. See Miner 1994, 13–14. Note the distinction in Savran (1988, 7) between "quoted direct speech" and "allusions, summaries, and oblique references to other words and phrases." For a broader discussion, see Hebel 1991, 135–64, and Irwin 2001.

9. See Miner 1994, 14; Irwin 2001, 288; Ben-Porat 1976, 108–9. It is the act of referencing another context that distinguishes allusion from simple repetition.

10. Elihu's speeches contain most of the quotations and allusions; cf. Dhorme 1967, c–cii, and Habel 1984, 94–95.

11. For example, there are instances in which the alluding text is an inversion of the source text (e.g. Job 34:21 → 31:4, or Job 25:4 → 15:14), or a conflation of two source texts (e.g. Job 34:21–23 → 22:13 + 24:23).

12. The negative use of סוך/שׂוך in Job 3:23 is possibly an ironic allusion to the positive use in 1:10, and the (deliberately?) non-anthropocentric use of the word in 38:4 might allude to the previous occurrences; see Schifferdecker 2008, 73–74. See also the use of רעה, "adversity," in Job 42:11 ("all the adversity which Yhwh brought upon him") as an allusion to 2:10–11 (where Job says it is right to accept "adversity" from God as well as good), and the use of שׂערה/סערה, "stormwind," in Job 38:1; 40:6 as an allusion to its occurrence in 9:17.

13. See, for example, Habel's (1985, 460–61) treatment of how Elihu in ch. 33 takes up Job's words from ch. 13, or Pyeon's (2003, 106–11) treatment of repetition in the speeches of the characters in chs. 3–14. I do not find all of Pyeon's examples (e.g. the repetition of the presentative הנה and the divine name אלוה) to be convincing instances of allusion.

where characters are made to respond explicitly to each other. While the direction of dependence and awareness of context are major issues in the study of allusion in other books, these are less significant in the book of Job. The challenges here lie in distinguishing probable allusions from other kinds of lexical repetition (i.e. repetition due to coincidence, to the author's unconscious recall of a word or phrase from an earlier context, to the use of fixed expressions,[14] or to the fact that the word is part of the author's idiolect[15]), and in explaining how the author is using the alluding text-segment to interact with the source text-segment.[16]

The Functions of Quotation and Allusion in the Book of Job

Cohesion
By using allusion to link speeches to other speeches and speeches to the narrative frame (both to the prologue[17] and the epilogue[18]), the author creates cohesion between the sections of the book.[19] These linkages are created even when the characters (and narrator) refer to the *fact* of another character's earlier utterance (e.g. Job 32:11–12, 14; 38:2; 42:7, 8).[20]

Plot Development
The following two examples demonstrate how the author uses allusion to shape the plot line of the book. First, the description of events and

14. For example, the use of ויאמר + PN + ויען (Job 4:1; 6:1; 8:1; 9:1, etc).

15. Examples of the author's idiolect in Job include the use of מלה (62× in the Hebrew Bible; 34× in Job) and the root מלל (5× in the Hebrew Bible, all in Job).

16. On criteria for the detection and analysis of allusion, see Sommer 1998, 20–31, 152–65; Schultz 1999, 211–15, 222–27, 231; Carr 2001; Leonard 2008; Lyons 2009, 59–75, 76–109.

17. Bildad's statement in Job 8:4 is likely an allusion to the events described in the prologue (Job 1:5, 18–19). The statement about fearing God and turning from evil in Job 28:28 may allude to the description of Job in the prologue (Job 1:1, 8; 2:3); cf. Newsom 2003, 181; Schifferdecker 2008, 48.

18. The description of Job's reversal of fortune in Job 42:10, 12 may also be an ironic allusion to the comment of Bildad in Job 8:7, though this does not involve verbal repetition.

19. On the relationship between allusion and coherence, see Nasciscione 2010, 107–20. This relationship could also be explained using the categories of anaphora and reiteration (Halliday and Hasan 1976, 31–34, 51, 277–82).

20. As Miner (1994, 14) notes, "although poetic allusion is necessarily manifested in words, what it draws on in another work need not be verbal. The words of the alluding passage may establish a conceptual rather than a verbal connection with the passage or work alluded to."

dialogue in ch. 2 is an allusion to an earlier scene in ch. 1 (Job 2:1–3 →
1:6–8 and Job 2:10 → 1:22). The repetition in these allusions causes the
reader to reflect on similarity and difference, on what changes (God's
admission of involvement, the heightening of affliction, the response of
Job's wife) and what does not (the opposition of the Satan, God's
confidence in Job, Job's integrity).[21]

Second, there are allusions in the epilogue that point back to the
prologue (Job 42:10, 12 → 1:3 and Job 42:13 → 1:2). These are cases of
reversal: Job's possessions and sons described as lost in the prologue are
replaced and the former exactly doubled in the epilogue, while Job's
daughters—who are replaced but not doubled—are heightened in beauty
and in legal status. This reversal is the means by which the author makes
a distinction between the concepts of a reward for piety and a bribe to
elicit piety (cf. Job 1:9–12).

Argument Structure

The characters in the book are made to argue with each other—about
Job's condition, about the connection between suffering and human
behavior, about divine justice—and the author uses quotation and allusion
to coordinate the arguments of the characters. In doing so, he replicates
the actual dynamics of hostile conversation (sarcasm, misunderstanding,
misrepresentation).

In a few instances, a speaker is made to allude to the words of another
in order to agree, or to use the words in the same way.[22] An example
would be Elihu's allusion (Job 34:12) to Bildad's statement (Job 8:3,
framed as a rhetorical question) that God will not "pervert justice"
(יְעַוֵּת מִשְׁפָּט).[23] Yet even here the allusion functions as an argument
against Job.

More frequently, a speaker alludes to the words of another in order to
contradict them, or to arrive at a different conclusion from them.[24] An
example would be Job's allusion (Job 9:10) to the words of Eliphaz (Job
5:9) that God "does great things that are unsearchable, wonders without
number."[25] Eliphaz's statement occurs in the context of his argument that
God's greatness should motivate Job to seek God (Job 5:8). However,

---

21. See Habel 1985, 28; Newsom 2003, 60–62.

22. See also (a) Job 34:12 → 8:3; (b) 34:35; 35:16; 36:12 → 38:2; 42:3a;
(c) 37:4–5 → 40:9–10; (d) 42:3a → 38:2.

23. Job 8:3 and 34:12 are the sole occurrences of this locution.

24. See also (a) Job 9:10 → 5:9; (b) 27:20 → 21:18; (c) 34:21–23 → 24:23;
22:13; (d) 36:6 → 21:7; (e) 36:11 → 21:13.

25. Job 5:9 may be an allusion to Ps 145:3, 5.

when Job utters the same words that Eliphaz used, Job is arguing that God is so great that he could *not* successfully communicate with God (Job 9:11–12, 14–16). In another instance of contradiction, Job seems to be depicted as *arguing that* a "stormwind steals away" (גנבתו סופה) the wicked (Job 27:20). This is an allusion to the use of the same locution in Job 21:18, where Job *questions whether* the "stormwind steals away" the wicked. This contradictory allusion is one of many features in Job 27:13–23 that challenges a reader's ability to understand this section as a straightforward argument by Job.[26]

There are a number of allusions that cannot be defined as simple agreement or contradiction. For example, Elihu alludes (Job 34:7) to the words of Eliphaz (Job 15:16), but turns Eliphaz's general reference ("one who is abominable and corrupt") into a more specific one by explicitly naming Job. A character may allude to an earlier speech in order to derive a different implication from the same words or use the same image in a different way (cf. Job 18:4 → 9:5; 14:18; or Job 41:2, 10 → 3:8, 9), or to reformulate ironically the words of an earlier speech (Job 15:14–15 → 4:17–18 and 7:17),[27] or to change a sarcastic challenge into a non-sarcastic statement (Job 42:4b → 38:3; 40:7).

In several cases, we see multiple allusions to the same passage.[28] In Job 33:12–13, Elihu argues that because God is greater than humanity, Job has no legitimate reason to "contend" (ריב, v. 13) with God; God is not bound to "answer" (ענה).[29] This is an allusion to Job 9:3, in which Job expressed his fear that if one desired to "contend" (ריב) in a lawsuit with God, he could not "answer" (ענה).[30] Elihu transforms Job's concern about his *inability* to conduct a lawsuit with God into a statement that Job has *no reason to expect* an answer from God. But we find another allusion to Job 9:3 in God's statement in Job 40:2: "Shall the one who

---

26. Gordis (1978, 536), Habel (1985, 385), and Clines (2006, 663) treat Job 27:13–23 as a displaced speech of Zophar; Hartley (1988, 355, 359) treats it as a displaced speech of Bildad. Newsom (1996, 524) argues that Job is imitating the speech of his friends to mock them; see the more developed argument in her later monograph (2003, 161, 167–68).

27. On these verses, see particularly Fishbane 1992, 93–98.

28. See the following complex network of allusions: Job 25:4–6 → 9:2 (מה אנוש + מה); and 25:4–6 → 15:14–16 (ילוד אשה + יצדק...יזכה + אנוש + מה); Job 15:14–15 → 4:17–18 (לא יאמין + יצדק + אנוש); Job 15:14 → 7:17 (מה אנוש כ...); and possibly Job 9:2 → 4:17 (עם־אל / מאלוה + יצדק + אנוש).

29. The verbs ריב and ענה occur in proximity only in Gen 31:36; Job 9:3; 33:13; 40:2.

30. The syntax of Job 9:3 is ambiguous; see Hartley 1988, 167; Clines 1989, 227–28; Newsom 1996, 409.

contends (רִיב) with the Almighty reprove? The one who argues with God must answer (יַעֲנֶה) it!" God transforms Job's *statement of concern* about his inability to answer God into a *challenge* to answer what God has been saying in the divine speeches.

Characterization

The author uses allusion to depict Job as respectfully submissive (though as some read Job's words, as ironically submissive or even resistant[31]) after God's challenge, and uses quotation to depict the speakers as hostile to each other and to each others' statements.[32] This hostility is manifested in outright misrepresentation: the book contains four quotations falsely attributed to Job (I include these because the formal features and rhetorical function of quotation are still employed in falsely attributed statements).[33] Even though it could be argued that the statements in Job 34:9 and 35:3 are legitimate *implications* of Job's speeches, the words that are put in his mouth are clearly designed to depict him in the worst possible—even contradictory[34]—light. For example, in Job 11:4, Zophar represents Job as saying, "My teaching (לֶקַח) is pure (זַךְ), and I am clean (בַר) in your eyes." Most commentators take Zophar's quote as an accurate representation of Job's claim to innocence (e.g. Job 9:20, 21; 10:7; 16:17b) that is nevertheless a distortion of Job's words,[35] turning his heartfelt complaint into abstract theologizing and reconfiguring his claim of innocence into a claim that what he is saying about God, justice, and suffering is "pure."

Even where a speaker quotes another character's speech using the character's own words (with minor modifications) and accurately represents his sentiments, the quotation may be meant to oppose and accuse

---

31.   These different interpretations of Job arise from how readers construe his words in Job 42:1–6. See Habel 1985, 577–83; Morrow 1986; Fox 2005, 355–56, 364–66; T. Krüger 2007, 217–29; Ho 2009, 711–14.

32.   For linguistic and pragmatic analyses of reported speech, see Coulmas 1986; Holt 1996; 2009. On the specifically adversarial use of quotation, see Goodwin 1980; Sternberg 1982, 108–9, 130–31; Lane-Mercier 1991, 206, 208; Matoesian 2000; Antaki and Leudar 2001; Galatolo 2007, 207–20.

33.   Job 11:4; 22:13–14; 34:9; 35:3.

34.   In two cases Elihu juxtaposes a quote of Job's *claim* to be righteous with a (falsely attributed) quote *questioning* the value of righteousness (Job 34:5–6, 9; 35:2–3). Analyses of reported speech in modern courtroom testimony show notable similarities to this use of quotation in Job; see Matoesian 2000. On the forensic qualities of the book of Job, see, e.g., Habel 1984; Magdalene 2007.

35.   Habel 1985, 206; Hartley 1988, 194; Clines 1989, 260; Newsom 1996, 419.

the speaker.[36] Ironically, the use of quotation is usually taken to represent a claim to neutrality and honesty ("I'm just repeating what you said!").[37] This allows characters to accuse their opponents from a higher ground by framing them negatively and using their own speech against them.[38] This is in fact what Job fears God will do to him (Job 9:20). Quotation therefore plays a key role in the author's strategy of characterization: the author presents the friends and Elihu as unsympathetic and unreliable characters, and Job as set in his opposition to them.

Effects on the Reader
The quotation and allusion in the book of Job have the effect of inviting the reader to read more closely and inquire: "Did I see these words before somewhere? Does this character represent the other fairly? Did the character being quoted really say *that*?" Then too, there is a sense of "aesthetic appreciation" when one recognizes an allusion.[39]

Conclusion

What, if anything, is unique about the text-referencing in the book of Job? It is not the techniques that are employed, or the local effects produced by individual examples of referencing. After all, we can find examples of irony and contradiction in allusion, or modifications of speech in quotation (whether to misrepresent or not) in other ancient Israelite texts. It seems to me that what is unique about quotation and allusion in the book of Job is the extent to which they are used, the scope

---

36.　Job 21:28 (*Job, quoting friends; source: Job 8:22; 15:28, 34; 18:14, 21; 20:28*); 33:8–9 (*Elihu, quoting Job; source: Job 16:17; 13:23; cf. 9:20, 21; 13:18*); 33:10–11 (*Elihu, quoting Job; source: Job 13:24, 27*); 34:5–6 (*Elihu, quoting Job; source: Job 9:15; 27:2; cf. 6:4, 28; 13:23*); Job 35:14 (*Elihu, quoting Job; source: uncertain; for similar sentiments, see Job 9:11; 23:9 [not seeing God]; 23:4 [setting case before God]; 31:35 [waiting for God]; for identical vocabulary, see Job 7:8; 17:15 [שׁור]; 19:29 [דין]; 6:11; 13:15; 14:14 [יחל]*). Job 35:2 (*Elihu, quoting Job; source: uncertain; cf. Job 13:18; 27:6?*) may be either an accurate paraphrase or an implication of Job's speech. Commentators differ on how Job 35:2 is to be understood: Is Job's righteousness "before God" (possibly an allusion to Eliphaz's words, Job 4:17) or is Job "more in the right than God"? See Gordis 1978, 400; Habel 1985, 491; Hartley 1988, 463; Newsom 1996, 580; Clines 2006, 795–96.
37.　Galatolo 2007, 207.
38.　Galatolo (ibid., 213–19) speaks of the "moral function" of direct reported speech, particularly in assigning blame.
39.　Gordis 1965, 203.

across which they are employed, and the atmosphere of relentless dis-agreement they create throughout the entire composition. The ambiguity, irony, and indirectness that are characteristic of the way quotation and allusion are employed in the book (see Habel 1985, 51) seem to be reflected in the argument structure of the book itself.

It seems to me that part of the reason for the enduring appeal of the book of Job lies in its mimetic qualities. Even today, victims of disaster really do speak as Job speaks, creating explanation after explanation in an attempt to provide a rationale for what has befallen them. Onlookers really do point their fingers and explain disaster as divine judgment. People really do argue in the way Job and the friends do, accusing and misrepresenting each other, reveling in the triumph of successfully wielding an opponent's words as weapons. In short, the book of Job is perceived as relevant because it reflects universal human experience. The use of quotation and allusion in the book plays an essential role in creating this mimetic realism.

Divine Discipline in Job 5:17–18, Proverbs 3:11–12, Deuteronomy 32:39, and Beyond

James L. Crenshaw

The initial reaction of Job's friend Eliphaz to his imprecation picks up the notion of hope in 3:9 and applies it to Job, first with reference to his integrity (4:6) and then in regard to his miserable condition (5:16). Eliphaz laces this speech with a variety of genres and topics: faint praise for Job's reputation as a comforter (4:3–4), standard fare about punishment for wicked conduct (4:7–11), an extraordinary claim to have received revelation from a mysterious visitor during the night (4:12), a low view of human nature (5:7), hymnic praise of the deity (5:9–15), and a treatise on divine discipline (5:17–27). In what follows, I shall focus on the last of these, God as disciplinarian as described in the first two verses of the unit:

> Look, happy is the one whom Eloah corrects;
>   don't reject Shaddai's instruction;
> for he bruises, but he binds up;
>   he strikes, but his hands[1] heal. (5:17–18)

My procedure is similar to that of W. A. M. Beuken (1994), who studied the relationship between Job's curse, Eliphaz's response, and Job's rejoinder. That approach involves a reading of literature with emphasis on identical lexemes and isotopes, as well as *Leitwörter* and even themes that link texts involving different speakers or authors. It also is attentive to formulaic constructions and traditional consensus, together with the possibility that the same idea may occur to different people whose common background has prepared them to think along the same lines. Above all, it recognizes that authors possessed a high degree of freedom to shape traditional beliefs in a way that best accorded with the aims of the new work.

---

1. Reading the *qere*.

This approach grafts intertextual concerns with tradition criticism. For, an appeal to a tradition creates intertextual connections with texts across the Hebrew Bible and beyond that also display that tradition. The lexemes related to the tradition of divine discipline discussed here become threads sewing together disparate texts from Job to 2 Samuel to the Epistle to the Hebrews. Thus the interaction between diachronic and synchronic intertextuality comes to the fore. I will trace the development of the tradition over time (diachronic), but when the breadth of this tradition is brought to bear on the passage in Job it informs our reading of that passage (synchronic). After all, we can only recognize a tradition when we synchronically look at texts from a long period of time and note similarities between them, even as their differences demonstrate its diachronic development. Though the author of Job is likely appealing to the broader tradition and not a specific text in Job 5:17–18, by doing so, he binds his text with others that interact with that same tradition throughout time.

In Eliphaz's treatise on divine discipline in 5:17–27, the first and last of eleven bicola begins with the particle הִנֵּה.[2] The argument moves from popular consensus (the traditional belief that the deity is compassionate even when disciplining wayward people) to the personal conclusions of Eliphaz. Assuring Job that he and his two friends have thoroughly investigated[3] the matter, Eliphaz urges him to recognize its validity. Possible aural associations and ambiguities reveal the psychological threat lurking within Eliphaz's response to Job's bitter curse.[4] The twofold occurrence of שׁד in vv. 21 and 22 echoes the name of the deity, Shaddai, in 5:17. In 5:24, נוה ("home") may be a metaphor for wife, with the negated verb תחטא implying sexual success resulting in his wife's pregnancy. Even the use of יד in vv. 18 and 20 links divine bruising and a sword wielded in a military skirmish. Perhaps the בשׁוט in 5:21 recalls the words of the provocateur in 1:7 and 2:2, whose slander inaugurated Job's test.[5]

---

2. The first speech by Eliphaz can be divided into seven units: (1) 4:1–6; (2) 4:7–11; (3) 4:12–17; (4) 4:18–21; (5) 5:1–7; (6) 5:8–16; and (7) 5:17–27. Clines (1989, 199–214) views 4:6 and 5:8 as nodal sentences, the first referencing Job's piety as his basis for hope and the second urging him to seek El in order to argue his case. The two sentences are at odds with one another.

3. On the verb חקר and related terms for the acquisition of knowledge, see Crenshaw 1998b, and Carr 2005.

4. Fishbane (1971) argues for a close textual relationship between Job's curse and that by Jeremiah.

5. Nevertheless, a difference in vowels remains (a final *u* in Job 1:7 and 2:2, an *o* in 5:21), even if one follows the versions.

The Analogy of Human Discipline to Divine

The idea that the deity adopted harsh measures when teaching individuals was at home among the sages, while prophets applied the concept to nations (Ezek 5:15; 25:17; Ps 94:10). Given the prominence of corporal punishment in the schools of ancient Egypt and Mesopotamia,[6] and its probable presence in scribal circles in Israel,[7] it is understandable that sages depicted YHWH in the image of human instructors.[8] Naturally, Eliphaz designates the deity by names more appropriate on the lips of non-Israelites.[9] Hence the use of Eloah and Shaddai in 5:17.

An Actual Tradition?

On what basis can one claim that Eliphaz appeals to common tradition about divine discipline? First, the similarities between Job 5:17–18 and Prov 3:11–12 ("The discipline of YHWH, my son, don't reject; and don't loathe his rebuke. For whom he loves YHWH rebukes, and he afflicts the son he favors"). Second, the affinities between Job 5:18 and Deut 32:39 ("See now that I, I am he, and there is no God besides me. I kill, and I make alive; I wound, and I heal. No one can deliver from my hand").[10]

6. For extensive treatment and relevant bibliography on ancient Near Eastern texts, see Crenshaw 1998a. The emphasis in Carr (2005) falls more on enculturation and the growth of literature.

7. Little information about scribes in Israel has survived, forcing scholars to resort to analogy from imperial cultures. The differences in power and in sophistication between the tiny states of Judah/Israel and its powerful neighbors to the South and East need to be taken into account (Hunter 2006). The subtitle of Perdue's 2008 edited volume, *Scribes, Sages, and Seers: The Sage in the Eastern Mediterranean World*, links three distinct groups that performed quite different functions. Not all scribes were sages, and seers belong to the ranks of prophets and authors of apocalyptic literature. Mantic wisdom hardly justifies the inclusion of seers in this otherwise excellent volume.

8. On the influence of the principle of similarity between humans and the deity, see van der Toorn 2002 and Crenshaw 2009. This projection of anthropology on depictions of YHWH both fostered intimacy with the deity and gave rise to concern about an immoral object of worship. This unflattering representation of YHWH issued in theodicy (Crenshaw 2005; Laato and de Moor 2003; Seibert 2009; Bergmann, Murray, and Rea 2011).

9. In the Hebrew Bible, foreigners are not permitted to use the name YHWH, and neither Job nor his three friends are depicted as Israelites. For an interesting exploration of the significance of Shaddai in the book of Job, see Janzen 2009.

10. The refrain, "There is no deliverer from my hand," has been analyzed by Chalmers (2005).

The astonishing linguistic consistency in the first example (Job 5:17–18; cf. Prov 3:11–12) stands out. Here one finds the verbal roots מאס, יכח,[11] and רפא,[12] as well as nominative forms מוסר[13] and תוכחת (the latter with a prefixed preposition and pronominal suffix). The verbal roots כאב and רפא link the two verses in the second example (Job 5:18; cf. Deut 32:39).

An examination of these lexemes reveals the rich variety of teachings about the positive role of the rod in education. According to Prov 29:15a, the combination of a rod and reproof yields wisdom. The addition of the root נגע to the nominal form of יכח in Ps 73:14 shows the close connection between suffering and learning. In a few instances, תוכחת even indicates destruction (Prov 15:10; Ps 149:7; Hos 5:9), although Ps 39:12 limits the loss to one's treasures. The result of rejecting divine reproof can be brokenness, the absence of healing (Prov 29:1). In the book of Job, יכח and תוכחת often have a juridical sense[14] (Job 13:6; 16:21; 22:4; 23:4) similar to the use in Hos 4:4; Isa 11:3; and Mic 6:2. By responding to reproof, one acquires honor (Prov 13:18), intelligence (Prov 15:32), and life (Prov 6:23). The connection of reproof and pain, both physical and psychic, is also recognized (Job 33:19).

The harsh aspect of divine discipline is seen in the parallel use of the verbs יכח and יסר in Pss 6:2 and 38:2 ("YHWH, don't instruct [יכח] me in your anger; don't teach [יסר] me in your fury"). Only the nouns for wrath differ here, אף and קצף. Similarly, the verb יסר and noun תוכחת reflect severe punishment in Ps 39:12, a painful lesson the psalmist hopes to avoid by fervent prayer. A third verb, למד,[15] is linked with strict divine discipline in Ps 94:10 ("Shall he who teaches [יסר] nations not punish [יכח], he who instructs [למד] men [in] knowledge?"). In Job 13:10 the combined infinitive absolute and verb reveal the full force of

11. According to Liedke (1997, 2:542), the verb יכח originally indicated judicial proceedings. That may explain its heavy use in the book of Job (15×).

12. Stoebe (1997, 1258) recognizes a "transformation in the conceptual field of רפא in Proverbs," where it no longer refers to "physical and spiritual healing in the proper sense" (cf. Prov 3:8; 12:18; 16:24).

13. Sanders (1955) stresses the theological abstraction of מוסר YHWH in Deut 11:2 and Prov 3:11, on which, see Sæbø 1997, 2:550.

14. The juridical sense of יכח is enhanced by the prominence of additional forensic vocabulary, especially ריב and משפט. As Job's speeches progress, his concern for a hearing in the court of law intensifies (cf. Habel 1985; Good 1990; Newsom 1996).

15. Besides "learning" in the religio-ethical sense, למד has the sense of (1) the training of animals, (2) training for battle, and (3) teaching and rehearsing songs (Jenni 1997a, 2:647). Its primary sense is "to be accustomed."

יכֹח as a means of chastising someone ("He would surely rebuke you if you secretly showed partiality").[16]

The noun מוּסָר occurs mostly in wisdom literature but is missing in Qoheleth.[17] It refers to verbal instruction and to corporal punishment. Not all מוסר is beneficial; in one instance, it seems to bear a negative sense unless it is figurative for punishment ("Acumen is a fountain of life to those who possess it, but folly is the instruction [מוּסַר] of fools," Prov 16:22). The usual synonym for מוּסָר is תּוֹכַחַת, but other possibilities exist. For example, in Prov 13:1 a derivative of the verb גָּעַר, "to roar," occurs. Its primary meaning approximates the impression of a rebuke, in some instances even indicating utter destruction (Ps 106:9; Isa 50:2; Nah 1:4, the drying of the sea; Ps 80:17, the perishing of a vine; Ps 76:7, horse and rider) or trembling (Job 26:11, heaven's pillars). The milder sense amounts to scolding, as in Ruth 2:16, Jer 29:27, and Gen 37:10. For an intelligent person, a rebuke is more effective than a hundred blows (Prov 17:10). That is why Qoheleth can say that it is better to hear the reproach of the wise than the praise of fools (Eccl 7:5).

Unwelcome Discipline

Just as students were not always eager to learn from their human mentors,[18] some individuals resisted divine discipline, in essence rejecting themselves (Prov 15:32a). The negated verb מָאַס in Job (7:16) addresses this possibility of refusing discipline, just as it does in Prov 3:11. Its use in the book of Job includes the concepts of rejecting and loathing, but an object is sometimes missing. That missing object is especially vexing in Job's crucial second response to YHWH (42:6).[19]

---

16. This verb also appears in a personalization of the tradition of divine discipline. The morally beneficial nature of divine chastisement was naturally applied to YHWH's favorite ruler. In 2 Sam 7:13–14, YHWH promises to be a father to David, who will be like a son to him, and when he goes astray YHWH will chastise him (הֹכַחְתִּיו) with a rod of men and with the affliction (וּבְנִגְעֵי) of mortals. Despite the presence of the image of a disciplining father, there is no mention of binding up or of healing in this context.

17. Sæbø (1997) counts 30 uses in Proverbs and four in the book of Job (plus a *hapax* יִסּוֹר in Job 40:2).

18. Crenshaw (1998a, 139–85) explores the many ways students resisted the rigors demanded by formal education.

19. Semantic vagueness in Job 42:6 allows for a number of possible translations. These are laid out nicely by Newsom (1996, 629); see also Patrick 1976, and J. B. Curtis 1979.

Some stated objects of loathing are Job's emaciated body (7:16), Job himself (19:18), his life (9:21), and the work of his hands (10:3). In 36:5, Elihu insists that mighty El does not despise, but the object of loathing is absent. In a number of instances מאס has the milder sense of rejection (5:17; 8:20; 30:1; 31:13; 34:33). The rejected objects are respectively Shaddai's discipline, Job's integrity (תם),[20] the fathers of urchins, the legal rights of servants, and either discipline or the deity.

In the Psalter and Lamentations מאס always has a stated object. It covers a broad spectrum including both humans and inanimate objects such as a cornerstone (Ps 118:22). Most distressingly, YHWH's utter rejection of Israel in Lam 5:22 uses the emphatic verb and infinitive absolute, a linguistic expression that carries more force than a mere verbal form of מאס followed by מאר as in Ps 78:59. Intensification takes another form in Jer 5:3, where the verb מאן occurs twice in the sense of refusing ("O YHWH, do your eyes not look for truthfulness? You have struck them, but they felt no pain; you consumed them, but they refused to accept [מאן] instruction. They hardened their faces more than stone; they refused [מאן] to turn back").

Divine Discipline as Proof of Love

Surprisingly, the harsh nature of divine discipline did not elicit complaint, at least from those who discuss it in the Bible. On the contrary, it gave rise to the notion of happiness. Here is what the author of Ps 94:12 says: "Happy is the man (הגבר) whom you instruct (תלמדנו)." A macarism also occurs in Job 5:17, followed by אנוש rather than הגבר.

It may seem strange to link happiness with suffering,[21] but Eliphaz is far from alone in doing so. Like the observation about divine discipline in 5:17, the statement that the deity both wounds and binds up, strikes and heals, has a proverbial ring. It gives expression to popular belief, one that has become almost formulaic.[22] The pronoun הוא identifies the deity as the active agent of the pain and initiating blows, just as the *qere* reading ידו leaves no doubt that the healing is the result of divine activity.

---

20. Job's integrity, vouched for by the narrator and YHWH but challenged by the provocateur and Job's three friends, is central to the book, on which, see Crenshaw 2011.

21. See Crenshaw 1993.

22. Chalmers (2011) identifies ten concise occurrences of this formula (Deut 32:39; Job 5:18; Isa 19:22; 60:10; Lam 3:32; Hos 6:1; and Tob 11:15; 13:2, 5, and 9) and three extended uses (Jer 30:12–17; 33:1–13; and Isa 57:14–19). He also finds a significant parallel in RS 25.460, line 34, with reference to Marduk.

Verbal Variety in Indicating Divine Discipline

The verbs for afflicting someone, יכאיב and ימחץ, indicate the result of the deity's action and the actual striking. There is no consistent language for the grief inflicted on individuals, for we also find the idea expressed by the verbs נכה and טרף in Hos 6:1 and נגף in Isa 19:22. In one instance, the striking is lethal (Deut 32:39).

A lack of consistency also characterizes references to positive divine activity. They range from bestowing life (Deut 32:39) to binding up (חבש) wounds (Job 5:18; Isa 30:2; Ps 147:3), and even to making one whole again (רפא, Job 5:18; Deut 32:39; Hos 6:1; Isa 19:22; Ps 147:3; and Isa 30:26). A late variant stresses divine compassion, a display of mercy following an act of inflicting pain (Isa 60:10).[23] A grateful Tobit gives voice to this theme in 11:15 with reference to his own temporary blindness and praises the "King of Heaven"[24] three times for showing mercy after afflicting people.

In this hymn of praise, Tobit uses two metaphors for the deity, father and king, that emerged in Mesopotamian thought when society became more urban than rural and when parental values began to shape religious teachings.[25] The actual metaphor father is rarely applied to YHWH in the Hebrew Bible (cf. Isa 63:16; 64:8; Mal 1:6; 2:10), although parental imagery occurs in a number of places, as does the comparison of God to human parents (cf. Prov 3:12).

Healing by the deity goes beyond broken bones and bruises. According to Ps 147:3a, "He [YHWH] heals their broken hearts."[26] In this theological interpretation of physical and psychic suffering as originating in the divine mind, two metaphors for YHWH in the book of Exodus have been joined. The divine warrior (Exod 15:3) has become the physician too (Exod 15:26). In most circles, the Deuteronomistic concept of reward and retribution prevails,[27] and divine restoration comes only to those who

23. For Chalmers (2011), the reference to showing mercy after afflicting someone is equivalent to the statement about healing and thus belongs to the formula about striking but healing.

24. The author's use of several titles for the deity in Tobit has not escaped notice. See Moore (1996, 283) for the observation that except for the pronoun "our" modifying Lord, God, and Father, the epithets for God in the psalm "seem rather august and regal."

25. Jacobsen (1976) detects this shift from the natural realm through the royal to the familial.

26. Israel's sages were not oblivious to the psychological dimension of humanity (Prov 13:12; 14:10, 13).

27. Chalmers (2011, 24) thinks the formula itself ("YHWH strikes and heals") naturally implied healing whether repentance took place or not. This reading of the

repent. Among some, however, YHWH's compassion falls indiscriminately on sinners and god-fearers, like sunshine and rain.[28]

A Full-Blown Tradition in Sirach

The dominant view can hardly find an abler advocate than Ben Sira. He remarks that the Lord has compassion on those who accept his discipline (Sir 18:13–14) and that anyone who fears the Lord will accept his discipline (Sir 32:14). For Ben Sira, the analogy with the refining of gold in fire serves to clarify the "furnace of humiliation" (Sir 2:5).[29] He goes far beyond Prov 3:12, suggesting that a father's love for his son can be measured by the frequency of whippings (Sir 30:1–6).[30] Even the notion of binding up a son's wounds is proof for Ben Sira that the boy is being spoiled (Sir 30:7).

Speculation about personified wisdom in Prov 8:22–31 is followed by the exhortation to obey מוסר and acquire wisdom, as well as a warning not to spurn it (תפרעו, v. 33).[31] Ben Sira advances this theological insight, describing Wisdom as inaugurating instruction by tormenting students and observing that she reveals her secrets to those burdened by her pedagogy after placing a heavy yoke on them (Sir 4:17; 6:30).[32]

The author of the Epistle to the Hebrews bears testimony to the attractiveness of the belief that God disciplines those who are special (Heb 12:5–6).[33] That view continues unabated in Psalms of Solomon. Here one reads "Happy is the man whom the Lord remembers with rebuking, and

---

situation does not reckon with the force of the argument, best articulated in Deuteronomy, that YHWH doles out reward and punishment on the basis of merit. This principle, however, was at odds with another emphasis in Deuteronomy, YHWH's חסד.

28.   No repentance is specified in Isa 57:16–18; Jer 30:12–17; 33:1–13.

29.   The metaphor from metallurgy also appears in Job 28, where the verb for binding up, חבש, refers to building a dam to stop the flow of water. The verb also is used to indicate saddling an ass.

30.   The sage Ahiqar similarly urges harsh treatment of boys to build character (col. VI.81–83) and school texts from Mesopotamia suggest that corporal punishment was not spared.

31.   Schroer (2000) and Sinnott (2005) give widely different but fascinating analyses of personified wisdom.

32.   The role of revelation in biblical wisdom has, for the most part, not garnered much attention among scholars, on which see Crenshaw 2010, 207–28.

33.   The rendering into Greek closely follows Prov 3:11a (μὴ ὀλιγώρει παιδείας κυρίου), except for putting the addressee first. Likewise ὃν γὰρ ἀγαπᾷ κύριος παιδεύει replicates 3:12a exactly. The second colon in both verses is translated more freely ("lose courage" for "abhor," "receive" for "love").

protects from the evil way with a whip" (*Pss. Sol.* 10:1).[34] This author implores the deity, "Discipline us as you wish," and concedes, "And we are under your yoke forever, and [under] the whip of your discipline" (*Pss. Sol.* 7:3, 9). The association of divine discipline and restoration continues in rabbinic Judaism of the first millennium C.E.[35]

Traditional Belief or Quoted Texts?

What can we make of this recurring theme over such a long time? Has a single text influenced the others, or is the theological connection between afflictions and healing a simple fact of experience that would occur to any devout worshipper?[36] It is often claimed that either Deut 32:39 or Prov 3:11–12 is the source of the idea that the deity both afflicts and heals.[37]

The accuracy of that claim is not easily proven. Why? First, because the dating of biblical texts is notoriously difficult. Proverbs 3:11–12 belongs to the latest major collection in the book, but chs. 1–9 undoubtedly have much early material that has been subjected to a particular theological understanding of reality.[38] The teaching about divine discipline may fall into this category. In short, we often need to distinguish between the time of composition and the date of specific units within a literary work. Even if Prov 1–9 were post-exilic, it could contain some very old proverbial sayings. The same caution pertains to the dating of Deut 32:39.[39]

Second, the inconsistent lexemes in texts about the deity's smiting and healing are troublesome to a view of literary dependence. Ancient writers exercised considerable freedom when repeating material already narrated,[40] and citations of textual units were usually from memory due

---

34. For the translation, see R. B. Wright 1985, 661.

35. According to Chalmers (2011, 29 n. 33), the formula occurs seven times in Jewish Aramaic texts that date to the second half of the first millennium C.E.

36. Two examples illustrate the point. The story in Gen 22:1–19 and the notion of originating in dirt and returning to dust may have existed as topoi familiar to many. References that echo both of these may have nothing to do with consulting a text, unless one thinks of cultural memory.

37. Habel 1985, 134–35; Clines 1989, 148–49.

38. Dell 2006.

39. See the discussion in Tigay 1996.

40. Vassar (2007) stresses the function of "recall" in intertextuality with attention to the Psalter and the Torah. Where narration is repeated in Ugaritic literature and in the Hebrew Bible, variation frequently occurs.

to the scarcity of manuscripts and lack of easy access to the few existing ones. In addition, the context into which the quotation is inserted may have encouraged minor alterations.[41] These changes may reflect favorite vocabulary,[42] aural links with the new context,[43] theological views different from those in the core text,[44] synonyms,[45] and regional differences in vocabulary.

Consider Wis 16:13–15, which attributes power over life and death to the Lord and states that it is impossible to escape from the divine hand. Does the author quote Deut 32:39 here? Clearly, the ideas merge the different traditions preserved in Deut 32:39 and 1 Sam 2:6, which links divine killing and resuscitating with bringing down to Sheol and raising up. The introductory polemic against rival deities and "I wounded and I will heal" in Deut 32:39 do not occur in Wis 16:13–15. Furthermore, the boast that no one can deliver from the deity's hand[46] takes the form of a declaration: "To escape from your hand is impossible." One could argue that the Alexandrian setting in which rival gods did not pose a problem the way they did in Israel, and that the shift from first person to third explain the missing polemic. Even then, however, the absence of the parallel line to "killing and making alive" remains unexplained.

It is more plausible to posit a common tradition as the source of Job 5:17–18 than to think a core text, either Deut 32:39 or Prov 3:11–12, is being quoted. The differences among the texts are considerable. The macarism in Prov 3:13 ("Happy is the person who finds wisdom, the one who acquires understanding") is in Eliphaz's formulation "Look, happy is the person whom Eloah corrects." אנוש occurs rather than אדם, and wisdom is acquired in a specific manner, by attending the school of hard knocks overseen by Eloah/Shaddai. Additionally, the general notion of Shaddai as the grand controller of cosmic events that affect human lives is far removed from the analogy of a father's personal care.

---

41. Crenshaw 2012.

42. An example is the substitution of the verb הוגה for הביתיך in Lam 1:5 as compared with Jer 30:14.

43. In a predominantly oral culture, listening was primary (Crenshaw 1997).

44. A text that attributes killing to YHWH was bound to provoke angst as well as attempts to soften its impact through an emphasis on a guarantee of healing based on the deity's intrinsic nature. The classic text, Exod 34:6–7, contains both emphases.

45. The demands of parallelism furnished a rich repertoire of synonymous lexemes.

46. What a difference there is in the deity's boast that no one could deliver from the grasp of such power and Qoheleth's twice-repeated ואין להם מנחם ("and no one to comfort them," Eccl 4:1) in the face of the "hand" of oppressors.

If Job 5:18 is influenced by Deut 32:39, important changes have taken place. The jarring merism "I kill and make alive" has been omitted, as have the polemical introduction and conclusion. In place of the merism is an assertion that Eloah (הוא) "afflicts and binds up." There follows a graded numerical saying about six/seven troubles that echoes the sevenfold punishment for Israel's transgression in Lev 26:18–30. Apparently, the idea that YHWH actually kills did not belong in a confessional statement about the relationship between God and the sick, a disputed issue as late as the second century when Ben Sira came to the defense of physicians (Sir 38:1–15) and connected prayer with healing from above. The preference for "he wounds and binds up" over "he kills and makes alive" addresses the charge of divine arbitrariness.[47] The less severe treatment belongs to a context in which a comforting word is expected, even if Eliphaz's assurance that "in seven harm will not touch you" misses the mark (Job 5:19).[48] It is no small stretch to imagine a psalmist viewing rebuke as choice oil on the head (Ps 141:5).

Conclusion

The preceding discussion has focused on individual lexemes across a broad spectrum of literature related to a specific tradition. In so doing, it has expanded the literary significance of *Leitwörter*, which often develop themes within a single book *intra*textually. For example, the use of חנם in the prose of Job to indicate arbitrary divine treatment and the provocateur's suspicion becomes especially poignant when the same lexeme occurs in the poetry to accuse Job of exacting pledges from his brothers for no reason (Job 22:6) and when Job accuses God of crushing him in a tempest and wounding him without cause (Job 9:17). Likewise, Qoheleth's use of הבל to indicate transience, futility, absurdity, mist, and foulness adds cohesion to teachings that abound with contradictions. Here the *Leitwörter* are restricted to a single work, unlike those indicating divine discipline (יסר, למד, מאס, and רפא), which pull texts from across biblical literature into conversation, dragging with them various theological perspectives on the issue. These various instances of the tradition are preserved in a variety of versions, each depending on its context, identifiable at least in part by clustered lexemes and isotopes. Each contributes to the theological debate about divine discipline, one in

---

47. For a classic analysis of the literary depiction of YHWH in an unflattering light, see Miles 1995.

48. After all, Job has already lost all his children, possessions, and health.

which a beneficial function of wounding among humans was analogically applied to divine conduct. Though the author of Job may not have had a specific text in mind when he appealed to this tradition, readers aware of the tradition cannot avoid considering its textual incarnations once they recognize the connection.

JOB AND ECCLESIASTES:
INTERTEXTUALITY AND A PROTESTING PAIR

Richard L. Schultz

Scholarly analyses of Hebrew wisdom literature commonly pair the authors of the books of Job and Ecclesiastes as two "wise men in revolt against the unexamined assumptions of their colleagues" (Scott 1971, 136, 165). It has become a commonplace to contrast the skepticism and pessimism, even the cynicism or nihilism, provoked by Qoheleth's and Job's broken worlds with the confident optimism of the book of Proverbs' tidy world. At the same time, scholars also acknowledge the divergent approaches of Job and Ecclesiastes. According to Genung (1906, 197, 143), while Ecclesiastes represents "the attack by the flank," Job represents "the attack by the centre," and, according to van Selms (1985, 15), "Ecclesiastes is an intellectual game, Job an existential cry."[1] Qoheleth's autobiographical-style wisdom treatise emphasizes the ubiquitous frustrations and inequities of life which primarily are *observed* rather than personally *experienced*, while Job presents the intense but innocent suffering of an individual in debate with his critics. Gerhard von Rad (1972, 237) summarizes their differences even more strongly: "Each of them goes its own way. They are comparable not even in their negations, only in their opposition to the didactic tradition."

Beyond these generalizations, what is the actual relationship between the rhetoric and the theological perspectives of these two wisdom critics, and how close is their intellectual alliance? There could be several viable ways of investigating these issues. One could, for example, examine how each book addresses a specific topic. One might then quickly discover that a prominent theme found in one book, such as oppressive government in Ecclesiastes or illness in Job, is virtually absent from the other. Another approach would be to compare passages which use nearly identical or at least notably similar expressions, which will be the focus of this essay.

---

1.   Any such brief summary contrastive statement runs the risk of minimizing similarities and overlaps between the two.

Methodological Reflections

In studying intertextual relationship, I utilize the essentially synchronic method for identifying and interpreting verbal parallels that I set forth in a 1999 monograph, *The Search for Quotation* (Schultz 1999, esp. 222–39), and further developed in a 2003 essay on the Book of the Twelve (Schultz 2003, esp. 26–33). In seeking to determine the degree to which the authors or editors of the prophetic books reused earlier prophetic material, I suggested three concentric categories—verbal parallels, verbal dependence, and quotation. The first simply involves demonstrable "verbal correspondence"; the second requires one to determine the "direction of borrowing"; the third demands evidence of "a conscious, purposeful reuse." Giving particular attention to the identification of quotation, I proposed a model that involves two complementary criteria (verbal and syntactical correspondence *and* contextual awareness, including interpretive re-use), a twofold analysis (diachronic and synchronic), and "an acknowledgement of the multi-functionality of quotation" (Schultz 1999, 222).

In my initial monograph, I noted that many verbal parallels are not the result of conscious repetition (i.e. those involving word pairs, similar imagery, physical gestures, and similar grammatical structures, including two-member construct chains). As a significant component of prophetic rhetoric, however, whether "intentional" or "unintentional," verbal parallels attract the attention of the careful reader of prophetic books, generating intertextual connections between the texts in which these verbal parallels are located. Similarly, repeated images or motifs, such as "light" (Miscall 1991) or the "way" (Lund 2007) can be traced through the book of Isaiah (or a major section thereof), thereby developing a multi-faceted theme. This would not necessarily require an interpreter to argue that an author or editor in each case is picking up and further developing the motif or theme in conscious dependence or reflection on a specific text or specific texts.

Additionally, I noted that (1) the establishment of literary dependence and the determination of the direction of borrowing are notoriously difficult, especially given the disputed compositional histories of the individual books within the Hebrew canon, and that (2) a reader will respond to obvious verbal correspondence regardless of its nature and origin. Accordingly, I offered a modified approach to intertextuality in a 2010 essay (Schultz 2010, 19–31), drawing on the intertextual theory of the French literary scholar Michael Riffaterre. His methodological emphases include noting the "layering of meaning" resulting from intertexts, asserting the independence of textual meaning from intertextual awareness, giving greater attention to intertexts that are clearly marked, and legitimating the use of later texts to shed interpretive light on earlier texts (Schultz 2010, 31, summarizing 26–29). I will also use this modified approach in examining some of the intertextual relationships between Job and Ecclesiastes.

Given the thematic and epistemological affinities that many scholars have noted between Job and Ecclesiastes,[2] it is surprising that little attention has been given to their intertextual relations. For example, Yohan Pyeon, in his monograph *You Have Not Spoken What Is Right About Me: Intertextuality and the Book of Job* (2003), gives no examples from Ecclesiastes.[3] An exception is Antoon Schoors' essay "(Mis)Use of Intertextuality in Qoheleth Exegesis" in which he cites three parallels (also noted by other scholars): (1) Eccl 3:20; 12:7a//Job 34:14–15, (2) Eccl 8:4 //Job 9:12, and (3) Eccl 5:14(15)//Job 1:21a (Schoors 2000, 46–47). Unlike most Job commentaries, which, in their introductory sections, note no parallels between these two books, Dhorme lists six parallels, which will be discussed below.[4]

This warrants an initial observation: Given how closely aligned Job and Ecclesiastes are in some of their major themes, it is striking how few explicit intertextual links can be noted between them; Job clearly has more verbal affinities with Psalms and Isaiah than with Ecclesiastes. This prompts Claude Cox (2007, 70) to conclude: "Though there is no direct line between Job and Ecclesiastes—for example, the latter never quotes or alludes to the former—they do share an interest in moving beyond simple maxims to take up the big questions of life." Is this, in fact, the case? Drawing on the methodology that I have just sketched, I will consider the validity and significance of intertextual links previously cited by various commentators.

2. According to O'Dowd (2009, 160–61), both books "oppose false ways of knowing," test "traditional wisdom against the perceptions of the lived life," and "undercut the human proclivity to certainty."

3. The same is true of Mettinger's essay (1993). An essay by Segal (1949, 45) mentions Ecclesiastes only once and not as a primary parallel, referring to Eccl 5:10 though appearing to have 5:14 in mind.

4. Dhorme 1984, clxxii–clxxiii. He labels one of these (Job 9:12//Eccl 8:4) as "proverbial" and therefore less significant. Hartley (1988, 12–13) only notes one parallel which Dhorme and others previously listed, as well. A thorough examination of the parallel passages listed in Torrey 2002 yielded no additional parallels with significant verbal and syntactical correspondence.

Intertextual Verbal Links Between Job and Ecclesiastes

Job 1:21//Ecclesiastes 5:14(15)

The initial and most frequently cited intertextual link between these two books is found in Job 1:21//Eccl 5:14(15):[5]

ויאמר ערם יצתי [יצאתי] מבטן אמי וערם אשוב שמה
יהוה נתן ויהוה לקח יהי שם יהוה מברך:

He said, "Naked I came from my mother's womb, and naked I shall return there. The LORD gave and the LORD has taken away. Blessed be the name of the LORD." (Job 1:21, NASB)

כאשר יצא מבטן אמו ערום ישוב ללכת כשבא
ומאומה לא־ישא בעמלו שילך בידו:

As he had come naked from his mother's womb, so will he return as he came.[6] He will take nothing from the fruit of his labor that he can carry in his hand. (Eccl 5:14[15], NASB)

Job 1:21 gives Job's entire response to the first wave of losses (children and animals) and is evaluated by the narrator in v. 22 as thereby avoiding sin by not accusing God of wrongdoing (ולא־נתן תפלה לאלהים). Accordingly, Job's remarks are formulated as a first-person existential statement introduced by "He said"; Eccl 5:14(15) is a generic third-person assertion. The initial clause of Job 1:21 (ערם יצאתי[7] מבטן אמי וערם אשוב שמה) closely parallels Eccl 5:14(15) (כאשר יצא מבטן אמו ערום ישוב ללכת כשבא). These texts are the only two occurrences of the verbal expression יצא מבטן אם in the Hebrew Bible, even though this could be an idiomatic expression for childbirth. These are also the only two texts that use the word "naked" (ערום) to refer to the state of a newborn, both also emphasizing the word by placing it at the beginning of the clause. A further feature that links these two texts is the surprising use of שוב to reverse the action of יצא. In the case of Job 1:21, it is unclear what is meant by "I shall return there" (NASB, אשוב שמה). Does Job really expect to return to his mother's womb? Clines suggests that "there" serves as a euphemism for the underworld or, more likely, refers to the womb of

---

5. When the Hebrew versification differs from the English translations, the English verse reference will be noted in brackets. All biblical citations are the NRSV except where noted.

6. The Masoretic accents indicate that "naked" belongs with "return" in the second clause rather than in the initial clause, as the JPS correctly translates it: "naked he shall go back."

7. Reading יצאתי with several MSS and *qere*.

Mother Earth, noting how the womb and earth as also linked in Ps 139:13, 15 (Clines 1989, 36–37).

The rarity of the shared expressions in these two texts makes it likely that some type of verbal dependence is present here. Although it is notoriously difficult to determine the direction of any borrowing between biblical texts, the possibility that Ecclesiastes is modifying Job is attractive. Both contexts use "naked" in the twofold sense of both "unclothed" and "bereft of possessions." Job has just lost his oxen, donkeys, camels, and servants, a primary measure of wealth in that period. Ecclesiastes 5:13(14) describes a similar situation: "those riches were lost in a bad venture (בעניין רע)" (NIV: "through some misfortune"). The expression used here need not refer to a poor investment (cf. 4:8—"an unhappy business") and could be used to describe Job's recent financial losses, as well. Ecclesiastes reinforces the metaphorical use of the word naked here by repeating the phrase "nothing in his hand" (my translation) in vv. 13(14) (ואין בידו מאומה) and 14(15) (בידו...מאומה־לא ישא). The first-person expression of Job understandably would be generalized and changed to third person in Ecclesiastes, since Qoheleth is evaluating "a grievous ill" that he has *seen* (יש רעה חולה ראיתי) rather than personally experienced (5:12[13]).[8] The more gnomic formulation is reinforced by the addition of כאשר, the preferred manner of expressing comparison or equivalence for the author of Ecclesiastes (see also Eccl 11:5). Then it also would be understandable that Ecclesiastes would also simplify the puzzling expression in Job 1:21, "return there," to simply "return." The latter would be clarified by the intratextual link to Eccl 3:20: "all are from the dust, and all turn to dust again" (הכל היה מן־העפר והכל שב אל־העפר; see also Eccl 12:7). Schoors notes a further modification in Ecclesiastes.[9] By beginning the verse with "As" (כאשר), rather than "Naked" as in Job 1:21a, and then adding "departing as he arrived" (my translation; כשבא ללכת) after "return," Qoheleth emphasizes the naked state of both the newborn and the deceased rather than their enigmatic destination.[10]

---

8. Even if dependent on Job, the author of Ecclesiastes is not referring to Job's experience, since Eccl 5:13(14) refers here only to a single child.

9. Schoors 2000, 47. Schoors draws here on the essay of Vall 1995, 325–42.

10. Given the prominence of the theme of death in Job and Ecclesiastes, it is not surprising that they employ similar expressions to describe it, such as the return to dust in Job 10:9 (ואל־עפר תשיבני, "and will you turn me to dust again?") and Eccl 12:7 (וישב העפר על־הארץ כשהיה, "and the dust returns to the earth as it was"). Both texts may well allude to Gen 3:19 (cf. 2:7), but it is unclear that either wisdom text depends on the other, especially in light of the divergent use of the Hebrew verb שוב in these two phrases and the intratextual parallels between Eccl 12:7 and 3:20, as

Whether or not one is convinced by a diachronic argument for the dependence of Ecclesiastes on Job, from a synchronic perspective, the reader who is familiar with Job will likely recall Job 1:21 when reading Eccl 5:14(15) and note the similar contexts and emphases and may note the key differences. Whether engaging in a diachronic or a synchronic analysis, there appears to be one striking difference. Job speaks these words while prostrating himself (Job 1:20: "and fell on the ground and worshiped"), attributing both the earlier acquisition and the recent loss of his material possessions to the LORD and nevertheless blessing the LORD: "the LORD gave, and the LORD has taken away; blessed be the name of the LORD" (Job 1:21). He does this despite the narrator's explicit mention of the Sabeans and Chaldeans (and Satan) as the direct perpetrators of these destructive actions. Qoheleth, in contrast, in the immediate context (5:9–16 [10–17]) portrays the gaining and losing of wealth as an exclusively this-worldly process. In the larger context, however, taking 5:9–6:9(5:10–6:9) as a carefully designed thematic unit on wealth,[11] Qoheleth describes the acquisition, loss, and (non-)enjoyment of wealth as directly dependent on God (see 5:17–6:2[5:18–6:2]). Although not using the language of blessing, Eccl 5:18(19) does call wealth, possessions, and their enjoyment "the gift of God" (מתת אלהים). Thus, despite the apparent divergence there is actually a striking agreement between Job and Ecclesiastes with regard to this topic, as presented in these two texts, and the close verbal correspondence between Job 1:21 and 5:14(15) invites the reader to consider them together.

Job 3:16//Ecclesiastes 6:3b–5
A second verbal parallel cited by Dhorme also refers to birth but, in this case, to a stillborn child:

well as between Job 10:9 and 34:15 (ואדם על־עפר ישוב, "and all mortals return to dust"). Dhorme (1984, clxxii) lists an additional parallel related to death, namely, between Job 14:21–22 and Eccl 9:5–6. The parallel here is not very close, however. Their verbal correspondence solely consists of their use of the negated Hebrew verb "to know," albeit expressed in a syntactically divergent manner (Job 14:21: ולא ידע// Eccl 9:5: אינם יודעים מאומה). Therefore this is best described as a *thematic* parallel, since both texts make an assertion about deceased individuals' lack of post-mortem knowledge, though Eccl 9:6 also emphasizes their lack of post-mortem participation in "under the sun" events.

11. Introduction (5:9–11[10–12]), negative portrait (5:12–16[13–17]), positive portrait (5:17–19[18–20]), negative portrait (6:1–6), conclusion (6:7–9). See Fredericks 1989.

או כנפל טמון לא אהיה כעללים לא־ראו אור:

Or why was I not buried like a stillborn child, like an infant that never
sees the light? (Job 3:16)

אמרתי טוב ממנו הנפל:
כי־בהבל בא ובחשך ילך ובחשך שמו יכסה:
גם־שמש לא־ראה ולא ידע נחת לזה מזה:

I say that a stillborn child is better off than he. / For it comes into vanity
and goes into darkness, and in darkness its name is covered; / moreover it
has not seen the sun or known anything; yet it finds rest rather than he.
(Eccl 6:3b–5)

The most significant verbal link between these two texts is the use of the
rare word for "stillborn," נפל, which occurs elsewhere in the Hebrew
Bible only in Ps 58:9(8). Psalm 58:9(8) is an isolated clause—"like the
untimely birth that never sees the sun" (נפל אשת בל־חזו שמש), the only
other text in the Hebrew Bible which uses the verb חזה to express "seeing the sun/light." The expression "to see [the] sun" using the Hebrew
verb ראה, as in Eccl 6:5, occurs in Deut 4:19 and elsewhere in Eccl 7:11
and 11:7. The expression "to see light" is more common in BH, occurring eight times (Gen 1:4; Job 3:16; 31:26; 33:28; 37:21; Pss 36:9[8];
49:20[19]; Isa 9:1[2]). It is interesting to note that the one expression is
favored in Ecclesiastes (which also reminds one of its repeated use of
"under the sun," 27×) while the other is preferred by Job. In sum, then,
all three references to a stillborn in the Hebrew Bible include the
description "not seeing light/sun."

Job 3:16 and Eccl 6:3b–5 are further linked in three ways: (1) the
stillborn is also described as experiencing "rest" (Job 3:7 [ינוחון]; Eccl 6:5
[נחת]); (2) the stillborn's fate is considered to be preferable to that of the
living—this is the emphasis of the entirety of Job 3, while in Eccl 6:3 it
is clearly stated as "a stillborn child is better off than he"; (3) depending
on how one understands the verb "buried" (טמון) in Job 3:16 (NIV:
"hidden"), this could be paralleled by the phrase "in darkness its name is
covered" (ובחשך שמו יכסה)[12] and by the reference to burial earlier in
Eccl 6:3.

Fredericks refers to these parallels, noting that the "preference" for
"definitive, premature death" in Eccl 6 is "not unique in the OT… Job
uses the same metaphors of darkness, light and rest" (Fredericks and
Estes 2010, 55). Can more be said regarding this parallel? These parallel
texts clearly lack the close verbal and syntactical correspondence that
characterize Job 1:21//Eccl 5:14(15), but despite the similarity in

12. "Darkness" (חשך) is also mentioned in Job 3:4, 5, 9.

formulation between Eccl 6:3b–5 and Ps 58:9(8), the multiple links between Job 3:16 and Eccl 6 indicate the presence of more than a similar metaphor, suggesting rather that one of the texts may involve an allusion to the other. As in Job 1:21//Eccl 5:14(15), this verbal parallel reflects the difference between Job's first-person perspective and Qoheleth's more general comments, as well as some wording differences, noted above, that reflect the preferences of each book. Within the flow of the discourse of Ecclesiastes, 6:3b–5 echoes and sharpens the sentiments of Eccl 4:2–3: "And I thought the dead, who have already died, more fortunate than the living, who are still alive; / but better than both is the one who has not yet been, and has not seen the evil deeds that are done under the sun." (The expression "better than" with טוב מן is also a favored formulation for Qoheleth which is absent from Job.)

One could employ similar arguments as with Job 1:21//Eccl 5:14(15) to claim that Ecclesiastes is dependent on Job, but the case is weaker here, though bolstered by the fact that Job 1:21//Eccl 5:14(15) involves the first "negative portrait" of wealth in Eccl 5:9–6:9(5:10–6:9), while this verbal parallel involves the second (see n. 11). Here again, however, the intertextual connection is sufficient to lead the competent reader to relate the two texts, noting that the two contexts and thematic emphases are similar. Job 3 is developed more fully and emotionally, beginning with Job's curse against his day of birth (3:1), while the individual contrasted with the stillborn in Eccl 6 is one who has possessions (and potentially many children and long life) yet is unable to enjoy them. For Qoheleth, wealth lost as well as wealth not enjoyed are both "grievous evils" (5:12 [רעה חולה], 13]; 15 [רעה חולה, 16]; 6:2 [חלי רע]) to which even death is preferable.

Job 9:12//Ecclesiastes 8:4

The next parallel noted by Dhorme is Job 9:12//Eccl 8:4:

הן יחתף מי ישיבנו מי־יאמר אליו מה־תעשה׃

He [i.e. God] snatches away; who can stop him? Who will say to him, "What are you doing?" (Job 9:12)

באשר דבר־מלך שלטון ומי יאמר־לו מה־תעשה׃

For the word of the king is powerful, and who can say to him, "What are you doing?" (Eccl 8:4)

Dhorme notes an additional parallel in Dan 4:32(35): "There is no one who can stay his [i.e. God's] hand or say to him, 'What are you doing?'" (ולא איתי די־ימחא בידה ויאמר לה מה עבדת). Not only is this claimed parallel in Aramaic, but it is also more of a thematic parallel expressing

God's irresistible power while displaying less verbal and syntactical correspondence.[13]

Is this merely a proverbial expression, as Dhorme (1984, clxxiii) claims? Although the interrogative particle "what" (מַה) is followed directly by some form of the verb "do" (עשׂה) 74 times in the Hebrew Bible, only six times does it occur with the second masculine imperfect verbal form (Josh 7:9; Job 9:12; 35:6; Prov 25:8; Eccl 8:4; Isa 45:9), and only Job 9:12//Eccl 8:4 and Isa 45:9 ("Does the clay say to the one who fashions it, 'What are you making'? or 'Your work has no handles'?") are formulated as a question in addition to being preceded by a question. Job 9:12//Eccl 8:4 are striking in that, in both texts, the basic question is preceded by an almost identical question: מִי־יֹאמַר אֵלָיו מַה־תַּעֲשֶׂה. Given the fact that four of the five words in this phrase as well as the syntax are identical, with the only difference being an interchangeable preposition. Furthermore, Dhorme does not explain what he means by "the proverbial character of the idea expressed" in this parallel, and it does not seem to be proverbial in either form or content.

It is worth noting here that, although these two texts have different referents—God in Job and the ruler in Ecclesiastes—they represent the two most powerful authorities operating on earth. Job 9:12, in effect, summarizes Job's emphasis in ch. 9 on one's utter inability to contend with or resist God's actions. Though focusing on the "power differential" (v. 19: "If it is a contest of strength, he is the strong one!"), Job's question may also reflect God's "knowledge differential" ("He is wise in heart, and mighty in strength" [Job 9:4]; "How then can I answer him, choosing my words with him?" [Job 9:14]), anticipating developments later in the book.[14] Either way, the futility of Job's efforts is highlighted.

The book of Ecclesiastes gives much more attention than Job to rulers and the abuse of authority, climaxing in ch. 8 (see Garrett 1987). Ecclesiastes 8:4 warns against the folly of rebelling against a ruler. Since I have tentatively suggested for the preceding two verbal pairs that Ecclesiastes might be dependent on Job rather than vice versa, it is worth considering whether reading the former in light of the latter might clarify the development of thought within Eccl 8:2–8. The initial command in 8:2, "Keep the king's command" (lit. "mouth"), parallels the concluding instruction in Eccl 12:13 to "fear God and keep his commandments," both verses using the same Hebrew imperatival form (שְׁמוֹר).

---

13. Dhorme 1984, clxxii–clxxiii. For example, the question in Daniel is not preceded by a question and the "do" verb is a perfect, not an imperfect form, as in Job and Ecclesiastes.

14. Compare also Job 12:13, 17, 21.

Similarly, the twofold use of the admonition אל־תבהל in Eccl 5:1(2) and 8:3, both with the meaning "do not be hasty,"[15] indicates that haste before both God and the ruler can be hazardous to one's health! The final clause in Eccl 8:3 (כי כל־אשר יחפץ יעשה, "for he does whatever he pleases") leads to the double question in v. 4. Since the ruler's word is powerful, one is not in a position to resist his actions. Thus the same attitude of caution and obedience is to mark one's attitude toward both God and the ruler.

God and the ruler are even more closely linked by the explanatory clause following the imperative in Eccl 8:2, "because of your divine oath" (ועל דברת שבועת אלהים), literally "the oath of God," more likely here to be an objective rather than a subjective genitive. 1 Kings 2:43 offers the closest parallel: "Why then have you not kept your oath to the LORD?" (ומדוע לא שמרת את שבעת יהוה). Ecclesiastes 8:2b may imply that the king's authority is delegated, so that submitting to the ruler may express submission to God. More clearly, however, both God and the king possess an authority that is not to be questioned, an authority that is highlighted by the fourfold use of the Hebrew root שלט in ch. 8 (vv. 4, 8 [2×], 9).[16] This would warrant the use of the same phrase in Job 9:12 and in Eccl 8:4 with different referents.

Job 34:14–15//Ecclesiastes 12:7 and 3:20
God's sovereign control over death itself is affirmed in another parallel, Job 34:14–15//Eccl 12:7 and 3:20, cited by both Dhorme and Schoors:

אם־ישים אליו לבו רוחו ונשמתו אליו יאסף׃
יגוע כל־בשר יחד ואדם על־עפר ישוב׃

If he should take back his spirit to himself, and gather to himself his breath, / all flesh would perish together, and all mortals return to dust. (Job 34:14–15)

וישב העפר על־הארץ כשהיה והרוח תשוב אל־האלהים אשר נתנה׃

and the dust returns to the earth as it was, and the breath returns to God who gave it. (Eccl 12:7)

הכל הולך אל־מקום אחד הכל היה מן־העפר והכל שב אל־העפר׃

All go to one place; all are from the dust, and all turn [NIV: "return"] to dust again. (Eccl 3:20)

15. In Eccl 8:3 the NIV ("Do not be in a hurry") is to be preferred to the NRSV ("Do not be terrified"). Compare also Eccl 7:9.

16. Eccl 8:8 may point indirectly to the limits of the ruler's power, unlike God.

The idea of the human spirit or breath (נשמה) being gathered (with אסף) is also found in Ps 104:29b:[17] "when you take away their breath, they die and return to their dust."

תסף רוחם יגועון ואל־עפרם ישובון׃

The verbal correspondence between Job 34:14–15 and Ps 104:29b is so close and extensive, including the use of גוע for "die" (eight times in Job), that some type of dependence seems likely here, one text either expanding or abbreviating the other. This raises the question of whether Ecclesiastes has been influenced here by Ps 104 rather than by Job 34. (Both Eccl 3:20 and Ps 104:29, as well as Gen 3:19, use the directive preposition עפר + אל rather than עפר + על, as in Job 34:15.)

The verbal correspondence between Job 34:14–15 and Eccl 12:7 certainly is minimal, consisting of merely the common use of the words עפר, רוח and שוב. The expression "and the breath returns to God who gave it" in Eccl 12:7, which may recall Eccl 3:21, "the human spirit goes upward,"[18] is a more passive way to say "If he should take back his spirit to himself, and gather to himself his breath," as in Job. Job 34:15 (ואדם על־עפר ישוב) admittedly more closely parallels Eccl 3:20 (הכל היה מן־העפר והכל שב אל־העפר), but it is likely that both Eccl 3:20 and 12:7 are dependent rather on Gen 3:19 (Clemens 1994, 5–8):

בזעת אפיך תאכל לחם עד שובך אל־האדמה כי ממנה לקחת
כי־עפר אתה ואל־עפר תשוב׃

> By the sweat of your face you shall eat bread until you return to the ground, for out of it you were taken; you are dust, and to dust you shall return.

In this case, the unparalleled expression על־הארץ in Eccl 12:7 would derive from אל־האדמה in Gen 3:19. In sum, in light of the striking divergences in wording between Job 34:14–15 and Eccl 3:20; 12:7, one can conclude that Job and Ecclesiastes are in agreement regarding God's control over the human spirit and thus over the termination of life and of the "dusty" destiny of human remains, but verbal dependence is uncertain.[19]

17. See also Judg 18:25 with נפש and Prov 30:4 (although רוח here means "wind").

18. For a discussion of whether Eccl 12:7 instead *contradicts* Eccl 3:21, see Longman 1998, 273. This depends largely on how one translates and understands the rhetorical thrust of the "Who knows…?" question in 3:21.

19. See also the discussion of these parallel verses in n. 10 above. The same probably is true of a final parallel cited by Dhorme (1984, clxxii)—Job 38:24//Eccl 11:5, in which "way" (דרך) is the only word found in both texts. If one follows the

Dhorme, the Job commentator whose list of parallels I have reexamined here, offers an appropriately modest summary of Job's influence on Ecclesiastes (Dhorme 1984, clxxii–clxxiii):

> The author of Ecclesiastes has perhaps taken from Job certain touches on the necessity of leaving everything at the moment of death, the abortion which is preferable to a birth, the unconsciousness of those who go down to Sheol, the origin and the end of things. But these two authors are so deeply original that they can have the same idea and imagery without the Book of Job having any direct influence on Ecclesiastes. The resemblance of Job 9:12 to Ec 8:4 (and also Dn 4:32) is due to the proverbial character of the idea expressed.

In employing my own strict criteria for identifying verbal parallels, I have disputed Dhorme's claim regarding Job 9:12 and Eccl 8:4 and argued that some of the noted parallels may involve verbal dependence while others simply reflect conceptual agreement. In all of the texts involved, however, these two sages express the same viewpoint regarding the topics addressed.

Conceptual Links Between Job and Ecclesiastes

As my discussion in the preceding section indicates, if one uses as criteria extensive verbal and syntactical correspondences between Job and Ecclesiastes, there are surprisingly few intertextual links between these two wisdom texts. But if one lowers the threshold, focusing instead on their similar use of key terms, a whole new horizon of intertextual readings opens up. That is, if one reads Job in light of the most significant repeated words of Ecclesiastes (or vice versa),[20] new areas of agreement, disagreement, and divergence emerge between these two texts. Of course, one author could intentionally use the key terms of another author/book in order to forge a conceptual link between two literary works by drawing on and further developing one or more of its major themes, but it would be difficult to demonstrate this. Even so, attentive

---

NIV, "As you do not know the path of the wind, or how the body is formed in a mother's womb," both Job and Ecclesiastes affirm human ignorance regarding the wind's course. It probably is preferable, however, to see a wordplay involving wind/Spirit (רוח) in Eccl 11:4–5, as indicated by the NRSV translation of v. 5—"Just as you do not know how the breath comes to the bones in the mother's womb"—in which case the meteorological parallel with Job 38:24 vanishes.

20. I am taking this approach simply because I have spent more time studying Ecclesiastes than studying Job and thus am more familiar with its terminology.

readers will likely note these thematic parallels, potentially enriching their readings of both books.

There are a number of shared terms that could merit such comparison: "time" (עת: Ecclesiastes, 40×; Job, 10×); "toil" (עמל [noun and verb]: Ecclesiastes, 35×; Job, 10×); "vanity" (הבל: Ecclesiastes, 38×; Job, 6×); "joy/rejoice" (שמח/שמחה [noun and verb]: Ecclesiastes, 17×; Job, 6×); "wind/spirit/Spirit" (רוח: Ecclesiastes, 24×; Job, 33×); "remember/remembrance" (זכר/זכרן: Ecclesiastes, 8×; Job, 12×); "portion/distribute" (חלק [noun and verb]: Ecclesiastes, 8×; Job, 9×).

Let me give just a brief sampling of this type of intertextual reading. Although Job does not offer a fully developed concept of the proper time such as one finds in Eccl 3:1–8 and 8:6 (Schultz 2005), Eliphaz, like Qoheleth, speaks of those who die at the appropriate time (בעתו, Job 5:26; cf. Eccl 3:2) as well as of the wicked who die prematurely (Job 22:16; cf. Eccl 7:17). Job, however, bemoans the fact that God apparently has not "set times" (Job 24:1)—presumably for the judgment of the wicked, in light of the descriptions of theft, injustice, and neglect of the needy in 24:2–12.[21] Qoheleth, however, maintains his confidence that divine judgment is coming, even if not now (Eccl 3:17). Ecclesiastes also speaks of "a time to be born" (Eccl 3:2); for Job this extends even to the wild animals (Job 39:1–3). Qoheleth claims that there is a set time for everything (Eccl 3:1); for Job, even the constellations have an assigned time for their movement (Job 38:32).[22]

In Ecclesiastes, the concept of הבל is thematically dominant, bracketing the book in 1:2 and 12:8, even though its proper translation and nuance continue to be disputed.[23] Job uses this noun only five times (Job 7:16; 9:29; 21:34; 27:12; 35:16), but the attentive reader who is familiar with Ecclesiastes will likely give attention to how Job uses this term, as well. Job 7:16 presents the same interpretive dilemma as the word הבל does in Ecclesiastes. Are Job's days without "meaning" (הבל, so NIV) and therefore despised by him (מאסתי), or are they insubstantial and brief ("breath," as in NRSV, NASB, and NKJV), not lasting forever (לא־לעלם), and thus unworthy of high regard? The preceding verse, Job 7:15 ("so that I would choose strangling and death rather than this body"), would

---

21. See the NIV and NJPS. Clines (2006, 601–2) sees here a reference to scheduled court sessions.

22. One also finds a more developed view of the enduring dimension of time in Ecclesiastes, i.e., 'eternity' (עלם; cf. especially Eccl 3:11, 14; 12:5). In Job 7:16, Job merely states his desire not to live "forever," without thereby implying the possibility of doing so.

23. See the recent summary of the options by Bartholomew 2009, 104–7.

appear to support the former. Job considers any effort to defend his innocence to be הבל (i.e. futile; 9:29), the same as Qoheleth's description of any effort to gain a permanent advantage by being wise (Eccl 2:15). Additionally, both Job and Ecclesiastes concede that human words can lack value and substance (Job 21:34; 27:12; 35:16; Eccl 5:6[7]; 6:11). Despite this agreement, the הבל-prone state of life "under the sun" is a major burden only for the author of Ecclesiastes.

Comparing the thematic emphases of Job and Ecclesiastes by means of close verbal parallels and broader conceptual (i.e. key word) links are only two possible ways of relating these two books. For example, these two books frequently address the subject of wisdom and folly, employing a wide range of terms and descriptions in the process, though no close verbal parallels connect these books with reference to this theme. While they express similar perspectives on the divine origin and relative but limited value of wisdom (Schultz 1997, 281–85),[24] Job emphasizes God's wisdom and Ecclesiastes focuses more on human efforts to acquire and employ wisdom. This is similar to what I have found in examining closer intertextual parallels between these books. At no point did I find them to offer contrasting viewpoints, despite divergent emphases. As a protesting pair within the canon, Job and Ecclesiastes stand in solidarity against overly optimistic views of the benefits of wisdom and wise living.

24. Here it is interesting to note that Job contains no "better than" sayings, in contrast with Ecclesiastes, cf. Eccl 4:13; 7:5; 9:16, 18.

THE INEVITABILITY OF READING JOB
THROUGH LAMENTATIONS

James K. Aitken

The Intertextual Relationship

There is undeniably a thematic connection between the books of Job and Lamentations. Both reflect on the themes of suffering and calamity; one expressed through personal experience and the other collective. Allusions in Job to psalms of lament rather than to the book of Lamentations have regularly been noted (e.g. Mandolfo 2007a, 2007b), but this does suggest that there could be shared themes with Lamentations itself. And yet the relation between the two books is rarely explored, Lamentations more often being seen in its relation to Deutero-Isaiah (e.g. Tull Willey 1997, 188–93; Linafelt 2000, 66–79). The lack of attention to the relation between these particular books in part can be attributed to uncertainty over their dates. It seems highly likely that Lamentations is to be dated to the exilic period and possibly early on in that era.[1] Job could also be dated to the same time if we take the character's suffering as emblematic of exilic experience, although numerous suggestions have been made for the date of the book. Doubt as to which book came first, or indeed whether the authors were contemporary but unaware of each other, renders it difficult to argue for any diachronic relation between the books. Were we able to identify an explicit allusion we would be able to establish the chronological sequence of one to the other. Of greater significance, though, is the fact that there simply does not seem to be dependence of one on the other or any place where a clear allusion is made between the texts. As we shall see, there are many tantalizing thematic and lexical correspondences, but none that can definitively be said to have been in the mind of either author.

---

1. For the date and setting of the book, the latest detailed discussion is that of Middlemas 2005, esp. 177–84.

Intertextuality in the sense in which it was coined by Kristeva (1969b; English translation 1980a) does allow us, however, to consider the relation. For, in those terms the presupposition of other texts is required for a text to have meaning. There is a dialogic engagement between the texts as they participate in a practice of encoding and recoding. As modern readers we inevitably have both texts in our minds as we read, and we cannot but make the connections ourselves. This leads, though, to an ambiguous participation of one text in another's exposition. While intertextuality can show to us how the one text is read in new ways and interpreted differently in the light of the other, it also shows how we cannot escape from the inevitable reading. We are bound to read the one in the light of the other, and therefore we cannot read it in ways not guided by those other texts. Our reading of the one is colonized by the other, as memory of one imports itself onto the other.

We will first consider here how far we might see a diachronic relationship,[2] namely, of intentional allusion to Lamentations in Job, and the few attempts among scholars to argue for such a relationship. Strikingly, the relation between the two texts has been recognized in pre-modern scholarship, as it is embedded in Jewish tradition. Despite that, there is a weak case for intentional allusion between the two books, although we are inevitably bound to read the two books in the light of each other. Reading the two books together will draw attention to certain themes that are highlighted by such intertextuality. As a result there is an inevitability to the reading that is already enshrined in our view of the book; indeed, the similar themes in both books arouse some surprise that there has been such a lack of interest in an intertextual perspective between the two.

Jewish Tradition

The surprising fact that the connections between the two books have not been more thoroughly explored is thrown into sharp focus by the attention given them in rabbinic literature. Jewish tradition has it that both are permitted to be read on the fast of Tisha b'Av, commemorating the destruction of the Temples. The study of the Torah for once is banned on this day,[3] with the exception, according to a Talmudic baraita (*b. Ta'an.* 30a), of the reading of Lamentations, Job and certain chapters from Jeremiah, if only the "sections of Jeremiah which deal with calamity."[4]

---

2. Adopting the terms of G. D. Miller 2011.

3. Cf. *m. Ta'an.* 4.6, since gladness must be diminished.

4. See Brady (2003, 4–6), including the introduction of the reading of blessings and curses from Lev 26 (*Sop.* 42a). On Job in liturgy, cf. Alexander 2008, 76.

Their thematic relationship is expressly recognized through this. None-theless, the Targumim, despite their role within the liturgy and the wider rabbinic recognition of the relation, hardly draw on one for the other. Thus Tg. Job 3:5 makes mention of the destruction of the Temple in a list of troubles, but seems not to have any explicit cognition of Lamentations. Tg. Lamentations by contrast does draw on Job to explicate certain verses,[5] but has no consistent exegetical approach to the relationship between the two.[6] And yet we find already in the early midrash *Lamentations Rabbati* (3:1 §1) R. Joshua b. Levi's view that Lam 3:1 ("I am the one [a man, גבר]")[7] is referring to Job, citing in support Job 34:7 ("Who is there [גבר] like Job"). This idea is taken up by the influential *payyetan* Eleazar Kallir, who uniquely connects Lamentations to Job 6:10 through the concept of comforting (נחם).[8] The clearest case, though, of rabbinic recognition of the intertextuality between the two books is in the *Pesiqta de Rab Kahana*.[9] This Byzantine midrash draws out the many verbal links between the two books in such a way that it is worth citing in full. It begins by associating Job with the consolations of Jeremiah through a wordplay on Job's name. Thereupon, Job is presented as representative of Israel, and therefore undergoing the same experiences as the destitute city in Lamentations:

> *All thy lovers have forgotten thee, [O Israel], they seek thee not; for I have wounded thee with the wound of an enemy* (Jer. 30:14). The words *the wound of an enemy* (אויב), however, are to be read *the wounds of Job* (איוב). Of Job it is written *The Chaldeans set themselves in three bands* (Job 1:17); and of Jerusalem it is written *The city is given into the hand of the Chaldeans* (Jer. 32:25). Of Job it is written *A fire of God* [אש] *is fallen from heaven* (Job 1:16); and of Jerusalem it is written *From on high He sent fire* [אש] *into my bones, and it prevaileth against them* (Lam. 1:13).

5.   Direct influence of Job on Lamentations in the Targum is rare. At Lam 3:15 the Targum's "gall of serpents" appears to derive from Job 20:14, "gall of asps" (although the Targum to Job reads differently there; see Alexander 2008, 147). In Lam 3:19 the Targum seems to have been influenced by Job 20:16 in its translation "serpent." Alexander (2008, 164) also notes the root in Lam 4:2 סלה II (BDB 699a), occurring in a similar context in Job 28:16, "it cannot be weighed against (estimated in) gold of Ophir" (note also Job 28:19, a connection already made by Rashi).

6.   As Alexander notes on Tg. Lam 3:1 (2008, 143), the Targum resists the temptation to identify the man.

7.   All translations are from the NRSV unless otherwise indicated.

8.   For the text see Stern (2004, 124–25), which includes a brief discussion (135 and n. 57). Cooper (2001) traces some of these connections through medieval Jewish commentators.

9.   For a critical edition, consult Mandelbaum 1987. For a discussion of its history, see Stemberger (1991, 317–22).

Of Job it is written *And he took him a potsherd* [חרש] (Job 2:8); and of Jerusalem it is written *The precious sons of Zion...how they are esteemed as earthen pitchers!* [חרש] (Lam. 4:2). Of Job it is written *So they sat down* [וישבו] *with him upon the ground* (Job 2:13); and of Jerusalem it is written *they sit* [ישבו] *on the ground, and keep silence* (Lam. 2:10). Of Job it is written *And have laid my horn in the dust* [עפר] (Job 16:15); and of Jerusalem it is written *They have cast up dust* [עפר] *upon their heads* (Lam. 2:10). Of Job it is written *Have pity upon me, have pity upon me* [חנוני], *O ye my friends* (Job 19:21); and of Jerusalem it is written *Forasmuch as I will show you no pity* [חנונה] (Jer. 16:13). Of Job it is written *For the hand* [יד] *of God hath touched me* (Job 19:21); and of Jerusalem it is written *That she hath received of the Lord's hand* [יד] *double for all her sins* (Isa. 40:2). (*Pesiq. Rab. Kah.* 16:6; trans. Braude and Kapstein 1975, 294)

The passage concludes with the reasoning that just as Job was given a double recompense (Job 42), so Jerusalem will also be given a double recompense, quoting the double "Comfort ye" of Isa 40:1. Jerusalem will one day be comforted when now there are none to comfort her. In this way the writer makes explicit the association between Job and the forsaken city of Jerusalem. We thus find that the figure of a desolated Job as an abandoned and ransacked city is present in the Jewish reception history of the book and will continue to have a force within our own readings of Job, if without conscious comparison to Lamentations.

Possible Intentional Allusions

Notwithstanding rabbinic awareness of the intertextual relation, scholarly attempts to draw out the connections between the books have been few. This is despite the fact that the figure of a suffering man (גבר) in Lam 3, as the rabbis were aware, is a fertile passage for comparison to Job. The *Pesiqta* has already identified a number of lexical parallels, and many more can be cited. Thus, the literary setting places Job in Uz in the "East" (Job 1:4), a location specified in Lamentations (Lam 4:21) as within Edom (see Habel 1985, 39–40; Clines 1989, lvii). Shared phrases and themes abound, focussing on both human experience and divine action. The wilderness is presented as a place of danger for the speakers in both (Lam 4:3, 18; Job 38:26), both characters (the city and Job) sit on the ground in mourning (Lam 2:10; Job 2:13; cf. Dhorme 1967, 23), they both express the bitterness that they feel (Job 9:18; Lam 3:15a), their stomachs churn (Lam 1:20; 2:11; cf. Job 30:27), and they become a laughingstock before their people (Job 12:4; Lam 3:14). God is also portrayed in similar fashion in each book: God sends his arrows against those suffering (Job 6:4; cf. Job 20:24; 5:17–18; Lam 3:12–15; see

Clines 1989, 171), and God's anger is vented on the day of God's wrath
(אף, Job 4:9; Lam 2:1; cf. Job 9:4, 13; 21:17; 35:15), an anger that is
presented as a punishing rod (Job 9:34–35; Lam 3:1; cf. Clines 1989,
243). General thematic parallels include wisdom-like themes in
Lamentations (Lam 3:25–30, 34–39) comparable to the speech of the
friends in Job, as noted by Dobbs-Allsopp (2002, 119–20), and the
reversal of joy and music-playing into mourning (Job 30:31; Lam 5:15).
All of these lexical and thematic similarities could be attributed, though,
to similar subject matter in both books rather than awareness by the
author of one book of the other or intentional allusions. The isolated
nature of each parallel would seem to confirm this, as much as in the
cases from the rabbinic midrashic texts, as there does not appear to be a
consistent attempt to draw from one text by another. The one possible
exception to this is the frequent allusions to Lam 3 in Job 19.

Job 16, 19 and Lamentations 3
The similarity between ch. 16 and 19 of Job and Lam 3 has been noted in
some commentaries. Habel (1985, 299–300), for example, recognizes
the siege imagery in Job 19:6 through its similarity to Lam 3:9, but does
not see a genetic relation. Clines recognizes the language of "psalmic
lament" in ch. 16, and draws various comparisons between Job and
Lamentations (e.g. Job 16:11 and Lam 2:7; Clines 1989, 383), although
others could be noted.[10]

The most sustained attempt to see a deliberate use of Lamentations by
the book of Job has been that of Lévêque (1970, 1:382–86), who believes
there is intentional citation in the book ("la principale source d'inspiration," 385). He describes Job 19 as an anthology of Lamentations, seeing
echoes of vocabulary from throughout Lamentations, especially ch. 3,
creating a mosaic of allusions. He identifies some fifteen words in
common to Job 19 and the book of Lamentations (1970, 1:384), and a
number of related themes, such as singing (Job 19:9; Lam 3:14), the
enemy (Job 19:11b; Lam 2:4b), lost hope (Job 19:10b; Lam 3:18), and
pity (Job 19:21; Lam 1:12, 18). That the chapter from Job incorporates
material from all five of the lamentations indicates both the unity of that
chapter in Job and that it must be dated later than the completion of the
book of Lamentations (Lévêque 1970, 1:385). The intention of the
allusions is the typical Joban practice of subversion of his source. An
image of God punishing Zion for its sin is reversed in Job into the image
of the experiences of an innocent sufferer, whose punishment is unjust.

---

10. The similarity of language, for example, in Job 16:8 and Lam 3 can be
observed (cf. Job 3:23; 6:4; 7:20; 10:16; 30:20).

Lévêque has been followed by Mettinger, who also makes comparison with Job 16 (1993).[11] Mettinger first notes the similarities between Job 16 and the lament genre, seen especially in Psalms but also in Lamentations (1993, 269–71). God in Job is the equivalent of the enemies in lament psalms, tearing like a wild animal (טרף, Job 16:9; cf. Pss 7:3; 17:12; 22:14) and gnashing his teeth (חרק, Job 16:9; cf. Pss 35:16; 37:12; 112:10; and Lam 2:16).[12] In addition God shooting arrows at Job (16:12–13; cf. 6:4; 34:6) seems to be a subversion of the divine archer shooting at the enemy or evildoers. Thus, for Mettinger Job is not so much alluding to a particular text, but to a whole genre of lament, and intentionally subverting it by turning God into the enemy. The absence of petition to God, however, which is so central to the lament genre (Mettinger 1993, 271), underscores this subversion or misuse of the genre (cf. Dell 1991, 110).

Specific comparison between Lamentations and Job 16 are found in the sufferer portrayed as a target (מטרא) of the divine arrows (Job 16:12; Lam 3:12), and the effect weeping has on the person (Job 16:16; Lam 1:20; 2:11; Mettinger 1993, 273). The strongest parallels, however, are to be found in Job 19, which in many ways continues the theme of Job 16 in its depiction of a hostile God. Mettinger focuses on certain terms identified by Lévêque. God is portrayed as an enemy who in a metaphor lays Job under siege in Job 19:6–12. While God enacting a siege against a person is surprising, it appears in Lam 3, where the man as personification of the besieged city Zion naturally lends itself to such imagery. Both texts speak of the blockading (גדר) of the person:

He has walled me about (גדר) so that I cannot escape. (Lam 3:7a)

He has blocked (גדר) my ways with hewn stones. (Lam 3:9a)

He has walled up (גדר) my way so that I cannot pass. (Job 19:8)

A similar imagery of God fencing someone in is found in Job 3:23 and 6:6 (cf. Clines 1989, 101). God likewise sets darkness on Job's paths (חשך, Job 19:8) and leads and makes the man sit in darkness in Lamentations (חשך, Lam 3:2, 6). This may suggest, as Mettinger proposes, that siege metaphors of a city, naturally applied in Lamentations, have generated the metaphor of attacking a human. Nevertheless, we may still wish to follow Clines, who recognizes the links between Job 19:7–12

---

11. I am grateful to Will Kynes for this reference.

12. In this Mettinger sets himself against other allusions seen in Job 16:7–17, such as Dell's view that it is a parody of passages where God strengthens a person, as in Ps 95:18–19 (1991, 130).

and Lam 3:7–9 but suggests that the imagery is of a "conventional stock available to both poets" (1989, 442). That Lévêque and Mettinger only point to a few comparisons, such as blockading and darkness, would support the idea that these are more typical features than a consistent allusion to Lamentations. Lévêque's mosaic is particularly problematic, since it does not imply a consistent allusion to one passage. As a result it is not possible to determine whether it is indeed intentionally drawing on particular sections or whether it expresses common motifs. As such there does appear to be an alignment of experience between the two books, but a distinct difference in their explanations and applications. Nevertheless, focussing on the shared experience expressed in each work does draw attention to themes that have been neglected particularly in Job and are highlighted by placing the two side by side.

Reading Job through Lamentations

The figure of the man in ch. 3 of Lamentations would be an obvious starting point for comparison. It indicates that the city as a mourning widow could also be portrayed as a person, and thereby that Job could be representative of a devastated city or country. Such a connection, however, does not do justice to the complex theological discussion in the book of Job, or the many reversals and surprises in the book that over-turn traditional biblical teaching (as Dell 1991). Rather, if we read Job in the light of the devastated city of Lamentations, our attention is drawn to certain thematic parallels. Commentators (e.g. Dhorme 1967, 29; Clines 1989, 63) have already noted the similarities between the city of Lam 1, sitting lonely, on the ground, with dust thrown on the head, and the Joban figure on the ash heap (comparing, e.g., Job 2:13 with Lam 2:10). Like Job and his friends, the elders of the city sit in silence and cast dust on their heads (cf. Josh 7:6):

> The elders of the daughter of Zion
> sit on the ground in silence;
> they have thrown dust on their heads. (Lam 2:10)

This draws attention to the dual roles of mourning and comfort in both books, and the important place in Job of the prose prologue for establishing the role of the friends and Job's predicament. The friends in particular serve an important purpose that shapes the context of the dialogues to follow.

Friends as Comforters

It was a recognized custom in ancient Israel that all mourners should have comforters (see, e.g., Olyan 2004, 46). This is recounted in David's concern for Hanun:

> Then said David, I will shew kindness unto Hanun the son of Nahash, as his father shewed kindness unto me. And David sent to comfort him by the hand of his servants for his father. And David's servants came into the land of the children of Ammon. (2 Sam 10:2)

The passage in Samuel continues that the servants are in fact comforters (2 Sam 10:3; cf. 1 Chr 19:2). This role of comforting is presented in both Job and Lamentations, but in quite different ways. The book of Lamentations dramatizes the need for comforting, portraying the devastated city of Jerusalem as a widow (Lam 1:1), and hence in mourning, and reminds the audience again and again that Jerusalem sits alone without comforters:

> ...among all her lovers she has no one to comfort her; all her friends have dealt treacherously with her, they have become her enemies. (Lam 1:2)

> ...her downfall was appalling, with none to comfort her. (1:9)

> For these things I weep; my eyes flow with tears; for a comforter is far from me, one to revive my courage. (1:16)

> Zion stretches out her hands, but there is no one to comfort her. (1:17)

> They heard how I was groaning, with no one to comfort me. (1:21)

Job's friends in similar fashion initially conform to what is expected of them, and it is explicitly stated that they set out to comfort him (Job 2:11). The introduction of friends who seek to offer consolation conforms to the proper behaviour of friends in Proverbs (e.g. Prov 12:26; 14:20; 17:17; 18:24) and to the expectations of Lamentations (cf. Davies 2010). The rich are said to have many friends (Prov 14:20; cf. 19:4), who are born to share adversity (Prov 17:17) and do not deceive with their lips (Prov 24:28), since only the godless would destroy their neighbours with their mouths (Prov 11:9). In Job the friends initially behave as they should, representing through their opinions the orthodox position. They echo Ps 37:25 ("I never saw a righteous man forsaken"), and presume Job must have done wrong to experience such suffering. However, they fail in their role, since their comfort is ineffective (Job 16:2; 21:34), leaving Job to seek an insufficient comfort in mere objects (Job 7:13; cf. 10:20). In effect the complaint of Lamentations that there is a lack of comforters is the same as Job's, for whom the comforters are ineffectual.

It is the elders' desire in Lamentations to offer comfort ("To what can I liken you, that I may comfort you," Lam 2:13), as much as it is the friends of Job.

The Mourning Rite

In the central image of Job upon his ash heap readers are confronted by the problem that the reason for Job's mourning is not clearly stated: it is ambiguous, and contributes to the characterization of the friends and their own misunderstandings. Comparison with Lamentations, where a similar mourning ritual is performed, sheds light on Job's actions. While in Lamentations the rite is clearly one of petition, in Job it is ambiguous, although commentators are for the most part content merely to identify Job as mourning without further clarification. Thus Habel, for example, speaks of "the customary rite of mourning" in 1:20, and "the traditional expressions of mourning" in 2:12 (Habel 1985, 93, 97), and Clines attributes to the sufferer in 1:20 merely the "ritual acts of mourning" (Clines 1989, 34; cf. Pope 1973, 15, 25; Tur-Sinai 1967, 19, 26). A particular problem lies in the relationship between Job's rites in chs. 1 and 2, such that Mathewson (2006, 38–39) argues that while Job could be mourning for the death of his children while on the ash heap, the second mourning rites in ch. 2 cannot be for that purpose. Job has already performed the rites in 1:20–21, such that 2:1–10 seems to be a separate narrative unit, at a time remote from the death of his children and in a section structured around the new calamity. When Job's friends arrive, upon seeing him, they also participate in mourning by weeping, tearing their clothes and throwing dust on their heads (Hebrew obscure; 2:12–13). For Clines (1989, 64), Mathewson (2006, 39) and others before them, the friends treat Job as if he is dead. They are now the ones mourning for him.

To understand the prologue, we need to identify clearly what Job might have been doing and then what the friends might have been intending. Rather than separate the two narratives of chs. 1 and 2, they can be seen as a continuity, since there is no evidence that his mourning rite in 1:20–21 had concluded or that he had moved from his spot (as Clines rightly notes). One rite might have developed into another in ch. 2. Certainly, Job in 2:8 is not to be seen as one close to death, but as one continuing the mourning rite, and in this he takes up the same position as the city of Lamentations.

The shared experiences in each book, already noted, draw attention to this comparison. In Job 1:20 the acts of rending his clothes (cf. Gen 37:9; Josh 7:6) and shaving his head (cf. Isa 15:2; Jer 7:29) are well-known signs of mourning, but some commentators also consider falling on the ground and prostrating as mourning rituals (e.g. Gordis 1978, 17; Pham 1999, 25). Others have been puzzled by Job's actions here. Clines says that the first two actions are those of mourning, but the second two a sign of Job's genuine piety (Clines 1989, 35). Lamentations, however, portrays the city members performing very similar acts: in addition to the elders' sitting on the ground and casting dust on their heads, the girls bow their heads to the ground (Lam 2:10). Lamentations presents the people as interceding for divine intervention. Such petitionary mourning is well attested, arising from disaster rather than death per se (e.g. Judith). Both Nehemiah (Neh 1:4–11) and Ezra (Ezra 9:3–15) perform mourning rites followed by prayer (Olyan 2004, 69). Since Job has also lost his livelihood through disaster, both from foreign attack and from natural catastrophes, his mourning is not merely for death. It might also be mourning for calamity, whether or not it is with a particular petitionary purpose to appease God. It is in this way a statement of Job's piety that he recognizes it is God's doing and that he must petition him. In this we come closer to the purposes of a city lament as exemplified in the book of Lamentations.

The Failed Comforters
As noted already, Job's friends recognize him as participating in the rite of mourning, and by tearing their clothes and throwing dust in the air, it may be presumed that they are also mourning. The suggestion by some that they are mourning since they think him dead does not account for their sitting with him and thereby joining him in the ritual. Rather, their sitting on the ground with him for seven days and seven nights, a standard time for mourning for the dead in some biblical traditions (cf. Gen 50:10; 1 Sam 31:13; Ezek 3:15; Sir 22:12; Jdt 16:24), indicates that they are joining him in the rite.[13] They remain silent since they respect the seven-day period, and observe the silence called upon in Lam 3:26, 28 (cf. Tur-Sinai's emendation [1967, 30]), and thereby fulfil the traditional role of comforters.[14] It is not that the friends or Job at the end of seven days cannot bear the silence anymore, as some commentators imply, or that after seven days Job is transformed as David was (Habel 1985, 98). Instead it is the traditional period that is to be respected, and therefore the friends rightly remain with him for that time. The surprise in the plot

13. They no doubt fasted too if they were joining him sitting in the one spot, as fasting would certainly accompany mourning (e.g. Neh 1:4; 2 Sam 1:12; 3:35–37; 12:23; Ezra 10:6; see Johnston 2002; Olyan 2004, 31 n. 11).

14. In Jewish tradition comforters were not permitted to say a word until the mourner opened the conversation (*b. Moʾed Qaṭ.* 28b; Pope 1973, 25).

is that Job does not end the mourning period after seven days (his friends are perhaps too naïve in thinking he might) but that instead he begins his complaint. This does imply we are moving into a different stage of mourning, and one better represented by the book of Lamentations, in which there is no immediate resolution.[15]

The comfort that the friends intend to offer is foiled since they only expected a brief period of mourning. Throughout the book it becomes clear that their comfort is offering advice based on traditional biblical wisdom, but that this is unacceptable to Job, as he declares in the first dialogue (Job 6:14–15):

> Those who withhold kindness from a friend forsake the fear of the Almighty. My companions are treacherous like a torrent-bed, like freshets that pass away.

In contrast to Lamentations, where the city has no comforters, Job has them, but they are ineffectual. It is not until the end of the book, when Job has been reconciled to God, that the friends and family are successful in their comforting:

> Then there came to him all his brothers and sisters and all who had known him before, and they ate bread with him in his house; they showed him sympathy and comforted him for all the evil that the LORD had brought upon him; and each of them gave him a piece of money and a gold ring. (Job 42:11)

In an ironic turn of fate, Job describes his former self as like one who comforts mourners (Job 29:25), although now he is the one in need of comforters.

Petitionary mourning does not seem to have any temporal constraints, as its aim is to secure the intervention of God on behalf of the petitioner (see Ezra 9–10; Joel 1–2). In this respect Job's mourning is the equivalent of the widowed city Jerusalem in Lamentations, and the comparisons noted already are striking in drawing out the expression of shared experience.[16] But the ambiguity in the mourning, and the failure of the friends in Job, leaves in the reader's mind a question over the efficacy of comforting and the nature of mourning. Lamentations is itself a traditional presentation of mourning, but without expectation of resolution since there are no comforters. In this way it is a condemnation of the

---

15. It is possible that Job is observing forty days rather than seven, another possible period of mourning in biblical tradition, but this would not account for the delineation of the seven-day period.

16. Rowley (1958, 200 n. 1) suggests an exilic setting for Job would make it hard not to draw such a comparison between Job's suffering and that of Israel.

present situation and a recognition of the extent of divine punishment. Job is not such a traditional presentation since the comfort offered is rejected, but through that rejection expectation is likewise lost. Job thereby brings into question any hope that the author of Lamentations might have had.

Conclusions

If we see in intertextuality a searching for new meaning through the dialogue between two texts, Lamentations encourages a reading of Job that brings into sharp relief the comforting role of friends. There has been a lack of attention to mourning within the book of Job, but such an intertextual reading renders both books as meditations on comfort. While we cannot with certainty assign Job to a similar time period as Lamentations, both books share similar experiences and reflect shared areas of interest. In this case Job is questioning the comforting that is lacking in Lamentations, and one wonders if there is a trace here of a dispute over the proper methods of mourning and thereby the inefficacy of certain types of comfort. Certainly, ongoing debates about mourning might have existed, reflected in the Holiness Code's restrictions on shaving and laceration (Lev 19:27–28; cf. 21:5; Deut 14:1) lest they leave long-term or permanent marks (according to the interpretation of Olyan 2004). Slightly later Ben Sira limits the length of time for mourning to seven days (Sir 22:11–12; cf. Sir 38:16), also implying mourning had become excessive in some circles. It is only through the comparison of the plea for comforting friends in Lamentations that our attention is drawn to the friends' comfort in Job.

This aspect of comfort has been little explored in Job, since the larger picture of a suffering Job has dominated tradition through scholarship, literature and art. Job on his ash heap is framed by forlorn Jerusalem lonely on the hill. Not only do both texts recount kindred struggles of suffering figures trying to reconcile their affliction with their understandings of God, but similar words and phrases comprise their conflicted anguish. In that respect the devastated city of Lamentations is the image that has colonized our view of Job. Therefore, inevitably we do see Job and Jerusalem as suffering figures, and we cannot escape that image. While Jewish tradition has drawn explicit connection between the two works, the focus in the tradition is still on the devastated city. Whatever else we might ourselves draw from the theology of Job, the perpetual intertextual dialogue between texts means Job will always be seen as the besieged city, a sufferer without comfort.

Part IV

JOB'S DIALOGUE BEYOND THE HEBREW BIBLE

"YOU DESTROY A PERSON'S HOPE": THE BOOK OF JOB AS A CONVERSATION ABOUT DEATH[*]

Christopher B. Hays

Introduction

The book of Job is a conversation about death. Or, in deference to the many things it has been to many readers over time, suffice it to say that that is one valid way to describe it. As Dan Mathewson observed, "*haśśatan*'s plan to test unmotivated piety has been set up as *a crisis of death*" (2006, 52, emphasis added).[1] The book portrays the destruction of Job's life, and then reports a conversation between Job, his friends, and God about how one should react to such a complete catastrophe.

The answers that Job entertains, and particularly the vocabulary of mythological motifs that underlies them, have a remarkable amount in common with Egyptian ideas about death and afterlife. Although Job has been most often compared to Mesopotamian literature, the Egyptian connections have been the topic of much previous scholarship based on both textual[2] and iconographic data (Keel 1978, 1981). Indeed, I have recently expanded the corpus of comparisons between Job and Egyptian texts (C. B. Hays forthcoming a, b). In this essay I step back from the minutiae of particular cases and survey the way that Egyptianizing motifs function in the book as a whole.

*   I would like to thank Carol Newsom and Dan Mathewson for their insightful comments on an earlier draft of this essay, and Sara Wells for her capable editorial assistance. Any remaining errors are my own.
1.   Walter Michel (1972, 184) notes "about 180 [expressions in Job refer] to the underworld and its realm. In addition, more than 100 different verbs are used to speak about the process of dying, going to the underworld, death, and the stay in the grave and the underworld."
2.   E.g. Gressmann 1925; Humbert 1929; Griffiths 1983; N. Herz 1913.

In a previous essay, I demonstrated that Julia Kristeva's original formulation of the concept of intertextuality explicitly invited consideration not only of literary texts, but of historical and social *con*texts as well (C. B. Hays 2008b). I argued that intertextuality should be understood not only as a literary theory but also as a historical and contextual one. Thus, the present essay is intertextual in that it shows how an author transposes and transforms materials supplied by his cultural context in the production of a new text. Within a well-known typology, the present essay should be considered a *production-oriented* approach to intertextuality;[3] that is, I argue that the Egyptianizing cultural elements found in Job would have been available to the author. Those elements probably would have been recognizable to educated hearers and readers as well, although ancient Near Eastern authors could employ esoteric wordplay for its own sake, even when it was unlikely to be understood.[4]

I am encouraged in thinking broadly about intertextual connections by Kristeva herself, who cautioned that intertextuality is not to be misunderstood in "the banal sense of 'study of sources'."[5] At times, comparative study of the Hebrew Bible in its ancient Near Eastern context has artificially limited its scope to instances of shared genre or vocabulary. By contrast, Kristeva's transformational/intertextual method encourages interpreters to consider texts within the whole cultural fabric of their environments, or as she put it, "to situate the literary structure within the social ensemble considered as a textual ensemble."[6] Job's employment of Egyptianizing imagery from different genres and a different linguistic family demonstrates the importance of conducting comparative study from this broader perspective, while still avoiding the potential errors of an ahistorical method. To be sure, this theoretical validation is not an innovation within comparative studies, it merely reinforces the subfield's best tendencies. The cultural riches of the ancient Near Eastern have been described as "treasures of darkness" (Jacobsen 1976), but year by year, the darkness shrinks as steady scholarly labor sheds greater light. The summons to comparativists is clear: to synthesize from these growing pools of data a picture of ancient Near Eastern intertextual relationships

---

3. Alkier (2005, esp. 6–11) suggests that one should distinguish between three types of intertextual interpretation: *production-oriented, reception-oriented,* and *experimental.*

4. See Rendsburg 1988, 354–56; Morrow 2010, 382; Roberts 1992; Casanowicz 1893, esp. the chart on 167; Schorch 2000.

5. "[L]e sens banal de 'critique des sources'" (Kristeva 1974, 60).

6. "La méthode transformationnelle nous mène donc à situer la structure littéraire dans l'ensemble social considéré comme un ensemble textuel" (Kristeva 1969a, 443).

that is more interconnected, more complex, and more aware of non-literary data than the one earlier generations constructed. In what follows, I am not arguing that the author of Job had direct access to the specific, identifiable Egyptian texts to which I will allude. Those texts express religious ideas that had fairly wide diffusion in the ancient Near East, and a Judean author might have come across them indirectly, for example through Phoenician mediation. For some, the difference between the terms "Egyptian" and "Egyptian*izing*" is a significant one, but I use the two terms almost interchangeably since we cannot know with any certainty how these ideas were transmitted.

Far from being naïve, this agnosticism reflects an awareness about the complexity of the ancient Near Eastern religious milieu. It is very likely that the "Egyptianizing" ideas that we may identify in Job and elsewhere actually had a significant constituency in ancient Judah, even alongside the more stringently YHWH-alone ideas of the prophets and Deuteronomists; the usual image of Yahwistic religion is highly conditioned by the theological preferences of the editors of the Hebrew Bible. For the purposes of this essay, the specific textual provenance of the ideas is not of the first importance; I call them "Egyptian" or "Egyptianizing" merely to differentiate them, because it so happens that it is in Egyptian texts that these ideas are most clearly and fully expressed. But it is the *dialogue* among various ideas within and beyond the biblical text that interests me here.

Job's Crisis of Death

One of the first and foremost answers to catastrophe that Job entertains is that death would be better than life. That outlook points to the book's similarities to pessimistic literature from various ancient cultures,[7] but the imagery of the book has particular affinities with Egyptian texts that will be summarized here. Job's "death wish" is as well known as it is unusual in the Bible, and certain elements of "foreign" religious belief about the afterlife have long been recognized as embedded within the book. This essay surveys a number of the passages concerning death and afterlife in order to show how Job plays with the ideas rhetorically, particularly with Egyptianizing hopes for the afterlife. The portrayed failure of those putatively "heretical" ideas is also what pushes the book towards its climax in the legal confrontation between Job and YHWH.

---

7. For example, the Egyptian text "Dialogue Between a Man and His Ba" (a.k.a. "The Man Who Was Weary of Life") (Lichtheim 1975, 1:163–69); or the Babylonian "Dialogue of Pessimism" (Lambert 1960, 139–49).

The death-wish that Job expresses looks both backwards and forwards. From a narrative perspective, it is contextualized by the death of Job's children and the destruction of his property in the prologue, which is sketched with maximal haste (1:13–19). Job becomes the epitome of the one who has nothing left to live for. It is not as well recognized that the prologue previews Job's hope for comfort in death. The resignation of 1:21a—"Naked I came from my mother's womb, and naked shall I return there"—is often noted, but almost none of the book's commentators remark on the *hope* this verse expresses.

The womb is of course a symbol of comfort even in our own times, but in the book's cultural context, that hope for a return has mythological significance because a return to the womb of a mother goddess was a central facet of ancient Egyptian hopes for the afterlife. In Egyptian funerary texts, there is "an astonishing consistency" throughout ancient history to the imagery of death as a return to a goddess's womb (Assmann 2005, 165–73; cf. 1989, 139–40). Images of a goddess giving birth to the deceased king as her son—causing him to "revive and live"—are found in numerous places, such as this example from the outer sarcophagus of Merneptah (thirteenth century), in which the goddess Neith says:

> I am your mother, who nurses your beauty,
> I am pregnant with you in the morning,
> and I deliver you as Re in the evening...
> When you enter me, I embrace your image,
> I am the coffin that shelters your mysterious form...
> I unite your limbs...[8]

I have argued in more detail elsewhere that such religious mythology was probably known to ancient Judean elites such as the author of Job (C. B. Hays 2008a; 2010; 2011, 60–66); the strongest argument is the presence of Egyptianizing motifs throughout the book.

The hope to return to the womb of a mother goddess is certainly not part of what became orthodoxy in postexilic Judah. (While one can affirm the diversity of religious ideas in biblical Judah in all periods, one can also speak of a nascent Yahwistic "orthodoxy," particularly in the postexilic period, to which Job's composition is most convincingly assigned.[9]) In the shape of the book as we read it now, it appears that Job

---

8. Cited in Assmann 2005. Robert K. Ritner's "A Uterine Amulet in the Oriental Institute Collection" (1984) is not strictly on topic, but does demonstrate the prominent place of womb imagery in the protecting and healing role of amulets in ancient Egypt.

9. I use the terms "orthodox" and "heterodox" with full awareness of the complexity and diversity of Israelite and Judean religions. The "orthodoxy" to which I

slips this heterodox hope into his otherwise hyper-pious exclamation, with its threefold use of the Divine Name: "YHWH gave, and YHWH has taken away; blessed be the name of YHWH" (1:21b).

The lament of Job 3 alludes to 1:21a, using the same term for womb, albeit in conjunction with a more traditional image of death as sleep:

> Why did I not die at birth,
>> come forth from the womb (בֶּטֶן) and expire?
> …
> Now I would be lying down and quiet;
>> I would be asleep; then I would be at rest (3:11, 13)

Here, death is associated with positive images of peaceful rest: both שָׁקַט (Isa 32:17; 1 Chr 22:19; Judg 3:11, etc.) and נוח frequently have positive connotations (note the combination of roots in Isa 14:7). This is not the same image as that of the dead who go to Sheol as disempowered mutes (e.g. Pss 31:18; 115:17), but rather death as a relaxing repose. This positive view of death has been compared to that of the Egyptian "Harper's Songs," funerary compositions that combine mourning and celebration (Blumenthal 1990). One such song asserts that "[the deceased] is happy… Death is a kindly fate" (Lichtheim 1975, 1:196).

Eliphaz's speech emphasizing God's justice misses the point spectacularly: "As for me, I would seek God, and to God I would commit my cause" (5:8), because "He will deliver you" (5:19). Job fires back with a speech identifying God himself as the *source* of Job's suffering (6:4). Therefore Job's next speech begins where the previous one left off, with a hope for death. Now, however, the cause of death is no longer impersonal, like a child's stillbirth (3:16), or caused by some third party, like abandonment (3:12); instead, the matter is now framed theologically as a confrontation between Job's will to die and God's apparent refusal:

> O that I might have my request,
>> and that God would grant my hope (תִקְוָתִי);
> that it would please God to crush me,
>> that he would let loose his hand and cut me off! (6:8–9)

At this point, Job abandons the idea of death as comfort and embraces death as escape. As Walter Crouch has nicely formulated it, "The will to live and the will to die are two different versions of hope" (2000, 158).

---

refer is essentially Deuteronomism, a code that was rarely if ever widely enforced in history, and is best treated as a literary construction. Nevertheless, it represents *one* of the significant streams of Judean theology. See Lang 1983 and Morton Smith 1987.

Job's Changing Hopes

"Hope" (תִקְוָה) becomes a *Stichwort* for the whole book, but Job 6:8 marks a shift in its referent. In Job's initial speech, hope is for light (3:9; although that hope is to be snuffed out). And twice in Eliphaz's opening speech (4:6; 5:16), hope is for justice and vindication from God. It recurs in the speeches of Bildad (8:13) and Zophar (11:18, 20), both of whom continue to press a "traditional" understanding of hope in God. In Job's speeches, however, hope undergoes a more complicated progression of meanings. Although he speaks in general of humans as exhausted laborers who hope for a wage (7:2)—implicitly casting God as an abusive taskmaster—he himself is "without hope" (בְּאֶפֶס תִקְוָה, v. 6). "Remember that my life is a breath," he says (7:7), looking forward to its expiration:

> The eye that beholds me will see me no more;
> while your eyes are upon me, I shall be gone.
> As the cloud fades and vanishes,
> so those who go down to Sheol do not come up. (7:8–9)

The phrase rendered "I shall be gone" by the NRSV is actually a pithier verbless construction (אֵינֶנִּי), which might better be translated: "No (more) me!" The same construction is repeated in 7:21, the final verse of Job's speech: "For now I shall lie in the earth; you will seek me—but no (more) me!" The exclamation points are an attempt to convey Job's apparent enthusiasm about the prospect of no longer existing. Again, he has given up the hope of rest and comfort in death, and retreats to the idea that at least death could be characterized by an absence of suffering.

Therefore Job vacillates between various kinds of hopes, but the matter comes into better focus as the book sets up a contrast between a hope for a contented afterlife and the afterlife that is actually offered. Job's preference for death (repeated in 10:18–19) is of course also very unusual in the Bible,[10] but it is more comprehensible if one conjectures that the author is aware of expectations of a happy afterlife like those of the Egyptians. That conjecture is supported by the image of rebirth that Job briefly entertains in 14:7–9:

> For there is hope (תִקְוָה) for a tree, if it is cut down,
> that it will sprout again,
> and that its shoots will not cease.
> Though its root grows old in the earth,
> and its stump dies in the ground,
> yet at the scent of water it will bud
> and put forth branches like a young plant.

---

10. Though not unique; see Wohlgelernter 1981.

There is a lengthy Egyptian iconographic tradition of portraying Osiris, the paradigmatic revivified one, as a tree.[11] In some manifestations, the Osiris-tree is portrayed with its base in a pool of water, a key element in Egyptian images of regeneration (Spieser 1997). Plutarch records a myth in which Seth tricks Osiris into entering a sarcophagus, which is cast into the river and eventually washes up in Byblos (i.e. on the Palestinian sea-coast), where a tree grows around it until it is fully enveloped (*Moralia* 356–57). The association with Byblos is probably not accidental, but rather a sign that the Osiris myth was known in Phoenicia, a major con-duit by which Egyptian culture reached Judah (Koemoth 2010).[12] Job's hope is entirely normal, one that is expressed in different ways in differ-ent cultures: that death would not be the end, but that life would go on.

Job briefly attempts to drive such hopes from his mind in vv. 10–12—"Mortals lie down and do not rise again"—yet he cannot dismiss his longing for revival in the afterlife, and he is willing to wait for it:

> Oh that you would hide me in Sheol,
>   that you would conceal me until your wrath (אַפְּךָ) is past,
> that you would appoint me a set time,
>   and remember me!
> If a man dies, will he live again?
> All the days of my term I would wait
>   until my relief should come.
> You would call, and I would answer you;
>   you would long for the work of your hands. (14:13–15)

It is hard to see what these verses could mean if they do not point to a hope that lies beyond judgment in the afterlife (of course, אַף commonly refers to God's judgment, but it has a particular afterlife aspect in, e.g., 4:9; 20:28; cf. Isa 66:15). Furthermore, this imagery of calling and answering, and the longing of a god for reunion with his (or her) creation is very similar to an Egyptian text from the tomb of the vizier Paser. There, Paser is depicted being embraced by his own mother, who is named in the caption. However, "Paser addresses his mother as a mani-festation of the goddess of the West," saying, "See, I have come to be at rest with you." And the mother/goddess responds, "How good it is! My heart is full of joy. My longing has been fulfilled" (Assmann 2005, 172).

---

11. See Koemoth 1993; 1994; Griffiths 1980, 31. Osiris is often thought of as a grain deity connected to vegetal fertility; suffice it to say that the Egyptians were not troubled by the multiplication of religious imagery.

12. The example of Berossus is only one indication of the extensive contacts around the Mediterranean world that had already existed before the Greco-Roman period. See also M. S. Smith 2008.

Job hopes for such a reunion with his own god, but the hope proves hard to sustain, and he descends again into despair:

> The waters wear away the stones;
>   the torrents wash away the soil of the earth;
>   so you destroy a person's hope.
> You prevail forever against him,
>   and he passes away;
> you change his countenance,
>   and send him away.
> His children are honored, and he does not know it;
>   they are brought low, and it goes unnoticed.
> He feels only the pain of his own flesh,
>   and his soul mourns because of it. (14:19–22)

Although this expression of despair about the afterlife is compatible with standard biblical disavowals of an empowered afterlife (e.g. Ps 88:11), it also reflects a tension between hope and pessimism present within Egyptian theology that is often overlooked. For example, a text from the Ramesside-period tomb of Nefersekheru mourns:

> Those in the West are in difficulty, their condition is bad.
> How motionless is the one who has gone to them.
> He cannot describe his condition.
> He rests in his lonely place,
> and eternity is with him in darkness. (Assmann 2005, 114)

The Egyptians were not uniformly optimistic about the afterlife, either. Job's abandonment of the hope of rebirth is described with further tree imagery in 19:10: "He has uprooted my hope like a tree" (ויסע כעץ תקותי). Although a tree may grow back if it is merely cut down (14:7), God denies that to Job, tearing him completely out of the ground of his hope.

Many exegetes have wanted to reduce Job's own speeches to a single view about death (Pinker 2007, 81–82), but what the book actually offers is a complex portrait of a man whose hopes flare, flicker, and recede; in short, a man who changes his mind.

The End of Job's Hope as a Turning Point

The point of despair that Job reaches by the end of ch. 14 becomes a turning point. Although another speech by Eliphaz intervenes, when Job resumes speaking in ch. 16, it is with deep exasperation concerning the supposed wisdom of his friends. They are windy and worthless, and Job sums up his indictment by saying, "I will not find a wise man among you" (17:10).

The frustration with the friends is synchronous with Job's abandonment of hope; it is at just this point that he definitively abandons the idea of embracing death:

> If I hope for Sheol as my house,
> if I make my resting-place in darkness,
> if I say to the Pit, "You are my father,"
> and to the worm, "My mother," or "My sister,"
> where then is my hope?
> Who can discern my hope? (17:13–15)

This is an extremely odd passage, except in the frame of afterlife mythology that we have already established: Job had entertained the idea of treating death as a return to family (notably to the mother in 1:21a), as a source of comfort, but he gives up that hope. He gives up hoping that death might be a return to family, which was a typical hope of ancient Near Eastern mortuary cults, and which even undergirded common biblical formulations such as "gathered to his kin" and "slept with his ancestors" (cf. Brichto 1973).

At this point, Job seems to realize that death cannot mean only reunion with family, but must also entail reunion with *God*—another vision of the afterlife well attested from ancient Syria-Palestine. It can be perceived in a muted form in the Psalms (21:4–6; 23:5–6; cf. 16:9–10) (Dahood 1966–70, 3:xlvi, xxxvi), and more plainly in an inscription by Panammuwa, king of the Aramean state of Samʾal in the eighth century. In the text written on his sarcophagus, he instructs whichever of his sons inherits his throne after he dies to make sacrifices and say to the deity Hadad: "May the soul of Panammuwa eat with you, and may the soul of Panammuwa drink with you."[13] This imagery of reunion with one's god is normally happy, but the thought of such a reunion terrifies Job, because, as he has just finished saying, it is *God* who has abused and terrorized him (16:11–14). The God to whom he goes in death is not the comforting mother he hoped for in 1:21, but Yahweh himself. He cannot go to a peaceful grave *because the God who torments him will be there waiting for him.* Although God has driven him to the point of death (19:20), still God continues to pursue him (19:20), continues to terrify him (23:15–16), and Job cannot hide even in the darkness of death (23:17).[14] Elihu also says "There is no darkness or shadow or death where those who do evil can hide from Him" (34:22), and this is the

---

13. האבל נבש פנמו עמך ותשתי נבש פנמו עמך (*KAI* 1.214:17; *COS* 2:36). See Greenfield 1973.

14. For instances of the word-pair חשך and אפל representing the darkness of death, see Job 10:21–22 and Amos 5:20.

same God who elsewhere boasts, "If they dig into Sheol, from there shall my hand take them" (Amos 9:2)—that is precisely Job's fear. His only comfort can be to establish his innocence in advance.

Therefore Job *must* confront God. He did not start off wishing to argue with God; he would rather hide in comfort and rejoin his lost family in death. It is only when his hope of escape is exhausted that he concludes it is the only way. Job's classic summons—"I would speak to the Almighty, and I desire to argue my case with God"—appears in 13:3, at the outset of the same speech where he abandons hope. Although the statements about the failure of Job's hope follow the summons to court, they are logically connected to it; they are part of the reason Job has settled on the course of action that drives the rest of the book.

Job's Legal Aspirations: Still Thinking in Egyptian Terms

Although Job gives up his initial hope for a happy afterlife, even his insistence on a hearing before God also turns out to have strongly Egyptianizing overtones. For example, there are references in biblical wisdom literature that suggest an awareness of longstanding Egyptian ideas about the judgment of the dead. The idea of judgment after death by some sort of tribunal is as ancient as the Old Kingdom; by the Middle Kingdom a distinct mythological tradition emerged in which Osiris oversaw the weighing of the heart of the deceased to determine its righteousness by the measure of Maat ($m3^ct$, "justice," both an abstract concept and a goddess). The god Thoth functioned as prosecutor; those who failed the inquisition would be drowned or devoured by the monster Ammut. Those who failed the judgment experienced the dreaded "second death." This traditional scene endured in Egyptian religious texts for thousands of years; in the Late Period, it was emblazoned in a band across the chests of sarcophagi.[15]

A key scene in the afterlife judgment in the Book of the Dead was the weighing of the heart against a feather, and references to weighing in the divine scales of justice include Job 31:6: "Let me be weighed in a just balance (מאזנים), and let God know my integrity!"[16]

An even more elaborate adaptation of the motif of the judgment of the dead appears in Job 33:22–26:

15. Gressmann 1925, 43–44; Scott 1965, 106; Griffiths 1991, 299–302.
16. Cf. Quirke 2001. E.g. Prov 21:2: "All a man's ways are right in his own eyes, but Y HWH weighs the heart" (also 16:2; 24:12). Job 6:2 might also be relevant here: "O that my vexation were weighed, and all my calamity laid in the balances (מאזנים)!"

His soul draws near the Pit,
  and his life to those who bring death.
Then, if there should be for him an angel,
  a mediator, one of a thousand,
  one who declares him upright,
  and he is gracious to him, and says,
"Deliver him from going down into the Pit;
I have found a ransom;
let his flesh become fresh with youth;
let him return to the days of his youthful vigor."

The rhetoric of restoring the flesh to youthfulness is quintessentially Egyptian—that is precisely the hope for the afterlife attested in numerous funerary texts. By contrast, such an image finds few comparisons in Semitic texts.[17]

A similar scene of afterlife judgment has been perceived in Job 19:25–27:

For I know that my redeemer lives,
  and that he will rise up last, over the dust of the earth;
and after my skin has been thus destroyed,
  then without[18] my flesh I shall see God...

Clearly, these are not precisely like the native Egyptian scenes. For example, the angelic mediator in 33:23 and the "redeemer" in 19:25 do not have a clear analogue in Egyptian texts.[19] Instead, they are adaptations, transpositions, or echoes that reflect fresh authorial creativity. But whatever one calls them, they cannot be rightly understood apart from the context provided by Egyptian culture, where their roots are wide, deep, and ancient.

There are also reflections in Job of the "negative confession" of the Book of the Dead, Spell 125, in which the deceased denies wrongdoing before his divine judges. A few lines of the lengthy composition give the sense of it:

I have committed no evil upon men.
I have not oppressed the members of my family.

17. A notable exception such as Ezek 37:1–12 should be understood to draw on a similar set of Egyptianizing imagery, extending national-resurrection imagery already introduced by the authors of Hosea and Isaiah.

18. Note the privative use of מִן also in Job 11:5; 21:9; 28:4.

19. Griffiths (1983, 196) sees in Thoth an analogue to the redeemer, but his role is typically to record the outcome of the judgment, not to support the one being judged. Job 19:25–27 is an example of a text that has echoes of Egyptian imagery but is very much adapted to a different religious context. For an analysis, see, e.g., Suriano 2010.

> I have not wrought evil in the place of right and truth…
> I have not oppressed servants.
> I have not scorned any god.
> I have not defrauded the poor of their property.
> I have not done what the gods abominate.

Job's assertion of his righteousness in 29:11–17 is reminiscent of those autobiographical assertions of goodness:

> …I delivered the poor who cried,
>   and the orphan who had no helper.
> The blessing of the wretched came upon me,
>   and I caused the widow's heart to sing for joy.
> I put on righteousness, and it clothed me;
>   my justice was like a robe and a turban.
> I was eyes to the blind,
>   and feet to the lame.
> I was a father to the needy,
>   and I championed the cause of the stranger.
> I broke the fangs of the unrighteous,
>   and made them drop their prey from their teeth.

Of course, such rhetoric of righteousness has other cognates, from Mesopotamian prayers to royal inscriptions from various places,[20] but the ensuing image that Job paints suggests that an Egyptian background figures prominently:

> Then I thought, "I shall perish among my clan,
>   and I shall multiply my days like the sand;[21]
> my roots spread out to the waters,
>   with the dew all night on my branches;
> my glory was fresh with me,
>   and my bow ever new in my hand." (29:18–20)

---

20. To address one specific argument of recent vintage: F. Rachel Magdalene's thesis that Job's "trial" reflects Neo-Babylonian trial law seems to me basically a productive one; however, in the specific case of these disavowals of guilt, her comment that Job's defense "turns [Sumero-Akkadian] incantations on their head" by listing not only possible offenses but also "a broad spectrum of righteous behavior" (Magdalene 2007, 183) seems to me an indication that its cultural roots are *not* to be sought primarily in Mesopotamia.

21. It has also been argued that this bicolon should be translated, "Then I thought, 'I shall die in my nest (עִמִּי קִנִּי), / and I shall multiply my days like the phoenix (חוֹל)'" (cf. NRSV), where the phoenix is understood to be related to the Egyptian *bennu*-bird, a symbol of revivification in the Book of the Dead. It is possible that there is a very complex play on words here, but if one must choose an interpretation, then the Hebrew words indicated are unlikely to be understood in such a way. Space limitations prevent a full discussion here; see further in Hays forthcoming b.

The imagery of the tree with its roots in the water evokes the image of rebirth in 14:7–9 (see above), and the renewed strength and vigor is very similar to the hopes expressed for rebirth in Egyptian afterlife texts as well. In particular, the image of the bow is more likely to be a reference to the restoration of the phallus (as has been recognized)[22] than to some martial aspiration; Job is not portrayed as a military man elsewhere in the book.

Having laid out the comparison between Job's rhetoric and Egyptian imagery, it may be necessary to allow, indeed to point out, that the author(s) of Job have not simply "borrowed" or "copied" Egyptian motifs. Rather, they seem to have *adapted* Egyptianizing mythological imagery in various ways—perhaps without even recognizing its specific sources (cf. Day 1996, 249). The mere identification of such borrowings is never the ultimate purpose of comparative study of the Hebrew Bible; instead, the goal is to understand a text's cultural context well enough to appreciate how it functioned within that context.

In Job's continuing to use Egyptianizing imagery even after God crushed his hopes of an Egyptian afterlife, one can see a very human stubbornness. There is a certain nobility to Job's persistence, but it really does turn out to be mere persistence, namely, the continuation of his old habits of thought. Job experiences a partial realization through his own thinking, but bringing Job and the reader to the book's radical theological conclusion still requires direct speech on God's part. The divine speeches are rightly understood to be no answer at all to Job's demands, but they are effective, finally crushing Job's aspirations: *Not only may you not have an afterlife apart from Me, you also may not summon Me to a court proceeding.* The Egyptian deceased aspired to "become an Osiris," the chief judge of the deceased in later Egyptian portrayals such as Book of the Dead, Spell 125, and standing like a peer of the gods in a divine court proceeding was a step on the way to that outcome. But Yahweh emphatically puts that hope to rest for Job.

---

22. קֶשֶׁת ("bow") as a euphemism for "penis" is noted in passing by Pope (1973, 216), who makes reference to Gen 49:24; Jer 49:35; and Hos 1:5. In Egyptian literature, the motif of the restoration of the penis in the happy afterlife is consistently attested in the afterlife books; see, e.g., Spells 376 and 486 of Pepi I in the Pyramid Texts, or chs. 42, 49, 93, and 162 of the Book of Going Forth By Day. The last of these reads: "You are lord of the phallus, strong when you rise."

Job Repents Concerning the Afterlife

This brings us to the book's final poetic verses, after the divine speeches. Job's response in 42:6 is the epitome of a *crux interpretum*, and has proved susceptible to various interpretations of the book's meaning (Morrow 1986). Though I renounce any hope of doing justice to the *Forschungsgeschichte*, when Job says, נחמתי על־עפר ואפר, it seems to me that (1) the likely sense of the Hebrew is "I repent *concerning* dust and ashes" (Patrick 1976), and (2) the word עפר is one that resonates with numerous instances of the imagery of death and afterlife throughout the book. For example, עפר characterizes dead bodies (7:5; 10:9; 34:15; 40:13), and it is repeatedly used to describe the location of the dead (7:21; 8:19; 14:8; 17:16; 19:25[?]; 20:11; 21:26; 30:19). Therefore, when Job "repents concerning dust," one has considerable warrant to interpret "dust" as shorthand for the hopes for the afterlife that were described above. Job had sought hopes for the afterlife other than the one that YHWH actually offers. Finally overwhelmed by the force of YHWH's rhetoric, he abandons that hope and submits to living his life despite the wreckage that it had become. Thomas Long (1988, 5–6) has written that Job "stands over against the prevalent religious impulse to fabricate a wishful picture of the world"—and this goes for the fabrication of wishful pictures of the afterlife as well.

Although that impulse is nearly universal, the book of Job allows the reader to construe the hopes described above as foreign, because Job is portrayed as a foreigner; wherever Uz was (and perhaps it was not meant to be any more clear then than it is to us), it was not Judah, but rather somewhere in the East (1:3) (Pope 1973, 3–7). The reception of Yahwistic faith and its adherents in foreign lands and among foreign peoples was a major preoccupation of postexilic Jewish literature (see Jonah, Ruth, Daniel, Ezra, Nehemiah, etc.). Furthermore, a popular tendency toward syncretism is condemned in, for example, Isa 55–66 and Ezra, whereas Dan 1–6 models faithful alternatives. In a postexilic perspective, then, Job can be understood as a text that seeks to inculcate a correct (i.e. stringently Yahweh-alone) perspective about suffering and death through the model of a foreigner. Job's brinksmanship, his toying with nominally foreign theological ideas, is projected onto a foreigner by the postexilic Judean author—perhaps because he would not have wanted even to admit the possibility in a fellow Judean. Job's subsequent submission to Yahweh could be compared (despite differences) to the faith of the foreigner Ruth; to the reverence of the sailors and Ninevites in Jonah; and to the confessions of various foreign kings in Daniel, Ezra, and Nehemiah.

After discussing and even longing for some other theological position that would be more palatable, Job finally resolves in accordance with what would have passed for orthodox Yahwism. Job will not, at the outset, accept the terror of death; or as Mathewson (2006, 54) puts it, Job "refuses to concede מות." The drama of the book is psychological as well as theological, focusing on Job's creeping recognition that he cannot escape death or have it his own way.

Carol Newsom (2003, 55) remarks that, in the book, cursing YHWH "could open a breach in the wholeness of the world…its presence would threaten the harmony upon which its vision is based. [Thus] the possibility of such cursing is raised (1:5, 11; 2:5) only to be defused (1:5) and rejected (1:22; 2:10)." The same can be said of Egyptianizing hopes for death and afterlife: they are raised and entertained, and eventually rejected. But Job's vacillation ends up reading as the expression of a complex character. The conversation in the book is not only among the characters, but also (and especially) *within Job himself.* The book's greatest achievement is its portrayal of an individual's struggle with YHWH. Like Jacob, Job is defeated and then blessed by YHWH. Hopes for the afterlife were at stake in the struggle.

THROUGH THE DUNG-HEAP TO THE CHARIOT: INTERTEXTUAL TRANSFORMATIONS IN THE *TESTAMENT OF JOB*

Anathea Portier-Young

Visionary Intertextuality

Early Jewish and Christian mysticism flourished at the juncture of "experience and exegesis" (DeConick 2006, 8). The mystic aimed to cross the threshold between earth and heaven, encounter God, and be transformed in the present time (DeConick 2006, 5–6). Stories and imagery from sacred scriptures could provide a model, path, and gateway for this mystical journey (DeConick 2006, 24; Rowland 2006, 56). For some mystics, reading, reciting, meditating upon, envisioning, and interpreting sacred scriptures were thus keys to experiencing transcendent, divine reality.

Yet reading alone would not lead a mystic to God, nor would traditional wisdom and ways of knowing. These were each necessary but not sufficient. Mystical experience could transcend limits of sensory perception, leading to new understanding, new revelation, and new interpretation (DeConick 2006, 7–8). A mystic or seer might thus aim not only to read but also to perform a text, with the goal of sharing the experience it narrated and seeing the vision it relayed (Rowland 2006, 48). Yet a single text alone did not generate its performance. Other scriptures, experiences, and practices simultaneously shaped religious experience, which in turn yielded a new, transformed hermeneutic, epistemology, and understanding. This "creative and experiential appropriation" of familiar texts generated new scripture and new scripts for future mystical experience (Rowland 2006, 48–50; DeConick 2006, 5–8).

It has often been noted that early Jewish mystics gave special attention to visionary models and imagery found in such prophetic and early apocalyptic texts as Isa 6, Ezek 1, and Dan 7 (Arbel 2003, 157; Schäfer 2011, 35, 44, 108). These texts provided a basis for speculation on and mystical ascent and descent to the heavenly throne-chariot or *merkabah*. In the *Testament of Job* (hereafter *T. Job*), throne symbolism holds a prominent place: the throne is a trope for earthly loss and heavenly gain. In response to the mocking refrain of Elious' royal lament over Iob ("now where is the glory of your throne?"), Iob locates the glory and majesty of his kingdom "in the chariots of the father" (33:9).[1] As I discuss further below, at *T. Job*'s conclusion the chariot becomes a focus of the visionary experience shared by Iob and his three living daughters, Day, Cassia, and Horn of Amaltheia, and the vehicle of heavenly ascent for Iob's soul (52:4–5).[2] As Lawrence Besserman has suggested, *T. Job* portrays Iob "as an initiate capable of initiating others in the secrets of the heavenly throne" (1979, 51). But it is not incidental that this hero is Iob. The primary intertext, model, and path to mystical experience of God in *T. Job* derive not from Isaiah, Ezekiel, or Daniel, but the biblical book of Job.[3]

T. Job creates from old signs—those borrowed from Old Greek (OG) Job—a new sign system in order to provide its readers a means for their own mystical transformation.

The Testament of Job *and the Biblical Book of Job*

The task of mapping lines of dependence between *T. Job* and OG Job is complicated by the plural extant text forms and translations of *T. Job*, as well as by the textual history of OG Job (see Ziegler 1982).[4] Yet their

---

1. I use the conventional titles to refer to the biblical book of Job (both MT and OG) and to *T. Job*. I transliterate the personal name Ιοβ as Iob and similarly transliterate the names of characters from LXX Genesis, following the practice of the *New English Translation of the Septuagint* (NETS).

2. See further Lesses 2007. But note Lesses's assertion that *T. Job* does not aim to instruct the reader in how to achieve the vision it describes (73).

3. See Kee (1974, 70) for the view that "the vision of God, mystically in the present age, and ultimately before the Throne itself in heaven" is the "highest aspiration" of humans in *T. Job*.

4. Although *T. Job* was originally composed in Greek, its earliest known witness is a fragmentary Coptic codex dating from the fourth or fifth century C.E., recently edited and translated by Schenke and Schenke Robinson 2009. The Greek witnesses consist of three Byzantine-era Greek manuscripts (commonly abbreviated as P, V, and S) dating from the eleventh to early fourteenth centuries C.E. (see critical edition of P in Brock 1967 and of S and V in Kraft 1974), as well as a sixteenth-century copy of P. There are also eight known Slavonic witnesses, some fragmentary, some complete, dating between the fourteenth and eighteenth centuries C.E. Textual analysis of the Slavonic traditions as well as the first English translation of Slavonic *T. Job* will appear in Haralambakis forthcoming.

literary relationship is well established, and there is wide consensus that *T. Job* depends upon and appropriates elements from OG Job. In a detailed analysis of material common to OG Job and *T. Job*, Berndt Schaller concluded that *T. Job* originally depended upon a prehexaplaric OG Job and that *T. Job*'s author knew OG Job well and made creative use of unmarked quotation as a literary technique. Building upon the earlier work of M. R. James, Schaller identified over fifty instances in which the author of *T. Job* appropriated and adapted phrasing from OG Job, ranging from a few words to multiple sentences in length. As Schaller and others have noted, the majority of shared material derives from the prose frame of OG Job (i.e. chs. 1–2 and 42:7–17). Other adapted material derives from OG Job 5:22; 7:1–2; 12:4; 14:11; 15:11; 29:6; 30:1, 19; 31:31, 32, 37; 36:1–2; and 38:1–3 (Schaller 1980).

Despite *T. Job*'s frequent appropriation of material from OG Job, the work is not simply a midrash or rewriting of OG Job, nor is its primary purpose to resolve exegetical problems arising from reading this biblical book. It is an artful literary composition in its own right, and, as Maria Haralambakis has argued, it "tells its own story" (Haralambakis forthcoming). It tells this story in conversation with OG Job.

Both OG Job and MT Job are deeply concerned with interpreting and responding to human suffering. Its approach to the problem of innocent suffering is bound up with questions about God and knowledge: Is God capricious or just? Can humans acquire wisdom? Can humans comprehend God's ways? The multiple genres and perspectives of Job's prose frame, wisdom dialogue, wisdom poem, human testimony, and divine speeches yield plural answers and non-answers to each of these questions. In this respect, OG Job and MT Job exemplify what Mikhail Bakhtin has called polyglossia (*mnogojazyčie*). That is, no one voice dominates the discourse, but instead a plurality of voices and signsystems interanimate one another, transforming a closed semiotic system into an open one (Bakhtin 1981, 12, 50–51, 61–67). The multiple genres and voices of OG Job and MT Job privilege dialogue and nonclosure and invite further reflection and debate (Newsom 2003).

T. Job similarly weaves together diverse genres, nesting a novella or "example story" (Haralambakis forthcoming) within a testamentary frame. The novella itself contains short dialogues and speeches, unsolvable riddles, and a variety of poetic compositions, including lament, taunt songs (one of which is styled as "royal lament," θρῆνος βασιλικός, 31:8), a "psalm of affirmation," and an execration hymn.[5] Yet the inclusion of

5. Unsolvable riddles, 37:8; 38:3; lament, 53:2–4; taunt songs, 25:1–8; 32:1–12; "psalm of affirmation," 33:3–9 (so labeled by Spittler 1983, 855); "execration

multiple genres does not signal a similar embrace of polyphony for its own sake. *T. Job* elides, renounces, and even condemns debate. The final word of Iob's promise in *T. Job* 5:1, ἄχρι θανάτου ὑπομενῶ καὶ οὐ μὴ ἀναποδίσω, a promise translated aptly by Kraft as "Till death I will endure and I will not retreat," could also be rendered "I will not call back and question" or "I will not cross-examine." The one who later does undertake such a cross-examination, namely Elious, is called a beast who is "filled with Satan" (41:7; 42:2); his words of challenge are not worthy to be included in *T. Job*, but remain among the "things left out" (ἐν τοῖς παραλειπομένοις, 41:7). *T. Job* omits not only these words but nearly all the poetic debate found in OG Job, eliding and critically summarizing this material in a brief declaration that "Eliphaz and the rest sat by me arguing and boasting against me" (41:1 SP; the summary in V is slightly longer). By contrast with the poetry of OG Job, the poems in *T. Job* do not create space for testing ideas and perspectives, but rather assign value. The text is not open-ended, but has a clear *telos*. This example story shows its readers a path and a goal. Suffering is not an unsolvable riddle. It is a way to heaven.

And while *T. Job* affirms with OG Job the limits of human knowing, it also narrates a transformation that enables human hearts and minds to regard the things of heaven and human mouths to speak and sing with the languages of those who inhabit the celestial realm: angels, archons, and cherubim. Day, Cassia, and Horn of Amaltheia, daughters of Iob, will cross the linguistic boundary between earth and heaven, achieving new language that corresponds and gives expression to their new mind, heart, and vision. Their transformations are a key to understanding *T. Job*'s visionary intertextuality.

George Aichele and Gary Phillips draw upon the work of Julia Kristeva to offer an account of intertextuality as a process of linguistic or semiotic transposition, redistribution, permutation, and transformation. That is, a system of signs from one textual system are transposed in and by another. In this process, not only texts but "readers are constantly made and remade...; worlds are remade as well" (Aichele and Phillips 1995, 10–11). *T. Job* transposes, transforms, and transvalues elements from Old Greek (OG) Job in order to provide its readers a means for their own mystical transformation. It also adumbrates an absolute transformation of signifiers from the realm of human signs to angelic, archontic,

hymn," 43:4–17 (so identified by Spittler 1983, 861 n. 43d). References to the Greek text of *T. Job* follow Kraft 1974. Translations or *T. Job* are mine unless otherwise noted.

and cherubic semiosis and hymnology (48:3; 49:2; 50:2). Only the latter are adequate to signify the eternal reality that is above and beyond the world-order (ὑπερκόσμιος 33:3) otherwise perceptible to human beings (cf. 49:3; 50:3). In this sense, *T. Job* is not polyglossic, like OG Job, but rather transglossic, even glossotelic (chs. 48–52). That is, *T. Job* has as its goal the transformation of language that signals and accompanies the mystical transformation of human body, mind, and spirit. This transformation brings with it a new capacity to see, understand, and communicate heavenly realities.

Textual Transformations:
Allusion, Elision, and Transvaluation

The first clue to this transformation appears in *T. Job*'s incipit. All three Greek manuscripts and one Slavonic witness identify Iob in the incipit as the one "called Iobab," taking up a tradition found in OG Job 42:17. As Annette Yoshiko Reed has noted, in *T. Job* the name change from Iobab to Iob takes on theological significance, foregrounding at the narrative's beginning the transformations Iob will undergo (Yoshiko Reed 2001, 51). In the book of Genesis, similar changes of name from Abram to Abraam (Gen 17:5), Sara to Sarra (Gen 17:15), and Iakob to Israel (Gen 32:28) accompany blessing, obedience, struggle, and transformation.

Iob's later statement in *T. Job* that "I was Iobab before the Lord named me Iob" (2:1) introduces Iob's account of his first experience of God. At the time of this encounter, Iobab's condition of unknowing (2:4) is remedied by direct revelation (chs. 3–4). His change of name thus signals epistemic transformation: Iob is now aware of the true nature of Satan's deceptions and gains knowledge of the future (3:3; ch. 4). In particular, as with Abraam, Sarra, and Israel, a blessing and call to obedience (5:7) accompany knowledge of struggle and suffering (4:4–5). Yet the revealing light (4:1) promises Iob that when he has endured difficult labors and achieved victory he will also have knowledge of divine justice, truth, and strength (4:10–11). Iob recognizes that the voice speaking to him has come for his "salvation" (3:5).

This focus on salvific epistemic transformation helps explain key differences in the beginnings of the two stories. While *T. Job* draws heavily from OG Job 1:2–5 and 1:7–11, it ignores entirely OG Job 1:1 and likewise omits any reference to the wager between God and the slanderer that provides the explanation for Iob's suffering in OG Job (cf. Kugler and Rohrbaugh 2004, 52). These omissions allow *T. Job* to focus on Iob's knowledge, free choice, and endurance, the contrast between earthly and heavenly glory, and the theme of inheritance. With the exception of Job's free choice, these themes are present in OG Job as well, but the two works develop them in different ways.

To this end, the story in *T. Job* begins not with the unique specimen of human righteousness found in OG Job but with a man suffering illness and facing death in the manner of all mortal beings (1:2). This introduction presents Iob not as exceptional but as exemplary. Moreover, when Iob begins his speech he identifies as his most important quality not righteousness or blamelessness (OG Job 1:1) but rather endurance (*T. Job* 1:3; Haas 1989). By contrast, in the biblical book, Iob voices his anger, sorrow, and loathing of his current state (6:2, 7) and declares that he has no strength to endure and no time for patience: τίς γάρ μου ἡ ἰσχύς ὅτι ὑπομένω ἢ τίς μου ὁ χρόνος ὅτι ἀνέχεταί μου ἡ ψυχή (6:11). Commenting on the closely parallel Hebrew text, Samuel Balentine (2006, 127) observes,

> Having committed to stand his ground by saying "No" to undeserved suffering and "Yes" to speaking the truth about God, Job is nevertheless convinced that he does not have the resources, physically or mentally, to do either (vv. 11–13). He does not have the strength to wait for death. He can not imagine any future…that provides the incentive to "prolong his life" (v. 11).

In OG Job, Iob hints that endurance might be possible if he could expect to be born again in a life beyond death (14:14), but he later denies this hope: "If I endure (ὑπομείνω), Hades is my house" (17:13). In *T. Job*, by contrast, Iob possesses abundant strength and is an athlete of endurance (Haas 1989).

A further contrast emerges in the elision of material from OG Job 1:6–12 and 2:1–6 and the addition of new narrative detail. As noted above, in *T. Job* there is no wager; suffering does not result from divine caprice. Satan attacks Iob because Iob destroys his temple (*T. Job* 5:2). Satan requests and receives authority over Iob's possessions (ch. 8; 16:2, 4) and body (but not his soul, 20:1–3 following OG Job 2:6), but the contest is not hidden from Iob. The luminous voice reveals the contest to Iob before the contest has even begun, and Iob freely chooses to enter into it and persevere (*T. Job* 3–4; 7:13; 18:7; 27:1). Iob is active in the struggle (Collins 1974, 36) and through his knowledge and endurance has power to overcome Satan (4:6, 10; 27:2–7).

By contrast, in OG Job, the hero and his human interlocutors are unaware of the contest that leads to Iob's loss of wealth, children, and bodily health; they debate his innocence and offer competing explanations for his suffering. In *T. Job*, the debate between Iob and the friends centers not on Iob's innocence (but see V 41:1) but on his wealth (30:3), his identity (ch. 31), his throne (chs. 32–33; 41), and his sanity (chs. 35–40). The friends do not share the knowledge that has been revealed to Iob and so lament his loss of earthly glory (chs. 31–32). When Iob declares that all earthly glory is transient and illusory (33:4, 8) and asserts his heavenly glory and eternal kingdom and throne (33:1, 5, 7, 9), they reject his testimony in favor of evidence they smell and see: the foul smell of Iob's body (34:4; 35:2) and the worms that infest his flesh (34:4).

T. Job develops the contrast between earthly and heavenly glory in Iob's tale of material wealth and loss (chs. 9–19). Details borrowed from OG Job 1:3 are amplified and woven into a dramatic account that emphasizes Iob's great wealth only to deny its value (*T. Job* chs. 9–13). His holdings of sheep, camels, donkeys, and oxen are multiplied by factors of three, two hundred and eighty, and seven; the smaller figures of OG Job now represent not the sum of his wealth but the numbers he freely gave for the benefit of those in need (*T. Job* 9:2, 4, 5; 10:5). Satan destroys the animals Iob had dedicated to the needy (16:1–2). Iob's countrymen seize the rest as spoil (16:3).

By transposing and multiplying the measures of Iob's earthly wealth, *T. Job* elaborates a new system of value, wherein vast earthly wealth is measured against the inheritance of even a portion of heavenly glory and deemed worthless. Iob now imagines himself like a merchant who throws away all his cargo in order "to enter a certain city, see its wealth, and inherit a portion of its glory" (18:6). He is willing to lose everything to enter this city and there inherit things better than the cargo or the ship (18:6). "So I too now valued the things that had belonged to me as nothing compared to drawing near to the city about which the angel had told me" (18:7).

The transvaluation of earthly status, rule, wealth, and power finds further expression in Satan's final encounter with Iob. In a simulacrum of the book's later theophany, Satan assumes the likeness of a hurricane (20:5). The wind topples king Iob from his throne, trapping him beneath it for three hours (20:5–6). Satan then afflicts him with disease. In OG Job the slanderer strikes Iob "from his feet to his head" (2:7). *T. Job* reverses the word order to emphasize first the affliction of Iob's head, the part of the body most closely associated with rule (*T. Job* 20:7). Indeed, Satan has not only assaulted Iob's body. He has removed him from the very seat of rule and overturned the symbol of Iob's earthly power. Iob's temporary immobility beneath the fallen chair provides a vivid image of reversal and loss of royal agency and power.

Yet Iob's disability is temporary only (cf. Cason 2007). Iob now rises and leaves one city to draw nearer to the one he has been shown. He also assumes a new seat. Readers more familiar with Hebrew Job may picture Job seated now on the ash heap, symbol of mortality, death, and mourning. But in OG Job and *T. Job* alike he sits not on an ash heap (but see *T. Job* 32:6, where "ash" provides poetic variation) but on a pile of dung (ἐπὶ τῆς κοπρίας, OG Job 2:8; *T. Job* 20:9; 24:1; 28:9; 32:5; cf. Lam 4:5). Its symbolism functions differently. Dung is waste, rejected by the body (cf. Philo, *QG* 2.6–7), yet can also provide manure (Philo, *Spec.* 1.74) and fuel and can be used to repair and fashion vessels. As manure, dung improves the structure of soil and nourishes plant life to provide food for other living beings. The dung of large cattle, horses, and camels provides a "slow-burning fuel" that transforms raw ingredients into sustaining food and generates light and warmth (J. S. Holladay 2009, 65–67; Borowski 1998, 58–59). Dung acts as a binding agent (Stager and King 2001, 134) and can be used to repair broken vessels and manufacture new ones. Vessels made of dung could, according to the mishnah, protect from impurity (*m. Kelim* 4:5; 10:1; Magness 2011, 75–76, 130–44; on dung and purity, see also *T. Benj.* 8:3). Seen in this light, the symbolism of Iob's dung-heap becomes clearer. What a body deems to be of no value is a source of light, warmth, and hidden life in the present and future. It can repair what is broken and be transformed into something new and pure. The dung-heap symbolizes the alternative system of value that Iob now embraces and the possibility and promise of transformation for Iob and others. Iob's years on the dung-heap (seven in V and Slav; 48 in P and S, *T. Job* 21:1) suggest a period of labor—in Iob's case, obedience and endurance—preceding jubilee, restoration, and new creation.

By contrast with Iob's patient endurance, his first wife (she is unnamed in OG and Slav; named Sitis, Sitida, and Sitidos in the Greek versions; and named Sitios in Coptic) grows weary of her labor and humiliation (24:4, 10). Even Iob protests her servitude (21:3), but he quickly regains his capacity for patient reasoning and abandons his complaint (21:4). By contrast, his wife succumbs to the deceptive reasoning of Satan, who propounds a logic similar to that of the friends in OG Job: if you did not deserve evil, it would not happen to you (*T. Job* 23:6; cf. OG Job 4:12). Just as Iob's patience derives from his epistemic transformation, his wife's lack of patience owes to her lack of knowledge and her failure to perceive rightly (on the latter, see Collins 1974, 43–44). She does not perceive Satan's disguise, the nature and purpose of Iob's contest, the worthlessness of what they have lost, the eternal reward of her children, or the goal toward which Iob strives.

In a lengthy parallel between OG Job 2:9 and *T. Job* 24:1–3, Iob's wife expresses her frustration and reveals the limits of her perception.[6] The writer of *T. Job* has added to her speech and to Iob's reply material that develops further the themes of earthly loss, heavenly gain, and the transformed system of signs and value. At the beginning of her speech the writer of *T. Job* has elided the question "how long will you persist (καρτερήσεις)…?" (OG Job 2:9) and substituted the question, "Iob, Iob, How long will you sit on the dung-heap?" (*T. Job* 24:1). Indeed, while one reference to the dung-heap suffices for all of OG Job, *T. Job* invokes the imagery not once but four times, each time inviting the reader to see in this unexpected image a path toward life and glory. Yet Sitis sees no reason to continue in her labor (25:10), just as she cannot see Satan standing behind her and disturbing her reasoning (26:6). She shares in the lament for her lost wealth and honor (25:1–7) without imagining that her material loss might become a path to heavenly gain.

The kings likewise remain anchored in and preoccupied by a system of value that prizes material wealth. *T. Job* closely follows OG Job (2:11–13) in narrating their approach and arrival, but Iob here adds commentary, explaining the cause of their distress: they previously admired Iob for his great wealth, surpassing even their own (*T. Job* 28:5–7, including a quotation transposed from OG 1:3). Now they find him destitute on a dung-heap (*T. Job* 28:9). They repeatedly ask about his possessions (28:11), insisting that the man they see cannot be Iobab (29:2; 30:2). They faint at the sight of him, and when they awake spend an entire week again discussing the possessions he once had (τὰ κτήνη καὶ τὰ ὑπάρχοντά μοι, 30:3). His current condition appears to them like a fall from life into death (νεκρότητα, 30:4). Their "royal lament" showcases Iob's lost wealth, contrasting his former jeweled throne and golden couches with the pile of dirt and dung he now occupies (32:5–6).

In response to this lament, Iob asserts the transience of all earthly wealth and kingdoms, including their own (34:8). The motif of transience is prominent in OG Job, and *T. Job* transposes an image from one of Iob's speeches in the earlier book to his speech here. In OG Job, Iob has contrasted human life with a tree and has likened human life to a river. A tree may be cut down but yet sprout new growth (OG Job 14:7–9). Not so human beings (14:10), "For a sea with time diminishes, and a river, laid waste, is dried up, but a person, once lying down, shall never

---

6. In both texts, the speech is significantly longer than that found in MT Job. Despite earlier conjectures that in this instance *T. Job* may have influenced a version of OG Job, Schaller (1980, 384–87) has demonstrated that here as elsewhere *T. Job* depends on OG Job and not the reverse.

rise again until the sky become unstitched" (OG Job 14:11 NETS). In *T. Job*, Iob repeats the image of the river, but dry rivers now signify the impermanence of the earthly realm by contrast with Iob's eternal kingdom, throne, and glory. "The rivers will dry up" (33:6), he declares, but the rivers of Iob's land, wherein sits his true throne, will not dry or vanish (33:7). Iob invokes a reality they cannot see. Still preoccupied with material wealth, the kings can offer only one explanation for his words: the memory of Iob's lost possessions has driven him insane (35:5–6; cf. 39:10). To test this theory, Baldas presses Iob further about his loss: "Who took away your belongings?" (37:3); if it was God, it would have been better for God never to have given anything in the first place (37:6). Like Iob's wife, Baldas cannot see loss as a path to greater gain.

I noted above that *T. Job* elides most of OG Job's poetic debate. It also elides nearly all of God's poetic speech to Iob from the whirlwind (OG Job 38:4–42:6). In OG Job, God's whirlwind speech reveals to Iob the limits of his comprehension. In *T. Job*, God's earlier revelation to Iob has already initiated Iob's epistemic transformation. God appears in the whirlwind (*T. Job* 42:1, adapting OG Job 38:1) to rebuke Elious and reveal his nature (*T. Job* 42:2), but this is all the reader learns of the Lord's speech to Iob before Iob reports its conclusion (*T. Job* 42:3, adapting OG Job 42:7).

Later, Iob will share with his three living daughters a final revelation that completes his own transformation and enables theirs as well. Iob presents Day, Cassia, and Horn of Amaltheia with shimmering, flashing bands from heaven (*T. Job* 46:8). They are each to wrap a band around their breasts (46:9). This is their inheritance, better than the property Iob has distributed to their brothers (46:1–5). The daughters are confused, and question how they might derive their livelihood from them (47:2). Iob assures them that they will have not merely livelihood, but life from these bands; the bands will lead them into the better world in the heavens (47:3). Iob understands that his daughters do not yet know the value (τιμήν, 47:4) of their inheritance, and so he relates how the Lord called him and presented these bands to him. Words that introduced God's challenge to Iob in OG Job, "Gird your loins like a man" (OG Job 38:3; 40:7; cf. 12:18), take on new meaning in *T. Job* (47:5). The instruction is no longer figurative, but literal. More importantly, it is not an invitation to learn the distance between human and divine knowing, but to bridge it. At the same time, when Iob girds himself, the bands heal and impart strength to his body. This physical transformation accompanies further revelation: God shows Iob "things that are and things that will be"

(47:10). From this time forward, "pain no longer touches him because of the sign (σημεῖον) of the girding with which he was girded" (52:1).

When the daughters wrap their breasts with the bands, they too are transformed, becoming like "heavenly beings" (Omerzu 2005, 95). Day receives another heart so that she no longer thinks of earthly things (48:2). She praises God in the language of angels (48:3) and has "Spirit" inscribed upon her stole (48:4). Cassia's heart is also transformed (ἀλλοιωθεῖσαν), relieving her from care about things of the world (τὰ κοσμικά, 49:1). Her mouth receives the dialect of archons (49:2). Horn of Amaltheia's heart is similarly changed (ἠλλοιοῦτο), and in the dialect of cherubim she speaks the glory of divine virtues (50:2). Soon the chariot comes to convey Iob's soul to the east. Iob and his daughters together behold the chariot (52:4–6).

Transforming Language and Vision

Despite its close intertextual relationship with OG Job, *T. Job* does not explicitly refer to that or any other biblical book. Instead, its scribal narrator Nereos presents himself as an eyewitness to Iob's final illness and testament, his daughters' receipt of their inheritance, their hymnody, the ascent of Iob's soul, and the death and burial of his body (ch. 51). In this way *T. Job* establishes its textual authority and priority. Old Greek Job, by contrast, makes no reference to its own writing and sets its story in generations past (42:17). The immediacy of *T. Job*'s contrasting present tense and first-person narration brings the reader a step closer to the presence of God and angels to which Nereos testifies (51:2).

And although *T. Job* does not name its biblical intertexts, Nereos names another set of writings recording the hymns and prayers of Day, Cassia, and Horn of Amaltheia. "Anyone who wishes to know the making of the heavens" (49:3) or "the trace of the glory of inheritance" (50:3 V) can "find" them in the Hymns of Cassia (49:3) and the Prayers of Horn of Amaltheia (50:3). According to V, Nereos himself has also written "the book of signs (σημείων) of most of the hymns" of the three women "to be a salvation with those" (51:3), that is, to provide a means of understanding and using the mystical hymns.

Traditional human sense-perception, wisdom, and reasoning fail to grasp the things of heaven; they cannot even give an account of the circuitry (πορείαν) of the human body (38:8). Rather, in *T. Job* these faculties share and are limited by the instability of earth and earthly creatures: earth's inhabitants are ἀκατάστατος (36:4), and susceptible to the deceptions of Satan (3:6; 6:4; 7:5; 17:2; 23:3). By the book's conclusion it is apparent that human language holds similar limitations. Day, Cassia, and Horn of Amaltheia transcend these limitations when they wrap around their breasts the shimmering, sparking bands they have inherited from their father (46:5, 8–9; chs. 47–50). What previously seemed to them to hold no value transforms their hearts and minds, their capacity to see and comprehend, and their languages (chs. 48–50; 52:7). So transformed, they share with Iob the mystical vision of the chariot.

Conclusion

T. Job transposed, transformed, and transvalued familiar signs from the Old Greek book of Job. In so doing, *T. Job* showed its readers a mystical path through the dung-heap to the chariot, toward personal transformation of heart, body, and mind. Iob's salvific divine revelation taught that suffering did not pose a challenge to the justice of God. It could be freely chosen and patiently endured in the knowledge of future victory. *T. Job* invites its readers to draw nearer to their heavenly inheritance, confident that heavenly glory surpasses all earthly wealth.

"HE MAKES PEACE IN HIS HIGH HEAVEN": JOB AND PAUL IN RESONANCE

J. Gerald Janzen

In this essay I shall explore aspects of resonance between Job and Paul's letters. At the level of theory and method, I am informed chiefly by Richard Hays (R. B. Hays 1989).[1] Hays concentrates on echoes, which occupy a particular point along an intertextual spectrum marked by *quotation*, *allusion*, and *echo*. He also considers *resonance*, and invokes John Hollander's image of a "cave of resonant signification" as a figure for Paul's scriptural canon. His discussion of resonance between Job 13:16 and Phil 1:19 suggests that he locates resonance *on* the spectrum, and *after* echo, as a fainter intertextual nexus, shading off into what may only be a ringing of the reader's own ears, or a "synthetic hermeneutical act" (R. B. Hays 1989, 24). In my view, resonance is not *on* the spectrum; it is the light that becomes visible *through* a point on it; it is the light of pre-understanding, the intuition of a richness of meaning that initially may elude focused recognition but that holds the involved texts in play toward eventual understanding. It may be analogized to Paul's "hearing" of ἄρρητα ῥήματα (2 Cor 12:4), a phrase I would paraphrase as "a wordless flow of inexpressible meaning." When it comes to expression, it takes the form of echo, allusion, quotation.

As the image implies, an "echo" is a one-way resonance. But echoes can rebound interactively; and texts which arose independently may resonate with one another. In a bad acoustical chamber such interaction may be heard as distorted meaning or noise; but under the right conditions it can produce mutually enhancing resonances. At a physical level tones generated by different instruments may interact to generate overtones not traceable to their respective sources, and audible only to the trained ear. Analogously, so-called synthetic interpretation of texts in

---

1. See also Alkier 2009 and Heimbrock 2009. For my own approach, see Janzen 2012.

synchronic interplay may be attributable to action occurring solely as overtones within the interpreter's own "cave of resonant signification." But such overtones do not feel as though they are occurring only within one's mind; they seem rather to arise before one in the resonant interaction between the texts themselves. Such "thick readings" of texts can, of course, easily be deconstructed by showing that none of the texts claimed in support, when taken individually in their respective contexts, will sustain such an interpretive move. To which the *sotto voce* response (echoing Galileo) is, *e pur si muove.*

In the nature of such a hermeneutics of resonance, the expository strategy is one of *eisegesis*, in that word's ancient meaning—of drawing another reader in among the texts to where that reader may also hear the overtones. The new reading of Job offered in the last section of this paper originated independently of my reading of Paul; but at a certain stage these two reading trajectories converged, and the result is the present study. Limits of space prevent significant engagement with the vast and rich scholarship on both Job and Paul.

Resonances of Job in Romans

Paul's exposition of the gospel of God (Rom 1:1) breaks into doxology at 11:33–36 over the "depth of the riches and wisdom and knowledge of God" manifest in God's unsearchable judgments and inscrutable ways, through which penultimate discriminations resolve into the ultimate result (11:32) that "God has consigned *all* to disobedience, that he may have mercy on *all*." The ultimacy of this "all" then forms the theme of the doxology's conclusion: "For *from* him and *through* him and *unto* him are *all things*." That Paul should back up this paean with a quotation from Deutero-Isaiah (Rom 11:34; cf. Isa 40:13) is not surprising, since he repeatedly quotes and echoes this prophet; so the paean implicitly invites his readers to ponder God's κρίματα/ὁδοί within that prophecy's overall "cave of resonant signification." The quotation from Job 41:11 in Rom 11:35, however, seems merely to exploit the point of that particular verse. But several considerations suggest that Job as a whole is as resonantly significant for Paul as Deutero-Isaiah.

First, the issue of God's *judgments* vis-à-vis the human cry for *justice* lies at the core of both books. To the cry in Isa 40:27 that "my way (דרך/ὁδός) is hid from the LORD, / and my right (משפט/κρίσις) is disregarded by my God," God responds by referring to cosmic creation as following a "path of justice (משפט/κρίσις)" and a "way (דרך/ὁδός) of understanding" derived from no counselor (איש עצה) (40:13–14), a

משפט/κρίσις made clear through God's servant (42:1–4), one who, his own משפט travestied (53:8), makes intercession for "the transgressors" (53:12). Similarly, God responds to Job's complaints concerning משפט/ κρίμα (e.g. 9:19; 19:7; 27:2) by referring to God's עצה (38:2) and משפט (40:8) as implicit in creation, but as obscured by the *quid pro quo* notion of משפט/עצה implicit in Job's bewildered accusations; and, following this disclosure ("now I see thee," 42:5) and its effect on him (נחמתי, "I change my mind/I am comforted," 42:6), Job intercedes for those whose accusations had exacerbated his sufferings by reinforcing his suspicion that they signify divine judgment. In each of these books, then, the issue of divine משפט/κρίμα revolves around a figure suffering unjustly precisely as God's servant who intercedes for his opponents. That Paul indicates Job and Deutero-Isaiah as primary scriptural contexts elucidating God's unsearchable judgments and inscrutable ways, is supported by the way in which, leading up to the quotations themselves, 11:33 is larded with echoes of these two books.

1. In the LXX ἀνεξιχνίαστος occurs only in Job (3×), translating אין חקר ("unsearchable") in 5:9; 9:10, and לא חקר in 34:24,[2] in connection with the theme of "searching" for wisdom or justice, a theme marked by the un-negated Hebrew noun חקר rendered with ἐξιχνίασον (8:8) ἴχνος (11:7) and ἴχνεσιν (38:16), and by the Hebrew verb חקר (6×, 4× rendered ἐξιχνιάζω). In no other book are these terms so concentrated in reference to divine wisdom and judgment.

2. ἀνεξεραύνητος does not occur in the LXX. The verb occurs once (Judg 18:2) for חקר, the related simple form, ἐρευνάω ("search, inquire") 14 times, twice translating חקר. Paul probably coined ἀνεξεραύνητα as a pair-word to ἀνεξιχνίαστοι, possibly aided by the rendering of אין חקר [*sic*] with οὐδὲ ἔστιν ἐξεύρεσις in Isa 40:28 [*sic*].

3. γνῶσις echoes דעת (σύνεσις) in Isa 40:14 (compare דעת in Job 38:2). The combination of the themes of depth, richness and wisdom (βάθος πλούτου καὶ σοφίας) is central to Job 28, where God alone "finds it out" (חקר, 28:27; compare 11:7; 12:22; 38:16).

4. In Rom 11:35 Paul takes the trouble to translate directly from the Hebrew of Job 41:11 (EVV3). This further suggests close study of the Job story, and not merely the adventitious memory of a stray text.

---

2. אין חקר occurs elsewhere only in Ps 145:3; Prov 25:3; and Isa 40:28 in continuation of 40:12–14.

5. One may note, further, the echo of Job 1:1, 8 in 1 Thess 5:22, and the quotation in 1 Cor 3:19 of Job 5:13 in a form "markedly different from the LXX" (Dunn 1988, 701).

6. Paul quotes Job 13:16 (τοῦτό μοι ἀποβήσεται εἰς σωτηρίαν) in Phil 1:19, "For I know that (οἶδα γὰρ ὅτι) through your prayers and the help of the Spirit of Jesus Christ this will turn out for my deliverance (τοῦτό μοι ἀποβήσεται εἰς σωτηρίαν)," which Hays examines as the case in point for his exploration of "how scriptural echoes lend resonant overtones to Paul's prose" (R. B. Hays 1989, 21). As he notes, Paul's introductory οἶδα γὰρ ὅτι occurs in the LXX only three times, all in Job. Further resonances between Paul and Job may be traced through the thematic interconnections between Paul's use of ἀποκαραδοκία in Phil 1:20 and in Rom 8:19 in the context of the general "groaning," sense of "futility," and persistence in "hope" that mark Rom 8 and Job. All these connections indicate that Paul had "meditated" (Dunn 1988, 703) long and hard on Job.

"Unto him are all things" in Romans 11:36 and Other Pauline Texts

In this section I want to lay the groundwork for a resonant convergence between Paul and my proposal for reading Job. The three-preposition formulation in Rom 11:36 may reflect Stoic formulas as already "domes-ticated through Jewish monotheism" (Dunn 1988, 701, 704); but, in view of the preceding scriptural focus on Job and Deutero-Isaiah, I take the formulation to resonate with Deutero-Isaiah's emphasis on Yahweh as "first" and "last" (אַחֲרוֹן/רִאשׁוֹן, 44:6; 48:12; cf. 41:4) such that "before me no god was formed, nor shall there be any after me" (Isa 43:10). Other gods are shown to be empty nothings (e.g. 41:21–24, 29), incapable of interpreting "the former things" and "the latter things," whereas Yahweh is at work, as creator and redeemer, in every "beginning" and every "end" (Isa 40:21; 41:4, 22, 26; 42:9, 10; 43:6, 9, 18–19; 44:7, 8; 45:21; 46:9–10; 48:3, 5, 6, 8, 16). Given how Paul echoes the τὰ ἀρχαῖα/καινά of Isa 43:18–19 in the τὰ ἀρχαῖα/καινά of 2 Cor 5:17 (in the context of Paul's point that "in Christ God was reconciling the world [κόσμος] to himself"), surely *this* is the template deeply informing Paul's eschato-logical sensibility, and imbuing the Stoic formula with new resonances of what he calls "the gospel of God."

This contrast between Yahweh and the gods is imaged graphically in Isa 46, where the idols of the latter, carried in procession on "weary beasts," are unable to "save the burden," but themselves "go into captivity," whereas Yahweh carries Israel from womb to old age (46:1–4) as one "declaring the end from the beginning and from ancient times things not yet done, saying, 'My counsel (עֵצָה; cf. 40:12–14) shall stand, and I will accomplish all my purpose (חֵפֶץ; βεβούλευμαι)'" (46:10).

But what is the scope of "all" God's purpose? And what is the scope of the "all things" in Rom 11:36? In Isa 40:10–11, God is portrayed like Jacob returning from exile, the imagery in 40:11 echoing Gen 33:13.[3] The mighty (40:10) divine shepherd's concern for this flock (עֵדֶר) is echoed in Isa 40:26 where the hosts of heaven are likewise objects of divine might, individually "called," so that "not one is missing (נֶעְדָּר)." The resonance between 40:10–11 and 40:26 plays on the promise to Abram of a progeny more numerous than the stars of heaven (Gen 15). But in Babylon the stars are (also) astral deities; in Isa 47:13 they are consulted in vain for help. If 40:26 connotes that they are under *Yahweh's* overlordship, what is *their* eschatological destiny? According to Job 38:7, at the foundation of the earth "the morning stars sang together, / and all the בְנֵי אֱלֹהִים sang for joy." In Ps 82 the gods who fail to do מִשְׁפָּט through lack of understanding are sentenced to death. But the drama in the sub-collection of Pss 93–100 moves from the rebellious noise of the "floods/sea" in Ps 93:3 to the "sea/floods" clapping their hands together with "all the earth" in the joy of the eschatological "new song" in Ps 98. And the Psalter draws near its conclusion with a vision (Ps 148) in which all beings in the heavens, on earth, and in "all deeps," are to praise God who has "raised up a horn for his people."

Such texts suggest the scope of Paul's εἰς αὐτὸν τὰ πάντα in Rom 11:36, which Käsemann (1980, 321) sums up this way: "As in 1:18ff., 5:12ff., 8:19ff., universal redemption is in view, with Christology as the center. Finally the acclamation, as in Revelation and Phil 2:11, takes up the cosmic veneration. In the praise of the community there is already uttered that which one day the whole world will have to confess and will have to confirm with its amen." The scope of Phil 2:11 ("every knee…, every tongue…, in heaven and on earth and under the earth," quoting Isa 45:23) appears again, liturgically, in Eph 1:10 and Col 1:15–20.

But *how* are all these "tongues" brought to say the "amen"? Are they violently subjected through fear of death? Such a path to the "amen" befits the wisdom of the rulers of this age (1 Cor 2:6–8), but not God's reconciling acts of "wisdom" and "power" (God's so-called folly and weakness) in and through a crucified messiah. To be sure, in 1 Cor 15:24

---

3.   עָלוֹת (RSV "giving suck") in Gen 33:13 and Isa 40:11 (RSV "those that are with young"); the word for "lambs," טְלָאִים, echoes טְלָאִים ("variegated flocks") in Gen 30:32, 33, 35, 39.

Paul speaks of Christ as "destroying (καταργέω) every rule and every authority and power." But the passage goes on (15:28) to speak of "all things" as "subjected to him," and of himself as then "subjected to him who put all things under him, *that God may be all in all* (πάντα ἐν πᾶσιν)"—as though the opposition of these authorities and powers (like the floods and sea of Ps 93 in Ps 98) is transformed into Christ's subjection to God. The verb καταργέω is crucial, meaning literally, "to empty of power, to render ineffectual." In Deutero-Isaiah (e.g. Isa 41) the gods are declared empty of power to announce or determine the course of universal history. Israel as Yahweh's witness not only *attests* their emptiness, but, by the all-encompassing hymnic outbursts that punctuate Deutero-Isaiah, *effectuates* that emptiness, in showing that these so-called gods have no power to determine Israel's praise. An analogous situation pertains in Phil 2:11; Eph 1:10; and Col 1:16–20—all occurring, like Rom 11:33–36 in acts of *worship*.

To be sure, such acts are commonly taken as *ascriptive*. On Eph 1:3 O'Brien (1999, 95) writes, "The same verb ['bless'] is used for men and women blessing God and for his blessing them, though in a different sense. In the former case *blessed* denotes the ascription of praise to God, while in the latter the verb describes God's providing his benefits." But in Ps 29:1–2 the "heavenly beings" (בני אלים) are called to "give (הבו; RSV 'ascribe') to the LORD glory and strength"; and I interpret such acts of "ascription" in accord with Erhard Gerstenberger's analysis in his paper, "The Dynamics of Praise in the Ancient Near East, Or: Poetics and Politics" (Gerstenberger 2010). His subtitle goes precisely to my point about praise and cosmic reconciliation. Gerstenberger's argument proceeds from exclamations like *halleluyah* and *allahu akhbar*, as "hymns in a nutshell, often condensed expressions of power," to the thesis that "praise is not only an aesthetic or stylistic speech form, with possible theological implications, but a real primordial force not to be tamed by modern interpretations." He observes that praise language, while situated in present reality, reaches out to the past and probes into the future, and that, in another aspect of its all-embracingness, it "emphasize[s] the unity of all existence...by recognizing participation of all agents in the universal powerplay." In such a reading of the relation between praise and politics, Paul's eschatological doxologies, hymns and *berakhah*'s not only envision but dynamically participate in, and indeed contribute to, the unification of all things "in heaven and on earth."[4]

---

4. Many now take Ephesians as the work of a disciple of Paul, or a "ghost-writer" drafting the particulars of a letter whose contents Paul has sketched. I take the letter's distinctive elements and general perspective to be accounted for as

The line of exegetical reflection that I am tracing comes to a head in Eph 3:10 where Paul, after referring to his calling to "preach to the Gentiles the *unsearchable riches of Christ*" as having to do with "the plan of the mystery hidden for ages in God who created all things" (3:8–9) refers to the church's participation in this mission, "that through (διά!) the church the manifold wisdom of God might now be made known to the principalities and powers *in the heavenly places*." If, as Andrew Lincoln writes, "the whole long sentence [in Eph 1:3–14] functions as a paean of praise into which its readers are invited" (Lincoln 1990, 44), their singing extends the invitation to the "principalities and powers in the heavenly places," including those currently in rebellion. I want, now, to draw together some of the resonances with Job that I hear in Eph 3.

The reference to "the unsearchable [ἀνεξιχνίαστον] riches of Christ" (as in Rom 11:33–36) echoes Job LXX, the term occurring only there. The "manifold wisdom (πολυποίκιλος σοφία) of God" may resonate with God's σοφία and ποικιλτικὴ ἐπιστήμη ("wisdom" and "variegated-embroidery of knowledge") in Job 38:36 (LXX).[5] When Paul bows his knee before the Father, "from whom every πατριά in heaven and on earth is named," he celebrates the love in which his readers are "rooted and founded (τεθεμελιωμένοι)," as, in Christ, "surpassing knowledge" in "breadth and length and height and depth," and yet as something they are "able to comprehend" (ἐξισχύσητε καταλαβέσθαι). On the one hand, the four-dimensional characterization of this "founding love" resonates with Job 11:7–9, Paul's verb ἐξισχύω interacting sonantly with the earlier ἀνεξιχνίαστον. In such a resonance the testimony of the earlier passage to the limitlessness of God is honored, while those depths are not simply "impenetrable and incomprehensible" (Dunn 1988, 704, on Rom 11:33) but "knowable" as a love that, however deeply one enters into it, one will never exhaust. Finally, in the focus on God as "Father," as one "from whom every πατριά in heaven and on earth is named " (3:15), the term

Pauline by its function (a) as a general letter for circulation among several churches, and (b) as, an attempt, finally, to articulate, so far as possible, the "pleromatic" eschatological implications of the "audition" reported in 2 Cor 12—an attempt, especially in the *berakhah* in Eph 1:3–14 and as intimated in 3:14–21, to convey through quotation, allusion, echo and resonance with his Scriptures the spectral colors of the light (Eph 5:14; 2 Cor 4:6; cf. Acts 26:13, 18, 23) of the "visions" accompanying the ἄρρητα ῥήματα.

5. Job 38:36 LXX: τίς δὲ ἔδωκεν γυναιξὶν ὑφάσματος σοφίαν ἢ ποικιλτικὴν ἐπιστήμην; ("Who has placed in a woman the woven-cloth of wisdom, / or the variegated-embroidery of knowledge?"). If Eph 3:10 echoes Job 38:36 LXX, the implication is that what has been hidden from and obscured by Job through his mindset is now disclosed in the church as conformed to its head.

πατριά refers to "family groupings or classes of angels," but "[i]t is not only good angels who are in view... For this writer all such spirit powers, even the rebellious ones, owe their origin to God" (Lincoln 1990, 202). These "family groupings" are the בני אלהים frequently encountered in the OT, associated at times with astral figures, as in Isa 14:12–14, and as in Job 38:7 where, at the founding of the earth, "the morning stars sang together, and all the בני אלהים shouted for joy" in a primordial version of Gerstenberger's power-laden praise and Käsemann's eschatological "Amen." This raises for me the following question: Do the thematics of Paul's εἰς αὐτὸν τὰ πάντα in Rom 11:36, and his expansions of that phrase in 1 Cor 15; Phil 2; Col 1:15–20, and Eph 1:10; 3:10, resonate with what I have recently come to suspect may be the *real* theological issue in Job? If, for example, the hymnic celebration of the *servant* figure in Phil 2:6–11 involves a hymnic participation in the work of that servant, in "making known to the powers" the true nature of God's creating and redeeming wisdom and power as the wisdom and power of love, in order to draw them into this amen chorus (Käsemann), what of Job's servant role vis-à-vis the Satan of the Prologue who, as one of the בני אלהים, presumably participated in the primordial paean of praise (Job 38:2)—a paean over God's עצה and משפט in cosmic creation and governance, but a paean now apparently obscured by the understanding of divine wisdom and power implicit in Satan's query concerning the grounds and nature of Job's piety? For behind Satan's query lies the assumption that Job's relation to God and to his human associates is grounded in the moral and spiritual axioms of reward and punishment; and that assumption in turn implies a similar basis for God's own עצה and משפט, a divine rule exercised according to the same logic.

"He Makes Peace in His High Heaven": The Central Issue in the Book of Job?

The preceding sentences imply a discordance between (a) Satan's understanding, in the Prologue, of the ground of human religion and piety, and also of the nature and logic of divine creative and world-governing wisdom and power, and (b) Satan's primordial understanding as one of the company in Job 38:2. This discordance within Satan himself issues in a discordance between Satan and Yahweh. Insofar as the Satan of Job 1–2 is a servant of God—now gathering information on God's subjects as loyal or disloyal—I suggest that Satan's current discordant "mind-set" results (as a sin besetting all specialized occupations) from taking the parameters and benchmarks appropriate to his limited function and universalizing them, construing the principles of *quid pro quo*—important as operational principles in human and divine affairs—as foundational and ultimate.

In Hardy and Ford's analysis of the hermeneutical implications of praise and blame (1985, 155), praise engages the object of praise in a wide perspective that, while not oblivious to the "warts" in the object, engages the object whole, while blame tends, in focusing narrowly on the "warts," to obscure what is praiseworthy. Put another way, a hermeneutics of praise involves trust while a hermeneutics of blame involves suspicion. It is significant, then, that the story of Job opens with God's praise of Job and Satan's contrasting blame in the sense that he reduces Job's motivation for uprightness and piety to a calculating *do ut des*. What is Yahweh to do with Satan? For the mindset displayed in Satan's query, if it is to deepen and to infect other members of the heavenly realm, can threaten the peace of heaven—throw it off key, as it were— and in this way shake the very foundations (Ps 82:5). How is Yahweh to "make peace [with Satan] in his high heaven"?

In earlier Joban studies I have developed, as a frame of reference, a two-paradigm model of divine–human relations attested in the Old Testament.[6] The first paradigm centers in God as divine father of the clan. As such, God is the giver of the blessings of conception and birth, prosperity in flock and field, guide and protector (cf. Gen 49:25). Under this aegis, the religious ethos centers in חסד ואמת ("steadfast love and faithfulness," e.g., Gen 24 passim) and רחמים ("compassion, mercy," Gen 43:13, 29–30). Though conflict, sometimes murderous, breaks out repeatedly between clan members—notably over Isaac and Ishmael; between Jacob and Esau; and between Joseph and his brothers—yet Jacob and Esau are reconciled (Gen 33); Isaac and Ishmael come together to bury their father, as do Jacob and Esau (Gen 25:9; 35:29); and the Joseph story ends in a scene of forgiveness and reconciliation (Gen 50) that in retrospect gives the ancestral narratives their ground and tenor. In these ways the narrative implies how the God of the Genesis ancestors, and of clan-type religion, would "make peace in his high heaven," were analogous tensions or challenges to arise there.

But Bildad, representing the friends, addresses the question within a different mindset (Job 25):

---

6. Most recently, Janzen 2009, 15–46; also 1997, passim. Similarly, Moberly 1992, though in my model the first paradigm remains foundational and is not superseded by the second.

Dominion and fear are with God; / he makes peace in his high heaven. / Is there any number to his armies? / Upon whom does his light not arise? / How then can man be righteous before God? / How can he who is born of woman be clean? / Behold, even the moon is not bright and the stars are not clean in his sight; / how much less man, who is a maggot, / and the son of man, who is a worm!

This mindset reflects the second paradigm, centering in God as divine king who rules through the promulgation of law undergirded by the sanctions of reward and punishment enforced through arms. It emerges into prominence at Sinai, and thereafter provides the *operational* basis for life as a covenant people before Yahweh. As such a basis, the laws are impartial and invariable, and enforced without favoritism. But the way in which grievous covenant defections are resolved indicates that the prior, ancestral paradigm remains foundational. When Israel commits the gravest covenant infidelity, in the idolatry of the golden calf, Moses *intercedes* (not a provision within the Sinai covenant itself), appealing to God to *remember the ancestors* "to whom you said, 'I will multiply your descendants as the stars of heaven [*sic*], and they shall inherit [this land] for ever," and God repents of the evil contemplated in wrath against the people (Exod 32:13–14). In Exod 33:19 (formalized in 34:6–7), God is identified in terms that evoke the ethos of clan religion. The logic of reward-and-punishment is operationally important; but when taken as foundational—obscuring the foundations in God's promises to the ancestors—it threatens to destroy the relationship and render impossible the realization of those promises. The import of this for what I may call intra-celestial relations may be appreciated from the portrayals of foundational actions and conflictual relations between the gods in *Enuma Elish*, the creation myth of Babylon, whose prominence provides the political and theological horizon within which the respective dramas in Deutero-Isaiah (cf. Isa 46; 47) and Job (cf. Job 1:17) are envisioned.

Enuma Elish opens with a primal divine pair, Apsu and Tiamat, acting "as one" to procreate all the other gods. When the younger gods foment rebellion, Apsu's vizier counsels destruction; but Tiamat shouts at Apsu, "How could we allow what we ourselves created to perish? / Even though their ways are so grievous, *we should bear it patiently*."[7] Her intercession [*sic*] on behalf of these young rebels, though unsuccessful, has as its aim that none of those whom she and Apsu have brought into being should perish. When Apsu, nevertheless, proceeds against the

---

7. In the concluding clause the verb *shadad* indicates a taking pains to attend carefully; if necessary, to endure the burdens of the current situation. See *CAD, shadadu.*

young rebels, he is killed. At this, Tiamat accedes to the pressures of older gods to take up Apsu's cause. In the event, she is slain by young Marduk (Bel/Nebo in Isa 46:1) who uses her dead body as the framework for his creation of the cosmos. Theologically, Marduk's victory over Tiamat represents the triumph of a *cosmogonic* myth, in which ultimate origins and continuing order are founded in conflict, over an earlier *theogonic* myth in which ultimate origins and continuing vitality arise through *generative* power (Cross 1976; Machinist 2005).[8] In the process, the motivation, means and goal of conflict-resolution briefly embodied in the intercessory cry of Tiamat are all but erased by their relegation to a mere prologue to the "real" account of current cosmic order. As James Crenshaw puts the matter (1995b, 469), "[t]he outcome of this struggle [between the gods] assured law and order, a universe that operated on a principle of reward for virtue and punishment for vice. This conviction that goodness paid worthy dividends and that evil produced an unwelcome harvest became axiomatic throughout the ancient Near East."

This is the mind-set reflected in Bildad's third speech in Job 25. In that speech, he echoes the logic of Eliphaz in 4:17–19 and 15:14–16, where Eliphaz asserts that God "puts no trust (לֹא יַאֲמִין/οὐ πιστεύει) in his servants / angels / holy ones / heavens," much less in frail, sinful, indeed wicked humans. This, of course, presents precisely the logic of Satan in so far as he has absolutized and universalized his limited, operational role. If Satan succeeds in fomenting dissatisfaction with Yahweh's rule within the ranks of the בְּנֵי אֱלֹהִים, peace in heaven will eventually be ruptured by the sort of rebellion we have witnessed in *Enuma Elish* (compare Isa 14:12–14); and if Yahweh responds as Bildad envisions, then precisely in losing *such* a battle Satan will have been proven right in his suspicions as to the nature of Yahweh's rule. How then *can* Yahweh prove Satan wrong without proving him right?

By confounding the assumptions of Eliphaz and Bildad and *trusting his human servant Job* to prove Satan wrong. By trusting Job to remain faithful even in the face of profound, unrectified injustice and, worse yet, in the face of apparent abandonment by a God whose "friendship" was once "upon my tent" (Job 29:4). And Job remains faithful. His calamities and suffering exacerbated by the theological interpretations placed upon them by his friends and by his own suspicions, Job unleashes strenuous complaints and accusations against God; but they differ only in boldness and intensity, not in kind, from those found within the Psalter. And, as Elie Wiesel notes in one of his stories, one can say anything to God

---

8. One may suggest a correlation between theogonic myths and clan religion, and between cosmogonic myths and city-state religion.

inside the synagogue; it is only when one steps *outside* that place, outside that relation, that what one says is blasphemy. And Job never steps outside the divine–human relation. Tellingly, while the friends speak only *about* God, Job speaks both about and *to* God. And in the end (27:1–6; ch. 31) Job swears an oath of clearance, in which, though the *form* of the utterance befits a legal (or law-based) frame of reference, the *spirit* of the utterance (using the very breath that Shadday gave him in his coming into life) is one in which Job *entrusts* the final disposition of his case to One whom he has viewed as both his judge and his accuser. In that self-entrustment, Job vindicates the trust placed in him by God. It remains only for God to appear to Job in those phenomena of storm and rain that renew the face of a drought-stricken earth to render it once again life-sustaining, and so to respond to his wistful words in 14:7–9, "there is hope for a tree, if it be cut down, that…at the scent of water it will bud…" And secondly, God must assure Job that the divine משפט is not a zero-sum game, but that Job can be—as advertised—innocent without God thereby being proven guilty; and thirdly, indicate to Job that in his zero-sum, *quid pro quo* reading of divine משפט/צדקה he was actually *obscuring* it.

The story ends with Job *comforted*[9] by this apocalyptic disclosure, and *interceding* for his friends. For, though they deserve the *quid pro quo* fate their own theology calls down on them, and though their behavior to Job *stirs up* divine wrath, Yahweh asserts that to *execute* that wrath on them would be to "do folly with them" (that being the most natural sense of the idiom in 42:8). Thus the breach between Job and his friends is healed, like the breach between Joseph and his brothers, the grave breach between Yahweh and Israel over the golden calf, and the conflict between God's servant and the nations in Isa 52:13–53:12.

What, then, of the breach that in the Prologue opens up between Yahweh and Satan? Is it healed? Is Satan, so to speak, drawn back into the divine choir by Job's confession in 42:1–6 and his intercession in the Epilogue? Or does Satan continue to sing off-key? The absence of any heavenly scene in the Epilogue is arresting. Why no heavenly scene to indicate some kind of closure, or a continuing rift, between Satan and Yahweh? I take the silence as deliberate—analogous to the silence at the end of the book of Jonah, where the reader is left to ponder whether Jonah is willing to relinquish his insistence on God's actions against Nineveh on a reward–punishment basis and to accept God's dealings with that city on the basis of the divine character proclaimed in Exod 34:6. The reader is drawn into that silence to ponder the issues the whole

---

9. For this interpretation of the verb נחמתי in 42:6, see Janzen 2009, 108–10.

book has raised, and to process for oneself, as voices within oneself—various competing voices *of* oneself—all the heavenly and earthly voices heard up to this point. Which voice(s) will prevail? Or will a synthetic voice emerge, as a soundless flow of ἄρρητα ῥήματα, moving one to worship? Does the silence concerning heaven intimate a silence *in* heaven—a silence perhaps connoting the resolution of the breach between Satan and Yahweh in a resumption of the primordial joy of 38:7? Whether or not such a resolution occurs behind the Epilogue's veil of silence, the reader who is able to join Job in his confessional response to God (42:1–6), and his intercession on behalf of his benighted friends (42:9), thereby testifies to Satan's inability to persuade concerning either the motivation for human piety and uprightness or the basis and character of divine counsel and judgment in heaven and on earth.

This resonates, for me, with the picture I have sketched in Pauline texts, where the hymnic testimonies that center in Christ's non-violent victory over the powers on the cross have as their function *both* to draw worshipers into the sphere of power set loose in the world through that victory, *and* to enlist those worshipers' own powers as participants in non-violent witness *to* the rebellious powers "in the heavenly places"—in a broadening of the vision in Isa 45:23 to draw *those powers* to rejoin the heavenly choir in an eschatological antiphon to the primordial chorus portrayed in Job 38:7—so that, as Paul says, the God "from whom and through whom and unto whom are all things," may be, according to 1 Cor 15:28, πάντα ἐν πᾶσιν.[10]

---

10. For my understanding of the general situation within which resonance operates, see the essay, "Toward a Hermeneutics of Resonance: A Methodological Interlude between the Testaments," in Janzen 2012.

An Intertextual Reading of Job in Relation to the Anti-Pelagian Augustine

Susannah Ticciati

In this essay I have chosen for Job a slightly surprising intertext from within the patristic period: Augustine's anti-Pelagian writings; surprising not only given the more likely candidate of Gregory the Great,[1] but also because Augustine's use of Job in his arguments against the Pelagians is apparently superficial, amounting to what seems like no more than proof-texting. Nevertheless, I hope to justify my choice by showing that, despite appearances, there are unexpected deeper resonances between the Joban worldview and the Augustinian one, which comes to pithy expression in Augustine's claim for original sin. Moreover, I hope to show that reading Job in intertextual relationship with Augustine awakens new meaning in the book of Job. I will focus on one work by Augustine in three books, *The Punishment and Forgiveness of Sins and the Baptism of Little Ones* (hereafter *Pecc. mer.*),[2] in which Augustine appeals to Job as an example of one of the most righteous people to have lived, but who is nevertheless not without sin.

After presenting the prima facie case that Augustine's use of Job as a prooftext does violence to the words of Job by taking them out of their context within the book, this essay will step back from the particular use to which Job's words are put and suggest that the wider tenor of Augustine's argument is less out of keeping with the book of Job than his prooftexts might otherwise suggest. It will identify three successive

---

1. Gregory the Great wrote an extensive and celebrated commentary on the book of Job. See *S. Gregorii Magni Moralia in Iob* (CCSL 143). Augustine himself wrote notes on the book of Job which are published as *Adnotationes in Iob* (CSEL 28). Since these are only fragmentary, and for reasons of space, I will not consider them here.

2. *De peccatorum meritis et remissione et de baptismo parvulorum ad Marcellinum* (CSEL 60); English translations taken from Teske 1997. The translation of the title above is Teske's.

moments of rapprochement between the worlds of Augustine and Job, the final one leading to the opening up of new meaning within Job. To anticipate, the God who speaks out of the whirlwind will come to be heard as the God of grace.

I

Augustine's *Pecc. mer.* is his first anti-Pelagian work, written in 411 or 412.[3] Most extensive reference to Job is made in Book II, which discusses whether it is possible to live a sinless life, and further whether anyone actually has. Job enters the discussion in the company of Noah and Daniel, those mentioned together in Ezek 14:14 as being of exemplary righteousness.[4] Along with them he is held up as proof that even the most righteous of human beings are not without sin, confirming an answer in the negative to the question of whether there has ever actually existed anyone without sin.

Augustine quotes at some length from Job 9 and 13–14, taking words from the mouth of Job which would seem to prove that Job admits his sinfulness, and even finding there an adumbration of the doctrine of original sin. In particular, Job 14:4–5a is used in this context and in others[5] to just this effect: "For who will be clean from filth? No one, not even if one's life lasts only a single day" (Augustine's Old Latin version follows the LXX[6]). This is surely a travesty of the intent and purpose of Job, who (read in context) is appealing to the impossibility of purity

---

3. Shortly after the condemnation of Pelagius's disciple, Caelestius, by the Council of Carthage. Books I and II are written in response to questions posed by the tribune of the Council, Flavius Marcellinus, about Caelestius's views. Book III is provoked by Augustine's reading of Pelagius's *Expositio XIII epistularum Pauli Apostoli* (to be found in Souter 1922), in particular his exposition of Rom 5:12 (*Pecc. mer.* III.1.1; Teske 1997, 22).

4. *Pecc. mer.* II.10.12–12.17. Noah and Daniel are discussed first in 10.12–13, and Job is discussed in 10.14–12.17.

5. See e.g., *Pecc. mer.* I.24.34 and III.6.12–7.13, where Augustine is citing Jerome. Cf. also *De natura et gratia* 7.8 (CSEL 60) and *De perfectione iustitiae hominis* 11.23 (CSEL 42), where Augustine dismisses the Pelagian interpretation of these verses.

6. The Latin reads: "quis enim erit mundus a sordibus? nemo, nec si unius diei fuerit uita eius" (CSEL 60, 85, lines 23–24). It would have been much more difficult for Augustine to use the Hebrew version in support of his argument for original sin. The Hebrew of 14:4–5a reads: מִי־יִתֵּן טָהוֹר מִטָּמֵא לֹא אֶחָד: אִם חֲרוּצִים יָמָיו, "Who can bring a clean thing out of an unclean? There is not one. Since his days are determined" (RSV). It has no reference to the newly born, and the first clause of v. 5 naturally goes together with the rest of v. 5 rather than being linked with v. 4.

before God as part of his accusation against God that God is humanly unaccountable: specifically, that God has the power to make human innocence appear wicked because of the sovereignty of his transcendent (and arbitrary) will. Thus Job 9:19, "Even if I am righteous, my mouth will speak wickedness," and Job 9:31, "Even if I shall be purer than snow and have clean hands, you have sufficiently dipped me in filth,"[7] refer to God's manipulative and abusive distortion of the truth. Yet both verses are cited by Augustine as proof of Job's confession of his own sin.

But not only is the immediate context of Job's words against Augustine's rendering; so is the thrust of the whole book, which vindicates Job not only in the face of the arguments of the friends, according to whom Job's suffering is caused by his sin, but also in relation to the Satan's test, which he passes by remaining faithful to God even in the throes of his suffering. Job is commended by God not only at the beginning (1:8), but also at the end (42:7–8). However, this is not to say that a Pelagian counter-reading of Job as sinless would fare much better. The question of sin is only in view in the book of Job in its relation to suffering: in the implicit question of the Satan ("Does suffering provoke sin, or more specifically, the cursing of God?"; cf. Job 1:11 and 2:5) and in the assertion of the friends ("Suffering is punishment for sin"). The abstract question of the possibility of absolute sinlessness is simply not in view. Thus the Pelagian Controversy is being fought on different terrain from that of the book of Job, and Augustine's use of Job in support of his argument is simply not warranted.

II

However, stepping back from this close-up view, we can discover a first moment of rapprochement between the worlds of Augustine and Job. Augustine's argument for original sin is also an argument for the sovereignty of God's grace. Human beings are dependent on God's grace not only for their existence and their power of free choice, but also for their choice of the good.[8] Thus God's agency precedes and undergirds human agency at every point (except where human beings depart from God's will in bad use of free choice). Moreover, God's precedence is not a matter of mere transcendent sovereignty: it is a transcendence which entails immanence. In Augustine's words:

---

7. Teske's translations of Augustine's Old Latin version, cited in *Pecc. mer.* II.10.14.

8. See *Pecc. mer.* II.6.7 and 18.30–31. From now on references to this work will be given in parentheses in the main text.

> So that we may love God, *love is poured out in our hearts*, not by us, but
> *by the Holy Spirit who has been given to us* (Rom 5:5). We human beings
> strive to find in our will some good that is ours and that we do not have
> from God, but I do not know how one can find such a good. (II.17.27–
> 18.28)

God operates on human beings not from the outside but within them,
generating the human will at its source.[9]

With this vision we may compare that of the book of Job. God's
speeches out of the whirlwind present a God who precedes and transcends
human machinations (human questions of wickedness and innocence), a
God who has brought into existence not only Job but also the whole
creation of which Job is a tiny part. The implication is that God does not
react to events in the world from an independent but co-ordinated van-
tage point, rewarding here and punishing there. Rather, God holds the
whole of creation in being, including Job's own place in it as a righteous
sufferer. Furthermore, as transcendent creator, God is also intimately
present to creation. The divine speeches make clear not only that God
knows the ins and outs of his creation, but that he knows them precisely
in creating them. God is present to the movement of the clouds (Job
38:36), to the dance of predator and prey (38:39–41), to the birthing
cycle of the goats and the deer (39:1–3)—as their cause and source. God
knows these creaturely movements from the inside.

The similarity between Augustine and Job on this macro-level is a
formal one. Both present a prevenient and transcendent God who is also
inwardly present to creation as its cause. For Augustine, God operates
internally to the human will, by his grace bringing about a good will
turned towards him. For the book of Job, God operates internally to a
creation which exceeds Job but includes him within it. For both, God is
at once sovereign and intimate, transcendent and immanent. The portrayals depart from one another materially, however, insofar as Augustine's
vision of God's transcendent immanence is allied to an anthropocentric-
ity which places the question of human salvation at the centre, while
Job's vision is of a creation which exceeds human concerns, decentring
them in their preoccupation with human justice. The God of the whirlwind speeches cannot simply be equated with Augustine's God of grace:
while we may have discovered a formal similarity, the rapprochement
between Augustinian and Joban worlds is only partial; they remain on
different planes.

---

9. For a more thorough examination of the relation between grace and free
choice in Augustine along these lines, see Ticciati 2010.

III

But a further moment of rapprochement becomes possible if we focus in on another aspect of Augustine's account. This aspect sounds only a minor note in the present work, but it is intensified considerably as the Pelagian Controversy proceeds, reaching its highest pitch of intensity in his much later works written to the monks of Hadrumetum and Marseilles, later labelled Semi-Pelagians.[10] The aspect in question is Augustine's appeal to the inscrutability of God's judgment, made in response to the question of why grace is given to one person and not to another—the question of the rationale of God's distribution of grace.[11] It is often accompanied by citation of Rom 11:33: "O the depth of the riches of the wisdom and knowledge of God! How inscrutable [*inscrutabilia*] are his judgments and unsearchable [*inuestigabiles*] his ways!" In the present work Augustine comes up against the problem about half-way through Book I (*Pecc. mer.* I.21.29–30), citing Rom 11:33 not just once but three times in response (once in the context of Rom 11:32–36). The passage begins as follows, weaving in other scriptural citations along the way:

> Why this grace comes to one person and does not come to another can have an hidden [*occulta*], but not an unjust cause. *Is there injustice* [iniquitas] *in God? Heaven forbid* (Rom 9:14). But we must first bend our necks before the authorities of the holy scriptures so that through faith each of us may come to understanding. Scripture did not, after all, say without a reason, *Your judgments are like a great abyss* (Ps 36:7). As if he were gasping at the depth of this abyss, the apostle cried out, *Oh the depth of the riches of the wisdom and knowledge of God!* (Rom 11:33). (I.21.29)

In Book II Augustine's argument forces him to the same austere conclusion at two points, but rather than citing Rom 11:33 he makes reference simply to "the decision (*ratio*) of his hidden justice [*aequitatis secretae*]" (II.5.6), and to the "plan of righteousness [*consilium iustitiae*] that lies more deeply hidden [*occultioris*] in him" (II.18.32).

This has immediate resonance with the book of Job, in which God's unsearchability is a keynote. In broad terms, just as Augustine's God transcends the categories of human justice, so does the God of the book of Job—as God's response to Job out of the whirlwind makes abundantly

---

10. *De gratia et libero arbitrio, De correptione et gratia, De praedestinatione sanctorum* (PL 44) and *De dono perseverantiae* (PL 45).

11. See Ticciati 2011, in which I interpret these appeals not as admissions of defeat in argument, but as significant moments in Augustine's theological vision. Another author to treat them constructively is Paul Rigby (2000; 2002).

apparent. But more specifically, it is possible that we find something approaching a verbal equivalent of Augustine's *inscrutabilia* and *inuestigabiles* in the Hebrew root חקר ("search out"), which pervades the book of Job and is used to indicate either the depths to be searched out, or (as negated) that which is unsearchable.[12] This root appears in God's first speech out of the whirlwind, describing the depths of the sea which exceed Job's imagination and experience, as God asks Job, "Have you entered into the springs of the sea, or walked in the recesses of the deep (בחקר תהום)?" (38:16).[13] While the reference is not directly to God's depths or unsearchability, the unplumbed depths of creation (which God expands upon in the following verses) suggest a fortiori God's unsearchability for Job.

A similar, if not identical, note is played in Job 28, the Hymn to Wisdom. While this is often thought to be an interpolation, it nevertheless captures an important aspect of the flavor of the book. The Hymn begins by evoking the spectacular human feats of natural discovery: "Men put an end to darkness, and search out (חוקר) to the farthest bound the ore in gloom and deep darkness" (28:3). But this is only so as to conjure up by comparison and contrast the even greater fathoms of wisdom, which only God can search out: "But where shall wisdom be found?... God understands the way to it... [H]e saw it and declared it; he established it, and searched it out (חקרה)" (vv. 12, 23, 27). The comparison works both negatively, insofar as it contrasts what human beings can discover with a wisdom which is beyond their reach, but also positively insofar as wisdom gains, in an intensified way, the resonance of the connotations of the human search. For our purposes, the implication is that God, like the wisdom only he can fathom, is unsearchable for human beings.

The unsearchability of God in both Augustine's work and the book of Job seems to bring their two worlds close together. However, we must not be too hasty in drawing this conclusion, since it is not just on the mouth of God and in the Hymn to Wisdom (both in their ways authoritative within the book of Job) that we find the evocation of God's unsearchability. The friends, too, sound this note, bringing blatantly home the message that appeals to God's unsearchability can serve different purposes. Thus, how can we be sure, without further investigation, whether Augustine's appeals and those which win out in the book of Job are in keeping with one another? Here is Eliphaz:

---

12. Cf., e.g., Job 11:7 and 5:9 respectively.

13. English biblical translations, when not in the context of Augustine's usage and unless otherwise stated, will be taken from the RSV.

As for me, I would seek God,
and to God would I commit my cause;
who does great things and unsearchable (וְאֵין חֵקֶר),
marvelous things without number. (Job 5:8–9)

And here is Zophar:

Can you find out the deep things of God (הַחֵקֶר אֱלוֹהַ)?
Can you find out the limit of the Almighty?
It is higher than heaven—what can you do?
Deeper than Sheol—what can you know? (Job 11:7–8)

On the basis of these isolated verses it is impossible to pick out the broader dynamic to which appeal to God's unsearchability contributes for either Eliphaz or Zophar. But without looking any further, might it not seem more likely that its role in Augustine is more similar to its role for the friends than that which it plays in God's speeches or in the Hymn to Wisdom—as a buffer to further argumentation and attack on God's justice? Does it not serve in both cases to keep God beyond questioning? Indeed, as we saw above, Augustine cites (alongside Rom 11:33) Rom 9:14: "Is there injustice in God? Heaven forbid."[14] Surely this is akin to such arguments as we find on the mouth of Bildad: "Does God pervert justice? Or does the Almighty pervert the right?" (Job 8:3). By contrast with this, God's speeches out of the whirlwind evoke an amoral God, or at least one who brings human categories of justice even more thoroughly into question than Augustine does: God so transcends them that even a "hidden justice" cannot be appropriately predicated of God (the gap being too wide for one and the same word to bridge). This goes together with Job's angry challenge of the transcendent, "amoral" God, whose tone is nowhere to be found in Augustine's more measured work.

IV

Thus the second attempted rapprochement gets us only so far, at most generating an ambivalence in Augustine between a dynamic akin to the trajectory from Job to God and one more akin to the speeches of Job's "miserable comforters" (Job 16:2). We embark, then, on the final step of the essay in the hope that it will bear more fruit. This will involve an investigation of the "Pelagian mindset" which Augustine's account of original sin is constructed to counter.[15] By filling in the details of this, we

14. *Pecc. mer.* I.21.29.
15. This will be constructed on the basis of the views Augustine critiques, not by examining extant Pelagian sources independently. Indeed, "Pelagianism" as a

will be in a better position to understand Augustine's own agenda, and consequently the way in which it resonates at a deeper level with that of the book of Job: for the Pelagian mindset will be exposed to be uncannily similar to that of the friends.

A primary concern for the Pelagians is to uphold the justice of God. Thus they argue that the human will must be in the position to do what God commands, and to do so independently of God's help (*Pecc. mer.* II.3.3). By contrast, Augustine argues that it is necessary to pray for God's help, without which the will lacks the requisite strength to do what is right (II.3.3–5.5), and thus that not only the will, but also the good will, is a gift of God (II.18.30). As becomes even clearer in Augustine's later anti-Pelagian works, the Pelagian view is that God's grace consists in the gift of free choice at creation, and in the external guidance of the law and Christ's teaching, while for Augustine God, by his grace, takes up residence within the ongoing operation of the human will.[16] In other words, Augustine's God operates internally to the human will (which is never just neutral, but oriented to the good or the bad) and the Pelagian God cooperates with human beings from the outside, never infringing upon their wills, which retain a fundamental neutrality and independence of God.

This Pelagian view of the will provides the foundation for a merit-based view of human action in relation to divine action. Because the will is independent of God's grace, grace can be conceived as given in response to human acts of will. This, in turn, allows the Pelagians to avoid imputing any arbitrariness to the divine distribution of grace which might bring the divine justice into question. This Pelagian nexus of thought begins to emerge in Augustine's discussion of the fate of unbaptised infants in Book I of *Pecc. mer.* Assuming with Augustine that infants have accrued no personal sins, the Pelagians argue that unbaptised infants cannot be condemned to damnation, apparently foreseeing the alternative (unpalatable) conclusion reached by Augustine, that God's gift of salvation to one infant rather than another depends not on human merit but on God's inscrutable judgments.[17] It becomes clear from

---

systematic theological schema, so it has been argued, is a creation more of Augustine than of his opponents (cf. P. Brown 1967, 345).

16. Cf. *De gestis Pelagii* 14.30–31 and *De gratia Christi et de peccato originali* I.3.3 (CSEL 42).

17. See *Pecc. mer.* I.18.23–21.30. Augustine has previously refuted another possibility entertained by the Pelagians that infants are forgiven personal sin at baptism, a view which likewise maintains the non-arbitrariness of divine grace (I.17.22). Augustine goes on to ridicule a merit-based view of grace in I.22.31–33.

Augustine's later anti-Pelagians works that the merit-based view can include the forgiveness of sin in response to human repentance,[18] though, as we have seen, it does not extend to God's future help of the will. Rather, the will stands alone, meriting what it does by its own discrete acts, and being forgiven those wrongful acts of the past for which forgiveness is asked.

This calculable, merit-based worldview has strong resonances with that of Job's friends, for whom divine reward and punishment correspond to human righteousness and wickedness respectively. Any number of verses could be picked out to demonstrate this. But the following from Bildad are exemplary:

> If you will seek God
> and make supplication to the Almighty,
> if you are pure and upright,
> surely then he will rouse himself for you
> and reward you with a rightful habitation.
> …
> Can papyrus grow where there is no marsh?
> Can reeds flourish where there is no water?
> While yet in flower and not cut down,
> they wither before any other plant.
> Such are the paths of all who forget God;
> the hope of the godless man shall perish. (Job 8:5–6, 11–13)

As in the Pelagian worldview there is room here also for supplication to God, and (as becomes clearer in Zophar's speech in Job 11) for a dynamic like that of repentance and forgiveness. At the root of both, however, is an assumption of the measurability of human life: for the friends in terms of the traditional categories of righteousness and wickedness, and for the Pelagians in terms of the moral categories of good and evil, or, for short, in terms of human merit. And in both, divine justice is just the mirror image of this, thereby becoming equally measurable. In the case of the friends this needs qualification in view of their appeals to the unsearchability of God, and the incommensurability between God and human beings expressed in Eliphaz's question: "Can mortal man be righteous before God? Can a man be pure before his Maker?" (4:17). But such a qualification is only made at the edges, and does not dislodge the core belief in a trustworthy and calculable doctrine of retribution. An important difference between the views of the Pelagians and of the friends lies in the contrast between the Pelagian

18. See, e.g., *De natura et gratia* 18.20.

eschatological and extrinsic understanding of divine reward and punishment and the friends' immanent earthly understanding according to which they are inherent within the workings of creation. But this does not disturb the more basic confluence of their views.

Given this resonance between the Pelagians and Job's friends, might we find a similar resonance between the views of Augustine and Job? I will begin by looking at Job 9, since it is here that Job casts the argument in legal terms, and by doing so exposes the flaws at the heart of the tidy system of the friends.[19]

> Truly I know that it is so:
> But how can a man win (יִצְדַּק) against God?
> If one wished to contend (לָרִיב) with him,
> he would not answer one in a thousand times.
> …
> Though I am innocent (צָדַקְתִּי), I cannot answer him;
> I must appeal for mercy to my accuser.
> If I summoned him and he answered me,
> I would not believe that he was listening to my voice.
> …
> If it is a contest of strength, behold him!
> If it is a matter of litigation (לְמִשְׁפָּט), who can summon him?
> Though I am innocent (אֶצְדָּק), my own mouth would condemn me
> (יַרְשִׁיעֵנִי);
> I am perfect (תָּם־אָנִי), and he declares me perverse.
> I am perfect (תָּם־אָנִי); I regard not myself;
> I loathe my life.
> It is all one; therefore I say,
> he destroys both the perfect (תָּם) and the wicked (וְרָשָׁע).
>
> (Job 9:2–3, 15–16, 19–22)[20]

This is Job's hypothetical trial against God, hypothetical because his complaint is precisely that God cannot be called legally to account.[21] But Job nevertheless revels in legal terminology, as the translation of various key words here attempts to bring out. The legal system in the terms of which Job is operating here might be summed up in the opposition between the root צָדֵק ("innocent/righteous") and the root רָשַׁע ("wicked"),

---

19. Cf. Zuckerman 1991, 104–17, in which Zuckerman (following others) argues that Job is conducting a *rīb* (lawsuit) against God. In particular, he points to the way in which Job gives a legal spin to the moral categories of the friends (compare 9:2 and 4:17) (106).

20. Translation taken from the RSV, but modified where necessary.

21. See Ticciati 2005: Chapter 5, and for a fuller account of the argument to follow, Chapter 6.

captured especially in v. 20a. Job shows how the God who transcends the law simply collapses the distinction, turning his innocence into wickedness. The law is a malleable tool in the hands of the arbitrary God at its root. But something unexpected emerges from this collapse: Job holds all the more confidently to his integrity. The word translated here as "perfect" (תם) is the very same word God used of Job in 1:1. It connotes a wholeness which is not captured by "perfect," nor by any possible legal rendition. Job's repeated exclamation, תם־אני (in vv. 20b and 21a), is thus strongly suggestive of his own transcendence of the legal system. Just like the "arbitrary" God to whom he appeals, Job exceeds all legal categories and cannot be bound by them.

By contrast with the worldview of the friends, according to which human life is measurable, calculable by way of the doctrine of retribution, Job's life is immeasurable, and any attempt to measure it by way of legal or other categories will leave the remainder of an unaccounted-for excess.[22] This is what Job discovers in his trial against God. And his discovery is more than confirmed by God's speeches out of the whirlwind, in which God appears to him as the creator, beyond the categories of the law, addressing him as a creature among other creatures, none of which can be summed up according to a finite (humanly defined) purpose. In this explosion of creaturely activity, God can nevertheless single out Job, addressing him in all his particularity.

Do we find any such excess in Augustine? What should immediately strike one in the light of this exposition of Job—but as a negative image of the immeasurability discovered there—is the negative excess of original sin, which precedes and exceeds any personal sin a human being might acquire over a lifetime. This original orientation away from God, which human beings have no power to turn about, indicates a "bad merit" which cannot be measured, and thus a human will which exceeds the calculability of the Pelagian will in its immeasurable depths.[23] And human immeasurability is complemented by a view of God's justice as more than the mirror-image of measurable acts of human will. Such is the fruit of Augustine's apparently troubling view that God condemns human beings for what they could not have helped.

This negative depth in Augustine has, in fact, a direct counterpart in Job (even if all the connotations of original sin are not present there). As Job grows in assurance of his own innocence, he is at once plunged more deeply into a wretchedness and humiliation also stemming from his relationship with the arbitrary God of the law: "yet you will plunge me

---

22. A similar contrast is drawn in Habel 1981.
23. These are explored brilliantly by Wetzel (1992).

into a pit, and my own clothes will abhor me" (9:31); "for I am filled with disgrace" (10:15); "and my leanness has risen up against me, it testifies to my face" (16:8). But if Job's excessive relationship to God is two-sided, can we find in Augustine a positive counterpart to the negative excess of original sin? I suggest that we do so in the good will issuing from grace. Just as human beings exceed their bad personal merits in their original sin, so as graced by God do they exceed their good personal merits. The latter are rooted in the fundamental liberating dependence of human beings on God. Such an orientation to God exceeds, upholds and infuses the particular creaturely orientations they express in their acts towards their fellow creatures. Correspondingly, God's gift of grace precedes and exceeds these acts: this is just what Augustine means by claiming that it is unmerited—or gratuitous.[24] God is beyond human measure.

V

In the worlds of both Job and Augustine the excess of human beings is their rootedness in God. While they operate according to different categories (law and creation in Job; sin and redemption in Augustine), the dynamics of each is fundamentally similar. However, such intertextual *resonance* may, in turn, invite the exploration of an intertextual *awakening of meaning* in each of the intertexts. I will conclude with just such an exploration, and specifically of the meaning Augustine's text awakens in Job.

When we look back at the God who upholds Job's integrity in the light of Augustinian grace, we are invited to see the God of the whirlwind speeches precisely as the God of grace. This is not a connection one would initially make, given the voice with which God speaks out of the whirlwind: one of power, whose moments of tenderness (as in the description of the birthing of the goats) cannot straightforwardly be equated with gracious love. But it is a connection Augustine himself makes, interpreting the whirlwind speeches as expressive of Christ, and Job's confession in 42:5–6 as a vision of Christ's righteousness (*Pecc. mer.* II.11). In other words, the power of God expressed in the whirlwind speeches is, for Augustine, the power of Christ—which is (implicitly) a power both to suffer and to heal as God incarnate. In this light we see the display of chs. 38–41 in a new way. They show forth the power of the creator as the one who is also redeemer, and therefore as the one who meets Job in his plight. It is not a power of indifference but a power

---

24. E.g. *Pecc. mer.* I.21.29 (*gratiam gratuitam*).

of victory over sin, suffering and evil. This rereading has profound implications also for the rest of the book, beyond those exploited by Augustine. Job's suffering (as unjust, even while he is subject to original sin) can be seen as a foreshadowing of the way taken by the suffering Christ. The prologue is therefore not an arbitrary wager of God with the Satan, but the catching up of Job into God's purposes in Christ; in Barth's terms, Job's election as a witness to Christ.[25]

What this exercise in intertextual reading shows is that the meaning of a text is neither something which is all already there for the finding (in the text), nor something created entirely by the reader (imposed on the text). Rather, insofar as meaning is *awakened*, we can say that it occurs at the interface between the text and reader; it is a relational product. Thus, new historical contexts are environments within which new meanings can be awakened. In this case, the context created by Augustine's doctrine of grace (not available at the time of the composition of the various layers of the book of Job) elicits new meaning according to which the sovereignty of the God of the whirlwind speeches is the sovereignty of grace, which in turn makes sense of God's singling out of Job both in the prologue and in the address of the whirlwind speeches. The new meaning is therefore also an illuminating one, making sense of aspects of the book which might otherwise have been puzzling. Thus Augustine's work, far from relegating Job to a prooftext which distorts its plain sense, operates as an intertext which evokes a series of increasingly deep resonances between the theological worlds of Augustine and Job, at the deepest level awakening new meaning in the book of Job.

25. Barth 1961, 388.

JOB IN MODERN AND CONTEMPORARY LITERATURE ON THE BACKGROUND OF TRADITION: SIDELIGHTS OF A JEWISH READING

Gabrielle Oberhänsli

(Translated from the German, Yiddish, and Hebrew by Anette Andrée)

In the book of Job I read
And from beyond the ages
His heart's blood calls out to me:
I have graves.
I don't even have graves.
My people have turned to ashes.
My world burnt by Cain.

You have been pitched into misery, man from the Land of Uz.
And yet—do you know the crematoriums of exile?
What is your disaster, Job, and what is your misery
Compared with the greatest tragedy of all
That of a people without graves?

I read and read.
Here, out of the storm
The word of the Creator,
Here is his thunder asking questions—
But for the soul there is no redeemer.
It aches in its own fashion.
And all of a sudden:
"Were the gates of death revealed to you
And did you see the gates of utter darkness?"
That is the question—the obvious,
The truly vital one
The answer to it?

Were the gates of death revealed you?
And what lies beyond them—do you know?
He who resurrects and kills and resurrects,
It is well-known: Only loss awaits its owners.

Beyond the gates of death—
Your sons and daughters, Job!
Beyond the gates of death, concealed, far away,
There is a people there—devoured by fire,
There are millions there, waiting,
There is the great assembly completely burnt—
And this assembly will appear when it sanctifies itself in the battle of
redemption,
The last battle,
When the gates of death open.[1]

This poem by the Belarusian-born, Hebrew-Jewish poet and dramatist Aaron Zeitlin (1898–1973) was written in 1946, immediately after the Shoah, in which his whole family was annihilated. Zeitlin belongs thus to the precursors of those Jewish writers who turn Job into the primary biblical Shoah-protagonist. Where the first literary testimonies dealing with Auschwitz have not wholly discarded a theological interpretive framework—for example, in the member of the French Resistance Charlotte Delbo (1946) or in the Italian chemist Primo Levi (1947)—Job is from the very beginning the principal interpretative figure of the Holocaust, most notably in Elie Wiesel, through whose life's work Job runs as a veritable leitmotif.[2] While militant tones, such as the battle motif or the figure of Cain, can already be discerned in Aaron Zeitlin's poem, this trait will intensify significantly in the following decades; Job's hatred grows. And just as in Zeitlin, in the contemporary literature the question of theodicy is raised by Job merely in a resigned fashion, without actually expecting an answer, to say nothing of accepting one.

Seen against the background of the traditional Jewish literature, this shaping of Job into a hate-filled embodiment of the suffering Jew is remarkable for two reasons: on the one hand, because Job is regarded neither in the Hebrew Bible nor in talmudic literature as a Jew and, on the other, because the topos of Job's hatred is alien to both the Bible and the Talmud.

In the following reflections, the path followed by Job through the Jewish literature will be traced in more or less rough outlines, in the course of which biblical and rabbinical literature will receive only a brief viewing, so that modern and contemporary texts can be given greater scope. My methodological starting point here is the investigation of the

1. Aaron Zeitlin, "Be-hippatah sha'arê mawet" ("When the Gates of Death Open"), in Shaked 2005, 342–43. Here, as in the concluding poem by Nathan Zach, the defective punctuation of the Hebrew text has been retained.

2. Wiesel 1958 (the title of the original Yiddish text: *Un die Welt hot geschwign* 1956), 1975, 179–99; 1979; Wiesel and Eisenberg 1986.

dialogic interactions between the book of Job, on the one hand, and talmudic-rabbinic, modern, and post-modern Jewish literature, on the other, revealing themes (the overlapping motifs or "Sondergut"), which show the direction the reception of Job tended to take. A subsequent examination of these themes in their dynamic interplay with their new intratextual and extratextual contexts provides answers to questions I am particularly interested in. What were the reasons—political, socio-cultural, religious—for entering into a dialogue with the book of Job? How and why are the meaning of the original biblical motifs altered in the course of dialogic interchanges through the centuries? In what way is the biblical book itself "changed" or updated by the conversations with later texts? In order to bundle together the many aspects resulting from my exploration of the long and fascinating dialogic interactions with Job, I have focused on two aspects: the possible answers the Joban material supplies to the problem of theodicy and the specific aspect of Job's hatred of God and humanity.

The Theodicy in the Biblical Book

The book of Job is in all probability one of the most philosophical texts in the Hebrew Bible in the sense that this book—even though in a narrative and not an analytical way—attempts to fathom the problem of theodicy intellectually. To what extent is God responsible for the evil in the world? Why do the righteous suffer? To these questions Job, his friends, God, and the narrative arrangement of the text as a whole provide completely different answers.[3]

In the course of reading the text, the following interpretive approaches gradually emerge. The prologue with its two scenes set in heaven offers an answer to the question of why the pious suffers guiltlessly in, at first glance, a most unexpected way, since his misery basically results from a wager between God, as capricious ruler of the world, and Satan, as malicious deuteragonist, setting the whole action into motion. Without sharing the cynicism inherent in this approach, Job declares—be it as a sufferer in the frame story or as a rebel in the dialogues—that everything, good as well as bad, has its origin in God, condensing this view in two sentences, as simple as they are stupendous: "The Lord has given and the Lord has taken" (Job 1:21) and "Shall we accept the good from the hand of God and not accept the bad?" (Job 2:10). With his submissive attitude,

---

3. For a historical-critical examination of the book of Job and biographical references, see Oorschot 1995.

however, the protagonist reaches the limit of what is conceivable, so that God's ambivalence induces him to unusually blasphemous tones—God, a sadist?—leading him to the point of breaking up God's oneness, as he accuses God before God:

> God delivers me to injustice, he casts me into the hands of the wicked. I was at peace, and he broke me apart, he took me by the neck and shattered me; he set me up as his target. His arrows threaten me from all around, he pierces my kidneys without mercy and spills my gall on the ground... Oh earth, do not cover my blood and let there be no resting-place for my cry! Even now, behold, there is a witness for me in heaven, testifying for me on high. My friends mock me, my weeping eye looks up to God that he administer justice to a man against God, to the son of man against his friend. (Job 16:11–13, 18–21)

Worlds apart from him are Job's friends, Eliphaz, Bildad, and Zophar—comforters of the worst sort! Preaching in numerous variations a connection between personal conduct and wellbeing, they attribute Job's misery to a sin of some kind: a genuine guilt of humanity in itself, a substantial offence against the law, a violation of social-ethical principles, or even just the improper way Job argues with God. Explaining suffering as a divine warning, Elihu, the latecomer to the group—and from a literary-critical point of view evidently somewhat lagging behind as well—advocates a hardly more differentiated doctrine of retribution. With all the more suspense, therefore, does the reader, on reaching the conclusion and climax of the dialogue section, look forward to the appearance of God, whose words, nevertheless, remain obscure—an indication that the universalistic ways of the Creator are incomprehensible to human beings or that God has to repeatedly subdue the powers of chaos, symbolized as Leviathan and Behemoth?[4] The epilogue, finally, seems utterly to confuse the different positions. While Job recants, God, contrary to the immediately preceding monologue, vindicates Job by rejecting the argumentation of the friends, and acts himself, however, according to the just-repudiated doctrine of retribution by rewarding the undisputedly loyal Job.

From all these refractions and disparities, from the plethora of contradictory resolutions of the problem of theodicy, as well as from the ambivalent attitude of the protagonist as sufferer and rebel, the biblical book of Job ultimately draws its huge potential for suspense. Further possibilities of confronting the problem of theodicy could be conceived, such as invoked, for instance, in the scenario "beyond the gates of death"

---

4. Cf. Keel 1978.

in the opening poem by Aaron Zeitlin. And, in actual fact, rabbinical thinking with its belief in a resurrection of the dead does venture into new domains to the effect that in the coming world God's justice would be able to show itself and thus resolve the problem of theodicy. This is a position that is, however, explicitly excluded in the biblical book in statements such as Job 7:9: "He who descends to the underworld does not ascend again."

Nonetheless, the answer to Job's question fails to materialize, hovering instead above the interplay between the various approaches, inciting the later history of the reception of Job to further reflection. A dominant feature of the (post-)modern Jewish literature dealing with Job is, however, that it consecutively examines and rejects the positions stated—first of all, the connection established between personal conduct and well-being. This, in the last analysis, the "Wiedergutmachung" at the end of the biblical book endorses, as well: a brief mention that everything is restored to Job in double measure, followed by a quick fading out, not a word about how Job contends with the death of his first ten children and what confidence he would be able to place in a good fortune he had already once before seen completely annihilated.[5]

The greatest distinction between the post-biblical, here specifically the contemporary, figures of Job and the biblical Job is, in fact, that the biblical protagonist adheres unwaveringly to God, and this may also be the reason why in Job no hatred grows, neither of God nor of humanity. In the biblical book of Job the words שׂנא ("to hate") and שׂנאה ("hatred") hardly appear, and if they do occur, then it is in statements categorically rejecting that feeling such as Job 31:28–29: "This too would be a penal crime…if I took pleasure in the downfall of him hating me." Hatred does not develop in the argument but in the turning away, there where all explanation is withheld and the theological investigation of the theodicy has been abandoned.

From the End of Classical Antiquity to the Twentieth Century

Surveying the—albeit here only roughly outlined—history of Job's reception from the beginning of classical antiquity to the twentieth century, one is rather surprised at how freely the literary production treats Job, indeed, how elastic the figure of Job proves to be in its interpretation.[6]

---

5. Shalev, "ʾîsh hayâ be-ʾerets ʿûts" ("Once Upon a Time There Was a Man in the Land of Uz: The Story of Job"), in Shalev 1985, 105–13.

6. On the reception of Job in the Jewish World, see Oberhänsli-Widmer 2003.

There is, to begin with, the *Testament of Job* (Schaller 1978) written around the first century C.E., a Hellenistic-Jewish text in which Job is transformed into a Jewish convert preaching the resurrection of the dead and acting as a model of social welfare—parts not specified or but little spelled out in the biblical version. Imperative for the whole further development of Job in the Jewish literature is at this point the question of Job's nationality. Job, the man from the Land of Uz, does not possess a patronym, and Uz, like all the other place names in the book of Job, lies outside the borders of Israel,[7] making Job and his friends non-Jews—as if the biblical authors recoiled from putting Job's daring talk about God into the mouth of an Israelite protagonist.

The Talmudic sages, on the other hand, argue vehemently among themselves about Job's ethnic provenance, some following the early Jewish *Testament of Job* and declaring Job to be a Jew, others denying him any Jewish provenance at all. Occurring between the first and the sixth century of the Christian calendar, this rabbinical debate is—as has been well established—of the greatest importance for all later Jewish tradition. The most comprehensive rabbinical passage dealing with Job is found in the tract *Baba Batra* 14b–16b of the Babylonian Talmud, and here—for all the rabbinical dialectic—a massive denigration of Job is evident. Job is declared a goy, a blasphemer, his name אִיּוֹב is etymologically linked with אוֹיֵב ("enemy"), his share in the coming world is cancelled, and, by reducing him to a מָשָׁל, a parable, his very existence disputed. For example:

> A certain rabbi sat in front of Rav Samuel bar Nahmani, sat and declared: Job has neither existed nor has he been created, but is, as matter of fact, a parable… An objection was raised: There was a certain pious man in the gentile nations named Job, but he only came into the world to receive his reward, and when the Holy One, blessed be he, brought chastisements upon him, he began to curse and blaspheme, so that the Holy One, blessed be he, doubled his reward in this world in order to oust him from the world to come. (*Baba Batra* 15a, b)

Job's exclusion from the Jewish family by the rabbis has serious consequences, since the talmudic sages dominate all later commentary literature, and Job, by not having a place assigned to him in the Jewish liturgy, becomes for centuries a peripheral minor figure in Jewish literature. It is, therefore, quite possible to leap boldly over the centuries in the Jewish reception of Job, for until the turn of the twentieth century Job remains an insignificant character. The two important medieval currents,

---

7. On the localizations, see Maag 1982, 14–19.

Kabbalah and religious philosophy, do in part rediscover Job (Maimonides for his treatise on predestination, Nahmanides for his concept of metempsychosis), but generally the commentaries follow the talmudic assertions. From late antiquity up to modern times, Job is a "goy," his message of only restricted relevance for Jewry.

A fundamentally new way of reading Job does not occur before the Enlightenment and consequent secularization, which in the Jewish world set in during the eighteenth century. It is worth noting that the Jewish emancipation implies not only an outward but also an inward emancipation, a dissociation from the *Hazal*, the great sages of the religious tradition. In the Jewish reception of Job this new intellectual independence leads to a break with tradition and to an exploration of new interpretive fields, since for the first time other voices beyond the rabbis' receive both a hearing and a significance.

Not until the great tragedies of modern history, however, does Job, treated by the rabbis as a minor figure, become one of the most important interpretive figures of modern Jewry. The disastrous persecutions of the nineteenth and twentieth centuries, the pogroms in Eastern Europe, and the Shoah make the question of theodicy more vital than ever for a people whose sacred literature presents the picture of a good and just God manifesting himself precisely in the history of his people—and what biblical figure could be better suited to accuse God for the terrible suffering brought upon his people than Job?

A number of the most important works dealing with Job—of which in the twentieth century some hundreds exist—will be mentioned here briefly (see Langenhorst 1995). Viewed in chronological succession, these works reveal a remarkable line of development. The modern Job mirrors, on the one hand, contemporary history reaching from the pogroms in Eastern Europe to the Jewish–Arabic wars in Israel and displays, on the other, an orientation that has become increasingly more psychological than theological.

In 1894 Isaac Leib Perez (1851–1915) composed his masterly short story *Bonze Schweig* (Perez 1994). Written under the impact of the pogroms and the destitution of the Jews in Eastern Europe, it tells the story of a poor Jewish labourer who only experiences misery in this world but is recompensed in heaven in a fairytale manner. Yet behind the sugary sweet scene in heaven with little angels wearing little silver slippers, a massive criticism of passively endured suffering can be detected. Even so, by explicitly identifying his Bonze Schweig, the small Jewish everyman, with Job, Perez returns Job to Jewry. Here is a short passage from the heavenly court scene, in which the divine advocate intercedes for Job:

"Never did he complain," continues the advocate, "neither about God nor about mankind, not a spark of hatred gleamed in his eyes, and never did he raise them towards heaven with an expression of reproach"…"Job could not endure it yet *he* was more miserable than Job—" (112)

A submissive sufferer, without a vestige of hatred is this Bonze-Job. The story is, nevertheless, far from being the idyll it pretends to be. The whole reparation consists, accordingly, in a slice of bread and butter served daily by the celestial kitchen, which in view of Bonze's suffering borders upon sheer cynicism.

Better known than Perez's short story is the novel *Hiob: Roman eines einfachen Mannes* (*Job: The Story of a Simple Man*) written in 1930 by Joseph Roth (1894–1939), which, particularly in the film version by Michael Kehlmann, appears to be a terrible foreshadowing of the Holocaust. As indicated by the subtitle, the central character, the Job figure by the name of Mendel Singer, is here also a simple and pious man, an Eastern Jew, haunted by bad luck, who emigrates to the United States and loses everything: possessions, home, sons, wife. When, finally, in addition to all this, his daughter develops a serious mental illness, the pain proves more than Mendel is able to bear, and he, who had previously adhered unfalteringly to his fear of God, now puts a drastic end to his relationship with God. Here is a short passage from the dramatic peripeteia, in which Mendel gets ready to burn his praying utensils:

> Thus Mendel stood in front of the open window, shouting and stamping his feet. He held the little red velvet bag in his arms, but he did not throw it in. A couple of times he lifted it up, but his arms let it drop again. His heart was angry with God, but in his muscles the fear of God was still alive. For fifty years, day by day, these hands had spread out the tallith and folded it again, had unrolled the phylacteries and wound them around his head and left arm, had opened this prayer book, turned the pages over and over and closed it again. Now his hands refused to obey Mendel's anger. (Roth 1979, 115)

In Roth's novel, for the first time in the Jewish reception of Job, feelings of hatred may be perceived, hatred of humankind and hatred of God, which notably find an expression in Mendel-Job's answer to the question of his appalled friends, when they ask what he actually would want to burn (116): "It is God I want to burn." Nevertheless, the novel—following the biblical text—does have a happy ending, which shall, however, not be disclosed here. Mendel-Job finds his way back from his hatred of God and humankind.

With their works Perez and Roth have shaped Job even before the Shoah into the interpretive figure of the poor Eastern Jew, thereby inspiring works dealing with Job immediately after the Shoah, for in the 1940s Job becomes the representative symbolic figure for a Jewry haunted by the Holocaust. While Jewish Holocaust theologies—which are indisputably predominately rabbinically influenced—scarcely turn back to Job in order to explain the break in Jewish history,[8] Jewish literature selects Job as one of its most preferred protagonists.

Leading the way here is Margarete Susman (1872–1966) with her wide-ranging essay *Das Buch Hiob und das Schicksal des jüdischen Volkes*, published in 1946 (and appearing in Susman 1996), in which she reads the biblical book of Job parallel to the history of the Jewish people.

In the same year and in a substantially more masterly fashion, the Yiddish author Zvi Kolitz (1919–2002) composed the poetic text *Jossel Rakovers Wendung zu Gott*.[9] This short work is the fictitious record of a combatant in the Warsaw Ghetto who, in the face of certain death, settles accounts with God in the manner of Job, concealing the record as a testament in a bottle. Kolitz's Jossel Rakover is a most poignant and convincing Job figure, intellectually joining Job's inner-division between devoutness and rebellion when he states:

> I die calmly, peacefully, but not appeased, beaten but not enslaved, bitter but not disillusioned. Believing but not praying, not pleading, loving God but not blindly saying "Amen" to him. (41 [94])

According to this declaration Jossel Rakover dies reconciled, without hatred. Nevertheless, no happy ending is to be found here anymore: the biblical epilogue is missing.

In our reading of Job, Jossel Rakover's death in the Warsaw Ghetto has brought us to the very focus of the Holocaust. Before turning to the work of Israeli authors writing in Hebrew, the following points may be noted in retrospect. While the Bible and the rabbis do not regard Job as a Jew, numerous writers in the twentieth century adopt Job as the interpretive figure of Jewry in the Shoah. In the prolongation of this interpretation, the founding of the state of Israel is partly equated with the wondrous rehabilitation of the biblical Job. In the contemporary develop-

---

8. Münz 1995. Münz points out explicitly (203) that in the interpretations of the Jewish Holocaust theologies Job as the best known biblical figure of suffering outside the Jewish world is of no relevance. The only notable exception here is Berkovits (1984).

9. Kolitz 2004 (1946). Kolitz's edition contains the original Yiddish text in facsimile which was used for the English translation here.

ment, on the other hand, a Job figure gradually evolves which, with the growing distance from the Shoah, progressively loses both sight of the divine dimension and faith in possible reparation.

Job in Israel

From the start, the forces were unequal: Satan a grand seigneur in heaven, Job mere flesh and blood. And anyway, the contest was unfair. Job, who had lost all his wealth and had been bereaved of his sons and daughters and stricken with loathsome boils, wasn't even aware that it was a contest.

Because he complained too much, the referee silenced him. So, having accepted this decision, in silence, he defeated his opponent without even realizing it. Therefore his wealth was restored, he was given sons and daughters—new ones, of course—and his grief for the first children was taken away.

We might imagine that this retribution was the most terrible thing of all. We might imagine that the most terrible thing was Job's ignorance: not understanding whom he had defeated, or even that he had won. But in fact, the most terrible thing of all is that Job never existed and was just a parable. (Pagis 1989, 11)

The cynical undertone struck by the poet and professor of medieval Hebrew literature Dan Pagis (1930–1986)—also a survivor of the Holocaust—in this poem, entitled "Homily," will become increasingly pronounced in Hebrew literature, and the dimension of hatred will articulate itself ever more in the decades following the Shoah.

In April 1981 the major Israeli dramatist Hanoch Levin (1943–1999) staged his play *Yissûrê Iyyôv*, the "Suffering of Job," in Jerusalem (1999). The plot is set in antiquity, the time of the Roman–Jewish wars. Job himself is here really an atheist perversely dying a martyr's death, while his outwardly pious friends all too eagerly and opportunistically renounce their God in the face of Roman oppression. It needs hardly to be mentioned that this tragedy knows of no reparation made to Job. Act VII, showing Job's impalement, destroys the last vestiges of faith in God and humanity, and in the brutal and obscene enactment of the ending— hardly bearable even in the written version—hatred pervades everything, in contrast to the biblical Job, who was wholly sustained by his devotion to God.

The most monumental work dealing with Job in contemporary Israeli literature was, however, published in 1995 by Jossel Birstein. In keeping with its status, his novel *ʿÂl tiqrâ lî Iyyôw* (*Don't Call Me Job*)

(Birstein 1995) shall be discussed here at some length. Birstein (1920–2003), a Polish survivor of the Holocaust, emigrated in 1950 to Israel, making a name there for himself as both a Yiddish and a Hebrew writer. Written fifty years after the end of World War II, the plot is superficially set in the Jerusalem of the 1990s, but it is, nonetheless, a novel about the Shoah. The outer frame, holding the story together, is a night of drinking spent by three men in a Jerusalem luxury apartment: the millionaire Shlomo Shapira (owner of the apartment), his friend (the first-person narrator), as well as a locksmith come to change the lock in order to prevent Shlomo's wife from entering the apartment. Shlomo and the first-person narrator are Polish survivors of the Holocaust, the locksmith is the son of a Romanian Jewess, who lost all her children in the Holocaust, but has been given "new sons and daughters" in Israel. At the beginning we learn that the first-person narrator has come with bad tidings, namely Job's news, for his friend Shlomo, and at the end we discover that the news concerns the death of Shlomo's son.

Even at this point it should be evident that every character possesses Job-like features, and—without entering here into the extremely rich and complicated plot—one could claim that Birstein's novel is a kaleidoscope of Job enactments, narratively realised by a profusion of retrospectives blending predominantly into the Shoah. Nearly every protagonist and even every secondary character is a different rendering of Job, and each existence is imbued with a specific, and, in its individual fashion, downright perverse, tragedy.

Various books accompany Shlomo, the protagonist, through life in the way of a leitmotif, among them the biblical Job, the *Histories* of the ancient historian Herodotus, who "loved episodes more than the red thread" (45; which patently characterizes the narrative technique of Birstein as well), and the *Guinness Book of Records*—as if it were really a question of which protagonist was the world-record holder in suffering, the most tragic of all the Job figures.

Only a few aspects of *Don't Call Me Job* can be mentioned here. There is, in the first place, the dubious rehabilitation of Job, the "Wiedergutmachung," in Hebrew פיצויים or שלומים, which in connection with the Holocaust acquires a different, specifically financial connotation. Then there is the rather strange statement that not every new beginning necessarily involves a catastrophe, implying that this is in keeping with the empirical value of the protagonists. Furthermore, we constantly meet Jews clipping their side locks or beards as a symbol that they are renouncing their relationship with God—consequently, they also no longer call themselves Jews, a Jew now being from their point of view merely a "co-religionist." And then there is the story from Herodotus's *Histories*, according to which Xerxes ordered the flogging of the sea after his fleet had been swallowed by it. This story, in view of Shlomo Shapiro's relationship with God, must be interpreted to suggest that it is as futile to flog the sea as it is to quarrel with God about one's misfortune.

Fundamentally, the interpretation of Job in Birstein's *Don't Call Me Job* consists in the insight that the Job syndrome is a tragic chain reaction in human relationships, an epidemic running through the generations, passed down in particular from Jewish fathers to their sons.

The conclusion of the novel is, consequently, a desperate attempt to escape from the fatal Job-heritage. In a fax, Shlomo's wife urges her husband to have done with the "Job games." Shlomo answers with the title (122), "Don't call me Job any longer, darling," and burns the biblical book of Job in an eerie final scene. The reader suspects, however, that the escape attempt is futile.[10]

At this point another retrospective view might be worthwhile. While immediately after the Shoah the tone of the Job literature was in part strangely conciliatory, towards the end of the twentieth century a growing aggression starts to spread. The protagonist "God" increasingly loses relevance. A review of the latest versions of Job shows that in Job feelings of hatred grow in the same measure that he loses his argument with God. As mentioned before, hatred develops in the turning away, not in the argument. The person one wants to understand, one does not hate, and the person one hates, one no longer wants to understand. Where Job cannot attain peace with God, hatred of humankind begins to spring up.

By the end of the twentieth century Job has become an atheist. For the post-modern Job, reparation has but a stale taste to it. Not even by means of a fresh start can the breakdown of life be coped with. A further examination of the development in the more recent Job texts reveals that Job's rehabilitation increasingly fades from view. It is to begin with, and in keeping with the biblical epilogue, wholly present (in Perez and Roth, for example). Immediately after the Shoah it is only alluded to in a subdued fashion (as in Susman). Two generations after the Shoah (in Lewin and Birstein) it has, however, disappeared completely from sight as if all visions of happiness and peace had evaporated. Contrary to the biblical text, the biography of Job is now no longer a purposeful development from misery to happiness but rather a fatal and repetitive vicious circle.

---

10. It is, incidentally, quite evident that the behaviour of Birstein's protagonists is in line with the late traumata of Holocaust survivors as analytically described in psychology and psychiatry, cf. Ludewig-Kedmi, Spiegel and Tyrangiel 2002.

Looking back on the course followed by the figure of Job through the centuries and millennia, the most tragic aspect of all would thus seem to be that the suffering of Job was neither parabolic nor unique, but remains real and recurrent. Illustrating this aspect of the dialogue between the book of Job and contemporary Israeli literature, the poem "With Job This Was Quite Unique" by Nathan Zach (born 1930) may serve here as an appropriate conclusion:

> With Job this was quite unique
> While this one was still talking, behold, that one came
> First the cattle, then the camels and the sons and daughters
> What is there to talk about, hearty blows.
> After that came the endless debates,
> The arguments and replies, and promises, promises.
>
> With me it wasn't all that dramatic.
> A slight stroke in the morning, from time to time
> Just a casual smack or slap.
> Sometimes even only an accident, not sent by God.
> And a little bruise, now and then a black eye
> Or just defective vision, or forms,
> Or the house owner, work, or letters, a woman, in the evening.
> And Fridays two blows, perfunctorily,
> And on the Sabbath you rest and recuperate.
>
> Once I was in another country,
> No one knew my name there,
> And God and Satan did not compete for my integrity
> And no one at all bothered me, no disaster and no scream and it was
> A little bit boring, but it was wonderful. And everything
> Was all right, but not as it should be. And I returned to my place
> And behold, I am a prophet,
> A nationalized Jobchik growing old, kicking and screaming
> I I.[11]

---

11. Nathan Zach, "ʿEtsel Iyyôv zê hayâ hadpaʾamî" ("With Job This Was Quite Unique") in Shaked 2005, 348–49. The poem was published in 1996.

THE BOOK OF JOB AND MARJORIE KEMPER'S "GOD'S GOODNESS"

J. Clinton McCann, Jr.

C. Michael Curtis, editor of both *The Atlantic Monthly* and an anthology of short stories that includes Marjorie Kemper's "God's Goodness," describes Kemper's story simply as "remarkable" (C. M. Curtis 2003, x).[1] Indeed it is! In addition to winning a prestigious 2003 O. Henry Prize for the best short stories of 2002, with this work Kemper added her name to a long list of philosophers, psychoanalysts, musicians, visual artists, poets, playwrights, novelists, short story writers, and more who have been drawn to the book of Job. Why? As Samuel Balentine suggests, citing and expanding upon J. Hempel's conclusion that Job is "the struggle for the last truth about God" (Hempel 1938, 73),

> The struggle for the truth about what it means to live in a world where order breaks down and chaos runs amok, where the innocent suffer and the wicked thrive, where cries for help go unanswered—by powers divine or human—is universal and, as far as we can know in this world, ongoing… If God is just and good, why do the innocent suffer and the guilty thrive? As the British novelist Muriel Spark has observed, the Joban problem is "the only problem, in fact, worth discussing." In short, the Joban drama is perhaps the longest-running story in the history of human experience. The biblical Job is but one, even if one of the best, of a cast of characters who has played this role. (Balentine 2006, 3–5)[2]

Kemper's title, "God's Goodness," alludes to what Balentine calls "the Joban problem"—often labeled by biblical scholars and theologians as the problem of theodicy (literally, "the justice of God")—how can a

---

1. "God's Goodness" first appeared in *The Atlantic Monthly* 289/3 (March 2002), 81–89. It is also included in Furman (2003, 84–99). Quotations from the story will be followed by page number(s) in parentheses. The page numbers are those in C. M. Curtis 2003.

2. See Spark 1984, 22.

good God allow the suffering of the innocent and the prosperity of the guilty? Beyond this allusion, however, Kemper explicitly makes the book of Job an integral part of her story. It is quoted four times; and even more importantly, as described in detail below, Job becomes the favorite piece of literature of one of the two main characters in the story. The fact that Kemper features the book of Job clarifies and simplifies the methodological issues involved. Because Kemper intends that her readers hear the story in conversation with the book of Job, her story invites what Geoffrey D. Miller (2011, 286) calls an "author-oriented" approach to intertextuality. Consequently, I shall consider how Kemper uses the book of Job; and I shall offer my understanding of what Kemper seems to want to accomplish.

At the same time, however, I shall venture over into what Miller calls the "reader-oriented" approach, which is, as he points out, more congruent with what Julia Kristeva meant by the term "intertextuality" (G. D. Miller 2011, 286, 304–5). That is to say, my analysis of "God's Goodness" will not be confined to my understanding of what Kemper may have intended. Especially since Kemper, by utilizing Job, is participating in (in Balentine's words) "perhaps the longest-running story in the history of human experience," it is only natural that her work evokes in me (and other readers) ideas and directions that she never intended, as well as connections to other texts that she did not have in mind. There is no reason that the "author-oriented" and "reader-oriented" approaches cannot be complementary rather than conflicting, even though they have often been viewed as mutually exclusive. Before any analysis, however, it is necessary to review the story.

A Synopsis of "God's Goodness"

The story opens with the introduction of Ling Tan, one of the two main characters, who immediately identifies herself as a "good Christian" (51). Ling, a Chinese immigrant to the United States, is looking for a job in the field of nursing; and her self-introduction happens during a job interview. The employment counselor is not impressed, nor is Ling particularly qualified. She is pleasant and persistent though, and the interview leads to her being hired to be the live-in caretaker for Mike, the other main character, a teenage boy who is dying of cancer.

Even before she begins her new job, Ling's particular version of Christianity is evident. She smiles incessantly; and despite a very difficult past and her unenviable financial situation, "Wherever she looked she could see evidence of his [God's] goodness" (52). In addition to her talk about divine goodness, Ling's vocabulary regularly features words like "blessings," "miracles," and "hope." In terms of Mike's terminal illness, this means that Ling prays for a miracle, and that she fully expects that Mike will be cured and not die. Such is Ling's hope as a "good Christian."

It is precisely this form of hope that upsets Mike's parents, who are resigned to his dying but are not dealing well with the situation. Mike's mother, who spends most of her time escaping into gardening, tells Ling "that it was a little late in the day" to "pray for a miracle" (54). Mike's father spends more time with his son, mostly in the evenings when they read Hegel together (see below). When he is informed that Ling is praying for a miracle, he firmly tells her not to let Mike know about it, because "We've spent two years choking on hope around here; hope is ancient history" (57).

There are two other minor characters: an oncologist who visits Mike occasionally but virtually ignores him, and a very cheerful psychiatrist whom the father employs to help Mike deal with his dying. Even Ling notices that the psychiatrist is "always so cheerful" (62), and Mike's assessment of him is revealing: "he's so damn hopeful" (60). The rhetorical function of the psychiatrist is to sharpen the question of what might constitute genuine hope (see below).

The other main character is Mike, an extremely intelligent and literate teenager who is dying. With no help from his parents, and no help from the psychiatrist, and no direct help from the content of Ling's hope, Mike increasingly develops a form of hope that he seems to find truly comforting. The help comes from the book of Job, which Mike chooses for himself and Ling to read together one night when Ling has suggested that they read the Bible. Ling's immediate reaction to Mike's choice is that Job is a "*sad* story" (59); but they proceed, and the book of Job quickly becomes a regular topic of conversation and "a favorite of Mike's" (61). He "read Job over and over. He memorized great hunks of it, and insisted on reading his favorite bits aloud to Ling. Sometimes he stopped mid-sentence and laughed" (61). In short, Mike finds Job comforting and consoling; and he even develops out of his reading of Job a conception of divine goodness and a profound sense of hope.

Mike's understanding of God's goodness and his form of hope differ significantly from Ling's. He knows that he is dying, and he never expects to be cured. His condition gradually worsens, and he dies. Among his last words are a recitation of Job 37:5 (see below). As for Ling, she retains her belief in God's goodness; but there are hints that her understanding of divine goodness has changed. We shall explore these hints in the next section.

One further aspect of the story needs to be mentioned. Over Mike's bed is the famous poster of Albert Einstein, looking rather disheveled and sticking out his tongue. Mike obviously likes Einstein and is conversant with his work. As the story proceeds, Ling notices that "Mike liked Job almost as much as he liked Einstein" (62–63). And among Mike's last words are his conclusion that the book of Job puts one in touch with a God who "*does* stuff we don't get. Hegel didn't get it. I'm not sure even Einstein got it" (65). Ling's immediate response is, "He get it. That's why he stick tongue out" (65). The last scene in "God's Goodness" consists of Ling leaving Mike's room on the morning after he has died during the night. She looks at the poster of Einstein, "'Goodbye, Mr. Genius,' she said softly. Then, before she sailed out of the door, and in recognition, or solidarity, or maybe just farewell, Ling stuck out her little pink tongue" (66). What Kemper intended by this conclusion is not entirely clear, but we shall explore some of the possibilities in the next section.

An "Author-Oriented" Approach

Most intertextual studies that involve the Hebrew Bible cannot claim any direct access to the author of either or any of the texts. In fact, one of the objections to the "author-oriented" approach is that discerning the author's intent in alluding to or citing another text is always speculative. To a degree, this objection is valid for my analysis in this section of the essay; therefore, I do not claim that I can discern precisely what Kemper intended by her use of the book of Job. Rather, I shall explore what Kemper may have intended, and I shall discuss what I discern that Kemper has accomplished. In the case of "God's Goodness," however, we do have at least a clue from the author herself.

The O. Henry Prize Stories 2003 contains a section entitled "The Authors on Their Work." Here is what Kemper offers concerning her creation of "God's Goodness":

> My friend Andrea has always maintained that her favorite book is the Book of Job. I'm the kind of person whose favorite book is Charles Portis's *Norwood*, so I'd always thought hers a pretty bleak choice. Since writing this story, I'm not so sure. The story went through a great many permutations. The one constant in all of them was Ling's voice and her steely determination to find God's goodness in the world. She just wouldn't give up on it. In the end, I couldn't either. (Furman 2003, 335)

Given this clue, we can discern parallels between Kemper's experience and the story. As is the case with her friend Andrea, the book of Job becomes Mike's "favorite book." As Kemper judged Andrea's to be "a pretty bleak choice," so Ling judged Mike's choice in the story. The very positive, transformative role that Job plays for Mike seems, however, to be indicative of Kemper's re-assessment of Job. In any case, as suggested above, the book of Job plays a pivotal role in the story. To be sure, the first three quotations of Job in "God's Goodness" seem more playful than substantive. Job 7:3, "Wearisome nights are appointed to me," is where Ling stops reading to Mike one night after he has fallen asleep (60); Mike quotes Job 10:8, "Thine hands have made me and fashioned me together round about; yet thou dost destroy me," in a humorous attempt to get a rise out of his psychiatrist (62); and Mike jokingly recites Job 6:6 every morning as a comment on Ling's delivery of his breakfast, "Or is there *any* taste in the white of an egg?" (63). But this very playfulness is a comment on the high value Mike places on the book of Job, and apparently Kemper grows to value it highly as well.

As Kemper suggests, like Ling, she could not give up on the attempt "to find God's goodness in the world." In essence, then, Ling's, Mike's, and Kemper's own search for "God's goodness in the world" becomes another episode in "perhaps the longest-running story in the history of human experience." Kemper does not claim, of course, to have found "God's goodness in the world," nor does her story provide a definitive solution to what Balentine calls "the Joban problem." But precisely at this point, Kemper is faithful to the book of Job itself, which also, according to many biblical scholars, provides no unambiguous answers.

For biblical scholars, the interpretive crux is usually the divine speeches (Job 38–41), along with Job's final response (Job 42:1–6, especially v. 6), which Kemper does not cite explicitly in "God's Goodness." Carol Newsom, for instance, offers five defensible translations of 42:6, each of which suggests a different interpretive direction. And she concludes:

> Asking which possibility is correct misses the interpretive significance of the ambiguity of Job's reply, which corresponds to the ambiguity of the divine speeches… The ambiguities inherent in the divine speeches and Job's reply resist every attempt to reduce them to a single, definitive interpretation. (Newsom 1996, 629)[3]

3. See also Morrow (1986, 223–25), who argues that 42:6 is intentionally ambiguous.

In short, the book of Job itself apparently does not claim to locate precisely "God's goodness in the world," nor to provide a definitive solution
to the question of theodicy. What the book of Job does clearly affirm is
that the question and the search are crucial. At the very least, Kemper's
story reinforces this affirmation as it raises the question and joins the
search for "God's goodness in the world."

But can we say more? Following her material quoted above, Newsom
goes on to suggest that the ambiguity inherent in Job should not prevent
readers from proposing and pursuing particular interpretive directions.
Newsom herself sees the divine speeches not as irrelevant, nor evasive,
nor intended to belittle Job. Rather, they are intended to expand Job's
view of the created universe beyond the narrow confines of a doctrine of
retributive justice. God describes "a world in which the chaotic, although
present, is contained within the secure boundaries of a created order that
is also rich with *goodness*" (Newsom 1996, 631, emphasis added). Given
this view of the divine speeches, Newsom prefers the fourth and fifth
possible translations of Job 42:6, those belonging to Janzen and Perdue:

> (4) "Therefore I retract my words and have changed my mind concerning
> dust and ashes" [i. e., the human condition];
> (5) "Therefore I retract my words, and I am comforted concerning dust
> and ashes" [i. e., the human condition]. (Newsom 1996, 629)[4]

Concerning Job's new understanding, which is apparently a real source
of comfort, Newsom explains:

> Now, given what has been disclosed to him in the divine speeches, Job is
> able to perceive a world in which the vulnerability of human existence
> can be understood, not in terms of divine enmity, but in terms of a
> creation within which the chaotic is restrained but never fully eliminated.
> Thus it is fitting that Job should speak of a change of mind and perhaps a
> consolation concerning the human condition. (Newsom 1996, 629)

Although Kemper had probably not read Newsom, and although she
does not quote nor directly mention the divine speeches or Job's response,
her reading of Job moves in the same directions as does Newsom's.
Thus, it is appropriate that I have made, and shall continue to make,
Newsom's work part of the intertextual conversation between Kemper
and Job. Although Kemper's comments about her story highlight Ling's

---

4. See Janzen (1985, 251), where his translation differs slightly from how
Newsom quoted it: "Therefore I recant and change my mind concerning dust and
ashes"; and see Perdue 1991, 232. For a brief summary of Janzen's argument and its
implications, see McCann 1997, 23–25.

voice and "her steely determination to find God's goodness in the world," it seems to be Mike who best communicates Kemper's understanding of God's goodness. Like Job, Mike comes to a new understanding of the universe and his place in it; and like Job, Mike seems genuinely comforted by this new understanding.

More specifically, Mike's reading of Job significantly expands his view of the universe and its possibilities, or perhaps God's possibilities within the universe. The fourth and final quotation of Job in "God's Goodness" is by Mike shortly before he dies: "'God thundereth marvelously with his voice; great things doeth he, which we cannot comprehend'" (65). In the book of Job, Elihu speaks these words (Job 37:5); but the rhetorical effect of Elihu's words seems to be to anticipate the expansive creational perspective of the divine speeches that immediately follow. In any case, much like Job is comforted by God's portrayal of the wild and wonderful universe, so is Mike comforted by the vision of a world greater than humankind can comprehend. Following Mike's quoting of Job 37:5, his next words to Ling are these: "You'll admit that the universe, or God—whatever you like to call it—*does* stuff we don't get. Hegel didn't get it. I'm not even sure Einstein got it" (65).

Mike is not necessarily renouncing Hegel nor the whole attempt of idealistic-oriented philosophy to comprehend the world. Nor is Mike renouncing his love of Einstein and the attempt of science to comprehend the world empirically. Indeed, the role of Einstein in "God's Goodness" is particularly interesting in view of Newsom's conclusion that Job learned that the universe contains chaotic forces that have been "restrained but never fully eliminated." Einstein's theory of relativity and the whole field of quantum physics posit a kind of randomness within the apparently ordered universe, and this whole branch of thought is sometimes known as chaos theory. Mike (and apparently Kemper) can acknowledge the chaotic forces that make humanity vulnerable; and at the same time, Mike (and apparently Kemper again) can discern God's goodness in the midst of it all. So Mike achieves a measure of comfort that allows him to die with dignity, even maintaining a sense of humor to the very end. In a way that his parents cannot do (see above), Mike demonstrates genuine hope. Beyond Ling's form of hope that amounts to optimism or wishful thinking that Mike will be cured, Mike's hope looks vulnerability and death squarely in the face. Mike is apparently able to entrust self, life, and future to a power greater than the philosophers can explain or the scientists can prove. Although we cannot be sure, perhaps this is Kemper's hope as well. In any case, her story helps us to visualize a contemporary manifestation of "the Joban drama" as Mike joins Job among the cast of characters in "perhaps the longest-running story in the history of human experience."

If there is a single word that describes Mike's expanded understanding of things, it is "humility." After he has become immersed in Job, Mike and Ling have a conversation about the book and what may be learned from it. Ling sees no value in Job, she tells Mike; but she still believes in God's goodness, because in her words, "Have to believe in that when I look at God's big world" (62). For Mike, the revelation of "God's big world" is precisely the value of Job; it puts one in touch with a world "beyond our understanding" (62). Ling objects, "But [I] used to understand" (62). And Mike tries to explain to her that her new inability to understand is a good thing: "And now you don't. You see, you've learned something already" (62). In response to Ling's immediate question, "What am I learning?" Mike replies, "That there's more to heaven and earth than oatmeal and a positive attitude. More than Ling Tan was born knowing. Humility—not to put too fine a point on it" (62).

At this point, both Mike and Ling are playing the role of Job in Kemper's contemporary version of "the Joban drama." From the vastness set before him in the divine speeches, Job too learned humility. At this point, "God's Goodness" may again be congruent with Newsom's (and others') construal of Job. Unlike many traditional interpretations of Job that conclude that Job was belittled and humiliated by God (see the NRSV of Job 42:6 that supports the traditional interpretation), Newsom (and others) suggest(s) that Job was educated by God. In short, Job was humbled, not humiliated. The difference is crucial and profoundly important. A humbled Job, just like a humbled Mike and a humbled Ling, will be able to discern meaning and hope in a chaotic world, whereas a humiliated Job would resort to the old world of alleged certainties, which is the system he inherited and the one that the friends staunchly defend throughout the book.

Ling, of course, is hesitant to give up the world of alleged certainties (as was Job), the world she "used to understand." It is not entirely clear in "God's Goodness" that she does so, but there are hints that her understanding of divine goodness has been transformed. The clearest is the final poignant exchange between Ling and Mike shortly before he dies. Ling offers to Mike, just after he has quoted Job 37:5, that "Maybe God blessing us this moment, and we not knowing it" (65). Mike replies, "Thanks for trying, Ling, but that may be the single most depressing thing you've said to me" (65). Ling's response is what indicates her changed understanding of blessing: "Not depressing, Mikey. I only mean he bless me with you and he bless you with me" (65). For Ling, blessing no longer means a cure. Rather, it is the communion shared by two vulnerable human beings who are humbly aware of the vastness of a universe that they cannot comprehend, much less control.

The other clue that Ling's understanding of God's goodness has been transformed is the final sentence of the story when she sticks out her tongue at the Einstein poster as she leaves Mike's room for the final time on the morning after his death. Earlier, Ling had suggested to Mike that Einstein was sticking out his tongue because he realized that the universe was even bigger than science can comprehend. If Ling's final act is a gesture of "solidarity" (66) with Einstein, as Kemper hints, then perhaps Ling has indeed humbly moved beyond her old world of alleged certainties.

In any case, it is worthy of note that Newsom in her reflections on Job 42:1–6 articulates a connection among community, creation, comfort, and humility, a connection that is also featured in "God's Goodness" by way of the bond that develops between Ling and Mike, a bond of comfort that is sealed in part by their mutual humility in the face of a vast universe. As Newsom points out, "A person who has suffered a great loss or who has finally faced up to a painful reality long denied often experiences an overwhelming sense of isolation, alienation, and godforsakenness" (Newsom 1996, 631). Such may well have been the case with Mike before Ling's arrival. Mike tells Ling that he has no friends, and Mike is essentially abandoned, at least emotionally, by his parents and the medical profession. But Mike and Ling find comfort in each other; and the communion they share is grounded in large part in Ling's natural inclination to discern God's goodness in "God's big world" (62) and in Mike's discovery of humility by way of his thorough immersion in Job and its portrayal of a God who does things "which we cannot comprehend" (65; Mike quoting Job 37:5).

Newsom quotes E. Kohak, who also discerns and articulates the connection among community, creation, comfort, and humility in the book of Job:

> When humans no longer think of themselves alone, masters of all they survey, when they discern the humility of their place in the vastness of God's creation, then that creation and its God can share the pain... That is the age-old wisdom of the book of Job... [God] speaks not of pain but of the vastness of the creation, of the gazelle in her mountain fastness and the mighty creatures of the deep sea. God is not avoiding the issue. [God] is teaching Job the wisdom of bearing the pain that can neither be avoided nor abolished but can be shared when there is a whole living creation to

> absorb it… When the human, in the solitude of dusk, surrenders his pride
> of place and learns to bear the shared pain, he can begin to understand the
> pain that cannot be avoided as a gift which teaches compassion and opens
> understanding… It opens him to receive, in empathy, the gift of the other,
> not in censure, but in gratitude and love. (Newsom 1996, 632)[5]

As Mike opens himself to the God of the universe portrayed in the book
of Job, and as Ling surrenders her old world of alleged certainties, their
new-found humility yields the gift of each other. It is appropriate that the
last words Mike hears are Ling's: "Not depressing, Mikey. I only mean
he bless me with you and he bless you with me" (65). This parting gift,
deriving as it does from pain that is shared, bespeaks the connection
among community, creation, comfort, and humility in "God's Goodness"
and in the book of Job.

A *"Reader-Oriented" Approach*

The reader of this essay may conclude that I have already ventured over
into a "reader-oriented" approach in the previous section, and that may
indeed be the case. If so, I make no apologies; indeed, proponents of the
"reader-oriented" approach to intertextuality would say this was inevitable! In any case, I attempted in the previous section to suggest how
Kemper used the book of Job, and to what effects. To be sure, Kemper
may not have intended everything that I heard; but I hope at least to have
demonstrated that reading "God's Goodness" and the book of Job
together can increase our understanding and appreciation of both. In this
section, I shall focus on two topics that are central both to Kemper's
story and the book of Job—hope and humility (see above)—but I shall
relate these two topics to issues that Kemper did not appear to have in
mind and to texts written after her work and therefore beyond the reach
of her authorial intent. In this way, I intend to illustrate briefly the
virtually limitless possibilities of a "reader-oriented" approach.

   As suggested above, hope is a major theme in "God's Goodness," and
it is also a major theme in the book of Job (see the character Job's words
about hope in 7:6; 14:7, 19; 17:15; 19:10). In Kemper's story, it is Mike,
scientifically trained and a lover of Einstein, who moves from despair to
a hope grounded in a religious perspective that he gained from the book
of Job. Thus, "God's Goodness" can help readers think about the relationship between religion and science, an issue that continues to be
current in the public arena, including politics in the United States of

---

   5. See Kohak 1984, 45–46.

America. Mike knows and loves Einstein; but without renouncing the knowledge that empirical scientific research achieves, Mike arrives at the realization that there is something or someone more—"the universe, or God—whatever you like to call it" (65). Thus, Mike models a position that integrates faith and science. John Polkinghorne, a contemporary physicist (like Einstein), does the very same thing. Like Mike, Polkinghorne takes the reality of death with supreme seriousness; and also like Mike, he discerns an abiding hope grounded in the ultimacy of God beyond explanation:

> We shall all die, and the cosmos will die, but the final word does not lie with death but with God… [T]his does not mean that death is not real, but it does mean that it is not the ultimate reality. Only God is ultimate, and that is a sufficient basis to enable us to embrace the Advent hope. (Polkinghorne 2003, 9)

To be sure, not all scientists agree with Polkinghorne; but there is a burgeoning field devoted to the study of the possible integration of religion and science; and "God's Goodness" is an eloquent invitation to join the discussion.

"God's Goodness" can also invite readers to think further about the implications of what Mike specifically tells Ling that she is learning— "Humility, not to put too fine a point on it" (62). In essence, Mike learned humility from creation by way of the book of Job; and as suggested above, creation and humility are connected both in "God's Goodness" and the book of Job. This connection has a crucial implication that Kemper may hint at when she has Ling observe that Mike's mother's blooming flowers are evidence that she is a "good steward" (53). While Kemper does not develop this observation, her story resonates at this point with the ecological perspective of Bill McKibben, who is also reading Job. Like Mike, McKibben highlights the crucial role of humility. According to McKibben, the divine speeches about creation in Job have the following effect: "Our anthropocentric bias is swept away." When McKibben poses the question, "what will replace it?" his answer is this:

> Humility, first and foremost. That is certainly Job's reaction. If we are not, as we currently believe, at the absolute epicenter of the created world, then we need to humble ourselves. Humility is usually regarded as a spiritual attribute, a state of mind. But I want to focus for a short while on its more practical aspects—on what it might mean to walk more lightly on this earth, with more regard for the other life around us. (McKibben 2005, 32)

Ling found humility "a hard lesson" (62) to learn, and so does an ego-centric humankind. But "God's Goodness" and the book of Job suggest that it can be learned; and so Kemper and Job can invite us, along with McKibben, to consider the crucial ecological implications of humility, among others.

Conclusion

Following Kemper's lead, we have taken a largely "author-oriented" approach that demonstrates the ongoing influence of the book of Job, and that suggests how a contemporary version of "the Joban drama" can help us hear anew the ancient work. The more brief application of a "reader-oriented" approach also suggests that "the longest-running story in the history of human experience" still addresses timely human and societal issues, and that it can help us address them as well.

BIBLIOGRAPHY

Aichele, George, and Gary A. Phillips. 1995. Introduction: Exegesis, Eisegesis, Intergesis. *Semeia* 69/70:7–18.

Aitken, J. K. 2010. Job's Diet: Comfort, Food and Suffering. Pages 47–68 in *Hiob Biblijny, Hiob Obecny w Kuluturze*. Edited by P. Mitzner and A. Szczepan-Wojnarska. Warsaw: Wydawnictwo Uniwersytetu Kardynala Stefana Warszawa.

Alexander, Philip S. 2008. *The Targum of Lamentations, Translated, with a Critical Introduction, Apparatus, and Notes*. Aramaic Bible 17B. Collegeville, Minn.: Liturgical.

Alkier, Stefan. 2005. Die Bibel im Dialog der Schriften und das Problem der Verstockung in Mk 4: Intertextualität im Rahmen einer kategorialen Semiotik biblischer Texte. Pages 1–22 in *Die Bibel im Dialog der Schriften: Konzepte intertextueller Bibellektüre*. Edited by Stefan Alkier and Richard B. Hays. Neutestamentliche Entwürfe zur Theologie 10. Tübingen: Francke.

———. 2009. Intertextuality and the Semiotics of Biblical Texts. Pages 3–21 in Hays, Alkier, and Huizenga 2009.

Allen, Graham. 2000. *Intertextuality*. London: Routledge.

Alter, Robert. 1981. *The Art of Biblical Narrative*. London: George Allen & Unwin.

———. 1985. *The Art of Biblical Poetry*. New York: Basic.

———. 1996. *The Pleasures of Reading in an Ideological Age*. New York: Norton.

Altheim, F., and R. Stiehl. 1970. Hiob und die prophetische Überlieferung. Pages 131–42 in *Geschichte Mittelasiens im Altertum*. Berlin: de Gruyter.

Andersen, Francis, and David Noel Freedman. 1989. *Amos: A New Translation with Introduction and Commentary*. New York: Doubleday.

Anderson, G. A. 1991. *A Time to Mourn, a Time to Dance: The Experience of Grief and Joy in Israelite Religion*. University Park, Pa.: Pennsylvania State University Press.

Antaki, C., and I. Leudar. 2001. Recruiting the Record: Using Opponent's Exact Words in Parliamentary Argumentation. *Text* 21:467–88.

Arbel, V. D. 2003. *Beholders of Divine Secrets: Mysticism and Myth in the Hekhalot and Merkavah Literature*. Albany: State University of New York Press.

Assmann, Jan. 1989. Death and Initiation in the Funerary Religion of Ancient Egypt. Pages 135–59 in *Religion and Philosophy in Ancient Egypt*. Edited by James P. Allen et al. Yale Egyptological Studies 3. New Haven, Conn.: Yale University Press.

———. 2005. *Death and Salvation in Ancient Egypt*. Translated by D. Lorton. Ithaca: Cornell University Press.

Bakhtin, Mikhail. 1981. *The Dialogic Imagination: Four Essays*. Edited by Michael Holquist. Translated by Caryl Emerson and Michael Holquist. Austin: University of Texas Press.

Balentine, Samuel E. 2002a. Job as Priest to the Priests. *ExAud* 18:29–52.

———. 2002b. *Leviticus*. Interpretation. Louisville: John Knox.

———. 2002c. My Servant Job Shall Pray for You. *Theology Today* 58:502–18.

———. 2003. For No Reason. *Int* 57:349–69.

———. 2006. *Job*. SCHBC. Macon, Ga.: Smyth & Helwys.

———. 2007. Inside the Sanctuary of Silence: The Moral and Ethical Demands of Suffering. Pages 63–79 in *Character Ethics and the Old Testament: Moral Dimensions of Scripture*. Edited by M. D. Carroll and R. J. Lapsley. Louisville: Westminster John Knox.

———. 2008. Traumatizing Job. *RevExp* 105:213–28.

Barr, James. 1995. The Synchronic, the Diachronic and the Historical: A Triangular Relationship? Pages 1–14 in de Moor 1995.

Barré, Michael L., ed. 1997. *Wisdom, You Are My Sister: Studies in Honor of Roland E. Murphy, O. Carm., on the Occasion of His Eightieth Birthday*. CBQMS 29. Washington, DC: Catholic Biblical Association of America.

Bartelmus, R. 1987. Tempus als Strukturprinzip: Anmerkungen zur stilistischen und theologischen Relevanz des Tempusgebrauchs im "Lied der Hanna" (1 Sam 2,1–10). *BZ* 31:15–35.

Barth, K. 1961. *Church Dogmatics* IV.3.1. Edited by R. W. Bromiley and T. F. Torrance. Edinburgh: T. & T. Clark.

Barthes, Roland. 1970. *S/Z*. Paris: Seuil. English translation by Richard Miller. *S/Z*. Oxford: Blackwell, 1990.

———. 1971. La lutte avec l'ange: analyse textuelle de Genèse 32.23–33. Pages 27–39 in *Analyse structurale et exégèse biblique*. Edited by R. Barthes et al. Neuchâtel: Delachaux at Niestlé). English translation by Alfred M. Johnson Jr. in *Structural Analysis and Biblical Exegesis: Interpretational Essays*. Pittsburgh: Pickwick, 1974.

———. 1977. The Death of the Author. Pages 142–48 in *Image/Music/Text*. Edited by Roland Barthes and Stephen Heath. Translated by S. Heath. New York: Hill & Wang.

———. 1986. Writing Reading. Pages 29–32 in *The Rustle of Language*. Edited by Roland Barthes. Translated by R. Howard. New York: Hill & Wang.

Bartholomew, C. G. 2009. *Ecclesiastes*. Baker Commentary on the Old Testament Wisdom and Psalms. Grand Rapids: Baker Academic.

Barton, John. 1984. *Reading the Old Testament: Method in Biblical Study*. 2d ed. London: Darton, Longman & Todd.

———. 1987. Reading the Bible as Literature: Two Questions for Biblical Critics. *Journal of Literature and Theology* 1:135–53. Reprinted in Barton 2007b.

———. 1995. Historical Criticism and Literary Interpretation: Is There any Common Ground? Pages 3–15 in *Crossing the Boundaries: Essays in Biblical Interpretation in Honour of Michael D. Goulder*. Edited by S. E. Porter, P. Joyce, and D. E. Orton. Leiden: Brill.

———. 1996. *Reading the Old Testament: Method in Biblical Study*. 2d ed. London: Darton, Longman & Todd.

———. 2000. Intertextuality and the "Final Form" of the Text. Pages 33–37 in Lemaire and Sæbø 2000.

———. 2002. Thinking About Reader-Response Criticism. *ExpTim* 113:147–51. Reprinted in Barton 2007b.

———. 2007a. *The Nature of Biblical Criticism*. Louisville: Westminster John Knox.

———. 2007b. *The Old Testament: Canon, Literature and Theology: Collected Essays of John Barton*. Aldershot: Ashgate.

Bastiaens, Jean Charles. 1997. The Language of Suffering in Job 16–19 and in the Suffering Servant Passages in Deutero-Isaiah. Pages 421–32 in *Studies in the Book of Isaiah*. Edited by J. Van Ruiten and M. Vervenne. BETL 132. Leuven: Peeters.

Baumgärtel, Friedrich. 1933. *Der Hiobdialog: Aufriss und Deutung*. Beiträge zur Wissenschaft vom Alten und Neuen Testament 61. Stuttgart: W. Kohlhammer.

Baumgartner, Walter. 1988. *Jeremiah's Poems of Lament*. Translated by D. E. Orton. Sheffield: Almond.

Bautch, Richard J. 2007. Intertextuality in the Persian Period. Pages 25–35 in *Approaching Yehud: New Approaches to the Study of the Persian Period*. Edited by Jon L. Berquist. SemeiaSt 50. Atlanta: Society of Biblical Literature.

Beal, Timothy K. 1992a. Glossary. Pages 21–24 in Fewell ed. 1992.

———. 1992b. Ideology and Intertextuality: Surplus of Meaning and Controlling the Means of Production. Pages 27–39 in Fewell ed. 1992.

Ben-Porat, Ziva. 1976. The Poetics of Literary Allusion. *PTL: A Journal for Descriptive Poetics and Theory of Literature* 1:105–28.

Ben Zvi, Ehud. 1996. *A Historical-Critical Study of the Book of Obadiah*. BZAW 242. Berlin: de Gruyter.

Bergmann, M., M. J. Murray, and M. C. Rea, eds. 2011. *Divine Evil*. Oxford: Oxford University Press.

Berkovits, Eliezer. 1984. *Faith After the Holocaust*. New York: Ktav.

Besserman, Lawrence L. 1979. *The Legend of Job in the Middle Ages*. Cambridge, Mass.: Harvard University Press.

Beuken, W. A. M. 1994. Job's Imprecation as the Cradle of a New Religious Discourse: The Perplexing Impact of the Semantic Correspondences between Job 3, Job 4–5 and Job 6–7. Pages 41–78 in *The Book of Job*. Edited by W. A. M. Beuken. BETL 114. Leuven: Leuven University Press.

Birtsein, Jossel. 1995. ʿ*Âl tiqrâ lî Iyyôw (Don't Call Me Job)*. Bne Braq: Ha-Qîbbûs ha-Meʾûhad (Hebrew).

Blank, S. H. 1950–51. The Curse, the Blasphemy, the Spell and the Oath. *HUCA* 23:73–95.

Block, D. I. 1997. *The Book of Ezekiel: Chapters 1–24*. NICOT. Grand Rapids: Eerdmans.

Bloom, Harold. 1973. *The Anxiety of Influence: A Theory of Poetry*. Oxford: Oxford University Press.

———. 1975. *A Map of Misreading*. New York: Oxford University Press.

Blum, E. 2005. Notwendigkeit und Grenzen historischer Exegese: Plädoyer für eine alltestamentliche Exegetik. Pages 11–40 in *Theologie und Exegese des Alten Testaments / der Hebräischen Bibel: Zwischenbilanz und Zukunftsperspektiven*. Edited by B. Janowski. SBS 200. Stuttgart: Katholisches Bibelwerk.

Blumenthal, Elke. 1982. Die Prophezeiung des Neferti. *Zeitschrift für ägyptische Sprache und Altertumskunde* 109:1–27.

———. 1990. Hiob und die Harfnerlieder. *Theologische Literaturzeitung* 115:721–30.

Borowski, Oded. 1998. *Every Living Thing: Daily Uses of Animals in Ancient Israel*. Walnut Creek, Calif.: AltaMira.

Brady, Christian M. M. 2003. *The Rabbinic Targum of Lamentations: Vindicating God*. Studies in the Aramaic Interpretation of Scripture 3. Leiden: Brill.

Braude, William G., and Israel J. Kapstein. 1975. *Pesikta de-Rab Kahana: R. Kahana's Compilation of Discourses for Sabbaths and Festal Days, Translated from Hebrew and Aramaic*. The Littman Library of Jewish Civilization. London: Routledge.

Braulik, Georg. 1996. Das Deuteronomium und die Bücher Ijob, Sprichwörter, Rut: Zur Frage früher Kanonizität des Deuteronomiums. Pages 61–138 in *Die Tora als Kanon für Juden und Christen*. Edited by Erich Zenger. HBS 10. Freiburg: Herder.

Brenner, Athalya. 1989. Job the Pious? The Characterization of Job in the Narrative Framework of the Book. *JSOT* 43:37–52.

Brett, M. G. 1990. Four or Five Things to Do with Texts: A Taxonomy of Interpretative Interests. Pages 357–77 in *The Bible in Three Dimensions*. Edited by D. J. A. Clines, S. E. Fowl, and S. E. Porter. JSOTSup 87. Sheffield: JSOT.

—————. 1991. *Biblical Criticism in Crisis?* Cambridge: Cambridge University Press.

Brichto, H. C. 1973. Kin, Cult, Land and Afterlife—A Biblical Complex. *HUCA* 44:1–54.

Bright, John. 1970. Jeremiah's Complaints: Liturgy or Expressions of Personal Distress? Pages 189–204 in *Proclamation and Presence*. Edited by J. I. Durham and J. R. Porter. London: SCM.

Brinks-Rea, Christina L. 2010. The Thematic, Stylistic, and Verbal Similarities Between Isaiah 40–55 and the Book of Job. Ph.D. diss., University of Notre Dame.

Brock, Sebastian. 1967. *Testamentum Iobi*. Leiden: Brill.

Brown, Peter. 1967. *Augustine of Hippo: A Biography*. London: Faber.

Brown, William P. 1999. *The Ethos of the Cosmos: The Genesis of Moral Imagination in the Bible*. Grand Rapids: Eerdmans.

Bruch, Johann Friedrich. 1851. *Weisheits-Lehre der Hebräer*. Strasburg.

Budde, Karl. 1896. *Das Buch Hiob*. Edited by D. W. Nowack. HAT 1. Göttingen: Vandenhoeck & Ruprecht.

Callender, Dexter E. 2000. *Adam in Myth and History: Ancient Israelite Perspectives on the Primal Human*. Harvard Semitic Studies 48. Winona Lake: Eisenbrauns.

Carr, David M. 1998. Intratextuality and Intertextuality—Joining Transmission History and Interpretation History in the Study of Genesis. Pages 97–112 in *Bibel und Midrasch: zur Bedeutung der rabbinischen Exegese für Bibelwissenschaft*. Edited by Gerhard Bodendorfer and Matthias Millard. FAT 22. Tübingen: Mohr Siebeck.

—————. 2001. Method in Determination of Direction of Dependence: An Empirical Test of Criteria Applied to Exodus 34,11–26 and Its Parallels. Pages 107–40 in *Gottes Volk am Sinai. Untersuchungen zu Ex 32–34 und Dtn 9–10*. Edited by Matthias Köckert and Erhard Blum. Gütersloh: Gütersloher Verlag-Haus Mohn.

—————. 2005. *Writing on the Tablet of the Heart: Origins of Scripture and Literature*. Oxford: Oxford University Press.

—————. 2012. The Many Uses of Intertextuality in Biblical Studies: Actual and Potential. Pages 505–35 in *International Organization for the Study of the Old Testament Congress Volume: Helsinki 2010*. Edited by Martti Nissinen. VTSup 148. Leiden: Brill.

Carroll, Robert P. 1981. The Confessions of Jeremiah: Towards an Image of the Prophet. Pages 107–35 in *From Chaos to Covenant: Uses of Prophecy in the Book of Jeremiah*. Edited by Robert P. Carroll. London: SCM.

—————. 1986. *Jeremiah: A Commentary*. OTL. London: SCM.

Casanowicz, Immanuel M. 1893. Paronomasia in the Old Testament. *JBL* 12:105–67.

Cason, Thomas Scott. 2007. The Rhetoric of Disablement and Repair in the Testament of Job. Ph.D. diss., Florida State University.

Chalmers, Aaron J. 2005. "There Is No Deliverer (from my Hand)": A Formula Analysis. *VT* 55:287–92.

————. 2011. A Critical Analysis of the Formula "Yahweh Strikes and Heals." *VT* 61:16–33.

Cheyne, T. K. 1880–81. *The Prophecies of Isaiah*. 2 vols. London: Kegan Paul.

————. 1887. *Job and Solomon: Or, The Wisdom of the Old Testament*. New York: Whittaker.

Clark, H. H., and R. R. Gerrig. 1990. Quotations as Demonstrations. *Language* 66:764–805.

Clayton, Jay, and Eric Rothstein. 1991. Figures in the Corpus: Theories of Influence and Intertextuality. Pages 3–36 in *Influence and Intertextuality in Literary History*. Edited by J. Clayton and E. Rothstein. Madison: University of Wisconsin Press.

Clemens, D. M. 1994. The Law of Sin and Death: Ecclesiastes and Genesis 1–3. *Themelios* 19: 5–8.

Clines, David J. A. 1989. *Job 1–20*. WBC 17. Nashville: Thomas Nelson.

————. 2006. *Job 21–37*. WBC 18A. Nashville: Thomas Nelson.

Clines, David J. A., and D. M. Gunn. 1976. Form, Occasion and Redaction in Jeremiah 20. *ZAW* 88:390–409.

Collins, John J. 1974. Structure and Meaning in the Testament of Job. *SBLSP* 1:35–52.

Cooper, A. M. 2001. The Message of Lamentations. *Journal of the Ancient Near Eastern Society of Columbia University* 28:1–18.

Coulmas, Florian, ed. 1986. *Direct and Indirect Speech*. Berlin: de Gruyter.

Course, John E. 1994. *Speech and Response: A Rhetorical Analysis of the Introductions to the Speeches of the Book of Job (Chaps. 4–24)*. CBQMS 25. Washington, DC: Catholic Biblical Association of America.

Cox, C. E. 2007. When Torah Embraced Wisdom and Song. *Restoration Quarterly* 49, no. 2: 65–74.

Crenshaw, James L. 1984. *A Whirlpool of Torment: Israelite Traditions of God as an Oppressive Presence*. OBT 12. Philadelphia: Fortress.

————. 1993. Suffering. Pages 718–19 in *The Oxford Companion to the Bible*. Edited by M. D. Coogan. Oxford: Oxford University Press.

————. 1995a. *Joel*. AB 24C. New York: Doubleday.

————. 1995b. The High Cost of Preserving God's Honor. Pages 468–76 in *Urgent Advice and Probing Questions: Collected Writings on Old Testament Wisdom*. Macon, Ga.: Mercer University Press.

————. 1997. The Primacy of Listening in Ben Sira's Pedagogy. Pages 172–87 in Barré 1997.

————. 1998a. *Education in Ancient Israel*. Anchor Bible Reference Library. New York: Doubleday.

————. 1998b. Qoheleth's Understanding of Intellectual Inquiry. Pages 205–24 in *Qohelet in the Context of Wisdom*. Edited by A. Schoors. BETL 114. Leuven: Leuven University Press.

————. 2005. *Defending God*. New York: Oxford University Press.

————. 2009. Sipping from the Cup of Wisdom. Pages 41–62 in *Jesus and Philosophy*. Edited by P. K. Moser. Cambridge: Cambridge University Press.

————. 2010. *Old Testament Wisdom*. 3d ed. Louisville: Westminster John Knox.

————. 2011. *Reading Job: A Literary and Theological Commentary*. Reading the Old Testament. Macon, Ga.: Smyth & Helwys.

————. 2012. The Journey from Voluntary to Obligatory Silence (Reflections on Psalm 39 and Qoheleth). Pages 177–91 in *Focusing Biblical Studies: The Crucial Nature of the Persian and Hellenistic Periods: Essays in Honor of Douglas A. Knight.* Edited by Jon L. Berquist and Alice Hunt. LHBOTS 544. New York: Bloomsbury T&T Clark.

Cross, F. M. 1976. The "Olden Gods" in Ancient Near Eastern Creation Myths. Pages 329–38 in *Magnalia Dei: The Mighty Acts of God: Essays on the Bible and Archaeology in Memory of G. Ernest Wright.* Edited by F. M. Cross, W. E. Lemke, and P. D. Miller. Garden City, N.Y.: Doubleday.

Crouch, Walter B. 2000. *Death and Closure in Biblical Narrative.* Studies in Biblical Literature 7. New York: Lang.

Culler, Jonathan. 1981. *The Pursuit of Signs: Semiotics, Literature, Deconstruction.* Augmented ed. London: Routledge & Kegan Paul.

Curtis, C. Michael, ed. 2003. *Faith Stories: Short Fiction on the Varieties and Vagaries of Faith.* Boston: Houghton Mifflin.

Curtis, John Briggs. 1979. On Job's Response to Yahweh. *JBL* 98:497–511.

Dahood, Mitchell J. 1966–70. *Psalms.* 3 vols. AB 16–17A. Garden City, N.Y.: Doubleday.

Daube, D. 1947. *Studies in Biblical Law.* Cambridge: Cambridge University Press.

Davidson, Robert. 1983. *The Courage to Doubt: Exploring an Old Testament Theme.* London: SCM.

Davies, G. I. 2010. The Ethics of Friendship in Wisdom Literature. Pages 135–50 in *Ethical and Unethical in the Old Testament: God and Humans in Dialogue.* Edited by Katharine J. Dell. LHBOTS 528. London: T&T Clark International.

Day, John. 1980. The Daniel of Ugarit and Ezekiel and the Hero of the Book of Daniel. *VT* 30:174–84.

———. 1996. The Development on the Belief in Life After Death in Ancient Israel. Pages 231–57 in *After the Exile: Essays in Honor of Rex Mason.* Edited by John Barton and David J. Reimer. Macon, Ga.: Mercer University Press.

DeConick, April D. 2006. What is Early Jewish and Christian Mysticism? Pages 1–24 in *Paradise Now: Essays on Early Jewish and Christian Mysticism.* Edited by April D. DeConick. Atlanta: Society of Biblical Literature.

Delbo, Charlotte. 1946. *Aucun de nous ne reviendra.* Paris: Les Éditions de Minuit.

Delitzsch, Franz. 1887–89. *Biblical Commentary on the Psalms.* Translated by David Eaton. 3 vols. Clark's Foreign Theological Library 29–31. Edinburgh: T. & T. Clark.

Dell, Katharine J. 1991. *The Book of Job as Sceptical Literature.* BZAW 197. Berlin: de Gruyter.

———. 1997. On the Development of Wisdom in Israel. Pages 135–51 in *Congress Volume: Cambridge 1995.* Edited by J. A. Emerton. VTSup 66. Leiden: Brill.

———. 2000. The Use of Animal Imagery in the Psalms and Wisdom Literature of Ancient Israel. *Scottish Journal of Theology* 53:275–91.

———. 2006. *The Book of Proverbs in Social and Theological Context.* Cambridge: Cambridge University Press.

———. 2010. The Suffering Servant of Deutero-Isaiah: Jeremiah Revisited. Pages 119–34 in *Genesis, Isaiah and Psalms.* Edited by Katharine J. Dell, Graham I. Davies, and Y. V. Koh. Leiden: Brill.

Dentith, Simon. 2000. *Parody.* London: Routledge.

Derrida, J. 1973. *Speech and Phenomena and Other Essays on Husserl's Theory of Signs.* Translated by D. B. Allison. Evanston, Ill.: Northwestern University Press.

DeWitt, Calvin B. 2000. Behemoth and Batrachians in the Eye of God: Responsibility to Other Kinds in Biblical Perspective. Pages 290–316 in *Christianity and Ecology: Seeking the Well-Being of Earth and Humans*. Edited by Dieter Hessel and Rosemary Radford Ruether. Cambridge, Mass.: Harvard University Press.

Dhorme, Edouard. 1967. *A Commentary on the Book of Job*. Translated by Harold Knight. London: Thomas Nelson & Sons. Original edition: *Le livre de Job*. Paris: Lecoffre, 1926.

Dietrich, W. 2003–2006. *Samuel*. BKAT 8. Neukirchen–Vluyn: Neukirchener Verlag.

Dillmann, August. 1891. *Hiob*. 4th ed. Kurzgefasstes exegetisches Handbuch zum Alten Testament 2. Leipzig: Hirzel.

Dobbs-Allsopp, F. W. 2002. *Lamentations*. Interpretation. Louisville: John Knox.

Douglas, Mary. 1999. *Leviticus as Literature*. Oxford: Oxford University Press.

Draisma, Sipke, ed. 1989. *Intertextuality in Biblical Writings: Essays in Honour of Bas van Iersel*. Kampen: Kok.

Driver, Samuel Rolles. 1916. *A Critical and Exegetical Commentary on Deuteronomy*. ICC. New York: Charles Scribner's Sons.

Driver, Samuel Rolles, and George Buchanan Gray. 1921. *A Critical and Exegetical Commentary on the Book of Job*. ICC. Edinburgh: T. & T. Clark.

Duhm, Bernhard. 1897. *Das Buch Hiob*. Kurzer Hand-Commentar zum Alten Testament 16. Freiburg: Mohr.

Dunn, J. D. G. 1988. *Romans 9–16*. WBC 38. Dallas, Tex.: Word.

Edenburg, Cynthia. 2010. Intertextuality, Literary Competence and the Question of Readership: Some Preliminary Observations. *JSOT* 35:131–48.

Eerdmans, B. D. 1939. The Conception of God in the Book of Job (El. Eloah. Shaddai). Pages 1–26 in *Studies in Job*. Edited by B. D. Eerdmans. Leiden: Burgersdijk & Niermans.

Eisenberg, J., and E. Wiesel. 1986. *Job ou Dieu dans la tempête*. Paris: Fayard.

Eliot, T. S. 1934. Tradition and the Individual Talent. Pages 13–22 in *Selected Essays*. Edited by T. S. Eliot. London: Faber.

Eslinger, Lyle. 1992. Inner-Biblical Exegesis and Inner-Biblical Allusion: The Question of Category. *VT* 42:47–58.

Fewell, Danna Nolan. 1992. Introduction: Writing, Reading, and Relating. Pages 11–20 in Fewell ed. 1992.

———, ed. 1992. *Reading Between Texts: Intertextuality and the Hebrew Bible*. Literary Currents in Biblical Interpretation. Louisville: Westminster John Knox.

Fichtner, J. 1933. *Die Altorientalische Weisheit in ihrer Israelitisch-Jüdischen Ausprägung*. Giessen: Töpelmann.

Fish, S. 1980. Interpreting the *Variorum*. Pages 147–73 in *Is There a Text in This Class? The Authority of Interpretive Communities*. Edited by S. Fish. Cambridge, Mass.: Harvard University Press.

Fishbane, Michael. 1971. Jeremiah IV 23–26 and Job III 3–13: A Recovered Use of the Creation Pattern. *VT* 21:151–67.

———. 1985. *Biblical Interpretation in Ancient Israel*. Oxford: Clarendon.

———. 1992. The Book of Job and Inner-Biblical Discourse. Pages 86–98 in *The Voice from the Whirlwind: Interpreting the Book of Job*. Edited by Leo G. Perdue and W. Clark Gilpin. Nashville: Abingdon.

———. 2000. Types of Biblical Intertextuality. Pages 39–44 in Lemaire and Sæbø 2000.

Fohrer, Georg. 1963. *Das Buch Hiob*. KAT 16. Gütersloh: Gütersloher Verlag-Haus Mohn.

Fox, Michael V. 1980. The Identification of Quotations in Biblical Literature. *ZAW* 92:416–31.

———. 2005. Job the Pious. *ZAW* 117:351–66.

Fredericks, D. C. 1989. Chiasm and Parallel Structure in Qoheleth 5:9–6:9. *JBL* 108:17–35.

Fredericks, D. C. and D. J. Estes. 2010. *Ecclesiastes & Song of Songs*. Apollos Old Testament Commentary 16. Downers Grove, Ill.: InterVarsity.

Frevel, Christian. 2004. "Eine kleine Theologie der Menschenwürde": Ps 8 und seine Rezeption im Buch Ijob. Pages 244–72 in *Das Manna fällt auch heute noch: Beiträge zur Geschichte und Theologie des Alten, Ersten Testaments*. Edited by Frank-Lothar Hossfeld and Ludger Schwienhorst-Schönberger. HBS 44. Freiburg: Herder.

———. 2007. Schöpfungsglaube und Menschenwürde im Hiobbuch: Anmerkungen zur Anthropologie der Hiob-Reden. Pages 467–97 in Krüger et al. 2007.

———. 2009. Dann wär' ich nicht mehr da: Der Todeswunsch Ijobs als Element der Klagerhetorik. Pages 25–41 in *Tod und Jenseits im alten Israel und in seiner Umwelt: Theologische, religionsgeschichte, archäologische und ikonographische Aspekte*. Edited by Angelika Berlejung and Bernd Janowski. FAT 64. Tübingen: Mohr Siebeck.

Frow, John. 1990. Intertextuality and Ontology. Pages 45–55 in Worton and Still 1990.

Fuchs, Gisela. 1993. *Mythos und Hiobdichtung: Aufnahme und Umdeutung altorientalischer Vorstellungen*. Stuttgart: Kohlhammer.

Furman, Laura, ed. 2003. *The O. Henry Prize Stories 2003*. New York: Anchor.

Galatolo, Renata. 2007. Active Voicing in Court. Pages 195–220 in *Reporting Talk*. Edited by Elizabeth Holt and Rebecca Clift. Cambridge: Cambridge University Press.

Garrett, Duane A. 1987. Qoheleth on the Use and Abuse of Political Power. *Trinity Journal* 8:159–77.

Genette, Gérard. 1997. *Palimpsests: Literature in the Second Degree*. Translated by C. Newman and C. Doubinsky. Lincoln: University of Nebraska Press.

Genung, J. F. 1906. *The Hebrew Literature of Wisdom in Light of To-day: A Synthesis*. Boston: Houghton Mifflin.

Gerstenberger, E. 2010. The Dynamics of Praise in the Ancient Near East, Or: Poetics and Politics. Paper presented at SBL Annual Meeting, Atlanta, Ga.

Gertz, J. C. 2012. The Formation of the Primeval History. Pages 107–35 in *The Book of Genesis: Composition, Reception, and Interpretation*. Edited by C. A. Evans, J. N. Lohr, and D. L. Petersen. Leiden: Brill.

Good, Edwin M. 1990. *In Turns of Tempest: A Reading of Job*. Stanford, Calif.: Stanford University Press.

Good, John Mason. 1812. *The Book of Job*. London: Black, Parry & Co.

Goodwin, M. H. 1980. He-said-she-said: Formal Cultural Procedures for the Construction of a Gossip Dispute Activity. *American Ethnologist* 7:674–95.

Gordis, Robert. 1939. Quotations in Wisdom Literature. *Jewish Quarterly Review* 30:123–47.

———. 1949. Quotations as a Literary Usage in Biblical, Oriental and Rabbinic Literature. *HUCA* 22:157–219.

———. 1965. *The Book of God and Man: A Study of Job.* Chicago: University of Chicago Press.

———. 1978. *The Book of Job: Commentary, New Translation, and Special Studies.* Moreshet 2. New York: Jewish Theological Seminary of America.

———. 1985. Job and Ecology (and the Significance of Job 40:15). Pages 189–202 in *Biblical and Other Studies in Memory of S. D. Goitein.* Edited by R. Ahroni. Columbus: Ohio State University Press.

Goshen-Gottstein, M. H. 1972. Ezechiel und Ijob. Zur Problemgeschichte von Bundestheologie und Gott-Mensch-Verhältnis. Pages 155–70 in *Wort, Lied und Gottesspruch: Beiträge zu Psalmen und Propheten. Festschrift für Joseph Ziegler.* Edited by J. Schreiner. Forschung zur Bibel 2. Würzburg: Echter.

Granowski, Jan Jaynes. 1992. Jehoiachin at the King's Table: A Reading of the Ending of the Second Book of Kings. Pages 173–88 in Fewell ed. 1992.

Gray, John. 2010. *The Book of Job.* Edited by D. J. A. Clines. Texts of the Hebrew Bible 1. Sheffield: Sheffield Phoenix.

Green, William Scott. 2002. Stretching the Covenant: Job and Judaism. *RevExp* 99:569–77.

Greene, Thomas M. 1982. *The Light in Troy: Imitation and Discovery in Renaissance Poetry.* New Haven: Yale University Press.

Greenfield, Jonas C. 1973. Un rite religieux araméen et ses parallèles. *Revue biblique* 80:46–52.

Greenstein, Edward L. 1989. *Essays on Biblical Method and Translation.* BJS 92. Atlanta: Scholars Press.

———. 1996. Deconstruction and Biblical Narrative. Pages 21–54 in *Interpreting Judaism in a Postmodern Age.* Edited by S. Kepnes. New York: New York University Press.

———. 2003. The Language of Job and Its Poetic Function. *JBL* 122:651–66.

———. 2004. Jeremiah as an Inspiration to the Poet of Job. Pages 98–110 in *Inspired Speech: Prophecy in the Ancient Near East: Essays in Honor of Herbert B. Huffmon.* Edited by John Kaltner and Louis Stulman. JSOTSup 378. London: T&T Clark International.

———. 2005. The Extent of Job's First Speech. Pages 245–62 in *Studies in Bible and Biblical Exegesis, 7, Presented to Menachem Cohen.* Edited by Shmuel Vargon. Ramat-Gan: Bar-Ilan University Press (in Hebrew with English abstract).

———. 2006. Truth or Theodicy? Speaking Truth to Power in the Book of Job. *Princeton Seminary Bulletin* 27:238–58.

———. 2007a. "On My Skin and in My Flesh": Personal Experience as a Source of Knowledge in the Book of Job. Pages 63–77 in *Bringing the Hidden to Light— The Process of Interpretation: Studies in Honor of Stephen A. Geller.* Edited by K. F. Kravitz and D. M. Sharon. Winona Lake: Eisenbrauns.

———. 2007b. Features of Language in the Poetry of Job. Pages 81–96 in Krüger et al. 2007.

———. 2007c. God's Test of Job. Pages 263–72 in *Shai le-Sara Japhet: Studies in the Bible, Its Exegesis and Its Language.* Edited by M. Bar-Asher et al. Jerusalem: Mossad Bialik (in Hebrew with English abstract).

———. 2008. The Poetic Use of Akkadian in the Book of Job. Pages 51–68 in *The Avi Hurvitz Festschrift (Meh)qarim be-Lashon 11–12.* Edited by S. Fassberg and A. Maman. Jerusalem: Hebrew University Press.

————. 2009. The Problem of Evil in the Book of Job. Pages 333–62 in *Mishneh Todah: Studies in Deuteronomy and Its Cultural Environment in Honor of Jeffrey H. Tigay*. Edited by N. S. Fox, D. A. Glatt-Gilad, and M. J. Williams. Winona Lake: Eisenbrauns.

————. 2011a. "Difficulty" in the Poetry of Job. Pages 186–95 in *A Critical Engagement: Essays on the Hebrew Bible in Honour of J. Cheryl Exum*. Edited by D. J. A. Clines and E. van Wolde. Sheffield: Sheffield Phoenix.

————. 2011b. Wisdom in the Book of Job—Undermined. Pages 41–50 in *Wisdom, Her Pillars Are Seven: Studies in Biblical, Post-Biblical and Ancient Near Eastern Wisdom Literature*. Edited by S. Yona and V. A. Hurowitz. Beer-sheva 20. Beer-sheva: Ben Gurion University of the Negev Press (Hebrew).

————. Forthcoming. Three Philological Notes on the Book of Job. In *Studies in Bible and Exegesis, 11, Presented to Rimon Kasher*. Edited by E. Assis et al. Ramat-Gan: Bar-Ilan University Press (Hebrew).

Gressmann, Hugo. 1925. *Israels Spruchweisheit im Zusammenhang der Weltliteratur*. Berlin: Curtius.

Griffiths, J. Gwyn. 1980. *Osiris and the Origins of His Cult*. Studies in the History of Religions 40. Leiden: Brill.

————. 1983. The Idea of Posthumous Judgement in Israel and Egypt. Pages 186–204 in *Fontes Atque Pontes: Eine Festgabe für Hellmut Brunner*. Edited by Manfred Görg. Ägypten und Altes Testament 5. Wiesbaden: Harrassowitz.

————. 1991. *The Divine Verdict: A Study of Divine Judgement in the Ancient Religions*. Leiden: Brill.

Haas, Cees. 1989. Job's Perseverance in the Testament of Job. Pages 117–54 in *Studies in the Testament of Job*. Edited by Michael Knibb and Pieter W. Van Der Horst. Cambridge: Cambridge University Press.

Habel, Norman C. 1976. Appeal to Ancient Tradition as a Literary Form. *ZAW* 88:253–72.

————. 1981. "Naked I Came…": Humanness in the Book of Job. Pages 373–92 in *Die Botschaft und die Boten*. Edited by Jörg Jeremias and Lothar Perlitt. Neukirchen–Vluyn: Neukirchener Verlag.

————. 1984. The Role of Elihu in the Design of the Book of Job. Pages 81–98 in *In the Shelter of Elyon: Essays on Palestinian Life and Literature in Honor of G. W. Ahlström*. Edited by W. Boyd Barrick and John R. Spencer. JSOTSup 31. Sheffield: JSOT.

————. 1985. *The Book of Job: A Commentary*. OTL. Philadelphia: Westminster.

Hagedorn, Ursula, and Dieter Hagedorn. 2004. *Die älteren griechischen Katenen zum Buch Hiob, IV*. Patristische Texte und Studien 59. Berlin: de Gruyter.

Halliday, M. A. K., and Ruqaiya Hasan. 1976. *Cohesion in English*. London: Longman.

Hallo, William W., ed. 1996. *Monumental Inscriptions from the Biblical World*. COS 2. Leiden: Brill.

Haralambakis, Maria. Forthcoming. *The Testament of Job: Text, Narrative and Reception*. Library of Second Temple Studies. London: T&T Clark/Continuum.

Hardy, D. W., and D. F. Ford. 1985. *Praising and Knowing God*. Philadelphia: Westminster.

Hartley, John E. 1988. *The Book of Job*. NICOT. Grand Rapids: Eerdmans.

Hatina, Thomas R. 1999. Intertextuality and Historical Criticism in New Testament Studies: Is There a Relationship? *BibInt* 7:28–43.

Hays, Christopher B. 2008a. Damming Egypt / Damning Egypt: The Paronomasia of *skr* and the Unity of Isa 19:1–15. *ZAW* 120:612–16.

———. 2008b. Echoes of the Ancient Near East? Intertextuality and the Comparative Study of the Old Testament. Pages 20–43 in *The Word Leaps the Gap: Essays on Scripture and Theology in Honor of Richard B. Hays.* Edited by J. Ross Wagner, C. Kavin Rowe, and A. Katherine Grieb. Grand Rapids: Eerdmans.

———. 2010. The Covenant with Mut: A New Interpretation of Isaiah 28:1–22. *VT* 60:212–40.

———. 2011. *Death in the Iron Age II and in First Isaiah.* FAT 79. Tübingen: Mohr Siebeck.

———. Forthcoming a. "My Beloved Son, Come and Rest in Me": Job's Return to His Mother's Womb (Job 1:21a) in Light of Egyptian Mythology. *VT.*

———. Forthcoming b. "There Is Hope for a Tree": Job's Hope for the Afterlife in the Light of Egyptian Tree Imagery.

Hays, Richard B. 1989. *Echoes of Scripture in the Letters of Paul.* New Haven: Yale University Press.

Hays, Richard B., Stefan Alkier, and Leroy A. Huizenga, eds. 2009. *Reading the Bible Intertextually.* Waco, Tex.: Baylor University Press.

Hebel, Udo J. 1989. *Intertextuality, Allusion, and Quotation: An International Bibliography of Critical Studies.* New York: Greenwood.

———. 1991. Towards a Descriptive Poetics of Allusion. Pages 135–64 in *Intertextuality.* Edited by Heinrich F. Plett. Research in Text Theory 15. Berlin: de Gruyter.

Heckl, Raik. 2007. Die Religionsgeschichte als Schlüssel für die Literargeschichte: Eine neu gefasste Überlieferungskritik vorgestellt am Beispiel von Ex 32. *Theologische Zeitschrift* 63:193–215.

———. 2010a. Augenzeugenschaft und Verfasserschaft des Mose als zwei hermeneutische Konzepte der Rezeption und Präsentation literarischer Traditionen beim Abschluss des Pentateuch. *ZAW* 122:353–73.

———. 2010b. *Hiob: Vom Gottesfürchtigen zum Repräsentanten Israels.* FAT 70. Tübingen: Mohr Siebeck.

———. 2011. Die Präsentation tradierter Texte in Dtn 31 zur Revision der dtr Geschichtstheologie. Pages 227–46 in *Deuteronomium—Tora für eine neue Generation.* Edited by G. Fischer, D. Markl, and S. Paganini. Beihefte zur Zeitschrift für altorientalische und biblische Rechtsgeschichte 17. Wiesbaden: Harrassowitz.

Heimbrock, Hans-Günter. 2009. Reading the Bible in the Context of "Thick Description": Reflections of a Practical Theologian on a Phenomenological Concept of Contextuality. Pages 205–20 in Hays, Alkier, and Huizenga 2009.

Helbig, Jörg. 1996. *Intertextualität und Markierung: Untersuchungen zur Systematik und Funktion der Signalisierung von Intertextualität.* Heidelberg: Winter.

Hempel, J. 1938. The Contents of the Literature. Pages 45–73 in *Record and Revelation: Essays by Members of the Society for Old Testament Study.* Edited by H. Wheeler Robinson. Oxford: Clarendon.

Herz, N. 1913. Egyptian Words and Idioms in the Book of Job. *Orientalistische Literaturzeitung* 16:343–46.

Hibbard, J. Todd. 2006. *Intertextuality in Isaiah 24–27: The Reuse and Evocation of Earlier Texts and Traditions.* FAT 2/16. Tübingen: Mohr Siebeck.

Ho, Edward. 2009. In the Eyes of the Beholder: Unmarked Attributed Quotations in Job. *JBL* 128:703–15.

Holladay, John S., Jr. 2009. "Home Economics 1407" and the Israelite Family and Their Neighbors: An Anthropological/Archaeological Exploration. Pages 61–88 in *The Family in Life and in Death: The Family in Ancient Israel: Sociological and Archaeological Perspectives*. Edited by Patricia Dutcher-Walls. LHBOTS 504. New York: T&T Clark International.

Holladay, William L. 1986–89. *Jeremiah*. 2 vols. Hermeneia. Philadelphia: Fortress.

Hölscher, Gustav. 1937. *Das Buch Hiob*. HAT 17. Tübingen: Mohr.

Holt, Elizabeth. 1996. Reporting on Talk: The Use of Direct Reported Speech in Conversation. *Research on Language and Social Interaction* 29:219–45.

———. 2009. Reported Speech. Pages 190–205 in *The Pragmatics of Interaction*. Edited by Sigurd D'hondt, Jan-Ola Östman, and Jef Verschueren. Amsterdam: John Benjamins.

Hossfeld, Frank-Lothar, and Erich Zenger. 2011. *Psalms 3: A Commentary on Psalms 101–150*. Hermeneia. Minneapolis: Augsburg Fortress.

Humbert, Paul. 1929. *Recherches sur les sources égyptiennes de la littérature sapientiale d'Israël*. Neuchâtel: Secrétariat de l'Université.

Hunter, Alastair. 2006. *Wisdom Literature*. London: SCM.

Hurvitz, Avi. 1974. The Date of the Prose-Tale of Job Linguistically Reconsidered. *Harvard Theological Review* 67:17–34.

Hutcheon, Linda. 1985. *A Theory of Parody: The Teachings of Twentieth-Century Art Forms*. New York: Methuen.

Irwin, William. 2001. What Is an Allusion? *The Journal of Aesthetics and Art Criticism* 59:287–97.

———. 2004. Against Intertextuality. *Philosophy and Literature* 28:227–42.

Iseminger, G., ed. 1992. *Intention and Interpretation*. Philadelphia: Temple University Press.

Jacobsen, Thorkild. 1976. *The Treasures of Darkness: A History of Mesopotamian Religion*. New Haven: Yale University Press.

Jacobsen, T., and K. Nielsen. 1992. Cursing the Day. *Scandinavian Journal of the Old Testament* 6:187–212.

Jacobson, Rolf A. 2004. *"Many Are Saying": The Function of Direct Discourse in the Hebrew Psalter*. JSOTSup 397. New York: T&T Clark International.

Jamieson-Drake, D. W. 1987. Literary Structure, Genre and Interpretation in Job 38. Pages 217–35 in *The Listening Heart: Essays in Wisdom and Psalms in Honor of Roland E. Murphy*. Edited by Kenneth G. Hoglund et al. JSOTSup 85. Sheffield: JSOT.

Jannidis, F., et al. 1999. Rede über den Autor an die Gebildeten unter seinen Verächtern: Historische Modelle und systematische Perspektiven. Pages in 3–35 *Rückkehr des Autors: Zur Erneuerung eines umstrittenen Begriffs*. Edited by F. Jannidis et al. Studien und Texte zur Sozialgeschichte der Literatur 71. Tübingen: Niemeyer.

Janzen, J. Gerald. 1985. *Job*. Interpretation. Atlanta: John Knox.

———. 1997. *Exodus*. Westminster Biblical Companion. Louisville: Westminster John Knox.

———. 2009. *At the Scent of Water: The Ground of Hope in the Book of Job*. Grand Rapids: Eerdmans.

———. 2012. Toward a Hermeneutics of Resonance: A Methodological Interlude Between the Testaments. In *When Prayer Takes Place: Exegetical and Theological Forays into a Biblical World*. Eugene, Or.: Wipf & Stock.

Jenni, E. 1997a. *lmd* to learn. Pages 646–48 in vol. 2 of Jenni 1997b.

———. 1997b. *Theological Lexicon of the Old Testament*. Translated by M. E. Biddle. 3 vols. Peabody, Mass.: Hendrickson.

Johnston, P. S. 2002. *Shades of Sheol: Death and Afterlife in the Old Testament*. Leicester: Apollos.

Joyce, P. M. 2007. *Ezekiel: A Commentary*. LHBOTS 482. New York: T&T Clark International.

Käsemann, E. 1980. *Commentary on Romans*. Grand Rapids: Eerdmans.

Kee, Howard Clark. 1974. Satan, Magic, and Salvation in the Testament of Job. *SBLSP* 1:53–76.

Keel, Othmar. 1978. *Jahwes Entgegnung an Ijob: Eine Deutung von Ijob 38–41 vor dem Hintergrund der zeitgenössischen Bildkunst*. FRLANT 121. Göttingen: Vandenhoeck & Ruprecht.

———. 1981. Zwei kleine Beiträge zum Verständnis der Gottesreden im Buch Ijob (XXXVIII 36f., XL 25). *VT* 31:220–25.

Kellett, E. E. 1940. "Job": An Allegory? *ExpTim* 51:250–51.

Kissane, Edward J. 1939. *The Book of Job*. Dublin: Brown & Nolan.

Knohl, I. 1995. *The Sanctuary of Silence: The Priestly Torah and the Holiness School*. Minneapolis: Fortress.

———. 2003. *The Divine Symphony: The Bible's Many Voices*. Philadelphia: Jewish Publication Society.

Koemoth, Pierre. 1993. Des défunts "Secrets-de-places" aux arbres sacrés des nécropoles divines Št3.w-s.wt. *Discussions in Egyptology* 25:29–37.

———. 1994. *Osiris et les arbres: Contribution à l'étude des arbres sacrés de l'Égypte ancienne*. Aegyptiaca Leodiensia 3. Liège: C.I.P.L.

———. 2010. Du Nil à Byblos: De la dérive du corps au périple maritime du roi Osiris. *Bibliotheca Orientalis* 67:461–88.

Kohak, E. 1984. *The Embers and the Stars: A Philosophical Inquiry into the Moral Sense of Nature*. Chicago: University of Chicago Press.

Köhlmoos, Melanie. 1999. *Das Auge Gottes: Textstrategie im Hiobbuch*. FAT 25. Tübingen: Mohr Siebeck.

Kolitz, Zvi. 2004 (1946). *Jossel Rakovers Wendung zu Gott*. Zurich: Diogenes.

Kraft, Robert A. 1974. *The Testament of Job: According to the SV Text*. Missoula, Mont.: Scholars Press.

Kraus, Hans-Joachim. 1993. *Psalms: A Continental Commentary*. Translated by Hilton C. Oswald. 2 vols. Minneapolis: Fortress.

Kristeva, Julia. 1969a. Narration et transformation. *Semiotica* 1:442–48.

———. 1969b. *Séméiotikè: recherches pour une sémanalyse*. Paris: Seuil.

———. 1970. *Le texte du roman: approche sémiologique d'une structure discursive transformationelle*. Paris: Mouton.

———. 1974. *La revolution du langage poétique*. Paris: Seuil.

———. 1980a. *Desire in Language: A Semiotic Approach to Literature and Art*. Translated by Thomas Gora, Alice Jardine, and Leon S. Roudiez. New York: Columbia University Press.

———. 1980b. Word, Dialogue, and Novel. Pages 64–91 in Kristeva 1980a.

————. 1984. *Revolution in Poetic Language*. Translated by Margaret Waller. New York: Columbia University Press.

Krüger, Annette. 2010. *Das Lob des Schöpfers: Studien zu Sprache, Motivik und Theologie von Psalm 104*. WMANT 124. Neukirchen–Vluyn: Neukirchener Verlag.

Krüger, Thomas. 2007. Did Job Repent? Pages 217–29 in T. Krüger et al. 2007.

Krüger, Thomas et al., eds. 2007. *Das Buch Hiob und seine Interpretationen: Beiträge zum Hiob-Symposium auf dem Monte Verità vom 14.–19. August 2005*. Abhandlungen zur Theologie des Alten und Neuen Testaments 88. Zurich: Theologischer Verlag.

Kuenen, Abraham. 1873. Job en de lijdende knecht van Jahveh. *Theologisch Tijdschrift* 7:492–542.

Kugler, Robert A., and Richard L. Rohrbaugh. 2004. On Women and Honor in the Testament of Job. *Journal for the Study of the Pseudepigrapha* 14:43–62.

Kynes, Will. 2011. Beat Your Parodies into Swords, and Your Parodied Books into Spears: A New Paradigm for Parody in the Hebrew Bible. *BibInt* 19:276–310.

————. 2012. *My Psalm Has Turned into Weeping: Job's Dialogue with the Psalms*. BZAW 473. Berlin: de Gruyter.

Laato, A., and J. C. de Moor, eds. 2003. *Theodicy in the World of the Bible*. Leiden: Brill.

Lambert, W. G., ed. 1960. *Babylonian Wisdom Literature*. Oxford: Clarendon.

Lane-Mercier, Gillian. 1991. Quotation as a Discursive Strategy. *Kodikas/Code Ars Semeiotica* 14:199–214.

Lang, Bernhard. 1983. *Monotheism and the Prophetic Minority: An Essay in Biblical History and Sociology*. Sheffield: Almond.

————. 2006. Das Buch der Kriege. Pages 66–81 in *Mythos 2. Politische Mythen*. Edited by P. Tepe. Würzburg: Königshausen &Neumann.

Langenhorst, Georg. 1995. *Hiob unser Zeitgenosse: Die literarische Hiob-Rezeption im 20. Jahrhundert als theologische Herausforderung*. 2d ed. Mainz: Mathias-Grunewald-Verlag.

Lee, Samuel. 1837. *The Book of the Patriarch Job*. London: Duncan.

Lemaire, A., and M. Sæbø, eds. 2000. *Congress Volume: Oslo 1998*. VTSup 80. Leiden: Brill.

Leonard, Jeffery M. 2008. Identifying Inner-Biblical Allusions: Psalm 78 as a Test Case. *JBL* 127:241–65.

Lesses, Rebecca. 2007. Amulets and Angels: Visionary Experience in the *Testament of Job* and the Hekhalot Literature. Pages 49–74 in *Heavenly Tablets: Interpretation, Identity and Tradition in Ancient Judaism*. Edited by Lynn LiDonnici and Andrea Liebeter. Leiden: Brill.

Lévêque, Jean. 1970. *Job et son Dieu: essai d'exégèse et de théologie biblique*. 2 vols. Études bibliques. Paris: Gabalda.

Levi, Primo. 1947. *Se questo è un uomo*. Turin: Einandi.

Levin, Hanoch. 1999. *Yissûrê Iyyôv* ("The Suffering of Job"). Pages 55–103 in *Mahazôth 3 (Plays 3)*. Tel-Aviv: Ha-Qîbbûs ha-Me'ûhad. Original ed. in Hebrew, 1981.

Levinson, B. M. 1988. *Deuteronomy and the Hermeneutics of Legal Innovation*. Oxford: Oxford University Press.

Lichtheim, Miriam. 1975. *The Old and Middle Kingdoms*. Ancient Egyptian Literature 1. Berkeley: University of California Press.

Liedke, G. 1997. *ykh* hi. to Determine What Is Right. Pages 542–44 in vol. 2 of Jenni 1997b.

Limburg, James. 1992. Psalms. *ABD* 5:522–36.

Linafelt, T. 1996. The Undecidability of ברך in the Prologue to Job and Beyond. *BibInt* 4:154–72.

———. 2000. *Surviving Lamentations: Catastrophe, Lament, and Protest in the Afterlife of a Biblical Book.* Chicago: University of Chicago Press.

Lincoln, A. T. 1990. *Ephesians.* WBC 42. Dallas, Tex.: Word.

Long, Thomas G. 1988. Job: Second Thoughts in the Land of Uz. *Theology Today* 45:5–20.

Longman, Tremper, III. 1998. *The Book of Ecclesiastes.* NICOT. Grand Rapids: Eerdmans.

Ludewig-Kedmi, Revital, Miriam Victory Spiegel, and Silvie Tyrangiel, ed. 2002. *Das Trauma des Holocaust zwischen Psychologie und Geschichte.* Zurich: Chronos.

Lund, Ø. 2007. *Way Metaphors and Way Topics in Isaiah 40–55.* FAT 2/28. Tübingen: Mohr Siebeck.

Lundbom, J. 1999. *Jeremiah 1–20.* AB 21A. New York: Doubleday.

Lyons, Michael A. 2009. *From Law to Prophecy: Ezekiel's Use of the Holiness Code.* LHBOTS 507. New York: T&T Clark International.

Maag, Victor. 1982. *Hiob: Wandlung und Verarbeitung des Problems in Novelle, Dialogdichtung und Spätfassungen.* FRLANT 128. Göttingen: Vandenhoeck & Ruprecht.

Machinist, P. 2005. Order and Disorder: Some Mesopotamian Reflections. Pages 31–61 in *Genesis and Regeneration: Essays on Conceptions of Origins.* Edited by Shaul Shaked. Jerusalem: The Israel Academy of Sciences and Humanities.

Magary, D. R. 2002. Response to Balentine. *ExAud* 18:53–56.

Magdalene, F. Rachel. 2007. *On the Scales of Righteousness: Neo-Babylonian Trial Law and the Book of Job.* BJS 348. Providence, R.I.: Brown University Press.

Magness, Jodi. 2011. *Stone and Dung, Oil and Spit: Jewish Daily Life in the Time of Jesus.* Grand Rapids: Eerdmans.

Mandelbaum, Bernard. 1987. *Pesikta de Rav Kahana According to an Oxford Manuscript With Variants From All Known Manuscripts and Genizoth Fragments and Parallel Passages, With Commentary and Introduction.* 2d ed. New York: Jewish Theological Seminary of America.

Mandolfo, Carleen. 2007a. A Generic Renegade: A Dialogic Reading of Job and Lament Psalms. Pages 45–63 in *Diachronic and Synchronic: Reading the Psalms in Real Time.* Edited by Joel S. Burnett, W. H. Bellinger, and W. Dennis Tucker. New York: T&T Clark International.

———. 2007b. *Daughter Zion Talks Back to the Prophets: A Dialogic Theological Reading of Lamentations.* SemeiaSt 58. Leiden: Brill.

Margalioth, R. 1981. *The Original Job: Discussion and Proofs of Its Antiquity and Singular Authorship.* Jerusalem: Marcus (Hebrew).

Marlow, Hilary. 2009. *Biblical Prophets and Contemporary Environmental Ethics: Rereading Amos, Hosea and First Isaiah.* Oxford: Oxford University Press.

Mathewson, Dan. 2006. *Death and Survival in the Book of Job: Desymbolization and Traumatic Experience.* LHBOTS 450. New York: T&T Clark International.

Matoesian, G. 2000. Intertextual Authority in Reported Speech: Production Media in the Kennedy Smith Rape Trial. *Journal of Pragmatics* 32:879–914.

McCann, J. Clinton. 1997. Wisdom's Dilemma: The Book of Job, the Final Form of the Book of Psalms, and the Entire Bible. Pages 18–30 in Barré 1997.

McKane, William. 1986. *Jeremiah*. 2 vols. ICC. Edinburgh: T. & T. Clark.

McKibben, Bill. 1994. The Comforting Whirlwind: God, Job, and the Scale of Creation. *Religion & Values in Public Life (Harvard Divinity Bulletin)* 2:12–13.

———. 2005. *The Comforting Whirlwind: God, Job, and the Scope of Creation*. Cambridge, Mass.: Cowley.

Meier, S. 1989. Job I–II: A Reflection on Genesis I–III. *VT* 39:184–85.

Mettinger, Tryggve N. D. 1993. Intertextuality: Allusion and Vertical Context Systems in Some Job Passages. Pages 257–80 in *Of Prophets' Visions and the Wisdom of Sages*. Edited by Heather A. McKay and D. J. A. Clines. JSOTSup 162. Sheffield: JSOT.

———. 1997. The Enigma of Job: The Deconstruction of God in Intertextual Perspective. *Journal of Northwest Semitic Languages* 23:1–19.

Meyers, Carol L., and Eric M. Meyers. 1993. *Zechariah 9–14: A New Translation with Introduction and Commentary*. AB 25C. New York: Doubleday.

Michel, Walter. 1972. Death in Job. *Dialog* 11:183–89.

Middlemas, J. 2005. *The Troubles of Templeless Judah*. Oxford Theological Monographs. Oxford: Oxford University Press.

Migne, J.-P., ed. 1844–64. *Patrologia latina*. 217 vols. Paris.

Miles, J. 1995. *God: A Biography*. New York: Knopf.

Milgrom, J. 1991. *Leviticus 1–16*. AB 3. New York: Doubleday.

Miller, Cynthia L. 1996. *The Representation of Speech in Biblical Hebrew Narrative: A Linguistic Analysis*. Harvard Semitic Monographs 55. Atlanta: Scholars Press.

Miller, Geoffrey D. 2011. Intertextuality in Old Testament Research. *Currents in Biblical Research* 9:283–309.

Miller, Patrick D. 1987. Cosmology and World Order in the Old Testament: The Divine Council as Cosmic-Political Symbol. *Horizons in Biblical Theology* 9:53–78.

Miner, Earl. 1994. Allusion. Pages 13–15 in *The New Princeton Handbook of Poetic Terms*. Edited by T. V. F. Brogan. Princeton: Princeton University Press.

Minnen, B. 2007. Le cult de Saint Job à Wezemaal aux XV and XVI siècles. Pages 603–9 in *Actes des VII Congrès l'Association des Circles Francophones d'Histoire et de Belgique et LIV Congrès de la Féderation des Circles d'Archéologie et d'Histoire de Belgigue.*

———, ed. Forthcoming. *De Sint-Martinuskerk van Wezemaal en de cultus van Sint Job, 1000–2000*. Averbode: Altiora.

Miscall, Peter D. 1991. Isaiah: The Labyrinth of Images. *Semeia* 54:103–21.

———. 1992. Isaiah: New Heavens, New Earth, New Book. Pages 41–56 in Fewell ed. 1992.

Moberly, R. W. L. 1992. *The Old Testament of the Old Testament: Patriarchal Narratives and Mosaic Yahwism*. Overtures to Biblical Theology. Minneapolis: Fortress.

Moor, Johannes C. de, ed. 1995. *Synchronic or Diachronic? A Debate on Method in Old Testament Exegesis: Papers Read at the Ninth Joint Meeting of the Oudtestamentisch Werkgezelschap in Nederland en Belgie and the Society for Old Testament Study, Held at Kampen, 1994*. OtSt 34. Leiden: Brill.

———. 1998. Introduction. Pages ix–xi in *Intertextuality in Ugarit and Israel: Papers Read at the Tenth Joint Meeting of the Society for Old Testament Study and het*

Oudtestamentisch Werkgezelschap in Nederland en België. Held at Oxford, 1997. Edited by Johannes C. de Moor. OtSt 40. Leiden: Brill.

Moore, C. A. 1996. *Tobit.* AB 40. New York: Doubleday.

Moore, Stephen D., and Yvonne Sherwood. 2011. *The Invention of the Biblical Scholar: A Critical Manifesto.* Minneapolis: Fortress.

Morgan, D. F. 1981. *Wisdom in the Old Testament Traditions.* Oxford: Blackwell.

Morrow, William S. 1986. Consolation, Rejection, and Repentance in Job 42:6. *JBL* 105:211–25.

———. 2010. "To Set the Name" in the Deuteronomic Centralization Formula: A Case of Cultural Hybridity. *JSS* 55:365–83.

Moyise, Steve. 2002. Intertextuality and Biblical Studies: A Review. *Verbum et Ecclesia* 23:418–31.

Münz, Christoph. 1995. *Der Welt ein Gedächtnis geben: Geschichtstheologisches Denken im Judentum nach Auschwitz.* Gütersloh: Gütersloher Verlag-Haus Mohn.

Naish, J. P. 1925. The Book of Job and the Early Persian Period. *Expositor* Series 9. no. 3:34–49, 94–104.

Nasciscione, Anita. 2010. *Stylistic Use of Phraseological Units in Discourse.* Amsterdam: John Benjamins.

Newsom, Carol A. 1996. The Book of Job. Pages 317–637 in *The New Interpreter's Bible.* Vol. 4, *1 & 2 Maccabees, Introduction to Hebrew Poetry, Job, Psalms.* Edited by Katharine Doob Sakenfeld. Nashville: Abingdon.

———. 2003. *The Book of Job: A Contest of Moral Imaginations.* Oxford: Oxford University Press.

Ngwa, K. N. 2005. *The Hermeneutics of the "Happy" Ending in Job 42:7–17.* BZAW 354. Berlin: de Gruyter.

Nogalski, James D. 1996. Intertextuality and the Twelve. Pages 102–24 in *Forming Prophetic Literature: Essays on Isaiah and the Twelve in Honor of John D. W. Watts.* Edited by James W. Watts and Paul R. House. Sheffield: Sheffield Academic.

———. 2000. Joel as Literary Anchor in the Book of the Twelve. Pages 91–109 in *Reading and Hearing the Book of the Twelve.* Edited by James D. Nogalski and Marvin A. Sweeney. SBL Symposium Series 15. Atlanta: Society of Biblical Literature.

———. 2011. *The Book of the Twelve: Hosea–Jonah.* Smyth & Helwys Bible Commentary 18A. Macon, Ga.: Smyth & Helwys.

Noth, M. 1951. Noah, Daniel und Hiob in Ezechiel 14. *VT* 1:251–60.

Nurmela, Risto. 1996. *Prophets in Dialogue: Inner-Biblical Allusions in Zechariah 9–14.* Åbo: Åbo Akademi University Press.

———. 2006. *The Mouth of the Lord Has Spoken: Inner-Biblical Allusions in Second and Third Isaiah.* Lanham, Md.: University Press of America.

O'Brien, P. T. 1999. *The Letter to the Ephesians.* Pillar. Grand Rapids: Eerdmans.

O'Dowd, Ryan. 2009. *The Wisdom of Torah: Epistemology in Deuteronomy and the Wisdom Literature.* FRLANT 225. Göttingen: Vandenhoeck & Ruprecht.

Oberhänsli-Widmer, Gabrielle. 2003. *Hiob in jüdischer Antike und Moderne: Die Wirkungsgeschichte Hiobs in der jüdischen Literatur.* Neukirchen–Vluyn: Neukirchener Verlag.

Oeming, Manfred. 2000. "Ihr habt nicht recht von mir geredet wie mein Knecht Hiob" (Hi 42,7): Gottes Schlußwort als Schlüssel zur Interpretation des Hiobbuchs und als kritische Anfrage an die moderne Theologie. *Evangelische Theologie* 60:95–108.

———. 2001. Hiobs Monolog—der Weg nach innen. Pages 57–75 in *Hiobs Weg: Stationen von Menschen im Leid*. Edited by M. Oeming and K. Schmid. Biblisch-theologische Studien 45. Neukirchen–Vluyn: Neukirchener Verlag.

———. 2007. Ijobs Frau (Sitidos): Von der Perserzeit bis heute. Pages 25–41 in *Frauen gestalten Diakonie*. Band 1, *Von der biblischen Zeit bis zum Pietismus*. Edited by Adelheid M. von Hauff. Stuttgart: Kohlhammer.

Olyan, S. M. 2004. *Biblical Mourning: Ritual and Social Dimensions*. Oxford: Oxford University Press.

Omerzu, Heike. 2005. Women, Magic and Angels: On the Emancipation of Job's Daughters in the Apocryphal Testament of Job. Pages 85–103 in *Bodies in Question: Gender, Religion, Text*. Edited by Darlene Bird and Yvonne Sherwood. Aldershot: Ashgate.

Oorschot, Jürgen van. 1995. Tendenzen der Hiobforschung. *Theologische Rundschau* 60:351–88.

Opel, Daniela. 2010. *Hiobs Anspruch und Widerspruch: Die Herausforderungsreden Hiobs (Hi 29–31) im Kontext frühjüdischer Ethik*. WMANT 127. Neukirchen–Vluyn: Neukirchener Verlag.

Orr, Mary. 2003. *Intertextuality: Debates and Contexts*. Cambridge: Polity.

Otto, E. 2000. *Das Deuteronomium im Pentateuch und Hexateuch*. FAT 30. Tübingen: Mohr Siebeck.

———. 2007. *Das Gesetz des Mose*. Darmstadt: Wissenschaftliche Buchgesellschaft.

Ozick, C. 2000. The Impious Impatience of Job. Pages 59–73 in *Quarrel and Quandary*. Edited by C. Ozick. New York: Knopf.

Pagis, Dan. 1989. Homily. Page 11 in *Variable Directions: The Selected Poetry of Dan Pagis*. Translated by Stephen Mitchell. San Francisco: North Point.

Parpola, S. 1997. *Assyrian Prophecies*. State Archives of Assyria 9. Helsinki: Helsinki University Press.

Patrick, Dale. 1976. The Translation of Job 42:6. *VT* 26:369–71.

Peake, Arthur S. 1904. *Job*. Edited by Walter F. Adeney. The Century Bible. Edinburgh: T. C. & E. C. Jack.

Perdue, Leo G. 1977. *Wisdom and Cult: A Critical Analysis of the Views of Cult in the Wisdom Literatures of Israel and the Ancient Near East*. Missoula, Mont.: Scholars Press.

———. 1986. Job's Assault on Creation. *Hebrew Annual Review* 10:295–315.

———. 1991. *Wisdom in Revolt: Metaphorical Theology in the Book of Job*. JSOTSup 112. Sheffield: Almond.

———. 1994. *Wisdom and Creation: The Theology of Wisdom Literature*. Nashville: Abingdon.

———. 2007. *Wisdom Literature: A Theological History*. Louisville: Westminster John Knox.

———, ed. 2008. *Scribes, Sages, and Seers: The Sage in the Eastern Mediterranean World*. FRLANT 219. Göttingen: Vandenhoeck & Ruprecht.

Perez, Isaac Leib. 1994. *Bonze Schweig.* Pages 109–16 in *Jüdisches Erzählen.* Edited by Peter Schünemann. Translated by Alexander Eliasberg. Munich: Deutscher Taschenbuch.

Petersen, D. 1984. *Haggai and Zechariah 1–8.* OTL. Philadelphia: Westminster.

Pfeiffer, Robert H. 1927. The Priority of Job Over Is. 40–55. *JBL* 46:202–6.

———. 1941. *Introduction to the Old Testament.* New York: Harper & Brothers.

Pfister, Manfred. 1985. Konzepte der Intertextualität. Pages 1–30 in *Intertextualität: Formen, Funktionen, anglistische Fallstudien.* Edited by Ulrich Broich, Manfred Pfister, and Bernd Schulte-Middelich. Konzepte der Sprach- und Literaturwissenschaft 35. Tübingen: Niemeyer.

Pham, Xuan Huong Thi. 1999. *Mourning in the Ancient Near East and the Hebrew Bible.* JSOTSup 302. Sheffield: Sheffield Academic.

Pilger, Tanja. 2010. *Erziehung im Leiden: Komposition und Theologie der Elihureden in Hiob 32–37.* FAT 2/49. Tübingen: Mohr Siebeck.

Pinker, Aron. 2007. Job's Perspectives on Death. *JBQ* 35:73–84.

Plett, Heinrich F. 1988. The Poetics of Quotation. Pages 313–14 in *Von der verbalen Konstitution zur symbolischen Bedeutung—From Verbal Constitution to Symbolic Meaning.* Edited by János S. Petöfi and Terry Olivi. Hamburg: Helmut Buske.

———. 1991. Intertextualities. Pages 3–29 in *Intertextuality.* Edited by Heinrich F. Plett. New York: de Gruyter.

Polk, T. 1984. *The Prophetic Persona: Jeremiah and the Language of the Self.* JSOTSup 32. Sheffield: JSOT.

Polkinghorne, John. 2003. *Living with Hope: A Scientist Looks at Advent, Christmas, and Epiphany.* Louisville: Westminster John Knox.

Pope, Marvin H. 1973. *Job.* 3d ed. AB 15. Garden City, N.Y.: Doubleday.

Pyeon, Yohan. 2003. *You Have Not Spoken What Is Right About Me: Intertextuality and the Book of Job.* Studies in Biblical Literature 45. New York: Lang.

Quirke, Stephen G. J. 2001. Judgment of the Dead. Pages 211–14 in vol. 2 of *Oxford Encyclopedia of Ancient Egypt.* Edited by Donald B. Redford. 3 vols. Oxford: Oxford University Press.

Rad, Gerhard von. 1972. *Wisdom in Israel.* Translated by J. D. Martin. Nashville: Abingdon.

———. 1983. The Confessions of Jeremiah. Pages 88–99 in *Theodicy in the Old Testament.* Edited by James L. Crenshaw. London: SPCK.

Rappel, D. 1996. *The Haʾazinu Song with Introduction and Commentary.* Tel Aviv: Yediʿot Aḥronot (Hebrew).

Remus, Martin. 1993. *Menschenbildvorstellungen im Ijob-Buch: Ein Beitrag zur alttestamentlichen Anthropologie.* BEATAJ 21. Frankfurt am Main: Lang.

Rendsburg, Gary A. 1988. Bilingual Wordplay in the Bible. *VT* 38:354–57.

Riffaterre, Michael. 1979. La syllepse intertextuelle. *Poétique* 40:496–501.

———. 1991. Compulsory Reader Response: The Intertextual Drive. Pages 56–78 in Worton and Still 1990.

Rigby, Paul. 2000. Augustine's Use of the Narrative Universal in the Debate Over Predestination. *AugStud* 31:181–94.

———. 2002. The Role of God's "Inscrutable Judgments" in Augustine's Doctrine of Predestination. *AugStud* 33:213–22.

Ritner, Robert K. 1984. A Uterine Amulet in the Oriental Institute Collection. *JNES* 43:209–21.

Roberts, J. J. M. 1992. Double Entendre in First Isaiah. *CBQ* 54:39–48.

Rofé, A. 2002. The End of the Song of Moses (Deuteronomy 32.43). Pages 47–54 in *Deuteronomy: Issues and Interpretations*. Edited by A. Rofé. London: T&T Clark International.

Rohde, Michael. 2007. *Der Knecht Hiob im Gespräch mit Mose: Eine traditions- und redaktionsgeschichtliche Studie zum Hiobbuch*. Arbeiten zur Bibel und ihrer Geschichte 26. Leipzig: Evangelische Verlagsanstalt.

Rose, Margaret A. 1993. *Parody: Ancient, Modern, and Post-modern*. Cambridge: Cambridge University Press.

Roth, Joseph. 1979. *Hiob: Roman eines einfachen Mannes*. Reinbek bei Hamburg: Rowohlt.

Rowland, C., with P. Gibbons and V. Dobroruka. 2006. Visionary Experience in Ancient Judaism and Christianity. Pages 41–56 in *Paradise Now: Essays on Early Jewish and Christian Mysticism*. Edited by April D. DeConick. Atlanta: Society of Biblical Literature.

Rowley, H. H. 1958. The Book of Job and Its Meaning. *BJRL* 41:162–207.

———. 1970. *Job*. Century Bible. London: Thomas Nelson.

Saadiah Ben Joseph Al-Fayyūmī. 1988. *The Book of Theodicy: Translation and Commentary on the Book of Job*. Translated by Lenn Goodman. Yale Judaica Series 25. New Haven: Yale University Press.

Sæbø, M. 1997. *ysr* to Chastise. Pages 548–51 in vol. 2 of Jenni 1997b.

Sanders, James A. 1955. *Suffering as Divine Discipline in the Old Testament and Post-Biblical Judaism*. Rochester, N.Y.: Colgate Rochester Divinity School.

Saur, Markus. 2011. Sapientia discursiva: Die alttestamentliche Weisheitsliteratur als theologischer Diskurs. *ZAW* 123:236–49.

Saussure, Ferdinand de. 1983. *Course in General Linguistics*. Edited by C. Bally and A. Sechehaye. Translated by Roy Harris. London: Duckworth.

Savran, George W. 1988. *Telling and Retelling: Quotation in Biblical Narrative*. Bloomington: Indiana University Press.

Schäfer, Peter. 2011. *The Origins of Jewish Mysticism*. Princeton: Princeton University Press.

Schaller, Berndt. 1978. *Das Testament Hiobs: Jüdische Schriften aus hellenistisch-römischer Zeit*. Gütersloh: Gütersloher Verlag-Haus Mohn.

———. 1980. Das Testament Hiobs und die Septuaginta-Übersetzung des Buches Hiob. *Bib* 61:377–406.

Schart, Aaron. 2007. The First Section of the Book of the Twelve Prophets: Hosea–Joel–Amos. *Int* 61:138–52.

Schenke, Gesa, and Gesine Schenke Robinson. 2009. *Der koptische Kölner Papyrus-kodex 3221. Teil I, Das Testament des Iob*. Paderborn: F. Schöningh.

Schifferdecker, Kathryn. 2008. *Out of the Whirlwind: Creation Theology in the Book of Job*. Harvard Theological Studies 61. Cambridge, Mass.: Harvard University Press.

Schmid, Konrad. 2007. Innerbiblische Schriftdiskussion im Hiobbuch. Pages 241–61 in Krüger et al. 2007.

———. 2008. The Authors of Job and Their Historical Setting. Pages 145–53 in Perdue 2008.

———. 2010a, ed. *Hiob als biblisches und antikes Buch: Historische und intellektuelle Kontexte seiner Theologie*. SBS 219. Stuttgart: Kath. Bibelwerk.

———. 2010b. Hiob als Buch der antiken Literatur. Pages 56–62 in Konrad 2010a.

————. 2010c. Hiob als Buch der Bibel. Pages 33–55 in Konrad 2010a.

————. 2011. *Schriftgelehrte Traditionsliteratur: Fallstudien zur innerbiblischen Schriftauslegung im Alten Testament.* FAT 77. Tübingen: Mohr Siebeck.

Schmidt, L. 1976. *De Deo: Studien zur Literarkritik und Theologie des Buches Jona, des Gesprächs zwischen Abraham und Jahwe in Gen 18,22ff. und von Hi 1.* BZAW 143. Berlin: de Gruyter.

Schniedewind, W. M. 2004. *How the Bible Became a Book: The Textualization of Ancient Israel.* Cambridge: Cambridge University Press.

Schoors, Antoon. 2000. (Mis)use of Intertextuality in Qoheleth Exegesis. Pages 45–59 in Lemaire and Sæbø 2000.

Schorch, Stefan. 2000. Between Science and Magic: The Function and Roots of Paronomasia in the Prophetic Books of the Hebrew Bible. Pages 205–22 in *Puns and Pundits: Word Play in the Hebrew Bible and Ancient Near Eastern Literature.* Edited by Scott B. Noegel. Bethesda, Md.: CDL.

Schroer, S. 2000. *Wisdom Has Built Her House.* Collegeville, Minn.: Liturgical.

Schultz, Richard L. 1997. Unity or Diversity in Wisdom Theology? A Canonical and Covenantal Perspective. *Tyndale Bulletin* 48:271–306.

————. 1999. *The Search for Quotation: Verbal Parallels in the Prophets.* JSOTSup 180. Sheffield: Sheffield Academic.

————. 2003. The Ties That Bind: Intertextuality, The Identification of Verbal Parallels, and Reading Strategies in the Book of the Twelve. Pages 27–45 in *Thematic Threads in the Book of the Twelve.* Edited by P. L. Redditt and A. Schart. BZAW 325. Berlin: de Gruyter.

————. 2005. A Sense of Timing: A Neglected Aspect of Qoheleth's Wisdom. Pages 257–67 in *Seeking Out the Wisdom of the Ancients: Essays Offered to Honor Michael V. Fox on the Occasion of His Sixty-Fifth Birthday.* Edited by R. L. Troxel, K. G. Friebel, and D. R. Magary. Winona Lake: Eisenbrauns.

————. 2010. Intertextuality, Canon, and "Undecidability": Understanding Isaiah's "New Heavens and New Earth" (Isa 65:17–25). *Bulletin for Biblical Research* 20:19–38.

Schwienhorst-Schönberger, L., and G. Steins. 1989. Zur Entstehung, Gestalt und Bedeutung der Ijob-Erzählung (Ijob 1f/42). *BZ* NF 33:1–24.

Scott, R. B. Y. 1965. *Proverbs. Ecclesiastes: Introduction, Translation, and Notes.* AB 18. Garden City, N.Y.: Doubleday.

————. 1971. *The Way of Wisdom in the Old Testament.* New York: Macmillan.

Segal, M. Z. 1949. Parallels in the Book of Job. *Tarbiz* 20:35–48 (Hebrew).

Seibert, E. A. 2009. *Disturbing Divine Behavior.* Minneapolis: Fortress.

Selms, A. van. 1985. *Job: A Practical Commentary.* Grand Rapids: Eerdmans.

Seow, C. L. 2007. Job's Wife, with Due Respect. Pages 351–73 in Krüger et al. 2007.

Shaked, M., ed. 2005. *I'll Play You Forever: The Bible in Modern Hebrew Poetry—An Anthology.* Tel-Aviv: Yedioth Akhronoth (Hebrew).

Shalev, Meir. 1985. Once Upon a Time There Was a Man in the Land of Uz: The Story of Job. Pages 105–13 in *The Bible Now.* Jerusalem: Schocken (Hebrew).

Shelly, H. 1983. *Hebrew Translation of Codex B of the Septuagint of the Early Prophets.* Tel-Aviv: Hotsaʾat Sheli, be-ḥasut "ha-Ḥevrah le-ḥeqer ha-Miqra" (Hebrew).

Sheppard, Gerald T. 2000. Biblical Wisdom Literature and the End of the Modern Age. Pages 369–98 in Lemaire and Sæbø 2000.

Sinnott, A. M. 2005. *The Personification of Wisdom*. Society of Old Testament Studies Monograph Series. Aldershot: Ashgate.

Sitzler, Dorothea. 1995. *"Vorwurf gegen Gott": Ein religiöses Motiv im Alten Orient (Ägypten und Mesopotamien)*. Studies in Oriental Religions 32. Wiesbaden: Harrassowitz.

Smith, Mark S. 2008. *God in Translation: Deities in Cross-Cultural Discourse in the Biblical World*. FAT 57. Tübingen: Mohr Siebeck.

Smith, Morton. 1987. *Palestinian Parties and Politics That Shaped the Old Testament*. 2d ed. London: SCM

Sommer, Benjamin D. 1996a. Allusions and Illusions: The Unity of the Book of Isaiah in Light of Deutero-Isaiah's Use of Prophetic Tradition. Pages 156–86 in *New Visions of Isaiah*. Edited by R. F. Melugin and M. A. Sweeney. JSOTSup 214. Sheffield: Sheffield Academic.

———. 1996b. Exegesis, Allusion and Intertextuality in the Hebrew Bible: A Response to Lyle Eslinger. *VT* 46:479–89.

———. 1998. *A Prophet Reads Scripture: Allusion in Isaiah 40–66*. Stanford, Calif.: Stanford University Press.

Souter, A. 1922. *Pelagius's Expositions of Thirteen Epistles of St. Paul*. Cambridge: Cambridge University Press.

Spark, Muriel. 1984. *The Only Problem*. New York: G. P. Putnam's Sons.

Spiegel, S. 1945. Noah, Daniel and Job: Touching on Canaanite Relics in the Legends of the Jews. Pages 305–55 in *Louis Ginzberg Jubilee Volume*. New York: The American Academy for Jewish Research. Reprinted as pages 193–241 in *Essential Papers on Israel and the Ancient Near East*. Edited by F. E. Greenspahn. New York: New York University Press, 1991.

Spieser, Cathie. 1997. L'eau et la régénération des morts d'après les représentations des tombes thé baines du Nouvel Empire. *Chronique d'Égypte* 72:211–28.

Spittler, R. P. 1983. Testament of Job: A New Translation and Introduction. Pages 829–68 in vol. 1 of *The Old Testament Pseudepigrapha: Apocalyptic Literature and Testaments*. Edited by James H. Charlesworth. New York: Doubleday.

Stager, Lawrence, and Philip King. 2001. *Life in Biblical Israel*. Louisville: Westminster John Knox.

Stead, Michael R. 2009. *The Intertextuality of Zechariah 1–8*. LHBOTS 506. New York: T&T Clark International.

Steck, Odil Hannes. 1998. *Old Testament Exegesis: A Guide to the Methodology*. Translated by James D. Nogalski. Society of Biblical Literature Resources for Biblical Study 39. Atlanta: Scholars Press.

Steins, Georg. 1999. *Die "Bindung Isaaks" im Kanon (Gen 22): Grundlagen und Programm einer kanonisch-intertextuellen Lektüre; mit einer Spezialbibliographie zu Gen 22*. Edited by Georg Steins. HBS 20. Freiburg: Herder.

———. 2003. Der Bibelkanon als Denkmal und Text: Zu einigen methodologischen Aspekten kanonischer Bibelauslegung. Pages 177–98 in *The Biblical Canons*. Edited by J.-M. Auwers and H. J. de Jonge. BETL 158. Leuven: Leuven University Press.

Stemberger, G. 1991. *Introduction to the Talmud and Midrash*. Edinburgh: T. & T. Clark.

Stern, Elsie R. 2004. *From Rebuke to Consolation: Exegesis and Theology in the Liturgical Anthology of the Ninth of Av Season*. BJS 338. Providence: Brown Judaic Studies.

Sternberg, Meir. 1982. Proteus in Quotation-Land: Mimesis and the Form of Reported Discourse. *Poetics Today* 3:107–56.

Stocker, Peter. 1988. *Theorie der intertextuellen Lektüre: Modelle und Fallstudien.* Explicatio: Analytische Studien zur Literatur und Literaturwissenschaft. Paderborn: Schöningh.

Stoebe, H. J. 1997. *rpᵓ* to Heal. Pages 1254–59 in vol. 3 of Jenni 1997b.

Strahan, James. 1913. *The Book of Job Interpreted.* Edinburgh: T. & T. Clark.

Stuart, Douglas. 1987. *Hosea–Jonah.* WBC 31. Waco, Tex.: Word.

Suriano, Matthew J. 2010. Death, Disinheritance, and Job's Kinsman-Redeemer. *JBL* 129:49–66.

Susman, Margarete. 1968. *Das Buch Hiob und das Schicksal des jüdischen Volkes.* Herder-Bücherei 318. Freiburg: Herder.

———. 1996. *Das Buch Hiob und das Schicksal des jüdischen Volkes.* Frankfurt a.M: Jüdischer Verlag.

Syring, Wolf-Dieter. 2004. *Hiob und sein Anwalt: Die Prosatexte des Hiobbuches und ihre Rolle in seiner Redaktions- und Rezeptionsgeschichte.* BZAW 336. Berlin: de Gruyter.

Talstra, Eep. 1994. *Dialogue in Job 21: "Virtual Quotations" or Text Grammatical Markers?* Edited by W. A. M. Beuken. BETL 114. Louvain: Leuven University Press.

Tawil, H. 2009. *An Akkadian Lexical Companion for Biblical Hebrew.* Jersey City: Ktav.

Terrien, Samuel. 1966. Quelques remarques sur les affinités de Job avec le Deutéro-Ésaïe. Pages 295–310 in *Volume du Congrès. Genève 1965.* VTSup 15. Leiden: Brill.

———. 1996. *The Iconography of Job Through the Centuries: Artists as Biblical Interpreters.* University Park, Pa.: Pennsylvania State University Press.

Teske, Roland J. 1997. *Answer to the Pelagians.* The Works of Saint Augustine: A Translation for the 21st Century I 23. New York: New City.

Thiselton, Anthony C. 1992. *New Horizons in Hermeneutics: The Theory and Practice of Transforming Biblical Reading.* London: HarperCollins.

Ticciati, Susannah. 2005. *Job and the Disruption of Identity: Reading Beyond Barth.* London: T&T Clark International.

———. 2010. Augustine and Grace Ex Nihilo: The Logic of Augustine's Response to the Monks of Hadrumetum and Marseilles. *AugStud* 41:401–22.

———. 2011. Reading Augustine Through Job: A Reparative Reading of Augustine's Doctrine of Predestination. *Modern Theology* 27:414–41.

Tidwell, N. 1975. *Waᵓomar* (Zech 3:5) and the Genre of Zechariah's Fourth Vision. *JBL* 94:343–55.

Tigay, J. H. 1996. *The JPS Torah Commentary: Deuteronomy* דברים. Philadelphia: Jewish Publication Society.

Toorn, K. van der. 2002. Sources in Heaven: Revelation as a Scholarly Construct in Second Temple Judaism. Pages 265–77 in *Kein Land für sich allein.* Edited by U. Hübner and A. Knauf. Göttingen: Vandenhoeck & Ruprecht.

———. 2007. *Scribal Culture and the Making of the Hebrew Bible.* Cambridge, Mass.: Harvard University Press.

Torrey, R. A. 2002. *The Treasury of Scripture Knowledge.* Rev. ed. Peabody, Mass.: Hendrickson.

Tull Willey, Patricia. 1997. *Remember the Former Things: The Recollection of Previous Texts in Second Isaiah.* Society of Biblical Literature Dissertation Series 161. Atlanta: Scholars Press.

Tull, Patricia K. 2000a. Intertextuality and the Hebrew Scriptures. *Currents in Research: Biblical Studies* 9:59–90.

————. 2000b. The Rhetoric of Recollection. Pages 71–78 in Lemaire and Sæbø 2000.

Tur-Sinai, N. H. (H. Torczyner). 1967. *The Book of Job: A New Commentary.* Rev. ed. Jerusalem: Kiryath Sepher.

————. 1981. *The Book of Job: A New Commentary.* Jerusalem: Kiryath Sepher.

Uehlinger, C. 2007. Das Buch Hiob im Kontext der altorientalischen Literatur- und Religionsgeschichte. Pages 97–163 in Krüger et al. 2007.

Ulrich, E. et al., eds. 1995. *Qumran Cave 4.IX: Deuteronomy, Joshua, Judges, Kings.* Discoveries in the Judean Desert 14. Oxford: Clarendon.

Vall, G. 1995. The Enigma of Job 1,21a. *Bib* 76:325–42.

Vassar, John S. 2007. *Recalling a Story Once Told: An Intertextual Reading of the Psalter and the Pentateuch.* Macon, Ga.: Mercer University Press.

Vattioni, Francesco. 1968. *Ecclesiastico: Testo ebraico con apparato critico e versioni greca, latina e siriaca.* Pubblicazioni del Seminario di Semitistica 1. Napoli: Istituto Orientale di Napoli.

Vinton, P. 1978. Radical Aloneness: Job and Jeremiah. *The Bible Today* 99:1843–49.

Wahl, H.-M. 1992. Noah, Daniel und Hiob in Ezechiel xiv 12–20 (21–3): Anmerkungen zum traditionsgeschichtlichen Hintergrund. *VT* 42:542–53.

Westermann, Claus. 1981. *The Structure of the Book of Job: A Form-Critical Analysis.* Translated by Charles A. Muenchow. Philadelphia: Fortress. Original edition: *Der Aufbau des Buches Hiob.* Tübingen: Mohr, 1956.

Wetzel, J. 1992. *Augustine and the Limits of Virtue.* Cambridge: Cambridge University Press.

Wiesel, E. 1958. *La nuit.* Paris: Les Éditions de Minuit. Original edition: *Un die Welt hot geschwign* (1956) (Yiddish).

————. 1975. Job ou le silence révolutionaire. Pages 179–99 in *Célébration biblique: Portraits et légendes.* Paris: Seuil.

————. 1979. *Le procés de Shamgorod tel qu'il se déroula le 25 février 1649.* Paris: Seuil.

Willi-Plein, I. 2002. ŠWB ŠWBT—eine Wiedererwägung. Pages 189–208 in *Sprache als Schlüssel: Gesammelte Aufsätze zum Alten Testament.* Edited by I. Willi-Plein. Neukirchen–Vluyn: Neukirchener Verlag.

Williamson, H. G. M. 1994. *The Book Called Isaiah: Deutero-Isaiah's Role in Composition and Redaction.* Oxford: Clarendon.

Willmes, Bernd. 2002. *Von der Exegese als Wissenschaft zur kanonisch-intertextuellen Lektüre? Kritische Anmerkungen zur kanonisch-intertextuellen Lektüre von Gen 22,1–19.* Fuldaer Hochschulschriften 41. Frankfurt a.M.: Knecht.

Wilson, Leslie S. 2006. *The Book of Job: Judaism in the 2nd Century BCE: An Intertextual Reading.* Lanham, Md.: University Press of America.

Winton Thomas, D. 1962. צלמות in the Old Testament. *JSS* 7:191–200.

Witte, Markus. 1994. *Vom Leiden zur Lehre: Der dritte Redegang (Hiob 21–27) und die Redaktionsgeschichte des Hiobbuches.* BZAW 230. Berlin: de Gruyter.

————. 1995. *Philologische Notizen zu Hiob 21–27.* BZAW 234. Berlin: de Gruyter.

————. 2004. Hiobs "Zeichen" (Hiob 31,35–37). Pages 723–42 in *Gott und Mensch im Dialog: Festschrift für Otto Kaiser zum 80. Geburtstag*. BZAW 345. Berlin: de Gruyter.

————. 2009. Orakel und Gebete im Buch Habakuk. Pages 67–91 in *Orakel und Gebete: Interdisziplinäre Studien zur Sprache der Religion in Ägypten, Vorderasien und Griechenland in hellenistischer Zeit*. Edited by Markus Witte and Johannes F. Diehl. FAT 2/38. Tübingen: Mohr Siebeck.

Wohlgelernter, Devora K. 1981. Death Wish in the Bible. *Tradition* 19:131–40.

Wolde, Ellen van. 1989. Trendy Intertextuality? Pages 43–49 in Draisma 1989.

Wolff, Hans Walter. 1964. Das Kerygma des Deuteronomistischen Geschichtswerks. Pages 308–24 in *Gesammelte Studien zum Alten Testament*. Edited by Hans Walter Wolff. Theologische Bücherei 22. Munich: Kaiser.

————. 1977. *Joel and Amos: A Commentary on the Books of the Prophets Joel and Amos*. Philadelphia: Fortress (German original 1975).

Worton, M., and J. Still, eds. 1990. *Intertextuality: Theories and Practices*. Manchester: Manchester University Press.

Wright, G. H. Bateson. 1883. *The Book of Job*. London: Williams & Norgate.

Wright, R. B. 1985. Psalms of Solomon. Pages 639–70 in *The Old Testament Pseudepigrapha*. Edited by J. H. Charlesworth. Garden City, N.Y.: Doubleday.

Yoshiko Reed, Annette. 2001. Job as Jobab: The Interpretation of Job in LXX Job 42:17b-e. *JBL* 120:31–55.

Zach, Nathan. 2005. With Job This Was Quite Unique. Pages 348–49 in Shaked 2005 (Hebrew).

Zeitlin, Aaron. 2005. When the Gates of Death Open. Pages 342–43 in Shaked 2005 (Hebrew).

Ziegler, Joseph. 1982. *Iob*. Septuaginta: Vetus Testamentum Graecum 11/4. Göttingen: Vandenhoeck & Ruprecht.

Zuckerman, Bruce. 1991. *Job the Silent: A Study in Historical Counterpoint*. Oxford: Oxford University Press.

INDEX OF AUTHORS